critique
influence
change

critique confronts the world. Without dogma, without new principles, it refuses to conform and instead demands insurrection of thought. It must be ruthless, unafraid of both its results and the powers it may come into conflict with. Critique takes the world, our world, as its object, so that we may develop new ways of making it.

influence is a step from critique towards the future, when effects begin to be felt, when the ground becomes unstable, when a movement ignites. These critiques of the state of our world have influenced a generation. They are crucial guides to change.

change is when the structures shift. The books in this series take critique as their starting point and as such have influenced both their respective disciplines and thought the world over. This series is born out of our conviction that change lies not in the novelty of the future but in the realization of the thoughts of the past.

These texts are not mere interpretations or reflections, but scientific, critical and impassioned analyses of our world. After all, the point is to change it.

ABOUT THE AUTHOR

Maria Mies is a Marxist feminist scholar who is
renowned for her theory of capitalist patriarchy, one
which recognizes third world women and difference.
She is a professor of sociology at Cologne University
of Applied Sciences, but retired from teaching in
1993. Since the late 1960s she has been involved
with feminist activism. In 1979, at the Institute
of Social Studies in The Hague, she founded the
Women and Development programme. Mies has
written books and articles that deal with topics
relating to feminism, third world issues and the
environment. Her other titles published by Zed Books
include *The Lace Makers of Narsapur* (1982),
Women: The Last Colony (1988), *The Subsistence
Perspective* (1999) and *Ecofeminism* (2014).

PATRIARCHY AND ACCUMULATION ON A WORLD SCALE

WOMEN IN THE INTERNATIONAL DIVISION OF LABOUR

MARIA MIES

WITH A FOREWORD BY

SILVIA FEDERICI

Zed Books
London

Patriarchy and Accumulation on a World Scale:
Women in the International Division of Labour
was first published in 1986 by Zed Books Ltd,
7 Cynthia Street, London N1 9JF, UK

This edition was published in 2014

www.zedbooks.co.uk

A catalogue record for this book is available from the British Library
Library of Congress Cataloging in Publication Data available

ISBN 978-1-78360-169-1 paperback
ISBN 978-1-78360-258-2 PDF
ISBN 978-1-78360-259-9 EPUB
ISBN 978-1-78360-260-5 Kindle

MIX
Paper from
responsible sources
FSC
www.fsc.org   FSC® C013604

Contents

Foreword
Silvia Federici

There are many reasons why this new edition of *Patriarchy and Accumulation on a World Scale* is a welcome event. Already in the 1990s considered a classic of feminist literature and required reading for activists and scholars of the burgeoning anti-globalization movement, the book is not only as relevant today as when it was first published, but now addresses an audience even more ready to appreciate its content and methodology. Proposing a vision of world history centred on the 'production of life' and the struggle against its exploitation, this book speaks directly to the crisis that many are currently experiencing faced with the constant destruction of human lives and the environment, especially when the seeming inability of even powerful mass movements to bring about positive social change generates a quest for new paradigms.

Patriarchy and Accumulation recuperates, for a younger generation radicalized by the Occupy movement and the movements of the squares, the radical core of feminism, buried under years of institutional co-optation and postmodern denial of any ground of commonality among women. It recuperates the sense, so strong in the early phase of the feminist movement, that to speak of women is to touch something very fundamental in history and our everyday lives. For, as Mies puts it, women are not one particular group of human beings among others; they are those who, in every time and in every society, have produced life on this planet and on whose work, therefore, all other activities depend. Thus, tracing the origins of women's exploitation is to ask why and where history 'took a wrong turn', what are the real forces by which world history has been driven, and what is the truth of the capitalist system in which we live.

This is the task *Patriarchy and Accumulation* takes on, and the outcome is a historical and theoretical reconstruction whose scope has often been described as 'breathtaking'. Following the trail of centuries of male violence against women, and crossing space, time and disciplinary boundaries, it relates hunter/gatherer societies with the development of capitalism and colonialism, demonstrates the pitfalls of national liberation movements, shows the essential continuity between capitalism and socialism, all the while unearthing the material foundations of the hierarchies that have characterized the sexual division of labour and highlighting the principles by which a non-exploitative society should be governed.

There is, therefore, a great wealth of historical and political knowledge to be gained from the book. *Patriarchy and Accumulation* also teaches an important methodological lesson, as an excellent example of what constructing a theory requires. More important, combining the theories produced by the Wages for Housework movement, especially its identification of women's unpaid domestic labour as the pillar of capitalist accumulation, with the third-worldist analysis of peasant economies and colonization, the book develops a theoretical framework that enables us to think together different forms of exploitation and social movements, enables us to acknowledge what divides as well as unites women, and makes of feminism a probe to grasp the main trends in the restructuring of the world economy.

Inevitably, a work of such scope will pose many questions. Some may baulk at the thesis sustaining this effort: that at the beginning of history a sexual division of labour arose, whereby men specialized in the arts of violence and destruction while women specialized in the activities by which life is daily and generationally produced, and, in time, this division consolidated into a 'patriarchal' system in which men's violent appropriation of women's labour has become the dominant force of production.

This is a provocative contention, turning upside down the tales of civilization that we have been taught from the first days of school, and I imagine that a few anthropological research projects will be fuelled by the quest for evidence. But whether or not the empirical details of Mies's theory of the origin of patriarchy can all be verified, the logical power of her argument should not be missed, as it challenges us to account for the pervasive presence of male violence against women, and confronts even the 'gender sceptics' with an undeniable ground of commonality in their situation. It also demystifies the presumed innovative, creative character of capitalism, 'patriarchy's latest manifestation', highlighting its parasitic dependence on the free appropriation of nature and the body and work of women.

As Mies demonstrates, only with the advent of capitalism has the use of violence as an economic force been universalized and intensified beyond that exercised in any previous system. For, as she argues, the formation of a world-system has enabled capitalism to externalize exploitation, multiply its colonial divisions, and accelerate its destruction of the planet's natural wealth. In this context, one of the most powerful parts of *Patriarchy and Accumulation* is its analysis of the continuity between the processes that characterized the first phase of capitalist development – witch-hunts, the slave trade, colonization – and those that have characterized the restructuring of the world economy in our time, showing that 'development at one pole has always been underdevelopment at the other', and that 'primitive accumulation' cannot be confined to the origins of capitalist society, for it has been an essential aspect of every phase of capitalist development and has now become a permanent process.

This is a 'truth' that social and political developments since the first publication of *Patriarchy and Accumulation* have verified time and time again. So has the book's assertion of a direct causal connection between the global extension of capitalist relations and the escalation of violence against women, as the punishment against their resistance to the appropriation of their bodies and labour. Not only are thousands of women, as well as many young men, continuing to be enslaved and to die in 'free export zones', the workhouses of our time. Violence against women has so much increased in recent years that the term 'femicide' is now commonly used even in government reports; in Italy, in 2013, 'femicide' was introduced as a crime in the legal code. Meanwhile, across the world we have witnessed a resurgence of witch-hunts.

It is to Mies's credit that in describing the destructive forces that 'patriarchal capitalism' has unleashed, she does not soften her critique, nor offers quick solutions, but instead validates the growing realization that capitalism cannot be reformed. *Patriarchy and Accumulation*, however, is also an indictment of Marxism. Like Mariarosa Dalla Costa and other Wages for Housework activists and political theorists, Mies criticizes Marx's reductive concept of work, and goes even further in her rejection of the terminology Marx developed – arguing, for instance, that such concepts as 'productivity' and 'surplus labour', in Marx's interpretation, contribute to the mystification of what constitutes production.

This at present is easily granted, even by many Marxists, theoretically at least, as decades of feminist writing and campaigning have removed any doubt that producing human beings is work, and work that capitalism depends upon. More controversial, but especially important in the present social context, where the hold of technology on our lives has never being as strong, is Mies's rejection of the Marxian dream of a fully industrialized society, in which machines perform all the work, as a condition for human liberation. As she powerfully argues, such a dream ignores the fact that it is not work as such that is oppressive, but the social relations of exploitation that sustain it.

This is a crucial message for the many among us who, despite the growing refusal of capitalist society, are still enthralled by its technological production, often assuming that their powers have been acquired through Facebook or Twitter. For them, and indeed for all of us, *Patriarchy and Accumulation* is a necessary political guide. It does not allow us to forget at what cost the new technologies are produced, what violence they unleash, and how destructive the generalization of capitalist technologies would be for the productive powers of the earth.

Here, too, history is on the side of Mies's analysis – in the post-Fukushima world the Marxian dream of a continuous industrialization has become humanity's nightmare. More than that, people's response to the present capitalist crisis has vindicated Mies's view that the real revolutionary subjects are not the computer programmers and other agents of mechanization, but the millions of women who on less than 'a dollar a day' have struggled to keep their communities alive, mostly through their subsistence work and the creation of more cooperative forms of social reproduction. It is their implicit presence, and the presence of the many who daily struggle to create forms of existence and social relations not governed by the logic of capitalist accumulation, that give power to Mies's work.

This is why, despite its uncompromising portrayal of the destructive powers of capitalism, *Patriarchy and Accumulation* does not encourage any form of historical pessimism, confident that capitalism so deeply threatens the reproduction of our life that our revolt against it cannot be tamed, but will resurface again and again on humanity's agenda until it has been ended.

Preface
to the critique influence change edition

I am very glad that my book *Patriarchy and Accumulation on a World Scale*, which was first published by Zed Books in 1986, is being published again. But I ask: is this book still relevant today and if so why? Are my analysis and my conclusions still the same in a world in which one crisis follows the other, and one war follows the other? And what has changed since 1986?

My first questions are these. Are the concepts of patriarchy and capitalism still valid in a world where free trade is dominating all economic, political and social life? And, as I wrote in 1986, are capitalism and patriarchy still interconnected? Is my analysis of women's labour under capitalist patriarchy still the same? Has violence against women, nature and other colonies not disappeared from our civilized society?

Before answering these questions I want to illustrate how I discovered concepts like patriarchy, capitalism, exploitation of women, nature and colonies. One thing was clear from the beginning: I did not gain my insights by sitting in the British Library, reading books on political economy; I did so by participating in a number of socio-political movements, particularly the feminist movement but also the student movement, the ecology movement, the peace movement and later the anti-globalization movement. In fact, writing and reading books came during and *after* these struggles. That means that practice came before theorizing. This was – and is – particularly true for the feminist movement, because no books were there to explain why women are still oppressed, exploited and do not get the same pay as men.

Patriarchy and Accumulation is the result of this interwoven process of action and reflection, of experience and theory. But it was also written in a particular historical moment when people from different parts of the world, particularly women, asked similar questions. And I was fortunate enough to meet the right people at the right time in the right place, people who saw the need to change the status quo and were confident that they could do so. Hence *Patriarchy and Accumulation* is the 'child' of the conjuncture of these different circumstances.

In the following I'll describe the main stages of this process when I discovered what patriarchy means, what capitalism is, why the two are necessarily connected and what the consequences of this 'marriage' are.

In 1963 I became a lecturer at the Goethe Institute (GI) in Pune in India. Our students, men and women, came from all over India. Why men wanted to learn German was clear: they wanted to get a job in Germany, or to study physics or other sciences. But why did Indian women want to learn German? What use would German have for them? I made a small investigation, which was later published under the title 'Why German?' (Mies 1967).

My hypothesis regarding the men was correct. But the answers of the women were a surprise: they studied German because they wanted to postpone the 'marriage talk'. I wondered what that was. They told me that they all had to undergo an arranged marriage, in which their parents decided which man of what family their daughter would marry. In all upper-middle- and lower-middle-class families such an arranged marriage was the rule. Neither bridegroom nor bride had much of a say in these decisions. In more traditional families they were not even allowed to see each other. What was important was that caste, class, family status and financial status would fit. One of the gravest difficulties of these 'marriage talks' was and is the bargain about the dowry which the bride's family has to pay to the bridegroom's family. Many poorer families with a num-ber of daughters would – and often still do – become deeply indebted in order to find bridegrooms for them. On the other hand, an unmarried daughter had no economic security or social status. She was a disgrace to her parents. This situation has changed today, but arranged marriages and high dowry demands are still common. In educated middle-class families, however, daughters could 'postpone' the marriage negotiations so long as they were still studying, since education has a high prestige for the Indian middle class, even for daughters. Thus parents would not start the 'marriage talk' as long as their daughter was studying for a B.A. or an M.A. For our female students, 'studying German' was therefore an excuse to postpone these marriage negotiations. But in the end they had to get married to a man they usually did not know.

I did not yet know what the concept 'patriarchy' really implied. But these talks with my students gave me the first experiential glimpse of what it means to be a woman in a patriarchal society. They opened my eyes to the social oppression of women and the patriarchal relations between men and women. But I did not yet understand that patriarchy is a system that does not exist only in India.

From Iravati Karve, a world-renowned anthropologist, I learned that what I had heard from my students was just one feature of an overall patriarchal social and family system which had existed in the Indian sub-continent for thousands of years. From then onwards I wanted to know more about this system. Therefore, when I returned to Germany in 1968 I wanted to research this question: why are modern Indian women still oppressed by a patriarchal family system? I went to the University of Cologne to meet professor René Koenig, the Dean of Sociology and an internationally known family sociologist. I told him about my experiences in India and my interest in further study on modern Indian women. At that time there was no university in Germany where women's studies was taught, let alone studies on modern Indian women. Professor Koenig was fascinated by the topic and said: 'Why don't you do a Ph.D. on this subject?' I answered, 'If that's possible, then I'll do it.'

I went back to India and undertook empirical research on the dilemmas and conflicts of modern middle-class women. The results confirmed what I had already observed five years before, namely that patriarchy is an overall social, cultural and economic and political system which determines a woman's life from birth to death. Another lesson I learned was that patriarchy is not a thing of the past but is still flourishing today in spite of 'modernization and development'. I wrote my dissertation on the conflicts and dilemmas of modern Indian women. It was published in India under the title *Indian Women and Patriarchy* (Mies 1980).

Yet, while I studied the status of women in the Indian patriarchy I discovered the German patriarchy!

I had returned to Germany at the right historical moment. In Germany in 1968 two new and decisive socio-political movements had emerged: the student movement and the new feminist movement. Both movements attacked the social, economic and political foundations of society. The student movement started its 'anti-authoritarian' rebellion against established institutions like the family, the university, the Church and the state. Students began to study Marxism – which had been taboo since the end of World War II in Germany – and to read the main works of Marx and Engels and other socialists. Feminists attacked the family laws, particularly the prohibition on abortion and violence against women, wife-beating, rape and inequality between men and women. We did not begin to read fundamental books about women's oppression, because such books did not yet exist. But we started with actions to fight against the oppression of women. Through these struggles I discovered many parallels between the situation of Indian and German women. In both cultures women were inferior to men. In Germany, too, women depended economically on their parents or their husbands. There was no equality between men and women regarding education, jobs, pay and the de facto legal situation. A woman was only allowed to get a job if her husband agreed. A woman's 'normal' status was that of a dependent housewife. Moreover, women were victims of male violence in Germany too.

I was much older than most of the students I joined in the student movement. The students had formed 'Marxist study circles'. There I read for the first time what Marx and Engels had written about class, class struggle, labour, religion, the family and revolution. This all was a great eye-opener for me.

From the beginning, the feminist movement in Germany was part of the international women' movement. The issue that interested me most was the question of the sexual division of labour between women and men. The debate on the role of domestic labour within the capitalist family and society was decisive for my understanding of capitalism. Around 1980 I became involved in this new debate and began to read Marx more carefully, in particular what he had to say about work, especially women's work in the household. For many years this debate was at the centre of the international feminist discourse. Marx called housewives' work 'reproductive labour', while the work of a man in the factory was 'productive labour'.

This was when I began writing 'Social Origins of the Sexual Division of Labour', an essay published in *Women: The Last Colony*, which was co-written with my friends Veronika Bennholdt-Thomsen and Claudia von Werlhof (Mies, Bennholdt-Thomsen and von Werlhof 1988). This book was widely read and discussed by women all over the world. All three of us had worked and studied in 'Third World' countries – Veronika and Claudia in Latin America; I in India. Therefore we not only looked at the effect capitalism had on women in Europe and the United States but also asked what this meant for women in the so-called developing countries. We called them simply colonies. Veronika and Claudia both looked particularly at the similarity between the work of housewives and that of peasants in South America. I did the same for India. We understood that not only domestic labour of women all over the world was 'a free resource' for capital, but also the work of small peasants and that of slum dwellers in the cities. The same was/is true for colonies and particularly for nature. For capitalists all these are 'colonies' whose production can be appropriated almost free of costs.

We were not the only ones who tried to understand whether Marxian concepts like 'relations of production' or 'modes of production' made sense with regard to people who worked not directly for the market but for their sustenance from day to day – for their *subsistence*. Subsistence then became the main concept for us, to understand how capitalist accumulation really takes place. We understood immediately that unpaid housework was 'reproductive work', because a woman worked to 'reproduce' the male worker so that he could sell his labour for a wage at the factory door. Moreover, she would also 'reproduce' the next generation of workers, so that the process of capital accumulation could go on. Marx considered this daily and intergenerational 'reproduction of the working class' a matter of biology. Most feminists in the West criticized Marx for this overly biologistic and sexist understanding of women's housework.

Veronika – who had studied Marx's as well as Rosa Luxemburg's work more thoroughly – told us that Luxemburg had also criticized Marx, not because he ignored women's unpaid work, but because he ignored peasants and other non-capitalist strata of non-waged labourers.

Rosa Luxemburg wrote that Marx's model of ongoing accumulation of capital was based on the assumption that capitalism was a closed system in which only wage labourers and capitalists existed. She wrote that capitalism always needed 'non-capitalist milieux and strata' for its extension. According to her thesis these strata were peasants, colonies and the imperialist system. Without the ongoing exploitation of non-waged workers and of natural resources, and a perpetual extension of markets, capitalism would not be able to continue its process of permanent 'primitive accumulation' (Luxemburg 1923). Luxemburg was not a feminist. But her analysis was crucial for us to understand why women as unpaid domestic workers, the colonies and finally nature's resources have to be exploited for the process of ongoing capital accumulation. This process is necessarily based on violence, and finally destroys the subsistence of people and nature.

To test our thesis about women's and peasant exploitation, we went back to the countries we had studied before – Veronika and Claudia to South America; I to India. In India, too, the new feminist movement had just begun. I met a group of young students in Hyderabad who had started a campaign to abolish the dowry system. I told them about my research project and asked them where I could find an area in which women were exploited as subsistence producers. I was told about Narsapur, a small town on the eastern coast in South India where poor women made lace for 'foreign lands'. One of the students, K. Lalitha, came along with me as my assistant and interpreter. I wanted to study the women and their work in such an archetypal home industry.

My study of the lace-making women in Narsapur was the most important lesson I learned as a sociologist and a feminist. These women made crocheted lace from morning to night, sitting in front of their mud huts until it was too dark to work. For their work they would get much less than the minimum wage of a seasonal female agricultural labourer.

The lace industry was organized according to the classic putting-out system. They had to buy the thread from the exporter, who then collected the lace goods and exported them to Australia and Europe. He had become a millionaire and owned a big house in Narsapur. Yet, apart from this 'wage labour', they had also to cook, clean the hut, wash the clothes, sleep with their husbands, give birth to their children, nurse them, take care of them and all the other 'unseen work' done by women the world over. Hence they had to combine 'reproductive work' with the lowest paid 'productive work'. Their 'products' were luxury items, which were exported to the rich countries – for women there. I called this combination of both types of work the 'houswifization of labour'. I published the results of my research in the book *The Lace Makers of Narsapur* (Mies 1982).

Today it is also men who have to sit 'at home' and work on a computer for the world market. Although they are not as poor as the lace makers of Narsapur, structurally their work conditions are similar. But today one calls this 'precarious work'.

The next stage of my learning process about the interconnection between patriarchy and capitalism began in 1979, when I was invited by the Institute of Social Studies (ISS) in The Hague to create an M.A. programme for women from developing countries. The title of this program was 'Women and Development', and it was sponsored by the Dutch government. This was when official institutions began to understand that the 'woman question' would be of importance for the future development of the industrialized world. I had no problem to find candidates for our programme. The women came from India, Bangladesh, Thailand, Sudan, Somalia, Trinidad and Tobago, the Philippines, Belize, South Africa, and there were also two Dutch women who were very keen to study the problems of Third World women.

Yet there was another problem, which I had to solve immediately. There was no curriculum for such an M.A. course, no books, no colleagues to consult. Therefore I had to develop such a programme myself. For that I needed the help of my students. I asked them to tell us what the main problems were that women had to face in their own countries. Their stories were fascinating and new to all of us, and we learned a great deal from each other. Despite all of the cultural differences, we learned that women in all countries of the world were treated similarly: that they were considered to be inferior to men, subordinated, oppressed, exploited and often had to face the violence of their husbands, his family and society. In short, they were all victims of patriarchy. In the Netherlands and Germany, too, violence against women was 'normal'.

This was the time when feminists began to study women's history, because this history had largely been erased in all countries. This new women's history was called 'her-story'. I wanted our students to find out in their respective countries about the her-story of their mothers and grandmothers. I asked the students whether there had been an earlier women's movement in their countries. We were surprised to find that such movements had existed earlier, but had been forgotten in the meantime.

When I asked myself what I knew of earlier women's movements in Germany, I realized that I really did not know much of that history myself. Therefore I had to do my own homework first. I began to study the social-democratic women's movement of the nineteenth and early twentieth centuries. When I read about that history I learned that German socialist women had formed their own, separate all-women's organization where they could also discuss women's issues. The socialist men did not like these separate women's organizations. But when the Socialist Party was prohibited, the women could go on with their agitation, because they called it 'cultural work'. The state did not consider the women politically 'dangerous', so they were left alone. But after the party was legalized again, the leaders dissolved the separate women's organizations and asked the women to join as individual members.

When I talked about this story in my seminar, most women in the course told of similar experiences, particularly during liberation struggles in the Third World. Our conclusion was that women are welcome to fight together with the men for the liberation from colonial, racist, imperialist and capitalist oppression, but when the war is over they are sent back home to resume their old role of being a mother and housewife.

Another problem was that there were no textbooks at the ISS on women generally, particularly not on Third World women. Therefore we had to write our own textbooks. With my colleague Kumari Jayawardena from Sri Lanka, who had joined me after a year, we began to write down what we knew about the earlier women's movements in our own countries, producing the book *National Liberation and Women's Liberation* (Jayawardena and Mies 1982). Kumari wrote about the earlier women's movement in Sri Lanka, I wrote about 'Marxist Socialism and Women's Emancipation: The Proletarian Women's Movement in Germany'.

We asked our students to write papers on what they knew of the history of women in their own countries. Later some of the students continued this research for their doctorates. For instance, Rhoda Reddock from Trinidad wrote her thesis on *Women, Slavery, Work and Politics in Trinidad and Tobago* (Reddock 1994). Through her study I learned that the slave trade was not a so-called 'pre-capitalist' mode of production, but was a direct result of global capitalism, where particularly women were traded as commodities. The slave traders calculated whether it was more profitable if slave women were allowed to 'breed' or to buy new slaves. They came to the conclusion that 'It is more profitable to purchase than to breed.' Therefore slave women were not allowed to have children. The insights that my friends and I had gained many years ago – namely that women were the cheapest labour force for capital and that they were treated like colonies and like nature – was confirmed by a number of such stories that our students told from their own countries.

But the students also did their own research on Dutch women. They could not understand why Dutch women or Western women needed a movement for emancipation. Didn't they have all they wanted? They could marry a man they loved. They had an education and could get a job. What else did they want? I said to them: 'Why don't you meet some of the feminist groups in Holland and find out?' We called this 'Fieldwork in Holland'. When they came back, I was flabbergasted by their reports. One woman from the Philippines wrote: 'I always thought that Western values are good for Western people and that Eastern values are good for Eastern people. Now I know that Western values are not even good for Western people.' An African woman wrote: 'I don't understand these Dutch women. All the time they talk of men. Whether they are unmarried, married or divorced. Don't they have anything more important to do?'

For the students who came from around the world their experience at the ISS was crucial. They learned that women's problems all over the world were similar, in spite of differences of culture. But they also learned that patriarchy and capitalism are connected and that we have to fight against both. Therefore they invented the great slogan: 'Culture Divides Us; Struggle Unites Us.'

Violence, the secret of capitalist patriarchy

The main lesson we learned from the Third World women as well as from our European history was that direct violence was the means by which women, colonies and nature were compelled to serve the 'white man', and that without such violence the European Enlightenment, modernization and development would not have happened.

In Europe the epoch of Enlightenment began with the brutal persecution and killing of women as witches. Germany was one of the centres of witch-hunts. Feminists, in search of the roots of sexism, from 1976 to 1980 rediscovered the atrocities and crimes committed by Church, state and modern science against the mostly poor women who were denounced as witches. Witch-hunts began in the twelfth century and lasted until the seventeenth century. A great deal of historical research was done on witch-hunts in Europe; the findings were shocking in every respect. Not only were the forms of torture used to force a woman to confess that she had used magic spells to harm a neighbour or that she had cooperated or slept with the devil unbelievably cruel, but so was the joint labour between Church, state, law and 'modern science' in these witch trials.

Philosophers and political scientists tried to eradicate 'magic' and bring about the birth of the 'New Man' (Bacon) or to increase the birthrate in absolutist states such as the French one. Modern scientists and doctors managed to demonize the skills of midwives and women healers to steal their knowledge in order to develop the new, scientific medicine. The torture chambers were indeed laboratories to find out what could be done to a human body. In the same period our Mother Earth was tortured so that she would reveal her secrets to Man (Federici 2004). Although the witch-hunt is supposed to be over, the world-view of this epoch, of the Enlightenment and of rationality is still the same. It is based on the belief that the earth, nature and human beings are not good enough as they are. They must be improved, developed, made better to reach a 'higher stage' of civilization on earth. This 'higher stage' can only be reached through torture and violence. Since the Enlightenment the keywords for Western civilization are *rationality* and *progress*. In modern capitalist economics, rationality means nothing but unlimited capital accumulation.

The socialist utopia is also based on the same logic of rationality: on progress and the development of science and technology. And these need violence to analyse nature, to find out her secrets, including those of the human being. As it was with the witches: before rationality, science, technology and modern economics could be established, all wild, untamed, magic and backward-looking thinking had to be violently eliminated. Today it is no different: violence is needed to 'civilize', 'improve' the 'underdeveloped world' and 'wild nature'. Violence is therefore still the secret of modern capitalist–patriarchal civilization.

What is different today?

What comes first to my mind when I ask this question is that the general *mood* is different today. In 1968 many people were still full of hope that they could change things, that they could build a better world, that they could stop ecological destruction and the nuclear industry from poisoning the world. This optimism is no longer there. The general mood in Western societies is pessimistic – if not depressive. There are reasons for this change. The world has changed dramatically since I wrote my book. Here I want to mention only some of the most important changes.

From 1979 to 1980 Margaret Thatcher and Ronald Reagan introduced neoliberalism as the new economic dogma in Britain and the USA. The main pillars of the free-market economy are globalization, liberalization, privatization and universal competition (GLPC). This free-market economy was quickly introduced into all countries of the world, promoted by the World Bank, the IMF and later the WTO. In the indebted countries of the South governments were forced to accept this model. But the rich countries of the North also quickly transformed their economies according to the principles of the free market. And finally, after the end of the 'cold war', erstwhile socialist or communist states like the former Soviet Union and China also adopted neoliberalism, because it promised quick wealth for everybody, more jobs, more democracy, lower prices for globally sourced goods, free movement of people and capital from one country to the other. Most governments believed these promises. But many people later realized that the costs of these changes were rising unemployment, a new wave of poverty, more exploitation of workers, more ecological destruction and a state which had given up its role of controlling the economy.

In the beginning there was strong international opposition from all over the world to this free-trade policy, from those who understood what this new economy really meant, particularly for poor countries. But in the long run this opposition became weaker, because the international corporations were able to throw more and cheaper commodities from 'low-wage countries' onto the global market. One of the countries with the lowest wages is Bangladesh; China also exports cheap consumer goods to all countries of the world. The result is that more and more people in the erstwhile rich countries lose their jobs and face poverty.

Perhaps the most radical change in all spheres of life has come through the Internet. This new 'communications technology' is able to connect people instantly from one end of the world to the other. But the deepest and most far-reaching changes the Internet has brought is a totally new understanding of reality. Hitherto we had thought that reality is something one can see, touch, smell and that can be perceived by all our senses. In short, reality means that we live in a material world, where life has a beginning and an end. The Internet, however, creates a 'virtual world' in which everything is possible, in which all borders are eliminated and death no longer exists. The Internet is not a tool but a kind of surrogate religion. Yet people believe in it and that it will create a 'new world'. The far-reaching consequences of this faith are not yet known.

But other events in the real world changed the world so deeply that their consequences are felt everywhere. The first was the attack on the World Trade Center in New York on 11 September 2001. George W. Bush blamed Islamist terrorists for this attack. From this date onwards not only the United States but also the world had a new enemy: terrorism and Islam. This new enemy had to be fought everywhere. Bush himself talked of the necessity of a new crusade. A wave of wars against this new enemy followed. It started with Iraq, followed by Afghanistan. The next candidate on the war list is Iran.

Today there are wars again all over the world. The hope that an era of peace would follow the end of the East–West confrontation has been disappointed. The wars in Iraq and in Afghanistan were legitimized by the argument that they would bring freedom, democracy and modernity. The most perverse of these promises is that these wars are necessary to 'emancipate' the women of these countries from their backward, medieval cultures and the violence of their men. All Western media were and are full of the propaganda that Muslim women have to be liberated from their 'patriarchal men'. When German NATO soldiers were asked why they were in Afghanistan, many answered: 'We have to fight that girls can go to school and that women are not forced to wear that full body veil.' Since when have wars ever been fought to liberate the women of the enemy from their violent men? Have wars ever 'liberated' women? Since time immemorial women have been the victims of wars. Rape of women has always been part of all wars. The worst part of all this is that most people believe this propaganda. There is no protest any more against these new wars.

For quite some time I thought that the real goal of these new wars was to get access to resources like oil and gas. But now I wonder: are these new wars not wars about women? To whom do the women of a land belong? To the men of that land or to the new invaders? Many years ago I answered this question thus: 'He who owns the land owns the women of the land' (Mies et al. 1988). But today I would say: 'He who owns the women of the land owns the land.' This is the law of the old and the new patriarchs.

Another reason for the mood of pessimism today is the fact that the world economy is facing one crisis after another. This has created a tremendous sense of insecurity. After the USA, Europe, particularly the countries in southern Europe, have been victims of this continuous crisis. And there is no realistic hope that this situation of permanent crisis will end (Sarkar 2012). The crises are not only economic; they have psychological and sociological repercussions. But this situation has also led more and more people to question this whole system and to look for alternatives. They begin to ask: where is a new perspective, where is a new vision?

Many years ago I and my friends called this new perspective *The Subsistence Perspective* (Bennholdt-Thomsen and Mies 1999). We understood quite early on that capitalist patriarchy will go on with its destruction of life as long as people believe that ever more money will bring a better life. The first requirement for a new perspective is that people give up their faith in money. The second is a new definition of the goal of the economy. The word 'economy' comes from the Greek word *oikonomia*, knowledge about the household. The goal of the *oikonomia* was not the accumulation of money but the satisfaction of the basic needs of all members of the household. This is what subsistence means.

In September 2003 I was invited to a women's conference in Trier. It was organized by the Catholic Rural Women's Association. The slogan of this conference was 'The World is Our Household'. I thought this could be the keyword for the new paradigm people were looking for. If everybody treated the whole world as their own household, the world would be a different place.

But today people in the North have different worries. For the first time, they realize that it is not only people in the poor South but they too who are threatened by poverty. After a long period of prosperity the Western countries have experienced one crisis after another. Economists once proclaimed that such crises were over for good in the developed countries. But now they are back, in the United States as well as in Europe. And the politicians do not know how to solve them. In fact the present crises are part and parcel of capitalism. Capitalism needs crises. The politicians are helpless vis-à-vis the huge banks and the all-powerful international corporations that are responsible for the present crises. Southern Europe is hit most by the present crisis, and Greece, Spain and Portugal in particular are now dependent on the richer countries of Northern Europe, particularly Germany, to save them from bankruptcy.

Yet the insecurity about the future of our economy has also created a new awareness about the causes of this new impoverishment and those who profit from it. For a long time the word 'capitalism' had been taboo. But now it is used again in public discourse. Today many people realize that the present crisis cannot be solved within the framework of capitalist patriarchy. They are looking for a new perspective, a new paradigm, a new civilization (von Werlhof 2011). Many new visions are discussed all over the world. Among them is the subsistence perspective. Today, the subsistence perspective is not only a romantic idea; it is a necessity.

In the twenty-eight years since this book was first published one thing has become clear to me. A new paradigm cannot be based on a violent revolution. None of the earlier revolutions has eliminated the interconnection of patriarchy and capitalism. Capitalism is just the latest avatar of patriarchy. If we want to overcome both, we have to take a different path. This is the path of sowing new seeds. My friend Farida Akhter from Bangladesh has described this path in her book *Seeds of Movements* (Akhter 2007).

Maria Mies,
Cologne, March 2014

References

Akhter, Farida. *Seeds of Movements* (Narigrantha Prabartana, Dhaka, 2007).

Bennholdt-Thomsen, Veronika, and Maria Mies. *The Subsistence Perspective* (Zed Books, London, 1999).

Federici, Silvia. *Caliban and the Witch: Women, the Body and Primitive Accumulation* (Autonomedia, Brooklyn NY, 2004).

Jayawardena, Kumari, and Maria Mies. *National Liberation and Women's Liberation* (Institute of Social Studies, The Hague, 1982).

Luxemburg, Rosa. *Die Akkumulation des Kapitals. Ein Beitrag zur ökonomischen Erklärung des Kapitalismus* (Vereinigung Internationaler Verlags-Anstalten, Berlin, 1923).

Mies, Maria. 'Why German?', *Bulletin of the Deccan College Research Institute* 27, 1967/68 (Poona).

Mies, Maria. *Indian Women and Patriarchy* (Concept Publishers, New Delhi, 1980).

Mies, Maria. *The Lace Makers of Narsapur: Indian Housewives Produce for the World Market* (Zed Books, London, 1982).

Mies, Maria, Veronika Bennholdt-Thomsen and Claudia von Werlhof. *Women: The Last Colony* (Zed Books, London, 1988).

Reddock, E. Rhoda. *Women, Labour and Politics in Trinidad and Tobago: A History* (Zed Books, London, 1994).

Sarkar, Saral. *The Crises of Capitalism: A Different Study of Political Economy* (Counterpoint, Berkeley CA, 2012).

von Werlhof, Claudia. *The Failure of Modern Civilization and the Struggle for a 'Deep' Alternative: On 'Critical Theory of Patriarchy' as a New Paradigm* (Peter Lang Verlag, Frankfurt am Main, 2011).

Introduction

The idea of writing this book arose out of my desire to clarify some of the recurring confusions regarding the issue of feminism. I realized that, while the feminist movement was spreading to ever more regions of the world, while women's issues were becoming more and more 'acceptable' to the rulers of the world, the questions of what this movement was fighting against and what it was fighting for were becoming increasingly blurred.

While many of us would agree that our enemy is capitalist patriarchy as a system, and not just men, we cannot deny that many feminists do not even talk of capitalism, or, if they do, have a rather limited notion of this system and simply try to add the feminist analysis to the traditional Marxist analysis. Others only want more equality with men, like the Equal Rights Amendment (ERA) supporters in the USA, and do not even aspire to transcend capitalist patriarchy as a system.

Similarly, most of us feel that the feminist rebellion has crossed all barriers of class, race and imperialism, because women everywhere are victims of sexism and male dominance. We, therefore, feel that there is a realistic base for international solidarity among women, or for global sisterhood. On the other hand, we cannot close our eyes to the stark fact that women of all classes in the West, and middle-class women in the Third World, are also among those whose standard of living is based on the ongoing exploitation of poor women and men in the underdeveloped regions and classes.

Obviously, it is not enough to say that all women are exploited and oppressed by men. There is not only the hierarchical division between the sexes; there are also other social and international divisions intrinsically interwoven with the dominance relation of men over women. That means the feminist movement cannot ignore the issues of class, the exploitative international division of labour, and imperialism. On the other hand, the old argument, put forward by scientific socialists, that the 'woman question' is a secondary contradiction and belongs to the sphere of ideology, the superstructure or culture, can no longer be upheld to explain reality for women, particularly since everywhere the feminist rebellion was sparked off around the issue of violence.

The unresolved questions concern the relationship between patriarchy and capitalism: in other words, the relationship between women's oppression and exploitation and the paradigm of never-ending accumulation and 'growth', between capitalist patriarchy and the exploitation and subordination of colonies.

These are not academic questions. They concern every woman in her everyday life, and the feminist movement in its political goals and existence. If we are unable to find plausible answers to these questions, the danger arises that the feminist rebellion may be co-opted by the forces that only want to continue the destructive model of capital accumulation and that need the vitality of this movement to feed the slackening 'growth' process.

The following is not the result of a systematic study of the questions raised. These questions have cropped up again and again in the course of many struggles, discussions and meetings in which I have participated in recent years. Many of the discussions took place between Third World and First World women, some of them in Third World countries. The insights gained are not, therefore, something I could have gained without the existence of the international women's movement. Many women – and some men – gave me valuable ideas or feedback. I cherish most those which challenged some of my assumptions and thus forced me to deepen and broaden my analysis. Thus the question of what unites and what divides women in overdeveloped and underdeveloped classes, countries and regions played a crucial role. So did the question of the role of violence in the establishment of patriarchal men–women relations, as well as in the process of capital accumulation.

In the course of time, it became clear to me that the confusions in the feminist movement worldwide will continue unless we understand the 'woman question' in the context of all social relations that constitute our reality today – that means in the context of a global division of labour under the dictates of capital accumulation. The subordination and exploitation of women, nature and colonies are the precondition for the continuation of this model.

The second thing which became clear was the realization that women in their struggle to regain their humanity have nothing to gain from the continuation of this paradigm. Feminists everywhere would do well to give up the belief expressed by scientific socialism that capitalism, through its greed for never-ending accumulation or 'growth', has created the preconditions for women's liberation, which then can be realized under socialism. Today, it is more than evident that the accumulation process itself destroys the core of the human essence everywhere, because it is based on the destruction of women's autarky over their lives and bodies. As women have nothing to gain in their humanity from the continuation of the growth model, they are able to develop a perspective of a society which is not based on exploitation of nature, women and other peoples.

Methodologically, this means that it is not sufficient to look only at one side of the coin, but it is necessary to study the connections that exist between the various parts which have been divided up by the sexual and international division of labour. It also means understanding that these divisions and connections have a material reality because the world market does indeed connect the remotest corners of the world and the strangest people. But though these connections factually exist, they are almost totally obscured from our consciousness. We factually consume a mass of commodities produced by people in Third World countries, of whom we are not even aware. In order to overcome this alienation brought about by commodity production in the international and sexual division of labour, I have tried to look not only at what has happened to women in the West, but also at what was happening at the same time to women in the colonies. By looking at both sides of the coin it became possible to identify the contradictory policies regarding women which were, and still are, promoted by the brotherhood of militarists, capitalists, politicians and scientists in their effort to keep the growth model going. It became possible to overcome the limited view of cultural relativism which claims that women are divided by culture worldwide, whereas in fact we are both divided and connected by commodity relations.

'Looking at both sides of the coin' was facilitated in my case by the fact that I had the opportunity to meet and discuss with many women from Asia, Latin America and Africa while I worked as a coordinator of the programme 'Women and Development' at the Institute of Social Studies at The Hague. In addition the fact that I lived and worked for many years in India and had many contacts with Indian feminists also helped me to look at both sides of the coin. Therefore, much of the following analysis is based on my experiential and empirical knowledge of India and the new Indian women's movement. I owe a great deal of my insights to my Indian sisters, both the rural and the urban ones. The courage with which they are waging a struggle against patriarchal structures and institutions has been a great source of inspiration to me.

I have also learned a lot from my Third World students at the Institute of Social Studies. Their eagerness to understand what feminism was all about, and what relevance it had for themselves and for the burning problems of poverty in their own countries, prompted me to look for answers which could be valid not only for Western feminists, but also for Third World feminists.

Starting with the recognition that patriarchy and accumulation on a world scale constitute the structural and ideological framework within which women's reality today has to be understood, the feminist movement worldwide cannot but challenge this framework, along with the sexual and the international divisions of labour which are bound up with it.

The first chapter tries to clarify what the main challenges of feminism are. After a discussion of the history of the new women's movement in the USA and Europe, with special reference to its main issues, campaigns and debates, it focuses on the question of what differentiates the new women's movement from the old one. Further, what the emergence of feminist movements in Asia, Latin America and Africa can mean for the solution of the old unresolved questions: namely, the character of capitalism, the issue of colonialism and a socialist vision of a future society. In this respect, the feminist analysis of violence and of housework and the feminist concept of politics have played a crucial role in challenging the old theories of women's liberation.

The second chapter tries to trace the social origins of the sexual division of labour. The common, mostly biologistic, assumptions on the origins of the dominance relationship between men and women are critically assessed, and the notion is challenged that this relationship evolved either out of biological or out of economic determinants. It is emphasized that the monopoly over arms in the hands of Man-the-Hunter/Warrior constitutes the political power necessary for the establishment of lasting relations of exploitation between men and women, as well as between different classes and peoples. Thus, the exploitative sexual division is the social paradigm upon which the international division of labour is built up.

The third chapter traces the history of the related and double-faced processes of colonization and housewifization. The conquest and exploitation of the colonies from the 16th century onwards was the basis for capital accumulation in Europe. But equally important was the destruction of the autonomy of women over their bodies and life during the witch pogroms during the same centuries. In this chapter, I try to trace the processes and policies by which other countries and women are defined as 'nature', or made into colonies to be exploited by WHITE MAN in the name of capital accumulation or progress and civilization.

The fourth chapter extends this analysis to the contemporary new international division of labour, and the role which women have to play as cheapest producers and consumers in this world market system. The policy of defining women everywhere as dependent housewives, or the process of housewifization, is identified as the main strategy of international capital to integrate women worldwide into the accumulation process. This implies the splitting up of the economy and the labour market into a so-called formal, modern sector, in which mainly men work, and into an informal sector, where the masses of women work who are not considered to be real wage-workers, but housewives.

The fifth chapter focuses on the role of violence against women in the establishment of production relations which are not based on wage-labour proper. The analysis is based mainly on the experiences of women in

India and on their struggles against dowry-murder and rape. The various forms of direct violence against women are analysed not as a result of some timeless inborn male sadism, but as a mechanism in the process of ongoing 'primitive accumulation' by which men try to accumulate wealth and productive capital, based not on economic but on direct coercion, and on the extension of patriarchal control over women. In this chapter it is shown that patriarchal violence is not a feature of some feudal past, but the 'necessary' correlate of the so-called modernization process.

The sixth chapter addresses itself to the question of whether socialist countries that have gone through a war of liberation or a revolution can provide the desired alternative for women's liberation ,which, according to the foregoing analysis, is not possible under the laws of capital accumulation. On the basis of the examples of the USSR, China and Vietnam, it is shown that, in spite of the socialist rhetoric about women's participation in social production, the socialist accumulation process is also in reality based on the same mechanism of housewifization and on the model of dualizing the economy into a male-dominated, 'progressive' socialized sector, and into a subsidiary, private or informal sector, where mostly women are found.

The last chapter is devoted to the attempt to develop a feminist perspective of a future society which would, indeed, transcend the accumulation model based on the ever-expanding growth of commodities, wealth and productive forces. A society in which nature, women and other peoples are not colonized and exploited for the sake of others and the abstract idea of progress would have to be based on the recognition that our human world is finite. It would require a new concept of work which would transcend the present division between necessary labour increasingly relegated to machines -and creative labour reserved for human beings. The maintenance of the combination of necessary and creative work is seen as a precondition for human happiness. Such a concept of labour would have to lead to the abolition of the present sexual division of labour, as well as the international division of labour. It would have to be based on an alternative economy, an economy which would not be based on exploitation of nature, women and colonies, but would attempt to be self-sufficient to a large extent. A first step towards such autarky and the regaining of control over our lives and bodies could be a consumer liberation movement, started by women in the overdeveloped classes and countries. Such a movement, combined with a production liberation movement in underdeveloped countries and classes, could go a long way towards women's liberation in a global context.

1. What is Feminism?

Where are we today?

The Women's Liberation Movement (WLM) is perhaps the most controversial, as well as the most far-reaching of the new social movements: the ecology movement, the alternative movement, the peace movement, and others. By its very existence it provokes people. Whereas one can lead a dispassionate intellectual or political discourse on the 'ecology question', the 'peace issue', the issue of Third World dependency, the 'woman question' invariably leads to highly emotional reactions from men, and from many women. It is a sensitive issue for each person. The reason for this is that the women's movement does not address its demands mainly to some external agency or enemy, such as the state, the capitalists, as the other movements do, but addresses itself to people in their most intimate human relations, the relationship between women and men, with a view to changing these relations. Therefore, the battle is not *between* particular groups with common interests or political goals and some external enemy, but takes place *within* women and men and *between* women and men. Every person is forced, sooner or later, to take sides. And taking sides means that something within ourselves gets torn apart, that what we thought was our identity disintegrates and has to be created anew. This is a painful process. Most men and women try to avoid it because they fear that if they allow themselves to become aware of the true nature of the man-woman relationship in our societies, the last island of peace, of harmony in the cold brutal world of money-making, power games and greed will be destroyed. Moreover, if they allow this issue to enter their consciousness, they will have to admit that they themselves, women and men, are not only victims, on the one side (women), and villains (men), on the other, but that they are also accomplices in the system of exploitation and oppression that binds women and men together. And that, if they want to come to a truly free human relationship, they will have to give up their complicity. This is not only so for men whose privileges are based on this system, but also for women whose material existence is often bound up with it.

Feminists are those who dare to break the conspiracy of silence about the oppressive, unequal man-woman relationship and who want to change it. But speaking up about this system of male dominance, giving it certain names like 'sexism' or 'patriarchy', has not reduced the ambivalence mentioned above, but rather intensified and broadened it.

There have been contradictory responses to the new women's movement right from its beginning at the end of the sixties. The women who came together in this movement in the USA and in Europe began to call themselves feminists and to set up all-women's groups in which they, for the first time, after the petering out of the old women's movement in the twenties, began to talk about the 'problem without a name' (Friedan 1968). Each of us had listened, time and again in private conversations, to one of our sisters telling us how badly they had been treated by fathers, husbands, boy-friends. But this was always considered the private bad luck of this or that woman. The early consciousness-raising groups, the speaking-out sessions, the all-women's meetings, the first spectacular actions of women who began to separate themselves from the mixed groups and organizations were all occasions where women could discover that their apparently unique personal problem was the problem of all women, was indeed a social and political problem. When the slogan, 'The personal is political' was coined, the taboo was broken that surrounded the 'holy family' and its sanctum sanctorum: the bedroom and the sexual experiences of women. All women were overwhelmed by the extent and depth of sexism that came to the surface in these speaking-out sessions. The new concern that arose, the commitment to fight against male dominance, against all humiliation and ill-treatment of women, and against continuing inequality of the sexes created a new feeling of sisterhood among women which was an enormous source of strength, enthusiasm and euphoria in the beginning. This feeling of sisterhood was based on a more or less clear awareness that all women, irrespective of class, race, nation, had a common problem and this was: 'how men treat us badly', as the women of the 'Sistren Theatre Collective' in Jamaica put it in 1977 when they were about to start their group in Kingston.[1]

And wherever women come together to speak up about these most intimate and often taboo experiences, the same feelings of indignation, concern and sisterly solidarity can be observed. This is also true for the women's groups emerging in underdeveloped countries.[2] In the beginning of the movement, the hostile or contemptuous reactions from large sections of the male population, particularly those who had some influence on public opinion, like journalists and media people, only reinforced the feelings of sisterhood among the feminists who became increasingly convinced that feminist separatism was the only way to create some space for women within the overall structures of male-dominated society. But the more the feminist movement spread, the more clearly it demarcated its areas as all-women areas where men were out of bounds, the more were the negative or openly hostile reactions to this movement. Feminism became a bad word for many men and women.

In underdeveloped countries, this word was mostly used with the pejorative attribute 'Western', or sometimes 'bourgeois' to denote that feminism belongs to the same category as colonialism and/or capitalist class rule, and that Third World women have no need for this movement. At many international conferences I could observe a kind of ritual taking place, particularly after the United Nations Women's Conference in Mexico in 1975. When women spoke from a public platform, they first had to disassociate themselves from 'those feminists' before they could speak as a woman. 'Feminists' were always the 'other women', the 'bad women', the 'women who go too far', 'women who hate men', something like modern witches with whom a respectable woman did not want to be associated. Women from Asia, Latin America and Africa, particularly those connected with development bureaucracies or the UN, usually set themselves apart from those 'Western feminists' because, according to them, feminism would sidetrack the issue of poverty and development, the most burning questions in their countries. Others felt that feminists would split the unity of the working class or of other oppressed classes, that they forgot the broader issue of revolution by putting the issue of women's liberation before the issue of class struggle or national liberation struggle. The hostility against feminism was particularly strong among the organizations of the orthodox left, and more among men than among women.[3]

But in spite of these negative pronouncements about feminism in general, and 'Western feminism' in particular, the 'woman question' was again on the agenda of history and could not be pushed aside again. The International Women's Conference in Mexico, in a kind of forward strategy in its World Plan of Action, tried to channel all the subdued anger and slow rebellion of women into the manageable paths of governmental policies, and particularly to protect the Third World women from the infectious disease of 'Western feminism'. But the strategy had the opposite effect. The reports which had been prepared for this conference were, in several cases, the first official documents about the growing inequality between men and women (cf. Government of India, 1974). They gave weight and legitimacy to the small feminist groups which began to emerge in Third World countries around this time. At the Mid-Decade International Women's Conference in Copenhagen in 1980, it was admitted that the situation of women worldwide had not improved but rather deteriorated. But what had grown in the meantime were the awareness, the militancy and the organizational networks among Third World women. In spite of a lot of Third World criticism of 'Western feminism' at this conference, it still marked a change in the attitude towards the 'woman question'. After the conference, the word 'feminism' was no longer avoided by Third World women in their discussions and writings. In 1979, at an international workshop in Bangkok, Third World and First World women had already worked out a kind of common understanding of what 'feminist ideology' was; and the common goals of feminism are spelt out in the workshop documentation entitled *Developing Strategies for the Future: Feminist Perspectives* (New York, 1980). In 1981, the first feminist conference of Latin American women took place in Bogota.[4] In many countries of Asia, Latin America and Africa, small women's groups emerged who openly called themselves 'feminists', although they still had to face a lot of criticism from all sides.[5] It seems that when Third World women begin to fight against some of the crudest manifestations of the oppressive man-woman relation, like dowry-killings and rape in India, or sex-tourism in Thailand, or clitoridectomy in Africa, or the various forms of *machismo* in Latin America, they cannot avoid coming to the same point where the Western feminist movement started, namely the deeply exploitative and oppressive man-woman relation, supported by direct and structural violence which is interwoven with all other social relations, including the present international division of labour.

This genuine grassroots movement of Third World feminists followed similar organizational principles as that of the Western feminists. Small, autonomous women's groups or centres were formed, either around particular issues or, more generally, as points where women could meet, speak out, discuss their problems, reflect and act together. Thus, in Kingston, Jamaica, the theatre-collective Sistren mentioned above, formed itself as an all-women group with the aim to raise the consciousness of poor women, mainly about exploitative men-women and class relations. In Lima, Peru, the group Flora Tristan was one of the first feminist centres in Latin America (Vargas, 1981). In India a number of feminist groups and centres were formed in the big cities. The most well-known of them are the Stri Sangharsh group (now dissolved), and Saheli in Delhi. The erstwhile Feminist Network (now dissolved), the Stree Mukti Sangathna, the Forum against Oppression of Women, the Women's Centre in Bombay, the Stri Shakti Sangathana in Hyderabad, Vimochana in Bangalore, the Women's Centre in Calcutta. Around the same time, the first genuinely feminist magazines appeared in Third World countries. One of the earliest ones is *Manushi*, published by a women's collective in Delhi. In Sri Lanka the *Voice of Women* appeared around the same time. Similar magazines were published in Latin America.[6]

Parallel to this rise of Third World feminism from 'below' and at the grassroots level was the movement from 'above', which focussed mainly on women's role in development, on women's studies and the status of women. It originated, to a large extent, in national and international bureaucracies, development organizations, UN organizations where concerned women, or even feminists, tried to use the financial and organizational resources of these bureaucracies for the furthering of the women's cause. In this, certain US organizations, like the Ford Foundation, played a particularly important role. The Ford Foundation contributed generously to the setting up of women's studies and research in Third World countries, particularly in the Caribbean, in Africa (Tanzania) and in India. Research centres were created and policies were formulated with the aim of introducing women's studies into the syllabi of the social sciences.

In India, a National Association of Women's Studies was formed which has already held two national conferences. A similar organization is at present being formed in the Caribbean. But whereas the Indian association still sticks to the more general term 'women's studies', the Caribbean one calls itself 'Caribbean Association for Feminist Research and Action' (CAFRA).

This designation is already an expression of the theoretical and political discussions that are taking place in Third World countries between the two streams – the one from below and the one from above – of the new women's movement. The more the movement expands quantitatively, the more it is accepted by institutions of the establishment, the more money is coming forward from international funding agencies as well as from local governments, the more acutely the conflicts are felt between those who only want to 'add' the 'women's component' to the existing institutions and systems and those who struggle for a radical transformation of patriarchal society.

This conflict is also present in the numerous economic projects for poor rural and urban women, set up and financed by a host of development agencies, governmental as well as non-governmental ones, local and foreign ones. Increasingly, the development planners are including the 'women component' into their strategies. With all reservations regarding the true motives behind these policies (see chapter 4), we can observe that even these projects contribute to the process of increasing numbers of women becoming conscious of the 'woman's question'. They also contribute to the political and theoretical controversy about feminism.

If we today try to assess the situation of the international women's movement we can observe the following:

1. Since the beginning of the movement there has been a fast and still growing expansion of awareness among women about women's oppression and exploitation. This movement is growing faster at present in Third World countries than in First World countries where, for reasons to be analysed presently, the movement appears to be at a low ebb.

2. In spite of their commonality regarding the basic problem of 'how men treat us badly', there are many divisions among women. Third World women are divided from First World women, urban women are divided from rural women, women activists are divided from women researchers, housewives are divided from employed women.

   Apart from these objective divisions, based on the various structural divisions of labour under international capitalist patriarchy, there are also numerous ideological divisions, stemming from the political orientation of individual women or women's collectives. Thus, there are divisions and conflicts between women whose main loyalty is still with the traditional left and those who are criticizing this left for its blindness regarding the woman question. There are also divisions among feminists themselves, stemming from the differences in the analysis of the core of the problem and the strategies to be followed to solve it.

3. These divisions can be found not only *between* different sets of women, separated along the lines of class, nation and race but also *within* sets of women who belong to the same race, class or nation. In the Western feminist movement the division between lesbian and heterosexual women played an important role in the development of the movement.

4. As each woman joining the movement has to integrate in herself the existential experience of a basic commonality of women living under patriarchy with the equally existential experiences of being different from other women, the movement is characterized everywhere by a high degree of tension, of emotional energy being spent on women's solidarity as well as on setting oneself apart from other women. This is true for First and Third World movements, at least those which are not under the directives of a party, but are organizing themselves autonomously around issues, campaigns and projects.

5. Many women react to this experience of being both united and divided with moralistic attitudes. They either accuse the 'other women' of paternalistic or even patriarchal behaviour, or – if they are the accused – respond with guilt feelings and a kind of rhetorical breast-beating.

The latter can be observed particularly with regard to the relationship between sex and race, which has in recent years emerged as one of the most sensitive areas in the women's movement in the USA, England and Holland where large numbers of Third World women live who have joined the feminist movement (Bandarage, 1983). In the beginning, white feminists were often either indifferent to the race problem or they took a maternalistic or paternalistic attitude towards women of colour, trying to bring them into the feminist movement. Only when black and brown women began to extend the principle of autonomous organization to their own group, and formed their separate black women's collectives, magazines and centres the white feminists began to see that 'sisterhood' was not yet achieved if one put men on one side and women on the other. Yet although most white feminists would today admit that feminism cannot achieve its goal unless racism is abolished, the efforts to understand the relationship between sexual and racial exploitation and oppression remain usually at the individual level, where the individual woman does some soul-searching to discover and punish the 'racist' in herself.

On the other hand, neither do the analyses of black women go much further than to give expression to the feelings of anger of black women who refuse to be a 'bridge to everyone' (Rushin, 1981).

There are, as yet, not many historical and political-economic analyses of the interrelation between racism and sexism under capitalist patriarchy. Following the general ahistorical trend in social science research, racial discrimination is put on the same level as sexual discrimination. Both appear to be bound up with biological givens: sex and skin colour. But whereas many feminists reject biological reductionism with regard to sex-relations and insist on the social and historical roots of women's exploitation and oppression, with regard to race relations, the past and ongoing history of colonialism and of capitalist plunder and exploitation of the black world by white man is mostly forgotten. Instead, 'cultural differences' between Western and non-Western women are heavily emphasized. Today this colonial relation is upheld by the international division of labour. This relation is not only often eclipsed in the consciousness of white feminists whose standard of living also depends to a large extent on this ongoing colonial relation, but also in that of black women in the 'white world'. The fact that they have the same skin colour as their sisters and brothers in the 'black world' does not yet automatically put them on the same side as them (cf. Amos & Parmar, 1984), because black women are also divided by capitalist patriarchy along colonial and class lines; and class division in particular is often forgotten in the discourse on sex and race. At the present juncture, 'black' or 'brown' or 'yellow' capitalism is the great hope of the lieutenants of the capitalist world system. There are some black women in the 'black world' whose standard of living is better than that of some white women in the 'white world', and particularly than that of most of the black women in the white and in the black world's. If we do not want to fall into the trap of moralism and individualism, it is necessary to look below the surface and to come to a materialist and historical understanding of the *interplay* of the sexual, the social and the international divisions of labour. For these are the objective divisions, created by capitalist patriarchy in its conquest of the world, which are at the base of our differences although they do not determine everything. And these divisions are closely bound up with particular cultural expressions.

The way in which sex, class and race, or rather colonialism, are interwoven in our societies is not just an ideological problem which can be solved by good will alone. Anyone who wants to reach a realistic foundation for international feminist solidarity has to try to understand how these divisions along sex, race and class lines are combined. A mere appeal to more 'sisterhood' or international solidarity will not be sufficient.

As regards the divisions on the ideological and political planes, there have been attempts to categorize and label the various tendencies in the new feminist movement. Thus, some tendencies are called 'radical feminism', others 'socialist feminism' or 'Marxist feminism', others 'liberal feminism'; sometimes, depending on the political affiliation of the speaker, a tendency may also be denounced as 'bourgeois feminism'. In my view, this labelling has not contributed to a better understanding of what feminism really is, what it stands for, what its basic principles, its analysis of society and its strategies are. Moreover, this labelling has relevance only for people who mainly look at the movement from outside and try to fit it into categories already known to people. The categories developed may have some value in some countries, for example in the Anglo-Saxon world, but not in others. But by and large, their explanatory value is rather limited. Thus, the label 'radical feminism', mostly used to characterize one main trend of feminism in the USA, does not explain to an outsider what it stands for. Only those who know the movement know that radical feminists are those who advocate a strategy of radical separatism of women from men, particularly in the realm of sexual relations as the centre of patriarchal power. In polemics, 'radical feminists' are often accused of being anti-men, of all being lesbians.

The main shortcoming of this labelling approach, however, is not only its explanatory poverty but also the fact that it tries to fit the 'woman question' into already existing theoretical and political frameworks. This means these frameworks as such are not criticized from the point of view of women's liberation, but are considered more or less adequate and only *lacking* the 'women's component'. If this 'women's component' were added, it is hoped, these theories would be complete. Most feminist theoreticians who follow this approach are obviously unaware of the fact that the nature of the 'woman question' is such that it cannot simply be added to some other general theory, but that it fundamentally criticizes all these theories and begs for a new theory of society altogether. This additive labelling approach can be observed particularly in the attempts to add feminism to socialism. Characterizations of some trends in the women's movement as 'socialist feminist' or 'Marxist-feminist' are manifestations of the tendency to fit the new feminist critique and rebellion into the existing theoretical body of Marxism. By simply postulating, as a slogan of some Dutch 'socialist feminists' does, that there will be no socialism without women's liberation and no women's liberation without socialism (Fem-Soc-Group), we do not yet understand what these women mean by socialism or feminism. (For the Dutch women who coined this slogan, 'socialism' was more or less identical with European social-democracy.) Such slogans or labels may appear useful at the level of everyday politics where people want to know into which pigeon-holes to put the members of such a diffuse movement as the women's movement. But they do not give us a clue as to how these people analyse the 'woman question', what solutions they are proposing and what the relationship between the political goal of women's liberation and a socialist vision of a future society is. Such a relationship cannot simply be postulated. What is needed is a new historical and theoretical analysis of the interrelation between women's exploitation and oppression, and that of other categories of people and of nature.

Women following other tendencies, labelled 'radical' or 'liberal' feminism, have tried to fit their analysis into some other theoretical framework. Thus psychoanalysis has been the theoretical point of departure for many feminists in the USA, in France and West Germany (Millet, 1970; Mitchell, 1975; Irrigaray, 1974; Janssen-Jurreit, 1976). This emphasis on psychology and psychoanalysis has to be seen against the backdrop of the individualistic tendencies among large parts of the feminist movement in the West.

Others have used functionalism, structuralism or interactionism as theoretical frameworks for their analysis of the 'woman question'.

Of course, a social movement aiming at a fundamental change of social relations does not operate in a theoretical vacuum. It is natural that women who began to clarify their theoretical positions had to refer to existing theories. In some cases this led to a critique of at least parts of these theories: for example, Freud's theory of penis envy and of femininity came under heavy attack from feminists. But the theory as such remained intact. In other cases such a critique did not even take place, but the basic concepts and categories of such theories were used uncritically in feminist analysis.

This is particularly true for structural functionalism and its role-theory. Instead of criticizing the role theory as the theoretical framework for the maintenance of the patriarchal nuclear family under capitalism, the role theory was rather re-inforced by many feminists. The emphasis on sex-role stereotyping and attempts to solve the 'woman question' by changing this sex-role stereotyping through non-sexist socialization not only strengthened structural-functionalist analysis, but by so doing blocked the understanding of the deeper roots of women's exploitation and oppression. By defining the man-woman problem as a question of social role stereotyping and of socialization it was immediately put on an ideological plane; it became a cultural affair. The structural roots of this problem remained invisible, and thus its connection with capital accumulation remained invisible.

The latter is likewise true for the attempts to use structuralism, and, too, in its Marxist modification (Althusser, Meillassoux, Lacan) as a theoretical framework for the analysis of women's oppression. These attempts also end up by maintaining a structural division between the economic base and the 'relative autonomy' (Althusser) of the ideology. And women's oppression is considered part of ideology or culture.

All these efforts to 'add' the 'woman question' to existing social theories or paradigms fail to grasp the true historical thrust of the new feminist rebellion, namely its radical attack on patriarchy or *patriarchal civilization as a system, of which capitalism constitutes the most recent and most universal manifestation*. Since practically all the above-mentioned theories remain within the paradigm of 'civil-ized society', feminism, which in its political aim necessarily wants to transcend this model of society, cannot be simply added onto, or fitted into some forgotten niche of these theories. Many of us who have tried to fill those 'blind spots' have finally found out that our questions, our analyses put this whole model of society into question. We may not yet have developed adequate alternative theories, but our critique, which first started with those lacunae, went deeper and deeper till we realized that 'our problem', namely the exploitative oppressive men-women relationship, was systematically connected with other such 'hidden continents', above all 'nature' and the 'colonies'. Gradually a new image of society emerged in which women were not just 'forgotten', 'neglected', 'discriminated' against by accident, where they had 'not yet' had a chance to come up to the level of the men, where they were one of the several 'minorities', 'specificities' which could not 'yet' be accommodated into the otherwise generalized theories and policies, but where the whole notion of what was 'general', or what was 'specific' had to be revolution-ized. How can those who are the actual foundation of the production of life of each society, the women, be defined as a 'specific' category? Therefore, the claim to universal validity, inherent in all these theories, had to be challenged. This, however, was not yet clear to many feminists.

It is a peculiar experience of many women that they are engaged in various struggles and actions, the deeper historical significance of which they themselves are often not able to grasp. Thus, they do in fact bring about certain changes, but they do not 'understand' that the changes they are aiming at are much more far-reaching and radical than they dare to dream. Take the example of the worldwide anti-rape campaign. By focussing on the male violence against women, coming to the surface in rape, and by trying to make this a public issue, feminists have unwittingly touched one of the taboos of civilized society, namely that this is a 'peaceful society'. Although most women were mainly concerned with helping the victims or with bringing about legal reforms, the very fact that rape has now become a public issue has helped to tear the veil from the facade of so-called civilized society and has laid bare its hidden, brutal, violent foundations. Many women, when they begin to understand the depth and breadth of the feminist revolution, are afraid of their own courage and close their eyes to what they have seen because they feel utterly powerless *vis-à-vis* the task of overthrowing several thousand years of patriarchy. Yet the issues remain. Whether we – women and men – are ready or not to respond to the historic questions raised, they will remain on the agenda of history. And we have to find answers to them which make sense and which will help us to restructure social relations in such a way that our 'human nature' is furthered and not crushed.

Fair-weather Feminism?

The structural and ideological divisions among feminists referred to above, and the difficulty in breaking away from basically patriarchal theoretical frameworks and in developing new approaches cannot be explained by some inherent weak-ness of the female sex. These difficulties are rather manifestations of the actual social and political powerlessness of women and of the ambiguity which follows from it. Powerless groups, particularly if they are totally integrated within a system of power and exploitation, find it difficult to define reality differently from the powerful. This is particularly true for people whose material existence depends largely on the goodwill of the powerful. Although many women have revolted against all kinds of 'male chauvinism', they often did not dare to antagonize those on whom their jobs, their livelihood depended. For middle-class women these were often the powerful men in the academic and political establishment or even their husbands.

As long as the Western economies were experiencing an ever-expanding growth of their GNPs they could afford to neutralize social dissent and social unrest like that of the women by throwing some crumbs to such disenchanted groups. Under the pressure of the women's movement, certain reforms were introduced like a certain liberalization of the abortion laws, reforms of divorce laws, etc. And in some countries, as in Holland, the state even created commissions for the emancipation of women, and women's action and consciousness-raising groups could demand state support for their activities. Also, in the USA departments of women's studies were established in most universities without great opposition. Although this all needed a lot of struggle from the women's movement, there was a certain paternalistic benevolence in granting 'the girls' a certain niche in the system. Already at this stage the various patriarchal establishments used their power to co-opt women and to integrate their rebellion into the system. But the deepening of the economic crisis at the beginning of the 1980s, and the rise of conservative governments and tendencies in most Western countries with their new policies of restructuring the economy also marked the end of fair-weather or welfare-state feminism (De Vries, 1980). In several countries, particularly in the USA and West Germany, conservative governments launched a virtual attack on some of the half-hearted reforms achieved under the pressure of the new women's movement, above all on the liberalized abortion laws. This roll-back strategy with its renewed emphasis on the patriarchal family, on hetero-sexuality, on the ideology of motherhood, on women's 'biological' destiny, their responsibility for housework and childcare, and the overall attack on feminism had the effect that women who had hoped that women's liberation could come as a result of some legal reforms or consciousness-raising withdrew from the movement or even became hostile to it. In the academic world, conservative, or even outright reactionary theories like socio-biology, came to the surface again and women either kept quiet or began to withdraw their earlier criticism of such theories. In the field of women's studies a tendency towards academic feminism could be observed. The goal was no longer to transform society and the man-woman relationship, but to get more women into the academic establishment and women's studies and research (Mies, 1984(b)).

This roll-back strategy, however, is only the political manifestation of more fundamental structural changes in the Western economies which are usually referred to as 'flexibilization of labour'. Women are the immediate targets of this strategy. The new strategy of rationalization, computerization and automation of production processes and jobs in the service sector has the effect that women are the first to be pushed out of well-paid, qualified and secure jobs in the 'formal sector'. But they are not just being sent back to home and hearth. They are in fact pushed into a whole range of unqualified, low-paid, insecure jobs which they have to do on top of their housework, which, more than ever, is considered their true vocation. And, contrary to the official conservative ideology on women and the family, the family is no longer a place where women can be sure to find their material existence secured. Man-the-breadwinner, though still the main ideological figure behind the new policies, is empirically disappearing from the stage. Not only does the rising unemployment of men make their role of breadwinner a precarious one, but marriage for women is also no longer an economic guarantee of their lifelong livelihood.

The immediate effect of these new economic policies has been a rapid process of pauperization of women in the Western economies. Women constitute the largest section among the 'new poor' in the USA, in France, in England and in West Germany. In West Germany their proportion among the unemployed is almost 40 per cent. In the job market women are faced with all-round competition from men. This is particularly true with regard to well-paid, secure, prestigious jobs in schools and universities. In West Germany the policy of cuts in the educational system has led to large-scale unemployment, particularly of female teachers, and to the pushing out of women from the better-paid qualified posts in the universities. With jobs getting scarce, the league of men closes its ranks again and puts women again into their place, which is, according to many, the family and the home. Many men who have some power in this formal sector use it to get rid of women, particularly if these are known as feminists. The restructuring of the Western economies largely follows the model already practised in most underdeveloped countries, namely of dividing the labour market and the production process into a formal sector in industry and services with well-paid, qualified, mostly male workers, the classical wage-workers, whose job security, wages and other interests are the concern of trade unions, and an informal or unorganized sector with a host of different production relations and types of production, ranging from part-time jobs, to non-free contract labour, so-called self-employment, the new putting-out-system in tele- and other types of homeworking to domestic labour proper and any other paid or unpaid or low-paid work. This sector is characterized by low wages, absence of any job security and high 'flexibility'.

Trade unions do not feel responsible for this sector which absorbs all the chronically unemployed, marginalized people, most of them women because, according to the classical definition, shared by capital, state and the trade unions, these people are not 'free' wage-workers. People working in this so-called informal sector are like housewives. They work, often more than the 'free' wage-workers, but their labour is invisible. And thus it can become a source of unchecked, unlimited exploitation. The dualization of the economies and labour markets along the pattern known from underdeveloped countries is the method by which Western corporate capital is trying to bring the real wage level down, to save production costs and to break the power of the trade unions, because workers in the informal sector, like housewives, have no lobby and are atomized. What the experts call 'flexibilization of labour', some of us have called the 'housewifization' of labour (Mies, 1981; v. Werlhof, 1984).

The strategy of dividing the economy up into 'visible' and 'invisible' sectors is not at all new. It has been the method of the capitalist accumulation process right from its beginning. The invisible parts were per definition excluded from the 'real' economy. But they constituted in fact the very foundations for the visible economy. These excluded parts were/are the internal and external colonies of capital: the housewives in the industrialized countries and the colonies in Africa, Asia and Latin America. Due to the welfare provisions and the social security systems in Europe and the USA, the creation of an informal sector does not yet by itself make this sector a lucrative hunting ground for exploitation and accumulation. Only by simultaneously cutting down state expenditure on social welfare can the governments force the people who are thrown out of the formal sector to accept any work at any wage and any condition in order to produce their own survival. This means, in the last analysis, that the conditions which are prevailing for the vast majority of people in the underdeveloped world are returning to the centres of capitalism. Although for the time being the standard of living of the masses of people in the overdeveloped countries is still much higher than that in Third World countries, *structurally* the situation of people in the informal sector is approaching that of most people in the underdeveloped countries.

For women and the women's movement in the Western countries these developments have far-reaching consequences. Women are the hardest hit by this combined strategy of cuts in social welfare and the rationalization and flexibilization of labour. They, therefore, constitute the bulk of the 'new poor' in the Western countries (Atkinson, 1982; Möller, 1983).

For the women's movement these developments present an enormous challenge. On the one hand, they mean the end of 'fair-weather feminism'. All those feminists who had hoped that women's liberation could be brought about by putting pressure on the state and thus getting more social welfare for women, *or* by demanding equal opportunities for women in the job market, particularly in the higher ranks of this market, *or* by increasing women's participation in political and other decision-making bodies, find their expectations shattered. They have to realize today that the fundamental democratic rights, the claim to equality and freedom, are also fair-weather rights, as far as women are concerned, and that these rights, in spite of the rhetoric of their universality, are suspended when the accumulation needs of capital require this.

On the other hand, this disillusionment about the possibilities of the democratic capitalist states to fulfil the promises of the bourgeois revolution also for women can have a very salutory effect: it forces women, at least those who are not giving up their commitment to women's liberation, to open their eyes to the reality in which we live, and to turn to those questions which have been neglected by many feminists because they appeared to lie *outside* their immediate concern. These are, in my view,

1. a new assessment of what *capitalism* actually is and how women's exploitation and oppression, or patriarchy, are bound up with the process of capital accumulation.

2. a new discussion on *colonialism*. As the colonial conditions are returning to

the metropoles and as women, more than others, are affected by this process, the structural division, of Third World and First World women, brought about by the international division of labour or colonialism is getting blurred. Western feminists therefore have to learn quickly that colonized women are not only in Africa, Asia or Latin America, but also in the USA and Europe. Moreover, they have to find an answer to the question of why this highly-developed 'democratic' capitalist system still needs such colonies, in which all the rules it has laid down for itself are suspended or, in other words, why the system of capital accumulation on a world scale cannot afford to liberate women or other colonies.

3. From the above discussion and analysis will follow a renewed discussion of what a feminist vision of a future society should be or the realistic prerequisites for women's liberation. This discussion would have to transcend the boundaries created by capitalist patriarchy and take into account the experiences and analysis of women at the various ends of the global market system. Only within a perspective that comprises *all* production relations created by capitalist patriarchy and not only those which we see immediately around us, only by a truly global and holistic approach can we hope to be able to develop a vision of a future society where women and nature and other people are not exploited in the name of 'progress' and 'growth'.

What is New About Feminism?
Continuities and Discontinuities

One of the important discoveries of the new feminist movement was the rediscovery and reassessment of women's history. Methodologically this new historical approach in the analysis of the 'woman question' is closely linked to the political goal of women's liberation. Unless we know how things became what they are, we are unable to know how we should change them.

A critical assessment of the feminist movement with a view to solving some of its basic open questions has, therefore, to consider the history of this movement, not only the relatively short history of the new womens' movement which started in the West at the end of the sixties, but also the history of the earlier women's movement which petered out in the late twenties. Only by assessing how these movements have dealt with the above-mentioned basic questions, and by clarifying what the continuities and the discontinuities in the old and the new women's movement are, can we hope to learn from history and avoid the ambiguities which have marked large stretches of our history.

Continuities: Women's Liberation – A Cultural Affair?

The first wave of the women's liberation movement started in the context of the bourgeois revolutions, particularly the French Revolution of 1789 and the American Revolution of 1776.

During the French Revolution, the principles of freedom, equality and fraternity were put forward ostensibly for all mankind as basic human rights – and not only for the benefit of the rising bourgeois class. Indeed, the very fact that these principles were radical and universal made it impossible for the bourgeoisie, which had a direct and immediate interest in espousing them, to keep them within its own control. It could not prevent various categories of the oppressed and the down-trodden – the proletariat, the colonized nations, the negro slaves, and last but not least, the women – from making these principles the base of their liberation struggle in the course of time. It is not surprising, then, that French women brought forward demands for equal rights for women for the first time during the revolutionary periods around 1789 and 1848. They hoped to make their own revolution within the Great Revolution by joining in the struggle on the streets of Paris, as well as in the many discussion groups and republican clubs that had sprung up all over the country. Large masses of women from the impoverished sections of Paris participated actively in the battle against feudalism. When, in 1793, the Declaration of the Rights of Man was read in the Convent, one woman, Olympe de Gouges, raised her voice, and read her famous 17 articles on the 'Rights of Women'. She declared that if women have the right to die on the guillotine they must also have the right to speak on the tribune. She died on the guillotine the same year. And, although they had been in the vanguard of the revolution, women remained excluded from the political scene.

Also Mary Wollstonecraft's 'Vindication of the Rights of Women', published in 1792, could not change this policy of excluding women, even of the same bourgeois class, from the public sphere and from political power. The nineteenth-century women's movement, in Europe as well as in the USA, was mainly sparked off by the contradiction between the universal principles of the Bourgeois Revolution: freedom, equality, fraternity, and the deliberate exclusion of women from these human rights. The struggles of the old women's movement were therefore mainly concerned with getting women access to this public or political sphere, which was monopolized by bourgeois men.

Although Clara Zetkin, who initiated and led the Proletarian Women's Movement in Germany in the last decade of the nineteenth century, ridiculed this preoccupation with 'women's rights' as outdated 'bourgeois feminism', the aim of the socialist strategy for women's liberation, based on the theoretical foundations of Marx and Engels, was basically not much different: women's participation in public or social production as wage-labourers was seen as the precondition for their liberation (cf. Zetkin, 1971).

The addressee of most of the old feminist struggles and demands was the *state*, as the organizer and controller of the public sphere, not the men or patriarchy as a system. The social division of labour between 'private' and 'public', the main structural characteristic of capitalist industrial society, was accepted as necessary and progressive. It was not challenged either by the left, the liberal or the radical feminists. What the old women's movement fought for was that women should also get their rightful place in this public sphere. The theoretical assumptions underlying this orientation of the old movement were that women since time immemorial had been excluded from this public (political and economic) sphere. But modern society with its tremendous development of technology and material wealth on the economic plane, and with bourgeois democracy on the political plane would provide the structural and ideological preconditions for bringing women out of their idiotic privatized existence into the public arena where they would work side by side with men in 'social production'. They therefore would have the 'right' to sit with them on the same public platforms where political power was wielded. The old feminist movement drew its inspiration largely from the hope that the democratic rights of the bourgeois revolution would eventually also reach women. The difference between the liberal and the left women was that the former considered political participation in the public sphere as the key to women's liberation, whereas the latter thought that only full economic participation in 'social production' could lead to women's emancipation.

Both tendencies also used the same methods of public agitation, of propaganda, of writing and talking from public platforms. And both considered women's education and training as one of the most important methods to raise women's economic, political and cultural status. For the proletarian women's movement this emphasis on women's education was seen as necessary to make them class conscious and to improve their job opportunities. For the liberal women's movement education of girls and young women was seen as the most important path to women's emancipation. Many, if not most, of the early feminists of the 19th and 20th centuries were teachers or social workers. The emphasis on women's education and culture in the liberal camp is based on a theory of society according to which all structural problems of inequality or exploitation are basically solved, and that women's oppression is a kind of 'cultural lag' and ideological anachronism, which can be abolished by education and affirmative action and reform.

The new women's movement was also initially seen as mainly a cultural movement. It may be due to the fact that it arose in the late sixties in the USA and Western Europe in the context of the big protest movements: the Anti-Vietnam War movement, the Civil Rights movement, the Black Power movement, the Hippy movement in the USA and the Students' movement in Europe, that it was seen as a cultural phenomenon affecting mainly young middle-class women who had had access to higher education. As Herbert Marcuse pointed out, the frustrations and rebellions of this generation and class did not stem from material deprivation or poverty. The after-war years of scarcity and reconstruction were over and the economies of the capitalist West had reached a level where most people had been able to acquire most of the durable consumer goods and where full employment and continual growth seemed to have banned poverty and the cyclical economic crises for good. The traditional working-class protest, stemming from the discrepancy between profits and the misery of the workers, was blunted by high real wages and the integration of the workers into what H. Marcuse called the one-dimensional consumer society. Trade unions, capital and state all worked together to create this one-dimensional society (Marcuse, 1970). Juliet Mitchell explains the emergence of the protest movements in the context of the necessity of the capitalist economies to open up new areas of production and consumption, new markets, which required that many more people got a much higher level of education. The expansion of higher education was a precondition for the expansion of the new communication technologies and/or a market for cultural commodities (Mitchell, 1973).

The access of many more young people to higher education than before produced, however, its own contradictions insofar as this group realized the tremendous discrepancy between universal ideals of freedom and civil rights, basic for parliamentarian democracies, and the stark facts of discrimination, oppression and exploitation of minorities at home and of Third World peoples abroad. Moreover, it was this group which became aware of and articulate about the dehumanizing and alienating effects of consumerism. For the first time after World War II it articulated that human dignity was destroyed in the midst of plenty of material commodities. Thus, many people of the protest movements emphasized cultural or political forms of protest and anti-consumerism. The frustrations arose out of the realization that material affluence did not satisfy the deeper human desires for happiness, justice, freedom, self-realization. 'Water water all around and not a drop to drink' could have been the expression of these sentiments. However, the root cause of this frustration was not yet sought (by most) in the inherent mechanisms of the capitalist industrial system. It was rather believed that a cultural revolution was necessary to do away with the negative effects of technology and growth. The growth model as such and technological expansionism were not yet criticized. One standard argument was that now that poverty had been conquered for good in Western society by technological progress, there was at last scope both for a redistribution of wealth and a cultural liberation of people. Many protest movements drew their legitimacy from the discrepancy between the *potential* for human realization, inherent in modern democratic societies and its factual non-realization. All factors were at last there to fulfil the promises of the bourgeois revolution, not only for some but for all people. If this did not happen, it was not due to structural faults or to scarcity but to a lack of consciousness or political will.

The women's movement initially shared this orientation to some extent. Women in the USA and in Europe, and also in Third World countries, realized that in spite of equality of the sexes, proclaimed by all democratic constitutions, they were still treated as a sociological minority; they were discriminated against everywhere – in politics, employment, education, *in* the family, and *by* the institution of the family. Due to the then optimistic hope that at last women could become full 'citizens', the American National Organization of Women (NOW) was founded by Betty Friedan in 1966, with its emphasis on fighting for the Equal Rights Amendment (ERA). Legal action, affirmative action, cultural action, change of role models through non-sexist socialization and education, fighting against sexist images in the media were and still are some of the main forms of the feminist struggle.

This emphasis on struggles in the sphere of consciousness, ideology or culture continued even after the first euphoric years of the new women's movement were over. Many feminists still believe that patriarchal men-women relations can be changed through education or different forms of socialization, that discrimination against women in the fields of politics and employment can be abolished by giving girls more access to higher education and training. Also Women's Studies, which have by now been accepted in many universities and colleges, draw much of their legitimacy from this 'cultural feminism', the claim that equal access to education as such and the emphasis on women-oriented contents of education would go a long way towards improving the status of women.

Particularly with the appearance of the 'new technologies', the computer technology, genetic engineering and biotechnology we can hear again that women should go in for more education, more training in these technologies, particularly in computer science and microbiology, otherwise they would again be left behind by this 'third technological revolution'. Even feminists, who are critical of this technological development feel that 'we first have to know these new technologies before we can say whether they should be rejected or not'.[7]

The belief in education, cultural action, or even cultural revolution as agents of social change is a typical belief of the urban middle classes. With regard to the woman's question it is based on the assumption that woman's oppression has nothing to do with the basic material production relations or the economic system. This assumption is found more among Western, particularly American, feminists who usually do not talk of capitalism. For many Western feminists women's oppression is rooted in the *culture* of patriarchal civilization. For them feminism is, therefore, largely a cultural movement, a new ideology, or a new consciousness.

But the socialist countries also consider women's emancipation as a cultural or ideological affair (see chapter 6). After the abolition of private property and the socialist transformation of production relations, it is assumed that all remaining problems in the man-woman relation are 'cultural lags', ideological survivals of the past 'feudal' or 'capitalist' society which can be overcome through legal reform, education, persuasion, cultural revolutions and, above all, constant exhortation and propaganda. As the man-woman relationship is not considered as part and parcel of the basic structural relations of production, these methods have had as little success in the socialist countries as they had in the capitalist countries. The gap between liberal or socialist ideology enshrined in formal laws and constitutions and patriarchal practice is equally wide in both systems.

'Cultural feminism' has also had great influence in the theoretical works of feminists. This is not the place to discuss this topic in detail, but one of the more important manifestations of cultural feminism is the conceptual distinction between *gender* and *sex*, first developed by Anne Oakley, but meanwhile almost universally used in feminist writings and discussions. According to this distinction, *sex* is connected with biology, is considered to be based on hormones, gonads, genitalia, whereas the *gender* identity of men and women in any given society is considered as psychologically and socially, and that means historically and culturally determined. In order to avoid the confusion about sex as being biologically determined, the concept *gender* was introduced to denote the socially and culturally determined differences between men and women. The internalization of these differences is then called 'gendering' (Oakley, 1972).

This distinction between sex as a biological, and gender as a socio-cultural, category may at first sight appear a useful one, because it removes the irritation that woman's oppression is time and again attributed to her anatomy. But this distinction follows the well-known dualistic pattern of dividing 'nature' from 'culture' (Ortner, 1973). For women this division has had a long, and disastrous tradition in Western thought because women have been put on the side of 'nature' since the rise of modern science (Merchant, 1983). If feminists now try to get out of this tradition by defining *sex* as a purely material, biological affair and *gender* as the 'higher', cultural, human, historical expression of this affair, then they continue the work of those idealist patriarchal philosophers and scientists who divided the world up into crude 'bad' matter (to be then exploited and colonized) and 'good' spirit (to be monopolized by priests, mandarins and scientists).

It is not surprising that this terminology has immediately been adopted by all kinds of people who may not otherwise feel much sympathy for, or even be hostile to, feminism.[8] If, instead of 'sexual violence', we talk of 'gender violence', the shock is somewhat mitigated by an abstract term, which removes the whole issue from the realm of emotionality and political commitment to that of scientific and apparently 'objective' discourse. If the woman's question is again removed to that level, many men and many women, who do not want to change the status quo, will again feel quite comfortable with the women's movement.

But let us not fool ourselves. Human sex and sexuality have never been purely crude biological affairs. Nor has the female or male body been a purely biological affair (see chapter 2). 'Human nature' has always been social and historical. Human physiology has throughout history been influenced and shaped by inter-action with other human beings and with external nature. Thus, sex is as much a cultural and historical category as gender is.

By the dualistic splitting up of sex and gender, however, by treating the one as biological and the other as cultural, the door is again opened for those who want to treat the sexual difference between humans as a matter of our anatomy or as 'matter'. Sex as matter can then become an object for the scientist who may dissect, analyse, manipulate and reconstruct it according to his plans. Since all spiritual value has been driven out of sex and encapsulated in the category of gender, the taboos which so far still surround the sphere of sex and sexuality may easily be removed. This sphere can become a new hunting ground for biological engineering, for reproduction-technology, for genetic and eugenic engineering and last but not least for capital accumulation (cf. Corea, 1984).

Certainly Anne Oakley and others who introduced this distinction between sex and gender may not have envisaged these developments; they considered these categories as analytical tools only or theoretical constructions which help clarify our ideas, but concepts are also means to construct reality. Therefore it is essential that our categories and concepts are such that they help us to transcend capitalist-patriarchy and help us construct a reality in which neither women, men, nor nature are exploited and destroyed. But this presupposes that we understand that women's oppression today is part and parcel of capitalist (or socialist) patriarchal *production relations*, of the paradigm of ever-increasing growth, of ever-increasing forces of production, of unlimited exploitation of nature, of unlimited production of commodities, ever-expanding markets and never-ending accumulation of dead capital. A purely cultural feminist movement will not be able to identify the forces and powers that stand in our way. Nor will it be able to develop a realistic perspective of a future society free of exploitation and oppression.

23

Discontinuities: Body Politics

A look at the recent history of the new women's movement can teach us that the main issues which sparked off women's rebellion were not the issues usually taken up by cultural feminism, the issues of inequality and discrimination, but other issues which were all in one way or the other connected with the *female body*. In contrast to the old women's movement the new feminist movement did not concentrate its struggles on the public sphere (politics and economy), but opened up, for the first time in history, the private sphere as an arena for women's struggles. Women had been relegated to this 'private' sphere in capitalist patriarchy, which apparently was an area free of politics. By speaking openly about their most intimate relations with men, their sexuality, their experiences with menstruation, pregnancy, childcare, their relationship to their own bodies, the lack of knowledge about their own bodies, their problems with contraception etc., the women began to socialize and thus politicize their most intimate, individualized and atomized experiences. 'Body politics' was and still is the area around which the new women's movement got sparked off, not only in the West, but also in many underdeveloped countries. By defining this privatized, segregated sphere of the man-woman relation as a political one, by coining the slogan 'the personal is political', the structural division of bourgeois society between private and public was challenged. This meant at the same time a critique of the concept of 'politics' as it was commonly understood (Millet, 1970). 'Body politics' was not developed as a deliberate strategy by the feminists. It rather grew out of the frustrations and the rebellion of masses of women in the Western societies about certain issues which demonstrated the basically violent and oppressive nature of the man-woman relationship in our societies. What were the issues?

In many countries, the USA, England, France, West Germany, and later in Italy and Spain, the women's movement became a mass movement only with the campaigns for the liberalization or the abolition of the abortion laws in the early 1970s.

In the USA, England and West Germany, the first phase of the feminist movement started when women who participated in the left students movement began to separate from these organizations and to form their own autonomous groups. These groups were concentrated in university centres, and although their first spectacular actions were widely published, the ordinary women did not yet admit that male dominance, or 'male chauvinism' as it was then called, was also a problem for them. This changed with the campaigns against the abortion laws.

In France a self-accusation campaign was started by prominent women in the *Nouvel Observateur* in April 1971. Many prominent women signed a declaration that they had had abortions. They thus challenged the state as the guardian of law and order to take legal action against them. A similar campaign was started by Alice Schwarzer in the magazine *Stern* in Germany in the same year. Three hundred and seventy-four women signed the declaration. This was followed by a large series of actions, demonstrations, rallies, which mobilized hundreds of thousands of women, and brought them into the streets and up in arms against the most powerful institutions which are the guardians of modern patriarchy: the state, the law, the church and the gynaecologists. This large movement put pressure on the ruling party, the social-democrats, to abolish the law which criminalizes abortion. The campaigns against the abortion laws petered out in the early seventies, after some legal reforms had been achieved. In the old movement, the achievement of legal or political aims was usually the end of the movement. Not so in the new WLM. One could even say that the end of the campaign against abortion laws had signalled the beginning of the movement. What happened was that women were not mobilized by a party, a trade union or other organization, but by small groups of women who began to establish nationwide networks (Schwarzer, 1980).

The mass demonstrations and rallies were accompanied and followed by a proliferation of small groups, which cropped up in all cities. The women who had come out into the streets did not want to disappear again in the anonymity of their isolated homes. They were keen to join or form new women's groups. These women's groups discussed initially the problems of the abortion laws. But soon they developed into consciousness-raising groups, where not only problems of abortion were discussed, but experiences were exchanged about one's sexuality, one's experience as a mother, a lover, a wife. In short, the hidden reality of women's private lives became a public issue and many women realized that their 'unique' problem with their man, their child, their boss etc., was the 'general' problem of all women. In these discussions it became clear that the 'enemies' were not only the state, the church, the law, the male doctors, but that each woman also had the 'enemy' in her bed. Thus the campaigns for the abolition of the abortion laws had the logical consequence that more and more women began to reflect and discuss the issues of sexuality, the question why the consequences of sexual intercourse had always to be borne by women, why women knew so little about their own sexuality, why the questions of women's orgasm, of masturbation and female homosexuality were such taboos. These discussions brought finally to the surface that the most intimate sexual relationship between women and men was experienced by many women as characterized by violence, humiliation and coercion.

Violence and coercion seemed to be the main mechanisms by which the unequal power relation in the area of body politics was maintained. Women discovered more and more that their own bodies had been alienated from them and had been turned into objects for others, had become 'occupied territory'. Many began to understand that male dominance, or patriarchy as it then began to be called, had its origin not in the realm of public politics only but in men's control over women's bodies, particularly their sexuality and their generative capacities (Millet, 1970).

From this followed a 'discovery' of and a struggle against other manifestations of male violence. The next issues around which women were mobilized were wife and *women beating*. Large numbers of groups in many countries launched a movement against wife beating, and the physical and psychological cruelty of men towards women. Shelters for battered women were set up in most Western countries by autonomous women's groups as a first self-help measure. Meanwhile, such shelters were also set up in underdeveloped countries like India.

The movement against women battering was followed and accompanied by a similarly broad movement against rape and the molestation of women, against violence against women in the streets, in the media, in advertisements, and in pornography. Whereas the campaign against the abortion laws, at least in its initial stages, had addressed itself to the state and its law-giving bodies, the movements around the issue of male violence focussed on women as the victims, whom the feminists tried to help by a number of self-help initiatives like rape crisis centres, houses for battered women, feminist health collectives, etc. It had become clear in the meantime that women would not be able to develop a new consciousness as long as they lived in constant fear of men's physical or psychological assault. And it had also become clear that legal reform or state support was of no avail at this level, because women who tried to appeal for state or police protection against male violence had soon realized that the state did not interfere with the individual man if he treated a woman badly in his private sanctuary, the family. Although the modern state as the general patriarch had assumed the monopoly over all direct violence, it had left some of it to the individual patriarch in his family. Therefore, rape, for example, cannot become a punishable offence as long as it takes place within marriage. Raped women in all countries have realized that all the laws pertaining to rape are biased against women, that rape is blamed on the victim herself, that a raped woman, if she accuses a man, is often 'raped' a second time in court by the lawyers who take all liberty to make inquiries about the sexual life of the victim, whereas the man's aggression is often played down as a cavalier act. The more the feminist movement mobilized around various manifestations of sexist violence, the more it dawned on women that some of the basic human rights, proclaimed and upheld by all democratic constitutions, particularly the right to the inviolability and integrity of one's body, were not guaranteed for women. The stark fact that all women are potential victims of such male violence, and that modern democratic states with all their might and sophistication are not capable of implementing these basic rights for women raised serious doubts in the minds of many feminists about the state as an ally in their struggle for women's liberation. All the claims that direct violence had disappeared from modern democratic 'civilized' societies could not be accepted by women who had experienced violence in many different forms. More and more women began to understand that the often praised 'peace' in these societies was based on the everyday direct and indirect aggression against women. In the German peace movement the feminists coined the slogan: 'peace in patriarchy is war against women'.

The movements against violence against women in the context of body politics taught perhaps the most important lesson to women, namely that, contrary to the hopes of the earlier women's movement, the participation of women in the public sphere, the achievement of voting rights and women's participation in wage-employment had not solved the basic problem of the patriarchal man-woman relationship which seemed to be based on violence. The mobilization around the manifestations of sexist violence enlarged women's awareness about the systematic connection between the apparently 'private' aggression of individual men and the main institutions and 'pillars' of 'civilized society': the family, the economy, education, law, the state, the media, politics. While starting with their personal experiences of various forms of male violence, women began to understand that rape, wife-beating, harassment, molestation of women, sexist jokes, etc., were not just expressions of deviant behaviour on the part of some men, but were part and parcel of a whole system of male, or rather patriarchal, dominance over women. In this system both direct physical violence and indirect or structural violence were still commonly used as a method to 'keep women in their place'.

The origins and political significance of male violence against women were interpreted differently by different feminist groups. Some saw in male violence the manifestation of a universal and timeless system of male dominance or sexual power politics (Millet, 1970) which, in the last analysis, was rooted in the male physique, or psychology. This interpretation leaves little room for historical development and specificity, but assumes that men everywhere and at all times have tried to build their own power on the subordination of women.

My view on this question is that if we as women reject a biologistic explanation of our subordination, we must also reject biologistic reductionism with regard to the phenomenon of male sexist violence. It is more realistic to interpret these forms of male violence, and particularly the fact that they seem to be on the increase (see chapter 5), as time-bound and specific, and inherently bound up with the social paradigm which dominates our present world called 'civilization' or, in other words, 'capitalist patriarchy'. This does not mean that earlier patriarchal systems did not know violence against women (cf. the Chinese, the Indian, the Jewish patriarchies), but these systems never claimed that they had done away with direct violence, that they had 'pacified', 'civilized', 'domesticated', 'rationalized' all direct aggression of men against men and men against women. But modern or capitalist patriarchy, or 'civilization', has risen particularly with this claim; it has proclaimed itself superior to all other 'savage', 'barbaric' systems precisely because it claims to have banned all direct violence in the interaction of its citizens and handed it over to the overall sovereign, the state (cf. Elias, 1978).

If now, in spite of all the highly praised achievements of 'civilization', women under this system are still raped, beaten, molested, humiliated, tortured by men, a few serious questions arise which beg an answer:

1. If violence against women is not accidental but part of modern capitalist patriarchy, then we have to explain why this is so. If we reject a biologistic explanation – as I do – we have to look for reasons which are central to the functioning of the system as such.
2. If we include the so-called private sphere into the sphere of the economy and politics – as feminists do – then the claim that capitalism has transformed all extra-economic violence or coercion into economic coercion – a position held by Marxists – cannot be upheld.
3. In the political sphere, the state monopoly over direct violence obviously stops at the door of the private family.
4. If this is so, then the line dividing the 'private' from the 'public' is necessarily the same line that divides 'private' unregulated male violence (rule of might) from regulated state violence (rule of right).
5. Hence, as far as women are concerned, the hope that in civilized or 'modern'

society the 'rule of right' would replace the 'rule of might' – as the old women's movement had hoped – has not been borne out. Both co-exist side by side (cf. Bennholdt-Thomsen, 1985).

6. Again, if this co-existence is not just accidental or the result of survivals of 'barbaric' times, as some interpret it, then obviously we have to come to a different understanding of what civilization or capitalist patriarchy is.

Hence, the problem of violence around which women in all countries mobilized leads to a radical questioning of the accepted views on the social system we live in.

Discontinuities: A New Concept of Politics

Already in the early consciousness-raising groups the division between 'private', and 'political' or 'public' was rejected and the private sphere was discovered as the foundation, the base of public sexual politics. The slogan, 'The personal is political' had the effect that women began to change their self-perception as 'non-political' beings and that they began to act as political subjects around issues which were close to them. In the context of the struggles around 'body politics', a new concept of politics emerged which, in the last analysis, radically criticizes the concept of politics in parliamentary democracy. For feminists, 'politics' is no longer identical with going to the polls, electing one's candidate to a parliament and hoping that he will change things *in the name of* the electorate. Feminists have tried to move from a concept of 'politics by delegation' or vicarious politics,[9] to a concept of 'politics in the first person'. Particularly the groups which called themselves 'autonomous' made it a point that they did not want to delegate the struggle for women's liberation to some male-dominated party or other organization. History had taught them that even women in these organizations were powerless when it came to the crucial problems of patriarchal man-woman relations. Contrary to the old movement, the new feminists rather believe in direct political action, campaigns, initiatives, in starting women's studies themselves, even before the political or academic establishments give their approval, in creating numerous women's self-help and other projects with their own means and without waiting for support and acknowledgement from the administration or politicians. Feminists learned very fast that even small and powerless groups could achieve their goals faster if they created publicity through non-parliamentary means and methods than by following the bureaucratic procedures of party or trade union politics. 'Politics in the first person' was not only much more fun, more inspiring, but obviously also more effective than 'politics by representation'.

It has been the experience in practically all countries where small autonomous feminist groups began to adopt this concept of politics in the first person and to mobilize around issues of body politics, that the women and the women's wings in the political parties, particularly the left parties, were put under pressure also to take up these issues, if they did not want to leave the whole mobilization to the feminists. Although the parties of the orthodox left had always been critical of, if not hostile to, feminism, when the campaigns for the liberalization of abortion or against rape or other brutalities against women started, the women in the left parties (from the Communist parties to the social-democratic parties) could not sit back and watch. But the initiative for such struggles never came from the party women.

The autonomous groups stuck to the principle of 'politics in the first person' also because they were afraid that their mobilization might get instrumentalized by those parties for their own electoral interest, an experience undergone by numerous other powerless groups which had asked some party leaders to take up their grievances and to struggle in their name. Against such 'vicarious politics' the principle of *autonomy* was upheld. It meant, above all, that women would not entrust their struggles, their analysis, their organization, their action to anybody else, but would take politics into their own hands.

The emphasis on autonomy and politics in the first person was different in different countries. In countries where the ruling parties were sympathetic to the new women's movement, as was the case for example with the social-democratic parties in Scandinavia and Holland, the distinction between 'autonomous feminists' and 'party women' was not so sharp. Many feminists in these countries worked in governmental organizations and hoped thus to move the state machinery in favour of women. As long as the weather was fair, this approach showed good results in these countries.

In West Germany the Social Democrats were also in power in those years, but patriarchal structures in this party were so dominant that not even its women's wing, the Working Group of Social-Democratic Women (ASF) could achieve anything. In the course of the years many party women were disillusioned and frustrated. After the election of 1980 many gave up party politics and formed an autonomous grouping called the 'Women's Initiative of 6th October'.

The concept of politics developed by the feminist movement, the principle of an autonomous programme and practice was not only a challenge to the established parliamentary parties, but even more so to the traditional left parties, particularly the orthodox CPs. The impact of this challenge can perhaps best be illustrated by the reaction of the Communist Party of Italy (CPI) to feminism. In 1976, at the national conference of communist women, Gerardo Chiaromonto officially introduced the word women's 'liberation', along with the word 'emancipation' traditionally used in the Communist Party of Italy, into the party discourse. 'Emancipation' was understood in the way Engels, Bebel, Zetkin and Lenin had understood it: the introduction of women into social production as a prerequisite for their emancipation. 'Liberation', the word used by the feminists, meant the total liberation of the whole person, not only of her labour power.

The official recognition of feminism by the powerful CPI, which had so far been hostile to and critical of feminists, was a reaction to the tremendous pressure on the women and men of the CPI, exerted by the activities and the mobilization of Italian feminists. As Carla Ravaioli remarks, feminism was the spectre that haunted the national women's conference of the CPI in 1976, but also many of the debates afterwards. For the first time a spokesman of the CPI openly admitted that the feminist movement was a reality, that the party had to make an effort to understand its origins and motives: 'We also have to study the reasons for certain shortcomings of the labour movement and of our party in dealing with certain problem areas like those of our customs, our sexuality and the interpersonal manners, relationships' (Chiaromonto, quoted by Ravaioli, 1977: 10, transl. M.M.).

But the challenge of feminism to the classical CP concept of politics went deeper than the emotional sphere of the man-woman relationship, which the CPI also defined as being part of the 'superstructure' or culture (see above). As Carla Pasquinelli points out, the real reason for the earlier reservations of the CPI against feminism was precisely that the principle, 'the personal is political' constitutes the most complete antithesis to Leninism with its democratic centralism and its dictatorship of the proletariat (Pasquinelli, 1981). The opening of the CPI to feminism was certainly part and parcel of the new strategy of Italian Eurocommunism, but it was also a reflection of the fact that feminism with its few radical principles, and in spite of its diversity and its often chaotic functioning, challenged the political and theoretical claim of the classical communist parties to possess the blueprint for a total transformation of society. For feminists these parties and their politics were not radical enough.

This is not the place to elaborate further on the repercussions the feminist movement has had among the organizations of the traditional left. In several countries a new discussion has started about the relationship between feminism and the left (Rowbotham, Segal, Wainwright, 1980; Hartmann, 1981; Jelpke (ed.), 1981). When feminists in Third World countries write the history of their own movement, they will most probably discover similar developments. The fact that today the earlier attitudes of open hostility to feminism or of ignoring it as irrelevant have given way to a strategy of 'embracing feminism', which can be observed with many traditional communist parties, is proof of the strength of its new concept of politics.

Moreover, the concept of 'politics in the first person', the rejection of the politics of representation, the rejection of the dividing line between the 'private' and the 'public' and the politicization of the private sphere were later also taken over by a number of new social movements like the citizens' initiative movement in West Germany, the alternative movement, the ecology movement and the Green Party, which made 'basis-democracy' one of their main political principles. A number of organizational principles of the feminist movement like nonbureaucratic, non-hierarchical functioning, decentralization and emphasis on grass-roots initiatives are today shared by most of the other social movements in Europe and the USA.

Thus, although the new feminist movement did not start with a unified programme and a fully developed analysis, but with women's rebellion against various forms of male dominance in the sphere to which they had always been relegated – the private sphere and the sphere of their bodies – this approach had its own dynamics and momentum which went further and reached deeper levels of the social fabric than most critics of the movement had initially thought. The feminist movement as a political movement has perhaps more far-reaching repercussions than any of the other new social movements today.

Discontinuities: Women's Work

Another area where the feminist movement broke with the traditions of the old women's movement as well as with those of the orthodox left was the area of women's work. Whereas the old movement and the orthodox left had accepted the capitalist division between private housework or – in Marxist terminology – reproductive work, and public and productive work – or wage-work, the only sphere from which they expected revolution as well as women's emancipation – the feminists not only challenged this division of labour but also the very definitions of 'work' and 'non-work'. This approach also put into question the accepted division, following from the other dualistic divisions, between politics and economics. It was only logical that, once women had begun to consider the personal and the 'private' as political, that they also began to re-evaluate and re-define the work that most women did in this 'private' sphere, namely housework.

One of the most fruitful debates which feminism had started was the debate on domestic labour. This debate, more than others, was a challenge not only to the concept of politics of the traditional left but also to some of its fundamental theoretical positions. Significantly, the debate on housework was the first instance that men participated in the feminist discourse.

But before this debate on domestic labour started and before it degenerated into a more or less academic discourse, the issue of housework was raised as a *political issue* in the context of the labour struggles in Italy in the early seventies. The first challenge to the orthodox Marxist theory on women's work came from Italy, from Maria-Rosa Dalla Costa's essay, 'The Power of Women and the Subversion of the Community', which was published together with Selma James's 'A Woman's Place' in 1972 in Padua and in the same year in Bristol.

In this essay the classical Marxist position that housework is 'non-productive' is challenged for the first time. Dalla Costa points out that what the housewife produces in the family are not simply use-values but the commodity 'labour power' which the husband then can sell as a 'free' wage labourer in the labour market. She clearly states that the productivity of the housewife is the precondition for the productivity of the (male) wage labourer. The nuclear family, organized and protected by the state, is the social factory where this commodity 'labour power' is produced. Hence, the housewife and her labour are not outside the process of surplus value production, but constitute the very foundation upon which this process can get started. The housewife and her labour are, in other words, the basis of the process of capital accumulation. With the help of the state and its legal machinery women have been shut up in the isolated nuclear family, whereby their work there was made socially invisible, and was hence defined – by Marxist and non-Marxist theoreticians – as 'non-productive'. It appeared under the form of love, care, emotionality, motherhood and wifehood. Dalla Costa challenged the orthodox left notion, first spelt out by Engels, but then dogmatized and codified by all communist parties, and still upheld today, that women had to leave the 'private' household and enter 'social production' as wage-workers along with the men if they wanted to create the preconditions for their emancipation. Contrary to this position, Dalla Costa identified the strategic link created by capital and state between the unpaid housework of women and the paid wage-work of men. Capital is able to hide behind the figure of the husband, called 'breadwinner', with whom the woman, called 'housewife', has to deal directly and for whom she is supposed to work out of 'love', not for a wage. 'The wage commands more work than what collective bargaining in the factories shows us. *Women's work appears as personal service outside of capital*' (Dalla Costa, 1973: 34; transl. M.M.).

Dalla Costa rejects the artificial division and hierarchy capital has created between wage-workers on the one side and non-wage-workers on the other:

> In the measure that capital has subordinated the man to itself by making him a wage-labourer it has created a cleavage between him – the wage labourer – and all other proletarians who do not receive a wage. Those who are not considered capable of becoming a subject of social revolt because they do not participate directly in social production (Dalla Costa, 1973: 33).

On the basis of this analysis, Dalla Costa also criticizes the notion held by many men and women of the left, that women are only 'oppressed', that their problem is 'male chauvinism'. As capital is able to command the unpaid labour of the housewife as well as the paid labour of the wage labourer, the domestic slavery of women is called *exploitation*. According to Dalla Costa, one cannot understand the exploitation of wage-labour unless one understands the exploitation of non-wage-labour.

The recognition of housework as productive labour and as an area of exploitation and a source for capital accumulation also meant a challenge to the traditional policies and strategies of left parties and trade unions which had never included housework in their concept of work and their struggles. They have always colluded with capital in its strategy to remove all non-wage work from public perception.

It is not accidental that the issue of domestic labour was first raised in Italy, one of the more 'underdeveloped' countries of Europe which nevertheless had a strong communist party. As Selma James points out in her introduction, Italy had only a small number of female factory workers, the majority of women being 'housewives' or peasant women. On the other hand, Italy had seen a number of labour struggles, influenced by the non-parliamentary opposition which had included 'reproductive struggles', that is, non-payment of rent, struggles in neighbourhoods and schools. In all these struggles women had played a prominent role.

Moreover, Dalla Costa already saw a structural similarity between women's struggles and the struggles of Third World countries against imperialism as well as that of the blacks in the United States and the youth rebellion as the revolt of all those who had been defined as being *outside* of capitalism (or as belonging to 'pre-capitalist', 'feudal', etc., formations). With Frans Fanon she interprets the divisions among women (as housewives and wage-workers) as a result of a colonizing process because the family and the household to her is a colony, dominated by the 'metropolis', capital and state (Dalla Costa, 1973: 53). Dalla Costa and James wanted to reintroduce women into history as revolutionary subjects.

As a strategy to overthrow capitalism they launched the 'Wages for Housework' campaign. Many women in Europe and Canada were mobilized by this campaign and a lively discussion took place about the prospects of this strategy. Eventually the campaign petered out because several questions inherent in it could not be solved, for instance, the problem that 'wages for housework' would not end the isolation and atomization of housewives, or that the total generalization of wage labour would not necessarily lead to an overthrow of capitalism but rather to a totalization of alienation and commodity production, or the question, who would pay the wages for housework, the capitalists, the state or the husband?

In spite of these unresolved questions, the 'Wages for Housework' campaign had put the issue of women's domestic labour on the agenda of feminist theorizing. The 'domestic labour debate' which followed the book of Dalla Costa and James, particularly in Britain, but also in West Germany, has been an important contribution to a feminist theory of work. However, as many of the women and men who participated in this debate came from the traditional left, their concern eventually seemed to be rather to 'save their Marx' than to promote women's liberation.

Hence much of the debate ended in typically academic arguments at the centre of which was the question whether Marx's theory of value could be applied to domestic labour or not. Following from this, the dividing line between orthodox Marxists and feminists continued to be the question whether housework was considered 'socially productive' labour or not.

I do not intend to go back to the domestic labour debate here. As far as the politics of the feminist movement are concerned, its contribution was limited. But it did confront the left organizations for the first time with the unresolved question of women's housework under capitalism. Today many women and men of the left admit that Marx left out housework in his analysis of capitalism, but they then proceed to say that this does not invalidate the central role Marx assigned to wage labour, as the wage-labour relation to capital still constitutes *the* capitalist production relation.

The domestic labour debate, which took place between 1973 and 1979, did not include other areas of non-wage work which are tapped by capital in its process of accumulation. This is particularly all the work performed by subsistence peasants, petty commodity producers, marginalized people, most of whom are women, in the underdeveloped countries. Thus, most people involved in the discussion on housework did not transcend the Eurocentric view of capitalism. According to this view, these other areas of human labour are considered to be lying outside of capitalism and society proper. They are called 'pre-capitalist', 'peripheral-capitalist', 'feudal' or 'semi-feudal', or simply underdeveloped or backward. Sometimes they are referred to as areas of 'uneven development'.

The discovery, however, that housework under capitalism had also been excluded per definition from the analysis of capitalism proper, and that this was the mechanism by which it became a 'colony' and a source for unregulated exploitation, opened our eyes to the analysis of other such colonies of non-wage-labour exploitation, particularly the work of small peasants and women in Third World countries. This discussion was mainly led by feminists in West Germany who extended the critique of Marx's blindness regarding women's work to the blindness regarding the other types of non-wage-work in the colonies.[10]

In an article called 'Women's work, the blind spot in the critique of political economy', Claudia v. Werlhof challenged the classical notion of capital versus wage labour as *the only* capitalist production relation. She identified two more production relations based on non-wage labour, namely housework and subsistence work in the colonies, as prerequisites for the 'privileged' (male) wage-labour relation. In the discussions that took place between Claudia v. Werlhof, Veronika Bennholdt-Thomsen and myself in these years on the various forms of non-wage labour relations and their place in a worldwide system of capital accumulation, Rosa Luxemburg's work on imperialism played a decisive role (Luxemburg, 1923).

Rosa Luxemburg had tried to use Marx's analysis of the process of extended reproduction of capital or capital accumulation (Marx, *Capital*, Vol. II) for the analysis of imperialism or colonialism. She had come to the conclusion that Marx's model of accumulation was based on the assumption that capitalism was a closed system where there were only wage labourers and capitalists. Rosa Luxemburg showed that historically such a system never existed, that capitalism had always needed what she called 'non-capitalist milieux and strata' for the extension of labour force, resources and above all the extension of markets. These non-capitalist milieux and strata were initially the peasants and artisans with their 'natural economy', later the colonies. Colonialism for Rosa Luxemburg is therefore not only the last stage of capitalism (Lenin, 1917), but its constant necessary condition. In other words, without colonies capital accumulation or extended reproduction of capital would come to a stop (Luxemburg, 1923: 254–367).

This is not the place to go further into the debate which followed Rosa Luxemburg's work. With the tendencies governing the Comintern in the twenties it is not surprising that her views were criticized and rejected. I am also not concerned with Rosa Luxemburg's final expectation that if all 'non-capitalist milieux and strata' have been integrated into the accumulation process, capitalism would come to its logical breakdown. But what her work opened up for our feminist analysis of women's labour worldwide was a perspective which went beyond the limited horizon of industrialized societies and the housewives in these countries. It further helped to transcend theoretically the various artificial divisions of labour created by capital, particularly the sexual division of labour and the international division of labour by which precisely those areas are made invisible which are to be exploited in non-wage labour relations and where the rules and regulations governing wage-labour are suspended. We consider it the most important task of feminism *to include all these relations* in an analysis of women's work under capitalism, because today there can be no doubt that capital has already reached the stage of which Rosa Luxemburg spoke. All milieux and strata are already tapped by capital in its global greed for ever-expanding accumulation. It would be self-defeating to confine our struggles and analysis to the compartmentalizations capitalist patriarchy has created: if Western feminists would only try to understand women's problems in overdeveloped societies, and if Third World women would only restrict their analysis to problems in underdeveloped societies. Because capitalist patriarchy, by dividing and simultaneously linking these different parts of the world, has already created a worldwide context of accumulation within which the manipulation of women's labour and the sexual division of labour plays a crucial role.

A look at the brief history of the feminist movement can teach us that the rejection of all dualistic and hierarchical divisions, created by capitalist patriarchy, viz., between public and private, political and economic, body and mind, head and heart, etc., was a correct and successful strategy. This was not a pre-planned programme of action, but the issues raised were of such a nature that feminists could expect success only by radically transcending these colonizing divisions, for it became increasingly clear that the capitalist mode of production was not identical with the famous capital-wage-labour relation, but that it needed different categories of colonies, particularly women, other peoples and nature, to uphold the model of ever-expanding growth.

At present, I think it is necessary that feminists worldwide began to identify and demystify all colonizing divisions created by capitalist patriarchy, particularly by the interplay between the sexual and the international division of labour.

An emphasis on these colonial divisions is also necessary from another point of view. Many feminists in the United States and Europe have, together with critical scientists and ecologists, begun to criticize the dualistic and destructive paradigm of Western science and technology. Drawing their inspiration from C.G. Jung's psychology, humanistic psychology, non-dualistic 'Eastern' spirituality, particularly Taoism and other oriental philosophies, they propose a new *holistic* paradigm, the New Age paradigm (Fergusson, 1980; Capra, 1982; Bateson, 1972). This emphasis on the fact that in our world everything is connected with everything and influences everything is definitely an approach which goes along with much of the feminist rebellion and vision of a future society. However, if this desire to 'become whole' again, and to build bridges across all the cleavages and segmentations White Man has created is not to be frustrated again, it is necessary that the New Age feminists, the eco-feminists and others open their eyes and minds to the real colonies whose exploitation also guarantees them the luxury of indulging in 'Eastern spirituality' and 'therapy'. In other words, if the holistic paradigm is nothing but an affair of a new spiritualism or consciousness, if it does not identify and fight against the global system of capitalist accumulation and exploitation, it will end up by becoming a pioneering movement for the legitimization of the next round of the destructive production of capitalism. This round will not focus on the production and marketing of such crude material commodities as cars and refrigerators, but on non-material commodities like religion, therapies, friendship, spirituality, and also on violence and warfare, of course with the full use of the 'New Age' technologies.

In the following, therefore, I shall deal with these colonizing divisions of capitalist patriarchy, particularly the interplay between the sexual and international division of labour.

Concepts

Before starting the discussion of the sexual and the international division of labour, I want to clarify why I use certain concepts in my analysis and not others. This does not mean that I propose *fully to define* these concepts, because the concepts which emerged in the feminist discourse were mostly *struggle concepts*, not based on theoretical definitions worked out by an ideological mastermind of the movement. Therefore, the concepts I am proposing are of a more open character than scientific definitions. They are derived from our struggle experiences and the reflection on these experiences, and have thus a certain explanatory value. I do not think that it will help us very much to enter into a purely academic debate on the use of this or that concept. But, as we saw already in the discussion of the use of the concepts 'gender' or 'sex', it is important to recognize that questions of conceptualization are questions of power, that is, they are political questions. In this sense, the clarification of conceptual positions is part of the political struggle of feminism.

Exploitation or Oppression/Subordination?

In the feminist discourse words are used to denote and explain the problems women are suffering from in our societies. The terms 'subordination' and 'oppression' are widely used to specify women's position in a hierarchically structured system and the methods of keeping them down. These concepts are used by women who would call themselves radical feminists as well as by those who come from a Marxist background or call themselves Marxist or socialist feminists. The latter usually do not talk of exploitation when discussing the problems of women, because exploitation to them is a concept reserved for *economic* exploitation of the wage-worker under capitalism. As women's grievances go beyond those of wage-workers and are part of the 'private' man-woman relation, which is not seen as an exploitative one, but an oppressive one, the term exploitation is avoided.

In the following discussion I shall, however, use the term exploitation to identify the root cause of the oppressive man-woman relationship. The reasons for this usage are the following:

When Marx specifies the particular capitalist form of exploitation which, according to him, consists in the appropriation of surplus labour by the capitalists, he uses this general term in a specific narrow sense. But 'exploitation', as is explained in the next chapter, has a much wider connotation. In the last analysis it means that someone gains something by robbing someone else or is living at the expense of someone else. It is bound up with the emergence of men's dominance over women and the dominance of one class over others, or one people over others.

If we do not talk of exploitation when we talk of the man-woman relationship, our talk about oppression, or subordination hangs somewhere in the air, for why should men be oppressive towards women if they had nothing to gain from it? Oppression or subordination, without reference to exploitation, becomes then a purely cultural or ideological matter, the basis of which cannot be made out, unless one has recourse to the notion of some inborn aggressive or sadistic tendencies in men. But exploitation is a historical – and not a biological or psychological – category which lies at the basis of the man-woman relation. It was historically created by patriarchal tribes and societies. Thus, with Maria-Rosa

Dalla Costa I speak of exploitation of women in the triple sense: they are exploited (not only economically, but as human beings) by men and they are exploited as housewives by capital. If they are wage-workers they are also exploited as wage-workers. But even this exploitation is determined and aggravated by the other two interlinked forms of exploitation.

I *do not* talk of *inequality* or *discrimination* in the following text because it should be clear from my discussion of the demands of the old women's movement that these demands of the French Revolution no longer constitute the core aspirations of the new feminist movement. Most feminists do not want even to be equal to men in the patriarchal system. The discussion on housework has revealed that the emancipation expected from wage-work has not come true anywhere, neither in the capitalist nor in the socialist countries. If the latter, and all orthodox communist parties still restrict their policy of women's emancipation to the demands of 'equality' and 'women's rights', basically bourgeois concepts, they ignore patriarchy as a reality of both capitalist and socialist society. And within a patriarchal system 'equality' for women can only mean that women become like those patriarchal men. Most women who call themselves feminists are not attracted by this prospect, neither do they have any hope that the demand for equality could ever be fulfilled within such a system. It is, therefore, wrong, as many men fear, that the feminists only want to replace male dominance by female dominance, because that is what 'equality' means for most of them: equality of privileges. But the feminist movement is basically an anarchist movement which does not want to replace one (male) power elite by another (female) power elite, but which wants to build up a non-hierarchical, non-centralized society where no elite lives on exploitation and dominance over others.

Capitalist-Patriarchy

The reader will have observed that I am using the concept *capitalist-patriarchy* to denote the system which maintains women's exploitation and oppression.

There have been discussions in the feminist movement whether it is correct to call the system of male dominance under which women suffer today in most societies a patriarchal system (Ehrenreich and English, 1979). 'Patriarchy' literally means the rule of fathers. But today's male dominance goes beyond the 'rule of fathers', it includes the rule of husbands, of male bosses, of ruling men in most societal institutions, in politics and economics, in short, what has been called 'the men's league' or 'men's house'.

In spite of these reservations, I continue to use the term patriarchy. My reasons are the following: the concept 'patriarchy' was re-discovered by the new feminist movement as a struggle concept, because the movement needed a term by which the totality of oppressive and exploitative relations which affect women, could be expressed as well as their systemic character. Moreover, the term 'patriarchy' denotes the historical and societal dimension of women's exploitation and oppression, and is thus less open to biologistic interpretations, in contrast, for example, to the concept of 'male dominance'. Historically, patriarchal systems were developed at a particular time, by particular peoples in particular geographical regions. They are not universal, timeless systems which have always existed. (Sometimes feminists refer to *the* patriarchal system as one which existed since time immemorial, but this interpretation is not corroborated by historical, archaeological and anthropological research.) The fact that patriarchy is today an almost universal system which has affected and transformed most pre-patriarchal societies has to be explained by the main mechanisms which are used to expand this system, namely robbery, warfare and conquest (see chapter 2).

I also prefer the term patriarchy to others because it enables us to link our present struggles to a past, and thus can also give us hope that there will be a future. If patriarchy had a specific beginning in history, it can also have an end.

Whereas the concept patriarchy denotes the historical depth of women's exploitation and oppression, the concept *capitalism* is expressive of the contemporary manifestation, or the latest development of this system. Women's problems today cannot be explained by merely referring to the old forms of patriarchal dominance. Nor can they be explained if one accepts the position that patriarchy is a 'pre-capitalist' system of social relations which has been destroyed and superseded, together with 'feudalism', by capitalist relations, because women's exploitation and oppression cannot be explained by the functioning of capitalism alone, at least not capitalism as it is commonly understood. It is my thesis that capitalism cannot function without patriarchy, that the goal of this system, namely the never-ending process of capital accumulation, cannot be achieved unless patriarchal man-woman relations are maintained or newly created. We could, therefore, also speak of neo-patriarchy (see chapter 4). Patriarchy thus constitutes the mostly invisible underground of the visible capitalist system. As capitalism is necessarily patriarchal it would be misleading to talk of two separate systems, as some feminists do (cf. Eisenstein, 1979). I agree with Chhaya Datar, who has criticized this dualistic approach, that to talk of two systems leaves the problem of how they are related to each other unsolved (Datar, 1981). Moreover, the way some feminist authors try to locate women's oppression and exploitation in these two systems is just a replica of the old capitalist social division of labour: women's oppression in the private sphere of the family or in 'reproduction' is assigned to 'patriarchy', patriarchy being seen as part of the superstructure, and their exploitation as workers in the office and factory is assigned to capitalism. Such a two-system theory is not capable, in my view, to transcend the paradigm developed in the course of capitalist development with its specific social and sexual divisions of labour. In the foregoing, we have seen, however, that this transcendence is the specifically new and revolutionary thrust of the feminist movement. If feminism follows this path and does not lose sight of its main political goals – namely, to abolish women's exploitation and oppression – it will have to transcend or overcome capitalist-patriarchy as one intrinsically interconnected system. In other words, feminism has to struggle against all capitalist-patriarchal relations, beginning with the man-woman relation, to the relation of human beings to nature, to the relation between metropoles and colonies. It cannot hope to reach its goal by only concentrating on one of these relations, because they are interrelated.

Overdeveloped–Underdeveloped Societies

If we say feminism has to struggle against all capitalist-patriarchal relations, we have to extend our analysis to the system of accumulation on a world scale, the world market or the international division of labour. The cleavages created by this division pose particular conceptual problems. What terminology should we use when we refer to the two divided, yet hierarchically related, sides of the world market? Should we continue to talk of 'developed' and 'underdeveloped' countries? Or, should we, in order to avoid the notion of a linear process of development, talk of 'First' and 'Third' world countries? Or should we use the concepts 'metropoles' or 'centres' and 'peripheries', stemming from the theoreticians of the dependency school? Behind each pair of concepts stands a whole theory which tries to come to grips with the historical phenomenon that, since the rise of Europe and later the USA as the dominant centres of the capitalist world economy, a process of polarization and division has been taking place by which one pole – the Western industrialized world – is getting richer and ever more powerful, and the other pole – the colonized countries in Africa, Asia and Latin America – are getting poorer and less powerful.

If we follow the feminist principle of transcending the divisions created by capitalist patriarchy in order to be able to establish that these divisions constitute only parts of the whole, we cannot treat the 'First' and 'Third' world as separate entities, but have to identify the relations that exist between the two.

These relations are based on exploitation and oppression, as is the case with the man-woman relation. And similar to the latter, these relations are also dynamic ones in which a process of polarization takes place: one pole is getting 'developed' *at the expense* of the other pole, which in this process is getting 'underdeveloped'. 'Underdevelopment', according to this theory, which was first developed by André Gunder Frank (1969), is the direct result of an exploitative unequal or dependent relationship between the core-countries (Wallerstein, 1974) in the capitalist world economy, and their colonies. It is not due to some inexplicable 'backwardness'. In this dynamic process of polarization between countries which are 'developing' themselves and countries which they in this process 'underdevelop', the rich and powerful Western industrial countries are getting more and more 'overdeveloped'. This means their development does not stop at a certain point where people would say: 'This is enough. We have enough development for our human happiness.' The very motor driving on this polarization of the world economy, namely, the capital accumulation process, is based on a world view which never says 'This is enough'. It is by its very nature based on limitless growth, on limitless expansion of productive forces, of commodities and capital. The result of this never-ending growth model are the phenomena of 'overdevelopment', that is, of a growth that has assumed the character of cancer, which is progressively destructive, not only for those who are exploited in this process but also for those who are apparently the beneficiaries of this exploitation. 'Overdevelopment and underdevelopment' are, therefore, the two extreme poles of an inherently exploitative world order, divided up and yet linked by the global accumulation process or the world market.

To use the concepts 'overdevelopment-underdevelopment' in this sense may, therefore, help to avoid the illusion that in a world system, structured along these principles, the problems of the underdeveloped peoples could be solved by development 'aid', or that the overdeveloped peoples could achieve human happiness by further exploiting the underdeveloped world. In a finite world an exploitative and oppressive relation between the two sides of the whole will necessarily be destructive for both sides. At the present stage of history this truth begins gradually to dawn also on people in the overdeveloped world.

Autonomy

While the concept 'capitalist patriarchy' summarizes the system or the totality of social relations against which the feminist struggle is directed, the concept 'autonomy' expresses the positive goal towards which the movement strives. This is true for at least a large section of the feminist movement. As was said before, the concept of autonomy, usually understood as freedom from coercion regarding our bodies and our lives, emerged as a struggle concept in the context of body politics, the sphere where women's oppression and exploitation was most intimately and concretely experienced.

There have also been different interpretations in the feminist movement of this concept and its content. One interpretation, rather common among Western feminists, is that which more or less identifies autonomy with 'individual independence', 'self-determination of the individual woman' or the 'right to individual choice'. In this emphasis on the individual there is the correct element that in the last analysis the individual woman, that is, the undivided and indivisible person, is the subject who either assumes the responsibility for her person and her life, or not. I interpret autonomy as this innermost subjectivity and area of freedom – small as it may be – without which human beings are devoid of their essential human essence and dignity, without which they become puppets or organisms without an element of free will and consciousness, or mere assemblies of organic matter, as is the model of reproductive engineers today.

In the concept autonomy, therefore, the feminist aspiration to maintain and strengthen or recreate this innermost subjective human essence in women is expressed and preserved. On the other hand, we cannot close our eyes to the fact that capitalism, by focussing on the atomized individual in its marketing strategies has, to a large extent, perverted the humanist aspiration inherent in the concept of autonomy. As the capitalist commodity market creates the illusion that the individual is free to fulfil all her/his desires and needs, that individual freedom is identical with the choice of this or that commodity, the self-activity and subjectivity of the person is replaced by individual consumerism. Thus, individualism has become, among Western feminists, one of the main obstacles for feminist solidarity and thus also for the achievement of feminist goals.

If we want to avoid this individualistic perversion, we have to make sure that autonomy means the preservation of the human essence in women. Autonomy, however, is not only used in the sense described above. It is also a struggle concept which was developed to demonstrate that women wanted to separate from mixed, male-dominated organizations and to form their autonomous organizations, with their own analysis, programmes and methods. Autonomous organization was particularly emphasized, as we saw, *vis-à-vis* the traditional left organizations which had always claimed supremacy of organization, ideology and programme over all 'mass movements'. The feminist claim to autonomy in this sense means a rejection of all tendencies to subsume the women's question and the women's movement under some other apparently more general theme or movement. Women's autonomous organization is an expression of the desire to preserve both the qualitatively different character and identity of the feminist movement, as well as an independent power base. Particularly the latter has been learned from the old women's movement. By joining male-dominated organizations (parties and trade unions), the old movement lost its identity and was finally dissolved. The principle of autonomy is not only upheld with regard to male-dominated organizations, movements and contexts. Also within the feminist movement as such the diverse groups and categories of women have maintained this principle. This can be observed in the way various sub-movements evolved in the course of time, for example, the lesbian movement. But this principle was also followed by the rising Third World feminist movement. As there is no centre, no hierarchy, no official and unified ideology, no formal leadership, the autonomy of the various initiatives, groups, collectives is the only principle that can maintain the dynamism, the diversity, as well as the truly humanist perspective, of the movement.

Notes

1. The thirteen women of the 'Sistren' Collective in Kingston, Jamaica, came together in 1977 when the Michael Manley government had started an 'Impact Programme' in order to create jobs for unemployed women, such as street cleaning. The thirteen women had been given training as teachers' aides. During the training they were asked to do a theatre piece for the annual Workers' Week celebrations. They asked Honor Ford-Smith from the Jamaican School of Drama to help them prepare a play. When she asked them what they wanted to do a play about, they said: 'We want to do plays about how we suffer as women. We want to do plays about how men treat us badly' (cf. Honor Ford-Smith: 'Women, the Arts and Jamaican Society', unpublished paper, Kingston, 1980; see also Sistren Theatre Collective: 'Women's Theater in Jamaica', in *Grassroots Development*, vol. 7, no. 2, 1983, p. 44).

2. I could observe this happening in India in 1973/74 when a small women's group came together in Hyderabad, out of which grew the first new women's organization in India, the Progressive Organization of Women (POW) (cf. K. Lalitha: 'Origin and Growth of POW: First ever Militant Women's Movement in Andhra Pradesh', in *HOW*, vol. 2, no. 4, 1979, p. 5). Meanwhile, feminist groups and organizations are coming up in many Third World countries.

3. The theoretical base of left anti-feminism is the Marxist position, first spelled out by Engels, Bebel and Clara Zetkin, that the 'woman question' is part of the class question and should not be dealt with separately. In the beginning, the

the new feminist movement was ignored and considered irrelevant by Marxist-Leninist parties. When they realized, however, that the movement continued to exist and continued to mobilize ever more women, even in underdeveloped countries, the policy changed. On the one hand, these parties claimed an avant-garde role for this new social movement by adopting the symbols, the slogans – partly even the concepts – of the new women's movement. On the other hand, they continued the old polemics against autonomous feminist groups and movements as being 'bourgeois' and 'deviationist'. This process can be clearly observed in the recent history of the *Deutsche Kommunistische Partei* (DKP), the Moscow-oriented communist party of West Germany. Their women's wing uses the colours, the symbols, and the slogans of the feminists and even claims to be 'autonomous'. Feminists in underdeveloped countries have had similar experiences with the orthodox left and their hostility and double strategy regarding the women's movement (cf. Datar: 'The Left Parties and the Invisibility of Women: A Critique', in *Teaching Politics*, vol. X, Annual No., Bombay, 1984).

4. India seems to be the country in Asia where the feminist movement is spreading most rapidly. In a recent 'Women's Liberation Pilgrimage' (*Stree Mukti Yatra*), organized by some women's liberation groups from Bombay, about 200,000 women and about 100,000 men attended the drama-shows, poster exhibitions, talks and discussions, slide-shows, book sales and other programmes on women's oppression and liberation. This 'mobile workshop' consisted of a bus with 75 women's liberation activists which, in 12 days, covered 1,500 kilometres and held programmes in 11 towns and 10 villages in the state of Maharashtra. As one of the participants wrote: 'The objective was to create an awareness of the secondary position of women in society and clear some of the misunderstandings surrounding the concept of women's liberation' (Nandita Gandhi in *Eve's Weekly*, 16–22 February 1985). The response to and the result of this pilgrimage were so overwhelming that the *Times of India*, one of the main Indian dailies, commented: 'As the two-week long Stree Mukti Yatra proved in Maharashtra, feminism has come to stay here. No longer can it be dismissed as an irrelevant Western import, the preserve of a handful of city women' (Ayesha Kagal, 'A girl is born', in *Times of India*, 3 February 1985).

5. When the second Feminist Conference of Latin America and the Caribbean took place in Lima, Peru, in July 1982, the number of participants had increased from 230 women at the first conference in Bogota, to 700. Women from 15 countries, ranging from urban, middle-class intellectuals to working-class and peasant women attended the conference. The organizers clarified why women responded so eagerly to their call: 'It is the feminist movement which has been crucial in countering the rebirth of conservatism in the industrialized countries. Without a change in patriarchal power, the problems will persist' (cf. Jill Gay, 'A Growing Movement: Latin American Feminism', in *NACLA Report*, vol. XVII, no. 6, Nov–Dec 1983).

6. In a short annotated bibliography, some 36 titles are listed of feminist journals and magazines published by women's groups in Latin America (cf. Unidad de Comunicacion Alternativa de la Mujer – ILET, publicaciones alternativas de grupos de mujeres en america latina, Santiago, Chile, 1984).

7. At the 2nd International Interdisciplinary Women's Congress in Groningen (Holland) in April 1984 the main concern of the organizers, and of many of the women who presented papers, was to mobilize women to jump on the bandwagon of the 'third technological revolution'. Women's liberation was

again seen as a function of their knowledge of modern science and technology.

8. One of these is Ivan Illich, who first got a number of ideas and concepts from feminists like Barbara Duden, Gisela Bock and Claudia von Werlhof, whose analysis of housework under capitalism inspired him to write his paper on 'Shadow-Work'. But by subsuming housework under the sex-neutral concept of shadow-work, he not only again obscured women's exploitation, but eventually gave the materialist feminist analysis an idealistic interpretation. In this process the English concept 'gender' came in handy to transport the whole analysis to the cultural sphere. The next step then was his outright attack on feminists who, according to him, were about to abolish all universal, culturally-determined, gender differences (cf. I. Illich: *Gender*, New York, 1983).

9. The terms 'vicarious politics' or 'politics by delegation' are translations of the German term *Stellvertreterpolitik*. In West Germany the feminists were the first to reject *Stellvertreterpolitik*. Later, other social movements like the alternative movement, the ecology movement, and the Greens, also began to challenge the concept of politics by delegation and to replace it by the new concept of basis democracy, or grassroots democracy.

10. This discussion was started around 1977 by Claudia von Werlhof, Veronika Bennholdt-Thomsen and myself. Our analysis was presented in a number of papers published in feminist journals, mainly in *Beiträge zur feministischen Theorie und Praxis*. A collection of some of the main articles was published in: Claudia v. Werlhof, Maria Mies, Veronika Bennholdt-Thomsen: *Frauen, die letzte Kolonie* (Women, the Last Colony), Reinbeck, 1983.

2. Social Origins of the Sexual Division of Labour

The Search for Origins Within a Feminist Perspective[1]

Since the rise of positivism and functionalism as the dominant schools of thought amongst Western social scientists in the 1920s, the search for the origins of unequal and hierarchical relationships in society in general, and the asymmetric division of labour between men and women in particular, has been taboo. The neglect, and even systematic suppression, of this question has been part of an overall campaign against Marxist thinking and theorizing in the academic world, particularly in the Anglo-Saxon world (Martin and Voorhies, 1975: 155ff). It is only now that this question is being asked again. Significantly, it was not first asked by academics, but by women actively involved in the women's movement. Whatever the ideological differences between the various feminist groups, they are united in their rebellion against this hierarchical relationship, which is no longer accepted as biological destiny, but seen as something to be abolished. Their search for the social foundations of this asymmetry is the necessary consequence of their rebellion. Women who are committed to struggle against the age-old oppression and exploitation of women cannot rest content with the indifferent conclusion put forward by many academics, that the question of origins should not be raised because we know so little about them. The search for the social origins of this relationship is part of the political strategy of women's emancipation (Reiter, 1977). Without understanding the foundation and the functioning of the asymmetric relationship between men and women, it is not possible to overcome it.

This political and strategic motivation fundamentally differentiates this new quest for the origins from other academic speculation and research endeavours. Its aim is not merely to analyse or to find an interpretation of an old problem, the purpose is rather to solve it.

The following discussion should, therefore, be understood as a contribution to 'spreading the consciousness of the existence of gender hierarchy and collective action aimed at dismantling it' (R. Reiter, 1977: 5).

Biased Concepts

When we began to ask about the origins of the oppressive relationship between

44

the sexes, we soon discovered that none of the old explanations put forward by social scientists since the last century was satisfactory. For in all explanations, whether they stem from an evolutionist, a positivist-functionalist, or even a Marxist approach, the problem which needs explanation is, in the last analysis, seen as biologically determined and hence beyond the scope of social change. Therefore, before discussing the origins of an asymmetric division of labour between the sexes, it is useful to identify the biological biases in some of the concepts we commonly use in our debates.

This covert or overt biological determinism, paraphrased in Freud's statement that anatomy is destiny, is perhaps the most deep-rooted obstacle to the analysis of the causes of women's oppression and exploitation. Although women who struggle for their emancipation have rejected biological determinism, they find it very difficult to establish that the unequal, hierarchical and exploitative relationship between men and women is caused by social, that is historical, factors. One of our main problems is the fact that not only the analysis as such, but also the tools of the analysis, the basic concepts and definitions, are affected – or rather infected – by biological determinism.

This is largely true of the basic concepts which are central to our analysis, such as the concepts of *nature*, of *labour*, of *the sexual division of labour*, of the *family* and of *productivity*. If these concepts are used without a critique of their implicit ideological biases, they tend to obscure rather than to clarify the issues. This is above all true for the concept of *nature*.

Too often this concept has been used to explain social inequalities or exploitative relations as inborn, and, hence, beyond the scope of social change. Women should be particularly suspicious when this term is used to explain their status in society. Their share in the production and reproduction of life is usually defined as a function of their biology or 'nature'. Thus, women's household and child-care work are seen as an extension of their physiology, of the fact that they give birth to children, of the fact that 'nature' has provided them with a uterus. All the labour that goes into the production of life, including the labour of giving birth to a child, is not seen as the conscious interaction of a human being *with* nature, that is, a truly human activity, but rather as an activity *of* nature, which produces plants and animals unconsciously and has no control over this process. This definition of women's interaction with nature – including her own nature – as an act *of* nature has had and still has far-reaching consequences.

What is mystified by a biologistically infected concept of nature is a relationship of dominance and exploitation, dominance of the (male) human being over (female) nature. This dominance relationship is also implicit in the other concepts mentioned above when applied to women. Take the concept of *labour*! Due to the biologistic definition of women's interaction with her nature, her work both in giving birth and raising children as well as the rest of domestic work does not appear as work or labour. The concept of labour is usually reserved for men's productive work under capitalist conditions, which means work for the production of surplus value.

Though women also perform such surplus-value-generating labour, under capitalism the concept of labour is generally used with a male or patriarchal bias, because under capitalism, women are typically defined as housewives, that means as non-workers.

The instruments of this labour, or the bodily means of production implicitly referred to in this concept, are the hands and the head, but never the womb or the breasts of a woman. Thus, not only are men and women differently defined in their interaction with nature, but the human body itself is divided into truly 'human' parts (head and hand), and 'natural' or purely 'animal' parts (genitalia, womb, etc.).

This division cannot be attributed to some universal sexism of men as such, but is a consequence of the capitalist mode of production which is only interested in those parts of the human body which can be directly used as instruments of labour or which can become an extension of the machine.

The same hidden asymmetry and biologistic bias, which we could observe in the concept of labour, also prevails in the concept of *sexual division of labour* itself. Though overtly this concept seems to suggest that men and women simply divide different tasks between themselves, it hides the fact that men's tasks are usually considered as truly human ones (that is, conscious, rational, planned, productive, etc.), whereas women's tasks are again seen as basically determined by their 'nature'. The sexual division of labour, according to this definition, could be paraphrased as one between 'human labour' and 'natural activity'. What is more, however, this concept also obscures the fact that the relationship between male (that is, 'human'), and female ('natural') labourers or workers is a relationship of dominance and even of exploitation. The term exploitation is used here in the sense that a more or less permanent separation and hierarchization has taken place between producers and consumers, and that the latter can appropriate products and services of the former without themselves producing. The original situation in an egalitarian community, that is, one in which those who produce something are also – in an intergenerational sense – its consumers, has been disrupted. Exploitative social relations exist when non-producers are able to appropriate and consume (or invest) products and services of actual producers (A. Sohn-Rethel, 1978; Rosa Luxemburg, 1925). This concept of exploitation can be used to characterize the man-woman relationship over large periods of history, including our own.

Yet, when we try to analyse the social origins of this division of labour, we have to make clear that we mean this asymmetric, hierarchical and exploitative relationship, and not a simple division of tasks between equal partners.

The same obfuscating biologistic logic prevails with regard to the concept of *family*. Not only is this concept used and universalized in a rather Euro-centric and ahistoric way, presenting the nuclear family as the basic and timeless structure of all institutionalization of men-women relations, it also hides the fact that the structure of this institution is a hierarchical, unegalitarian one. Phrases like 'partnership or democracy within the family' only serve to veil the true nature of this institution.

Concepts like the 'biological' or 'natural' family are linked to this particular ahistorical concept of the family which is based on the compulsory combination of heterosexual intercourse and the procreation of consanguine children.

This brief discussion of the biologistic biases inherent in some of the important concepts has made clear that it is necessary systematically to expose the ideological function of these biases, which is to obscure and mystify asymmetric and exploitative social relations, particularly those between men and women.

This means with regard to the problem before us, namely the analysis of the social origins of the sexual division of labour, that we are *not* asking: When did a division of labour between men and women arise? Our question is rather: What are the reasons why this division of labour became a relationship of dominance and exploitation, an asymmetric, hierarchical relationship? This question still looms large in all discussions on women's liberation.

Suggested Approach

What can we do to eliminate the biases in the above-mentioned concepts? Not use the concepts at all, as some women suggest? But then we would be without a language to express our ideas. Or invent new ones? But concepts summarize historical practice and theory and cannot voluntaristically be invented. We have to accept that the basic concepts we use in our analysis have already been 'occupied' – like territories or colonies – by dominant sexist ideology. Though we cannot abandon them, we can look at them 'from below', not from the point of view of the dominant ideology, but from the point of view of the historical experiences of the oppressed, exploited and subordinated and their struggle for emancipation.

It is thus necessary, regarding the concept of the *productivity of labour*, to reject its narrow definition and to show that labour can only be productive in the sense of producing surplus value as long as it can tap, extract, exploit, and appropriate labour which is spent in the *production of life*, or *subsistence production* (Mies, 1980(b)) which is largely non-wage labour mainly done by women. As this *production of life* is the perennial precondition of all other historical forms of productive labour, including that under conditions of capitalist accumulation, it has to be defined as *work* and not as unconscious 'natural' activity.

In what follows, I will call the labour that goes into the production of life *productive labour* in the broad sense of producing use values for the satisfaction of human needs. The separation from and the superimposition of surplus-producing labour over life-producing labour is an abstraction which leads to the fact that women and their work are being 'defined into nature'.

In his discussion of the labour process in *Capital*, Volume I, Marx first uses a broad definition of 'productive labour' which, by a change of natural matter, produces a product for human use, that is, for the satisfaction of human needs (*Capital*, Vol. I, 1974). But in a footnote he already warns that this definition, correct for the simple labour process, is not at all adequate for the capitalist production process, where the concept of 'productive labour' is narrowed down to mean only the *production of surplus value*: 'Only that labourer is productive who produces surplus for the realization of capital' (*Capital*, Vol. I, 1974). Marx uses here the narrow concept of productivity of labour which was developed by Adam Smith and other political economists (see *Grundrisse*, p. 212). He still criticizes this concept in the sense that he states that to be a 'productive labourer under capitalism is not good luck but bad luck' (p. 532) because the worker becomes a direct instrument of valuation of capital. But by focussing only on this capitalist concept of productive labour and by universalizing it to the virtual eclipse of the more general and fundamental concept of productive labour – which could include women's production of life – Marx himself has theoretically contributed to the removal of all 'non-productive' labour (that is, non-wage labour, including most of women's labour) from public visibility. The concept of 'productive labour', used henceforth both by bourgeois as well as by Marxist theoreticians, has maintained this capitalist connotation, and the critique which Marx had still attached to it is long forgotten. I consider this narrow, capitalist concept of 'productive labour' the most formidable hurdle in our struggle to come to an understanding of women's labour both under capitalism and actually existing socialism.

It is my thesis that this general production of life, or subsistence production – mainly performed through the non-wage labour of women and other non-wage labourers as slaves, contract workers and peasants in the colonies – constitutes the perennial basis upon which 'capitalist productive labour' can be built up and exploited. Without the ongoing subsistence production of non-wage labourers (mainly women), wage labour would not be 'productive'. In contrast to Marx, I consider the capitalist production process as one which comprises both: the *superexploitation* of non-wage labourers (women, colonies, peasants) upon which wage labour exploitation then is possible. I define their exploitation as super-exploitation because it is not based on the appropriation (by the capitalist) of the time and labour over and above the 'necessary' labour time, the *surplus* labour, but of the time and labour *necessary* for people's own survival or subsistence production. It is not compensated for by a wage, the size of which is calculated on the 'necessary' reproduction costs of the labourer, but is mainly determined by force or coercive institutions. This is the main reason for the growing poverty and starvation of Third World producers. In their case, the principle of an exchange of equivalents underlying the wage negotiations of workers in the West is not applied (see chapters 3 and 4).

The search for the origins of the hierarchical sexual division of labour should not be limited to the search for the moment in history or prehistory when the 'world-historic defeat of the female sex' (Engels) took place. Though studies in primatology, prehistory and archaeology are useful and necessary for our search, we cannot expect them to give an answer to this question unless we are able to develop materialist, historical, non-biologistic concepts of men and women and their relations to nature and history. As Roswitha Leukert puts it: 'The beginning of human history is primarily not a problem of fixing a certain date, but rather that of finding a materialist concept of man [the human being, M.M.] and history' (Leukert, 1976: 18, transl. M.M.).

If we use this approach, which is closely linked to the strategic motivation mentioned earlier, we shall see that the development of vertical, unequal relationships between women and men is not a matter of the past only.

We can learn a lot about the actual formation of sex-hierarchies if we look at 'history in the making', that is, if we study what is happening to women under the impact of capitalism both at its centres and at its periphery, where poor peasant and tribal societies are now being 'integrated' into a so-called new national and international division of labour under the dictates of capital accumulation. Both in the capitalist metropoles and in the peripheries, a distinct sexist policy was and is used to subsume whole societies and classes under capitalist production relations.

This strategy usually appears in the guise of 'progressive' or liberal *family laws* (for example, the prohibition of polygamy), of family planning and development policies. The demand to 'integrate women into development', first voiced at the International Women's Conference in Mexico (1975), is largely used in Third World countries to recruit women as the cheapest, most docile and manipulable labour force for capitalist production processes, both in agro-business and industry, as well as in the unorganized sector (Fröbel, Kreye, Heinrichs, 1977; Mies, 1982; Grossman, 1979; Elson/Pearson, 1980; Safa, 1980).

This also means that we should no longer look at the sexual division of labour as a problem related to the family only, but rather as a structural problem of a whole society. The hierarchical division of labour between men and women and its dynamics form an integral part of the dominant production relations, that is, the class relations of a particular epoch and society, and of the broader national and international divisions of labour.

Appropriation of Nature by Women and Men

To search for a materialist concept of men/women and history, however, means to search for the *human nature* of men and women. But human nature is not a given fact. It evolved in history and cannot be reduced to its biological aspects, but the physiological dimension of this nature is always linked to its social dimension. Therefore, human nature cannot be understood if we separate its physiology from its history. Men's/women's human nature does not evolve out of biology in a linear, monocausal process, but is the result of the history of women's/men's interaction with nature and with each other. Human beings do not simply live, animals live. Human beings *produce* their lives. This production takes place in a historical process.

In contrast to the evolution in the animal world (natural history) human history is *social history* right from the beginning. All human history is characterized, according to Marx and Engels, by 'three moments' which existed at the beginning of mankind and also exist today: 1. People must *live* in order to be able to make history; they must produce the means to satisfy their needs: food, clothing, a shelter, etc. 2. The satisfaction of needs leads to new needs. They develop new instruments to satisfy their needs. 3. Men who reproduce their daily life must *make other men*, must procreate – 'the relation between men and women, parents and children the family' (Marx/Engels, 1977: 31).

Later on, Marx uses the expression 'appropriation of the natural matter' to conceptualize 'work' in its broadest sense: work as appropriation of nature for the satisfaction of human needs:

> Labour is, in the first place, a process in which both man and nature participate, and in which man on his own accord starts, regulates, controls the material re-actions between himself and nature. He opposes himself to nature as one of her forces, setting in motion arms and legs, head and hands, the natural forces of his body, in order to appropriate[2] Nature's productions in a form adapted to his wants. By thus acting on the external world and changing it, he at the same time changes his own nature. (Marx, *Capital*, vol. I: 173)

We must stress that this 'appropriation of nature' is the characteristic of *all* human history, including the earliest, primitive stages.

Engels, strongly influenced by evolutionist thinking, separates these earliest stages as pre-history, from the actual human history, which, according to him, begins only with civilization. This means it begins with fully-fledged class and patriarchal relations. Engels is not able to answer the question how humanity then jumped from pre-history to social history; moreover, he does not apply the method of dialectical historical materialism to the study of these primitive societies which have 'not yet entered history'. He thinks that the laws of evolution prevailed up to the emergence of private property, of family and the state.

In the first two sentences of the preface to 'The Origin of the Family, Private Property and the State' of 1884, he stresses:

> According to the materialistic conception, the determining factor in history is, in the last resort, the production and reproduction of immediate life. But this itself is of a two-fold character. On the one hand, the production of the means of subsistence, of food, clothing and shelter and the tools requisite therefore; on the other, the production of human beings themselves, the propagation of the species. The social institutions under which men of a definite historical epoch and of a definite country live are conditioned by *both kinds of production* (emphasis mine): by the stage of development of labour, on the one hand, and of the family, on the other (Marx, Engels, 1976: 191).

Whereas, as Anke Wolf-Graaf observes, every materialist feminist would happily agree that a materialist analysis must deal with the two *kinds of production*, Engels himself gives up this materialist conception immediately when he deals with 'production of human beings' (cf. Wolf-Graaf, 1981: 114–121), which according to him is determined by the 'development of the *family*', whereas the production of means of subsistence is determined by the development of *labour*. This distinction is not accidental because throughout the book Engels follows this line of thinking. As long as he describes the development from gens to tribe to the family, Engels does not apply an economic analysis but an evolutionary one which, for example, explains the introduction of the incest taboo and of monogamy by the 'natural' desire of women for monogamous relations. Only when it comes to private property and the monogamous patriarchal family does Engels bring in economic and historical materialistic explanations: 'With the patriarchal family we enter the field of written history' (Marx, Engels, 1976: 234). The monogamous patriarchal family 'was the first form of the family based not on natural but on economic conditions, namely on the victory of private property over original naturally developed, common ownership' (Marx, Engels, 1976: 239).

This distinction between 'natural' (that is, ahistorical) processes related to the 'production of human beings or procreation', and historical processes related to the development of the means of production and labour is essentially responsible for the fact that within Marxist theory a historical materialist conception of women and their labour is not possible. The idealistic (naturalistic, biologistic) concept of women's labour in the production of human beings as 'natural' is already clearly spelt out in the early analysis of Marx and Engels in the 'German Ideology'. Although Marx and Engels are eager to establish the historicity and the material basis of the '*three moments*' that constitute human life, they quickly exclude or drop the 'third moment', namely the production of new people from the sphere of history. They still begin their discussion on the 'third moment' as follows:

> The third circumstance which, from the very outset, enters into historical development is that men, who daily remake their own life, begin to make other men, to propagate their kind: the relation between man and woman, parents and children, the *family* (emphasis in the original). The family, which to begin with is the only social relationship, becomes later, when increased needs create new social relations and the increased population new needs, a subordinate one . . . (Marx, Engels, 1977: 31).

This means the man-woman relation is no longer considered as a driving force in history, but 'industry'. They continue:

> The production of life, both of one's own in labour and of fresh life in procreation, now appears as a double relationship: on the one hand, as a natural, on the other as a social relationship. By social we understand the co-operation of several individuals, no matter under what conditions, in what manner and to what end (Marx, Engels, 1977: 31).

A feminist would now expect that in the following analysis Marx and Engels would continue to include the relationship between men and women in the production of new life in the category of 'social relationship'. But this aspect is immediately forgotten when they continue:

> It follows from this that a certain mode of production, or industrial stage is always combined with a certain mode of co-operation, or social stage, and this mode of co-operation is itself a 'productive force'. Further that the multitude of productive forces accessible to men determines the nature of society, that the 'history of humanity' must always be studied and treated in relation to the history of industry and exchange (Marx, Engels, 1977: 31).

That they conceive of the 'production of new life' as a 'natural' and not a historical fact becomes even clearer when they talk of the development of the division of labour. This division of labour 'which was originally nothing but the division of labour in the sexual act' (p. 33), or 'the natural division of labour in the family' (p. 34) only becomes truly a division of *labour* 'from the moment when a division of material and mental labour appears'. Before that stage every activity is mere animal activity or 'sheep-like or tribal consciousness'. What leads from this sheep-like existence (which women still lead today, according to this concept), to a truly human, historical social existence is the increase of productivity of (male) labour (p. 33), the increase of needs and of population growth (p. 33). The co-operation of man and woman in the sexual act and the work of women in the rearing and nursing of children obviously do not belong to the realm of 'productive forces', of 'labour', 'industry and exchange' but to 'nature' (Marx, Engels, 1977: 33, 34). By separating the production of new life from the production of the daily requirements through labour, by elevating the latter to the realm of history and humanity and by calling the first 'natural', the second 'social' they have involuntarily contributed to the biological determinism which we still suffer today. With regard to women and their labour, they remain as idealistic as the German ideologues whom they criticized.

If we want to find an historical and materialist concept of women and men and their history, we have first to analyse their respective interaction with nature and how, in this process, they build up their own human or social nature. If we were to follow Engels, we would have to relegate women's interaction with nature to the sphere of evolution. (This, in fact, is being done by functionalists and behaviourists all over the world.) We would have to conclude that women have not yet entered history (as defined by Engels) and still basically belong to the animal world.

Women's/Men's Appropriation of Their Own Bodies

The labour process, in its elementary form, is, according to Marx, a conscious action with a view to producing use-values. In a wider sense, it is 'the appropriation of natural substances for human requirements'. This 'exchange of matter' (*Stoffwechsel*) 'between human beings and nature' is the everlasting nature-imposed condition of human existence, or rather is common to every historical phase (*Capital*, Vol. I: 179). In this 'exchange of matter' between human beings and nature, human beings, women and men, not only develop and change the external nature with which they find themselves confronted, but also *their own bodily nature*.

The interaction between human beings and nature for the production of their human requirements needs, like all production, an instrument or a means of production. The first means of production with which human beings act upon nature is their own body. It is also the eternal precondition of all further means of production. But the body is not only the 'tool' with which human beings act upon nature, the body is also the aim of the satisfaction of needs. Human beings do not only use their body to produce use-values, they also keep their bodies alive – in its widest sense – by the consumption of their products.

In his analysis of the labour process in its widest sense as appropriation of natural substances, Marx does not make a difference between men and women. For our subject, however, it is important to stress that men and women act upon nature with a qualitatively different body. If we want to achieve clarity with regard to the asymmetric division of labour between the sexes, it is necessary not to talk of *man*'s (the abstract generic being) appropriation of nature, but of women's and men's appropriation of nature. This position is based on the assumption that there is a difference in the way women and men appropriate nature. This difference is usually obscured because 'humanness' is identified with 'maleness'.[3]

Maleness and femaleness are not biological givens, but rather the results of a long historical process. In each historic epoch maleness and femaleness are differently defined. This definition depends on the principal mode of production in these epochs. This means the organic differences between women and men are *differently interpreted and valued*, according to the dominant form of appropriation of natural matter for the satisfaction of human needs. Therefore, throughout history, men and women have developed a qualitatively different relationship to their own bodies. Thus, in matristic[4] societies femaleness was interpreted as the social paradigm of all productivity, as the main active principle in the production of life.[5] All women were defined as 'mothers'. But 'mothers' meant something other than it does today. Under capitalist conditions all women are socially defined as housewives (all men as breadwinners), and motherhood has become part and parcel of this houswife syndrome. The distinction between the earlier, matristic definition of femaleness and the modern one is that the modern definition has been emptied of all active, creative (subjective), productive (that is, human) qualities.

The historically developed qualitative difference in the appropriation of the male and female bodily nature has also led to 'two qualitatively different forms of appropriation of external nature' that is, to qualitatively distinct forms of relations to the objects of appropriation, the objects of sensuous bodily activity (Leukert, 1976: 41).

Women's and Men's Object-Relation to Nature

First, we must stress the difference between animal and human object-relation. Human object-relation is *praxis*, that is, action + reflection; it becomes visible only in the historical process, and it implies social interaction or cooperation. The human body was not only the first *means of production*, it was also the first *force of production*. This means the human body is experienced at being able to bring forth something new and hence change the external and the human nature. Human object-relation to nature is, in contrast to that of the animals, a productive one. In the appropriation of the body as a productive force, the difference between woman and man has had far-reaching consequences.

What characterizes women's object-relation to nature, to their own as well as to the external nature? First, we see that women can experience their *whole* body as productive, not only their hands or their heads. Out of their body they produce new children as well as the first food for these children. It is of crucial importance for our subject that women's activity in producing children and milk is understood as truly *human*, that is, *conscious, social activity*. Women appropriated their own nature, their capacity to give birth and to produce milk in the same way as men appropriated their own bodily nature, in the sense that their hands and head, etc., acquired skills through work and reflection to make and handle tools. In this sense, the activity of women in bearing and rearing children has to be understood as *work*. It is one of the greatest obstacles to women's liberation, that is, humanization, that these activities are still interpreted as purely physiological functions, comparable to those of other mammals, and lying outside the sphere of conscious human influence. This view that the productivity of the female body is identical with animal *fertility* – a view which is presently propagated and popularized the world over by demographers and population planners – has to be understood as a *result* of the patriarchal and capitalist division of labour and not as its precondition.[6]

In the course of their history, women observed the changes in their own bodies and acquired through observation and experiment a vast body of experiential knowledge about the functions of their bodies, about the rhythms of menstruation, about pregnancy and childbirth. This appropriation of their own bodily nature was closely related to the acquisition of knowledge about the generative forces of external nature, about plants, animals, the earth, water and air.

Thus, they did not simply breed children like cows, but they appropriated their own generative and productive forces, they analysed and reflected upon their own and former experiences and passed them on to their daughters. This means they were not helpless victims of the generative forces of their bodies, but learned to influence them, including the number of children they wanted to have.

We are in possession of enough evidence today to conclude that women in pre-patriarchal societies knew better how to regulate the number of their children and the frequency of births than do modern women, who have lost this knowledge through their subjection to the patriarchal capitalist civilizing process (Elias, 1978).

Among gatherers and hunters and other primitive groups, various methods existed – and partly still exist today – to limit the number of births and children. Apart from infanticide, most probably the earliest method (Fisher, 1978: 202), women in many societies used various plants and herbs as contraceptives or to induce abortions. The Ute Indians used litho-spermium, the Bororo women in Brazil used a plant which made them temporarily sterile. The missionaries persuaded the women not to use the plant any more (Fisher, 1979: 204). Elisabeth Fisher tells us about methods used by women among the Australian aborigines, certain tribes in Oceania, and even in ancient Egypt, which were predecessors of modern contraceptives. Women in Egypt used a vaginal sponge, dipped in honey, to reduce the mobility of sperm. There was also the use of acacia tips which contained a spermicidal acid (Fisher, 1979: 205).

Another method of birth control used widely among contemporary gatherers and hunters is a prolonged period of breastfeeding. Robert M. May reports on studies which prove that 'in almost all primitive gatherers' and hunters' societies fertility is lower than in modern civilized societies. Through prolonged lactation ovulation is reduced, which leads to longer intervals between births'. He also observed that these women reached puberty at a much later age than civilized women. He attributes the much more balanced population growth, which can be observed today among many tribes as long as they are not integrated into civilized society, to 'cultural practices which unconsciously contribute to a reduction of fertility' (May, 1978: 491). Though he criticizes correctly those who think that the low rate of population growth in such societies is the result of a brutal struggle for survival, he still does not conceive of this situation as a result of women's conscious appropriation of their generative forces.[7] Recent feminist research has revealed that before the witch hunt women in Europe had a much better knowledge of their bodies and of contraceptives than we have today (Ehrenreich & English, 1973, 1979).

Women's production of new life, of new women and men, is inseparably linked to the production of the means of subsistence for this new life. Mothers who give birth to children and suckle them necessarily have to provide food for themselves *and* for the children. Thus, the appropriation of their bodily nature, the fact that they produce children and milk, makes them also the first providers of the daily food, be it as gatherers, who simply collect what they find in nature, plants, small animals, fish, etc., or as agriculturists. The first division of labour by sex, namely that between the gathering activities of the women and the sporadic hunting of the men, has its origin most probably in the fact that women *necessarily* were responsible for the production of the daily subsistence. Gathering of plants, roots, fruits, mushrooms, nuts, small animals, etc., was right from the beginning a collective activity of women.

It is assumed that the necessity to provide for the daily food and the long experience with plants and plant life eventually led to the invention of regular cultivation of grain and tubers. According to Gordon Childe, this invention took place in the Neolithic Age, particularly in Eurasia, where wild grains were first cultivated. He and many other scholars attribute this invention to women, who were also the inventors of the first tools necessary for this new mode of production: the digging stick – which was already in use for digging out wild roots and tubers – and the hoe (Childe, 1976; Reed, 1975; Bornemann, 1975; Thomson, 1965; Chattopadhyaya, 1973; Ehrenfels, 1941; Briffault, 1952).

The regular cultivation of food plants, mainly tubers and grains, signifies a new stage and an enormous increase in the productivity of female labour which, according to most authors, made the production of a *surplus* possible for the first time in history. Childe, therefore, calls this transformation the neolithic revolution which he attributes to the regular cultivation of grain. On the basis of recent archaeological findings in Iran and Turkey, Elisabeth Fisher, however, argues that people had been able to collect a surplus of wild grains and nuts already in the gathering stage. The technological precondition for the collection of a surplus was the invention of containers, baskets of leaves and plant fibres and jars. It seems plausible that the technology of preservation preceded the new agricultural technology, and was equally necessary for the production of a surplus.

The difference between the two modes of production is, therefore, not so much the existence of a surplus, but rather that women developed the first truly *productive* relationship to nature. Whereas gatherers still lived in a society of simple appropriation, with the invention of plant cultivation we can speak for the first time of a 'production-society' (Sohn-Rethel, 1970). Women did not only collect and consume what grew in nature, but *they made things grow*.

Women's object-relation to nature was not only a productive one, it was also, right from the beginning, *social production*. In contrast to men, who could gather and hunt only for themselves, women had to share their products at least with their small children. This means, their specific object-relation to nature (to their own bodily nature as well as to the external nature), namely, to be able to *let grow and make grow*, made them also the inventors of *the first social relations*, the relations between mothers and children.

Many authors have come to the conclusion that mothers-children groups were the first social units. They were not only units of consumption but also units of production. Mothers and children worked together as gatherers and in early hoe-cultivation. These authors are of the opinion that adult men were only temporarily and peripherally integrated or socialized into these early matricentric or matristic units (Briffault, 1952; Reed, 1975; Thomson, 1965).

Martin and Voorhies argue that these matricentric units coincided with a vegetarian phase of hominid evolution. 'Adult males would maintain no permanent attachment to these mother-child units, except to the unit of their birth' (Martin and Voorhies, 1975: 174). This would mean that the permanent integration of males into these units has to be seen as a result of social history. The productive forces developed in these first social units were not only of a technological nature, but were above all the capacity for human cooperation, and reflected the ability 'to plan for tomorrow', to anticipate the future, to learn from one another, to pass this knowledge on from one generation to the next and to learn from past experiences, or, in other words, to constitute history.

To summarize women's historically developed object-relation to nature, we can state the following:

a. Their interaction with nature, with their own as well as with the external nature, was a reciprocal process. They conceived of their own bodies as being productive and creative in the same way as they conceived of external nature as being productive and creative.

b. Though they appropriate nature, this appropriation does not constitute a relationship of dominance or a property relation. They are not owners of their own bodies or of the earth, but they co-operate with their bodies and with the earth in order 'to let grow and to make grow'.

c. As producers of new life they also become the first subsistence producers and the inventors of the first productive economy. This implies, from the beginning, social production and the creation of social relations, that is, of society and history.

Men's Object-Relation to Nature

Men's object-relation to nature, like that of women, has both a physiological and an historical dimension. The physiological side of this relation – which exists at all times as long as men and women live – means that men appropriate nature by means of a qualitatively different body than women.

They cannot *experience* their own bodies as being productive in the same way as women can. Male bodily productivity cannot *appear* as such without the mediation of external means, of *tools*, whereas woman's productivity can. Men's contribution to the production of new life, though necessary at all times, could become *visible* only after a long historical process of men's action on external nature by means of tools, and their reflection on this process. The conception men have of their own bodily nature and the imagery they use to reflect upon themselves are influenced by the different historic forms of interaction with external nature and the instruments used in this work-process. Thus, the male self-conception as human, that is, as being productive, is closely linked to the invention and control of technology. Without tools man is no MAN.

In the course of history, men's reflection of their object-relation to external nature found expression in the symbols with which they described their own body-organs. It is interesting that the first male organ which gained prominence as the symbol of male productivity was the phallus, not the hand, though the hand was the main instrument for tool-making. This must have happened at the stage when the plough replaced the digging stick or the hoe of early female cultivators. In some Indian languages there is an analogy between plough and penis. In Bengali slang the penis is called 'the tool' (*yantra*). This symbolism, of course, not only expresses an instrumental relationship to external nature, but also to women. The penis is the tool, the plough, the 'thing' with which man works upon woman. In the north-Indian languages the words for 'work' and 'coitus' are the same, namely '*kam*'. This symbolism also implies that women have become 'external nature' for men. They are the earth, the field, the furrow (*sita*) upon which men sow their seeds (semen).

But these analogies of penis and plough, seed and semen, field and women are not only linguistic expressions of an instrumental object-relation of men to nature and women, they also indicate that this object-relation is already characterized by dominance. Women are already defined as part of the physical conditions of (male) production.

We do not know much about the historic struggles which took place before men's object-relation to nature could establish itself as one of superior productivity to that of women. But from the ideological battles that went on in ancient Indian literature for several centuries over the question whether the nature of the 'product' (grain, children) was determined by the field (woman) or by the seed (man), we get the idea that the subordination of female productivity to male productivity was by no means a peaceful process, but was part and parcel of class struggles and the establishment of patriarchal property relations over land, cattle and women (Karve, 1963).[8]

It would be revealing to study the analogies between the words for men's sexual organs and the tools which men have invented in different historical epochs and for different modes of production. It is not accidental that in our time men call their penis a 'screwdriver' (they 'screw' a woman), a 'hammer', a 'file', a 'gun', etc. In the harbour of Rotterdam, a trading port, the male sexual organs are called 'the trade'. This terminology tells us a lot about how men define their relationship to nature, but also to women and to their own bodies. It is an indication of the close link in the minds of men between their work-instruments and their labour process, and the self-conception of their own bodies.

Yet before men could conceive not only of their own bodies as more productive than women's, but also establish a relationship of dominance over women and external nature, they had first to develop a type of productivity which at least *appeared* independent of and superior to women's productivity. As we have seen, the appearance of men's productivity was closely linked to the invention of tools. Yet men could develop a productivity (apparently) independent of women's only on the basis of developed female productivity.

Female Productivity as the Precondition of Male Productivity

If we keep in mind that 'productivity' means the specific capacity of human beings to produce and reproduce life in an historic process, then we can formulate for our further analysis the thesis that female productivity is the precondition of male productivity and of all further world-historic development. This statement has a timeless material dimension as well as an historical one.

The first consists in the fact that women *at all times* will be the producers of new women and men, and that without this production all other forms and modes of production lose their sense. This sounds trivial but it reminds us of the goal of all human history. The second meaning of the above statement lies in the fact that the various forms of productivity which men developed in the course of history could not have emerged if they could not have used and subordinated the various historic forms of female productivity.

In the following, I shall try to use the above thesis as a guiding principle for the analysis of the asymmetric division of labour between the sexes during some of the major phases of human history. It will help us to de-mystify some of the common myths which are put forward to explain the social inequality between women and men as nature-given.

The Myth of Man-the-Hunter

Women's productivity is the precondition of all other human productivity, not only in the sense that they are *always* the producers of new men and women, but also in the sense that the first social division of labour, that between female gatherers (later also cultivators) and predominantly male hunters, could take place only on the basis of a developed female productivity.

Female productivity consisted, above all, in the ability to provide the daily subsistence, the guarantee of survival, for the members of the clan or band. Women necessarily had to secure the 'daily bread', not only for themselves and their children, but also for the men if they had no luck on their hunting expeditions, because hunting is an 'economy of risk'.

It has been proved conclusively, particularly by the critical research of feminist scholars, that the survival of mankind has been due much more to 'woman-the-gatherer' than to 'man-the-hunter', in contrast to what social-Darwinists of old or of new preach. Even among existing hunters and gatherers, women provide up to 80 per cent of the daily food, whereas men contribute only a small portion by hunting (Lee and de Vore, 1976, quoted by Fisher, 1979: 48). By a secondary analysis of a sample of hunters and gatherers from Murdock's Ethnographic Atlas, Martin and Voorhies have proved that 58 per cent of the subsistence of these societies was provided by gathering, 25 per cent by hunting, and the rest by hunting and gathering done together (1975: 181). Tiwi women, in Australia, who are both hunters and gatherers, got 50 per cent of their food by gathering, 30 per cent by hunting and 20 per cent by fishing. Jane Goodale, who studied the Tiwi women, said that bush-hunting and collecting was the most important productive activity:

> . . . the women not only could but did provide the major daily supply of a variety of foods to members of their camp . . . Men's hunting required considerable skill and strength, but the birds, bats, fish, crocodiles, dugongs and turtles they contributed to the household were luxury items rather than staples (Goodale, 1971: 169).

It is obvious from these examples that, among existing hunters and gatherers, hunting does by no means have the economic importance which is usually ascribed to it and that the women are the providers of the bulk of the daily staple food. In fact, all hunters of big game depended on the supply by their women of food which is not produced by hunting, if they want to go on a hunting expedition. This is the reason why the old Iroquois women had a voice in the decision-making on war and hunting expeditions. If they refused to give the men the necessary supply of food for their adventures, the men had to stay at home (Leacock, 1978; Brown, 1970).

Elisabeth Fisher gives us further examples of still existing foraging peoples among whom women are the main providers of the daily food, particularly in the temperate and southern zones. But she also argues that the gathering of vegetable food was more important for our early ancestors than hunting. She refers to the study of coprolites, fossil excrement, which reveals that groups that lived 200,000 years ago on the southern French coast mainly survived on a diet on shellfish, mussels and grains, not meat. Twelve-thousand-year-old coprolites from Mexico suggest that millet was the main staple food in that area (Fisher, 1979: 57–58).

Though it is obvious from these examples, as well as from common sense, that humanity would not have survived if man-the-hunter's productivity had been the base for the daily subsistence of the early societies, the notion that man-the-hunter was the inventor of the first tools, the provider of food, inventor of human society and protector of women and children persists not only in popular literature and films, but also among serious social scientists, and even among Marxist scholars.[9]

The man-the-hunter hypothesis has been popularized particularly by anthropologists, and behaviourists and recently by sociobiologists who follow the line of evolutionist thinking developed by Raymond Dart, a South African anthropologist, who maintained that the first hominids had made their first tools out of the bones of slain members of their own kind (Fisher, 49–50). Following this hypothesis, Konrad Lorenz (1963), Robert Ardrey (1966, 1976), Lionel Tiger and Robin Fox (1971) argue that hunting was the motor of human development and that the existing relationship of dominance between women and men originates in the 'biological infrastructure' of stone-age hunters (Tiger and Fox, 1971). According to these authors, the (male) hunter is not only the inventor of the first tools – which of course are weapons – but also of the upright gait, because man-the-hunter needed to have his hands free for the throwing of projectiles. According to them, he is also the 'breadwinner', the protector of weak and dependent women, the social engineer, the inventor of norms and hierarchical systems which have only one aim, namely to curb the biologically programmed aggressiveness of the males in their fight for control over the sexuality of the females. They draw a direct line from the observed behaviour of some of the primates to the behaviour of the human male, and maintain that the male primates strive to come to the top of the male hierarchy in order to be able to subject the females for their own sexual satisfaction.

> The efforts of the human primate to get to the top of the male hierarchy, which apparently is only slightly, but in fact fundamentally, different from that of the apes, aim at gaining control over the female members of his own group *in order to exchange them against the women of another group* (emphasis Tiger and Fox). Thus he gets for himself sexual satisfaction and political advantages (Tiger and Fox, 1971).

The 'cultural' achievement of these human hunter-primates seems to be that they have risen (or 'evolved') from the stage of Rape to the stage of Exchange of Women. The exploitative dominance relationship between men and women has been ingrained into the 'biological infrastructure' of the hunting behaviour: men are the providers of meat, for which women have a craving. Therefore, the hunters were able to subject and subordinate the women permanently as sexual objects and worker bees. What gave the hunters this tremendous advantage over women was, according to these authors, the 'bonding principle', which evolved out of hunting in groups. Tiger already advanced the idea of the 'male bonding' principle as the root cause of male supremacy in his book *Men in Groups* (1969), when the US were in the middle of another adventure of man-the-hunter, the Vietnam War. Although he knew, as Evelyn Reed points out, that meat eating constituted only a tiny proportion of the baboon diet, he claims that hunting and meat eating constitute the decisive factor in pre-human primate evolution, and that male bonding patterns reflect and arise out of man's history as a hunter.

> So, in the hunting situation, it was the hunting group-male-plus-male-plus-male – which ensured the survival of the entire productive community. Thus was the male-male bond as important for hunting purposes as the male-female bond was important for productive purposes, and this is the basis for the division of labour by sex (Tiger, 1969: 122, 126).

The man-the-hunter model as the paradigm of human evolution has been the basis of numerous scientific works on human affairs and has been popularized by the modern media. It has influenced the thinking of millions of people, and is still constantly advanced to explain the causes of social inequalities. Feminist scholars challenged the validity of this model on the basis of their own research and that of others. They unmasked this model, including its basic premises of the male bonding principle, the importance of meat as food, etc., as a sexist projection of modern, capitalist and imperialist social relations into pre-history and earlier history. This projection serves to legitimize existing relations of exploitation and dominance between men and women, classes and peoples as universal, timeless and 'natural'. Evelyn Reed has rightly denounced the hidden fascist orientation behind this model, particularly in the writings of Tiger and his glorification of war (Reed, 1978).

Though we are able to de-mystify the man-the-hunter hypothesis and show that the great hunters would not have been able even to survive had it not been for the daily subsistence production of the women, we are still faced with the question why women, in spite of their superior economic productivity as gatherers and early agriculturists, were not able to prevent the establishment of a hierarchical and exploitative relation between the sexes.

If we ask this question in this way, we assume that political power automatically emerges from economic power. The foregoing discussion has shown that such an assumption cannot be upheld, because male supremacy did not arise from their superior economic contribution.

In the following, I shall try to find an answer to the above question by looking more closely at the various tools invented and used by women and men.

Women's Tools, Men's Tools

The man-the-hunter model is, in fact, the latest version of the man-the-toolmaker model. In the light of this model, tools are above all weapons, tools to kill.

The earliest tools of mankind, the stone axes, scrapers and flakes, were of an ambivalent character. They could be used to grind, smash and pulverize grains and other vegetable food, and to dig out roots, but they could also be used to kill small animals, and we can assume that they were used by men and women for both purposes. However, the invention of arms proper, of projectiles, of the bow and arrow, is an indication that the killing of animals had become a major specialization of one part of the society, mainly of men. The adherents to the hunter hypothesis are of the opinion that the first tools were invented by men. They ignore women's inventions connected with their subsistence production. But, as was previously discussed, the first inventions were most probably containers and baskets made of leaves, bark and fibres and later jars. The digging stick and the hoe were the main tools for gathering as well as for early agriculture. Women must have continued with their technology while some men developed specialized hunting tools.

What is important here is to note that women's technology remained productive in the true sense of the word: they produced something new. The hunting technology, on the other hand, is not productive, that is, hunting equipment proper cannot be used for any other productive activity – unlike the stone axe. The bow and arrow and spears are basically means of destruction. Their significance lies in the fact that they cannot only be used to kill animals, they can also be used to kill human beings. It is this characteristic of the hunting tools which became decisive in the further development of male productivity as well as of unequal, exploitative social relations, not the fact that hunters as providers of meat were able to raise the standard of nutrition of the community.

Hence, we conclude that the significance of hunting does not lie in its economic productivity as such, as is wrongly assumed by many theoreticians, but in the particular object-relation to nature it constitutes. The object-relation to nature of man-the-hunter is distinctly different from that of woman-the-gatherer or cultivator. The characteristics of this object-relation are the following:

a. The hunters' main tools are not instruments to produce life but to destroy life. Their tools are not basically means of production, but means of destruction, and they can be used as means of coercion also against fellow human beings.
b. This gives hunters a power over living beings, both animals and human beings, which does not arise out of their own productive work. They can appropriate not only fruits and plants (like the gatherers) and animals, but also other (female) producers by virtue of arms.
c. The object-relation mediated through arms, therefore, is basically a *predatory* or *exploitative* one: hunters' *appropriate* life, but they cannot produce life. It is an antagonistic and non-reciprocal relationship. All later exploitative relations between production and appropriation are, in the last analysis, upheld by arms as means of coercion.
d. The object-relation to nature mediated through arms constitutes a relationship of dominance and not of cooperation. This relationship of dominance has become an integral element in all further production relations which men have established. It has become, in fact, the main paradigm of their productivity. Without dominance and control over nature, men cannot conceive of themselves as being productive.
e. 'Appropriation of natural substances' (Marx) now becomes a process of one-sided appropriation, in the sense of establishing property relations, not in the sense of humanization, but in the sense of exploitation of nature.
f. By means of arms, hunters could not only hunt animals, but they could also raid communities of other subsistence producers, kidnap their unarmed young and female workers, and appropriate them. It can be assumed that the first forms of private property were not cattle or other foods, but *female slaves who had been kidnapped* (Meillassoux, 1975; Bornemann, 1975).

At this point, it is important to point out that it is *not the hunting technology as such* which is responsible for the constitution of an exploitative dominance-relationship between man and nature, and between man and man, man and woman. Recent studies on existing hunting societies have shown that hunters do not have an aggressive relationship with the animals they hunt. The pygmies, for example, seem to be extremely peaceful people who know neither war, nor quarrels, nor witchcraft (Turnbull, 1961). Their hunting expeditions are not aggressive affairs, but are accompanied by feelings of compassion for the animals they have to kill (Fisher, 1979: 53).

This means that the emergence of a specialized hunting technology only implies the *possibility* of establishing relationships of exploitation and dominance. It seems that, as long as the hunters remained confined to their limited hunting-gathering context, they could not realize the exploitative potential of their *predatory mode of production*. Their economic contribution was not sufficient; they remained dependent for their survival on their women's subsistence production.

Pastoralists

Though there may have been inequality between men and women, the hunters were not able to establish a fully-fledged dominance system. The 'productive forces' of the hunters could be fully released only when pastoral nomads, who domesticated cattle and women, invaded agricultural communities. This means that the full realization of the 'productive' capacity of this predatory mode of production presupposes the existence of other really productive modes, like agriculture.

Elisabeth Fisher is of the opinion that a dominance relationship between men and women could be established only after men had discovered their own generative capacities. This discovery, according to her, went hand in hand with the domestication – and particularly the *breeding* – of animals as a new mode of production. The pastoralists discovered that one bull could impregnate many cows, and this may have led to the castration and elimination of weaker animals. The main bull was then used at periods the pastoral nomads considered to be the most appropriate to impregnate the cows. Female animals were subjected to sexual coercion. This means that the free sexuality of wild animals was subjected to a coercive economy, based on breeding, with the object of increasing the herds. It is plausible that the establishment of harems, the kidnapping and raping of women, the establishment of patriarchal lines of descent and inheritance were part of this new mode of production. Women were also subjected to the same economic logic and became part of the movable property; they became chattels.

This new mode of production, however, was made possible by two things: the monopoly of men over arms, and the long observation of the reproductive behaviour of animals. As men began to manipulate the reproductive behaviour of animals, they discovered their own generative functions. This led to a change in their relation to nature as well as to a change in the sexual division of labour. For pastoral nomads, women are no longer very important as producers or gatherers of food, as is the case among hunters. They are needed as breeders of children, particularly of sons. Their productivity is now reduced to their 'fertility' which is appropriated and controlled by men (cf. Fisher, 1979: 248ff).

In contrast to the hunters' and gatherers' economy, which is mainly appropriative, the economy of the pastoral nomads is a 'productive economy' (Sohn-Rethel). But it is obvious that this mode of production presupposes the existence of *means of coercion* for the manipulation of animals and human beings, and for the extension of territory.

Agriculturists

It is, therefore, most probably correct to say that the pastoral nomads were the fathers of all dominance relations, particularly that of men over women. But there are enough data which suggest that exploitative relations between men and women also existed among agriculturists, not only after the introduction of the plough, as Esther Boserup believes (1970), but also among hoe-cultivators in Africa, where even today farming is done mainly by women. Meillassoux (1974) points out that in such societies, which he characterized as 'économies domestiques', the old men were in a position to establish a relationship of dominance over younger men and women because they could acquire more wives to work for them only. The marriage system was the mechanism by which they accumulated women and wealth, which in fact were closely related. Meillassoux, following Lévi-Strauss, takes the existence of an unequal system of exchange of women for granted, and mentions only passingly the probable roots of this system, namely, the fact that, due to the ongoing subsistence production of the women, the men were free to go from time to time on hunting expeditions. Hunting was for the men in these domestic economies a sporting and political activity rather than an economic one. On such expeditions, the men also kidnapped isolated gathering women and young men of other villages or tribes.

In a recent study on slavery in pre-colonial Africa, edited by Meillassoux, one finds numerous examples that show that such hunters not only kidnapped and appropriated people whom they surprised in the jungle, but they also organized regular *razzias* into other villages to kidnap women. The women thus appropriated did not become members of the community, but were usually privately appropriated by the leader of the expedition, who would either use them as slaves to work for him, or sell them against bridewealth to other villages. These kidnapped women thus became a direct source for the accumulation of *private property*.

Slavery, hence, obviously did not emerge out of trade, but out of the male monopoly over arms. Before slaves could be bought and sold, they had to be captured, they had to be appropriated by a master by force of arms. This predatory form of acquisition of labour power, both for work on 'private' plots and for sale, was considered the most 'productive' activity of these warrior-hunters, who, it has to be kept in mind, were no longer hunters and gatherers, but lived in an economic system based on women's productive agricultural work; they were the 'husbands' of female agriculturists. Their productivity was described by an old man of the Samos in Upper Volta as the productivity of bow and arrow, by which all other products – millet, beans, etc., and women – could be obtained:

> Our ancestors were born with their hoe, their axe, their bow and arrow. Without a bow you cannot work in the jungle. With the bow you acquire the honey, the peanuts, the beans, and then a woman, then children and finally you can buy domestic animals, goats, sheep, donkeys, horses. These were the riches of old. You worked with bow and arrow in the jungle, because there could be always someone who could surprise and kill you.

According to this old man there were 'commandos' of five or six men who would roam through the jungle trying to surprise and kidnap women and men who were alone. The kidnapped were sold (Heritier in Meillassoux, 1975: 491).

This passage shows clearly that the Samo men conceived of their own productivity in terms of arms, that they surprised lonely gatherers in the jungle in order to sell them. The reason for this was: what had been captured by surprise in the jungle was *property* (private property). This private property was appropriated by the lineage of the hereditary chief (formerly the rain-makers' lineage), who then sold these captives to other lineages, either as wives against bride price (in this case, against cowrie shells as money), or as slaves for agricultural work, or they were returned against ransom money back to their own village. These raids were thus a means for *some men* to accumulate more wealth than other men.

Female slaves were preferred, and fetched a higher price because they were productive in two ways: they were agricultural workers and they could produce more slaves. The Samo usually killed the men in these inter-village raids because they were of no economic use to them. But women and children were captured, made slaves and sold.

Jean Bazin, who studied war and slavery among the Segu, calls the capture of slaves by warriors the 'most productive' activity of the men of this tribe.

> The production of slaves is indeed a production . . . in the whole of the predatory activity this is the only activity which is effectively productive, because pillage of goods is only a change of hands and place. The dominant moment of this production is the exercise of violence against the individual in order to cut her/him off from the local and social networks (age, sex, relatives, alliances, lineage, clientele, village) (Bazin in Meillassoux, 1975: 142).

On the basis of his studies among the Tuareg, Pierre Bonte draws the conclusion that slavery was the precondition for the expansion of the 'économies domestiques' into a more diversified economy, where there is a great demand for labour. He sees slavery as the 'result and the means of unequal exchange' (Bonte in Meillassoux, 1975: 54).

The examples from pre-colonial Africa make clear that the predatory mode of production of men, based on the monopoly of arms, could become 'productive' only when some other, mostly female, production economies existed, which could be raided. It can be characterised as *non-productive production*. They also show the close link between pillage, loot and robbery on the one hand, and trade on the other. What was traded and exchanged against money (kauri shells) *was not the surplus produced over and above the requirements of the community; but what was stolen and appropriated by means of arms was, in fact, defined* as '*surplus*'.

In the last analysis, we can attribute the asymmetric division of labour between women and men to this predatory mode of production, or rather appropriation, which is based on the male monopoly over means of coercion, that is, arms, and on direct violence by means of which permanent relations of exploitation and dominance between the sexes were created and maintained.

This concept of surplus goes beyond the concept of surplus developed by Marx and Engels. The existence of a surplus constitutes, according to them, the crucial material-historical precondition for the development of exploitative social relations, for class-relations. They ascribe this emergence of a surplus to the development of more 'productive' means of production. In those societies which could produce more than they needed for their own subsistence, some groups of people could appropriate this surplus and thus establish long-lasting class relations, based on property relations. What is left unanswered in this concept is the question how and by which means this appropriation of surplus took place. We have enough empirical evidence from ethnological sources to show that the existence of surplus *per se* does not yet lead to a one-sided appropriation by one group or class of people (cf. the potlatch or sacrifices). Obviously, the definition of what is 'necessary' and what is 'surplus' is not a purely economic question, but a political and/or cultural one.

Similarly, *'exploitation'*, following this analysis, is not only the one-sided appropriation of the surplus produced over and above the necessary requirements of a community, but also the robbery, pillage and looting of the *necessary requirements* of *other* communities. This concept of exploitation, therefore, always implies a relationship created and held up in the last resort by coercion or violence.

From this follows that the establishment of classes, based on one-sided appropriation of 'surplus' (as I have defined it), is intrinsically interwoven with the establishment of patriarchal control over women, as the main 'producers of life' in its two aspects.

This non-productive, predatory mode of appropriation became the paradigm of all historical exploitative relations between human beings. Its main mechanism is to transform autonomous human producers into conditions of production for others, or to define them as 'natural resources' for others. It is important to stress the historical specificity of this patriarchal paradigm. Patriarchy was not developed universally all over the globe but by distinctive patriarchal societies. They include the Jews, the Arians (Indians and Europeans), the Arabs, the Chinese, and their respective great religions. The rise and the universalization of all these civilizations, but particularly the Judeo-European one, is based on conquest and war. Europe was not invaded by Africans, but Africa was invaded by predatory Europeans. This also means that a concept of a unilinear, universal process of history that evolves in successive stages everywhere from Primitive Communism, over Barbary, Feudalism, Capitalism to Socialism and Communism may have to be given up in our analysis of patriarchy.

'Man-the-Hunter' under Feudalism and Capitalism

The full potential of the predatory mode, based on a patriarchal division of labour could be realized only under feudalism and capitalism.

The patriarchal predatory mode of appropriation of producers, products and means of production was not abolished totally when new, and apparently more 'non-violent' modes of production replaced older ones. It was rather transformed and dialectically preserved, in the sense that it reappeared under new forms of labour control.

Similarly, so far new forms of the patriarchal sexual division of labour have not replaced the old forms, but only transformed them, according to the requirements of the new modes of production. None of the modes of production, which emerged later in the history of civilization, did away with predatoriness and violent acquisition by non-producers of producers, means of production and products. The later production-relations have the same basic structure of being asymmetric, and exploitative relations. Only the forms of dominance and appropriation have changed. Thus, instead of using violent raids and slavery for acquiring more women as workers and producers than were born in a community, hypergamous marriage systems were evolved, which made sure that the BIG

MEN could have access not only to more women of their own community or class, but also to the women of the Small Men. Women became a commodity in an asymmetric or unequal marriage market, because control over more women meant accumulation of wealth (Meillassoux, 1975). The BIG MEN (the state) then became the *managers* of social reproduction as well as of production. In all patriarchal civilizations, the relationship between men and women maintained its character of being coercive and appropriative. The asymmetric division of labour by sex, once established by means of violence, was then upheld by means of institutions like the patriarchal family and the state and also by means of powerful ideological systems, above all by patriarchal religions, law, medicine, which have defined women as part of nature which has to be controlled and dominated by man.

The predatory mode of acquisition saw a renaissance during the period of European feudalism. Feudalism as a specific mode of production based on owner-ship of land was built up with extensive use of violence and warfare. In fact, had there been but the endogenous processes of class differentiation in peasant societies, feudalism might not have evolved at all, at least not in its European version which figures as the 'model' of feudalism. The predatory form of acquisi-tion of new lands and the large-scale use of pillage and looting by the armed feudal class form an inseparable part of and a precondition for the rise and maintenance of this mode of production (Elias, 1978; Wallerstein, 1974).

Later, not only new lands were thus acquired, but with the lands, the means or conditions of production – the peasants – were also appropriated and tied to the feudal lord in a specific production-relation, which did not allow them to move away from that land. They were seen as part of the land. Thus, not only the women of these peasants, but also the male peasants themselves, were 'defined into nature', that is, for the feudal lord they had a status similar to that of women: their bodies no longer belonged to themselves, but to the lord, like the earth. This relationship is exactly preserved in the German term with which the serf is described, he is *Leibeigener*, that is, someone whose body (*Leib*) is the property (*Eigentum*) of someone else. But, in spite of this change-over from direct violent acquisition of land and the peasants who worked on it, to a 'peaceful' relation of *structural violence*, or, which is the same, to a dominance relation between lord and serf, the feudal lords never gave up their arms or their military power to expand and defend their lands and their wealth, not only against external enemies, but also against rebellions from within. This means that even though there were 'peaceful' mechanisms of effective labour control, actually under feudalism these production relations were established and maintained through the *monopoly over the means of coercion* which the dominant class enjoyed. The social paradigm of man-the-hunter/warrior remained the base and the last resort of this mode of production.

The same can be said of *capitalism*. When capital accumulation became the dominant motor of productive activity in contrast to subsistence production, wage labour tended to become the dominant form of labour control. Yet these appar-ently 'peaceful' production-relations, based on mechanisms of *economic coercion* (structural violence), could be built up only on the base of a tremendous expansion of the predatory mode of acquisition. Direct and violent acquisition of gold and silver and other products, mainly in Hispanic America, and of producers – first the Indians in Latin America and later African slaves – proved to be the most 'productive' activity in what has been described as the period of 'primitive accumulation'.

Thus capitalism did not do away with the former 'savage' forms of control over human productive capacity, it rather reinforced and generalized them: 'Large scale slavery or forced labour for the production of exchange value is prominently a capitalist institution, geared to the early pre-industrial stages of a capitalist world economy' (Wallerstein, 1974: 88).

This institution was also based on the monopoly over effective weapons and the existence of breeding grounds of enough 'human cattle' which could be hunted, appropriated and subjugated. This involves a re-definition of the rising European bourgeoisie's relation to nature and to women. Whereas under pre-capitalist production-relations based on ownership of land, women and peasants were/are defined as 'earth' or parts of the earth, as nature was identified with Mother Earth and her plants, under early capitalism slaves were defined as 'cattle' and women as 'breeders' of this cattle. We have seen that pastoral nomads also defined women mainly as breeders, not of labour power, but of male heirs mainly. But what fundamentally distinguishes the earlier pastoral patriarchs from the early capitalist patriarchs is the fact that the latter are not at all concerned with the production of the labour force and the 'breeders' of this labour force. In the first instance, the capitalist is not a producer, but an appropriator, who follows the paradigm of predatory acquisition, the precondition for the development of capitalist productive forces. Whereas the ruling classes among the pastoralists and the feudal lords were still aware of their own dependence on nature, including women (which they, therefore, tried to influence by magic and religion), the capitalist class saw itself right from the beginning as the master and lord *over* nature (cf. Merchant, 1983). Only now a concept of nature arose which generalized man-the-hunter's dominance-relation to nature. The division of the world which followed defined certain parts of the world as 'nature', that is, as savage, uncontrolled and, therefore, open for exploitation and civilizing efforts, and others as 'human', that is, already controlled and domesticated. The early capitalists were only interested in the muscle-power of the slaves, their energy to work. Nature for them was a reservoir of raw material and the African women an apparently inexhaustible reserve of human energy.

The change-over from production relations based on a master-servant pattern to one of a contractual character between capital and wage labour would not have been possible without the use of large-scale violence, and the 'definition into exploitable nature' of vast areas of the globe and their inhabitants. It enabled the capitalists 'to take off' and to give concessions to the European workers out of the loot of the colonies and the exploitation of slaves (see chapter 3).

In fact, one could say that to the same degree that the workers of the European centre states acquired their 'humanity, were humanized', or 'civilized', the workers – men and women – of the peripheries, that is, Eastern Europe and the colonies, were 'naturalized'.

The 'pacification' of the European workers, the establishment of a new form of labour control through the wage-nexus, the transformation of direct violence into structural violence, or of extra-economic coercion into economic coercion, needed, however, not only special *economic* concessions, but also *political* concessions.

These political concessions are not, as most people think, the male worker's participation in the democratic process, his rise to the status of a 'citizen', but his sharing the social paradigm of the ruling class, that is, the hunter/warrior model. His 'colony' or 'nature', however, is not Africa or Asia, but the women of his own class. And within that part of 'nature', the boundaries of which are defined by marriage and family laws, he has the monopoly of the means of coercion, of direct violence, which, at the level of the state, the ruling classes invested in their representatives, that is, the king and later the elected representatives.

However, the process of 'naturalization' did not affect only the colonies as a whole and the women of the working class, the women of the bourgeoisie also were defined into nature as mere breeders and rearers of the heirs of the capitalist class. But, in contrast to the African women who were seen as part of 'savage' nature, the bourgeois women were seen as 'domesticated' nature. Their sexuality, their generative powers as well as all their productive autonomy were suppressed and strictly controlled by the men of their class, on whom they had become dependent for their livelihood. The domestication of the bourgeois women, their transformation into housewives, dependent on the income of the husband, became the model of the sexual division of labour under capitalism. It was also necessary in order to gain control over the reproductive capacities of women, of all women. The process of proletarianization of the men was, therefore, accompanied by a process of housewifization of women (see chapter 4).

In this process, the sphere where labour power was reproduced, the house and the family, was 'defined into nature', but private, domesticated nature, while the factory became the place for public, social ('human') production.

Just as the process of 'naturalization' of the colonies was based on large-scale use of direct violence and coercion, so also the process of domestication of European (and later of North American) women was not a peaceful and idyllic affair. Women did not voluntarily hand over control over their productivity, their sexuality and their generative capacities to their husbands, and the BIG MEN (Church, State). Only after centuries of most brutal attacks against their sexual and productive autonomy European women became the dependent, domesticated housewives that we are in principle today. The counterpart of the slave raids in Africa was the witch hunt in Europe. The two seem to be connected through the same dilemma with which the capitalist version of man-the-hunter is faced: however much he may try to reduce women to a mere condition of production, to nature to be appropriated and exploited, he cannot produce living human labour power without women. Arms give him the possibility of an exclusively male mode of production, namely slavery or war which Meillassoux considers to be the male equivalent for the reproduction within a kinship system (Meillassoux, 1978: 7), an effort of the men of a certain society to become independent of their women's reproduction. But this male mode of production has its natural limitations, particularly when the hunting grounds for human cattle are exhausted. It was, therefore, necessary to bring the generative and productive forces of the European women under patriarchal control. Between the fourteenth and the eighteenth centuries, the male guilds and the rising urban bourgeoisie managed to push craftswomen out of the sphere of production (Rowbotham, 1974; O'Faolain and Martines, 1973). Moreover, millions of women, mostly of poor peasant or poor urban origin, were for centuries persecuted, tortured and finally burnt as witches because they tried to retain a certain autonomy over their bodies, particularly their generative forces. The attack of church and state against the witches was aimed not only at the subordination of female sexuality as such, although this played a major role, but against their practices as abortionists and midwives. The feminist literature which has appeared in recent years gives ample evidence of this policy (Rowbotham, 1974; Becker-Bovenschen-Brackert, 1977; Dross, 1978; Honegger, 1978; Ehrenreich and English, 1973, 1979). Not only were women artisans pushed out of their jobs and their property confiscated by the city authorities, the state and the church, but women's control over the production of new life – that is, their decision to give birth to a child or to abort – had to be smashed. This war against women raged throughout Europe for at least three centuries (Becker-Bovenschen-Brackert, 1977).

The witch hunt had not only the direct disciplinary effect of controlling women's sexual and reproductive behaviour, but also the effect of establishing the superiority of male productivity over female productivity. These two processes are closely connected. The ideologues of the witch hunt found no end in denouncing the female nature as sinful ('sin' is synonymous with 'nature'), as sexually uncontrollable, insatiable and ever ready to seduce the virtuous man. What is interesting to note is that women were *not yet* seen as sexually passive or even as asexual beings, as was the case later in the nineteenth/twentieth centuries. On the contrary, their sexual activity was seen as a threat to the virtuous man, that is, the man who wants to control the purity of his offspring, the heirs of his property. Therefore, it is man's obligation to guarantee the chastity of his daughters and his wife. As she is 'nature', 'sin', she has to be permanently under his guardianship; she becomes a permanent minor.

Only men are capable of becoming adults and citizens in the true sense. To control their own women's sexuality, the men were advised to resort to beatings and other violent devices (Bauer, 1917). But all direct and ideological attacks on the sinful nature of women also served the purpose of robbing women of their autonomy over other economically productive functions and establishing the male hegemony in the economic, political and cultural spheres.

Sexual autonomy is closely connected with economic autonomy. The case of the professionalization of male doctors who drove out and denounced women healers and midwives as witches is the best documentation of this onslaught on female productive activity. The new capitalist class rose on the subjugation of women (see chapter 3; also Rowbotham, 1974; Ehrenreich and English, 1979).

At the end of this 'civilizing process', we have the women disciplined enough to work as housewives for a man or as wage labourers for a capitalist, or as both. They have learned to turn the actual violence used against them for centuries against themselves, and to internalize it; they defined it as voluntariness, as 'love', the necessary ideological mystification of their own self-repression (Bock/Duden, 1977). The institutional and ideological props necessary for the maintenance of this self-repression were provided by the church, the state, and through the family. Women were confined to this institution by the organization of the labour process (division of household from workplace), by law, and by their economic dependence on the man as the so-called 'breadwinner'.

It would be an illusion, however, to think that with the full development of capitalism the barbarous features of its bloody beginnings would disappear, and that fully-developed capitalist production relations would mean the end of the social paradigm of man-the-hunter/warrior and the transformation of extra-economic coercion into economic coercion.[10]

On the contrary, we can observe that for the maintenance of an asymmetric exploitative division of labour on a national and international plane – both are interlinked – fully-fledged capitalism needs an ever-expanding state machinery of repression, and a frightening concentration of means of destruction and coercion. None of the capitalist states has done away with the police or the military; they are still, as among the hunters, warriors and warrior-nomads, the most 'productive' sectors because, through the monopoly of now legalized violence, these states are able effectively to curb any rebellion among the workers within their orbit, and also to force subsistence producers and whole peripheral areas to produce for a globally interlinked accumulation process. Though world-scale exploitation of human labour for profits has mainly taken the 'rational' form of so-called unequal exchange, the maintenance of the unequal relationship is guaranteed everywhere, in the last analysis, by means of direct coercion, by arms.

To summarize, we can say that the various forms of asymmetric, hierarchical divisions of labour, which have developed throughout history up to the stage where the whole world is now structured into one system of unequal division of labour under the dictates of capital accumulation, are based on the social paradigm of the predatory hunter/warrior who, without himself producing, is able by means of arms to appropriate and subordinate other producers, their productive forces and their products.

This extractive, non-reciprocal, exploitative object-relation to nature, first estblished between men and women and men and nature, remained the model for all other patriarchal modes of production, including capitalism which developed it to its most sophisticated and most generalized form.[11] The characteristic of this model is that those who control the production process and the products are not themselves producers, but appropriators. Their so-called productivity pre-supposes the existence and the subjection of other – and, in the last analysis, female – producers. As Wallerstein puts it: '. . . crudely, those who breed manpower sustain those who grow food who sustain those who grow other raw materials who sustain those involved in industrial production' (Wallerstein, 1974: 86). What Wallerstein forgets to mention is that all those sustain the non-producers who control this whole process, ultimately by means of arms, because at the heart of this paradigm lies the fact that non-producers appropriate and consume (or invest) what others have produced. Man-the-hunter is basically a parasite, not a producer.

Notes

1. This chapter is the result of a longer collective process of reflection among women in the years 1975–1977, when I conducted courses on the history of the women's movement at Frankfurt University. Many of the ideas discussed here emerged in a course on 'Work and Sexuality in Matristic Societies'. The thesis of one of my students, Roswitha Leukert, on 'Female Sensuality' (1976), helped to clarify many of our ideas. I want to thank her and all women who took part in these discussions.

The chapter is the revised version of a paper which was first given at the Conference 'Underdevelopment and Subsistence Reproduction', University of Bielefeld, 1979. It was published as an Occasional Paper in 1981 by the Institute of Social Studies, The Hague.

2. 'Appropriation of Nature' (*Aneignung der Natur*) has a double meaning in German, and this ambiguity can also be found in the way Marx uses this expression. On the one hand, he uses it in the sense of 'making nature our own, humanizing nature'. In his earlier writings the formulation 'appropriation of nature' is used in this sense. On the other hand, it defines a relationship of dominance between Man and Nature. This is the case in *Capital*, where Marx has reduced the broader definition to mean 'dominance over, control over, mastership over nature'. As we shall see, such an interpretation of this concept proves to be problematic for women.

3. This sexism prevails in many languages. They cannot, like English, French and all Romanic languages, differentiate between 'man' (male being) and 'man' (human being). In the German language this difference can still be expressed: *Mann* is the male, *Mensch* the human being, though *Mensch* has also assumed a male connotation.

4. With Bornemann I use the term 'matristic' instead of 'matriarchal', because 'matriarchal' implies that mothers were able to establish a political system of dominance. But not even in matrilineal and matrilocal societies did women establish such lasting political dominance systems (Bornemann, 1975).

5. The Indian mother-goddess (Kali, Durga, etc.) are all embodiments of this active and practical principle, whereas many of the male Gods are passive, contemplative and ascetic. For a discussion of the relationship between a certain concept of nature and the appropriation of female bodies, see also Colette Guillaumin, 1978.

6. A comparison of the terminology used in population research today with that of an earlier period would be very revealing.

Up to the 1930s, the production of new life was still conceptualized as 'pro-creation', that is, it still had an active, creative connotation. But today the generative productivity is conceptualized in passive, biologistic, behaviouristic and mechanistic terms like: 'fertility', 'biological reproduction', 'generative behaviour'. This definition of human generative productivity as passive fertility is a necessary ideological mystification for those who want to gain control over this last area of human autonomy.

7. This is not surprising as May also uses the concept 'fertility' in the same sense as most population researchers and family planners do, namely, as the result of unconscious, physiological behaviour.

8. For a discussion of the seed-and-field analogy in ancient Indian literature, see also Maria Mies, 1980; Leela Dube, 1978.

9. See, for instance, Kathleen Gough, 'The Origin of the Family', in Rayna Reiter (ed.), *Toward an Anthropology of Women*, New York, 1975.

10. At the present moment in history we can no longer share the opinion of the earlier Marxists, including Rosa Luxemburg, that warfare and violence were necessary as methods to solve conflicts of interest as long as the productive forces had not reached their highest development, as long as human beings had not achieved total control and dominance over nature (cf. Rosa Luxemburg, 1925: pp. 155–6). Our problem is that this definition of 'development of productive forces' *implies* violence and warfare against nature and human beings.

11. At this point, it would be appropriate to extend our analysis to the sexual division of labour under socialism. But this would require a much broader analysis. From what can be gathered from information about the status of women in socialist countries, we can only conclude that the division of labour by sex is based on the same social paradigm as in the capitalist countries. One of the reasons for this may be that the concept of the 'development of productive forces' and man's relation to nature have been the same as under capitalism, meaning namely man's lordship over nature, which implies his lordship over women (see chapter 6).

3. Colonization and Housewifization

The Dialectics of 'Progress and Retrogression'

On the basis of the foregoing analysis, it is possible to formulate a tentative thesis which will guide my further discussion.

The historical development of the division of labour in general, and the sexual division of labour in particular, was/is not an *evolutionary* and peaceful process, based on the ever-progressing development of productive forces (mainly technology) and specialization, but a violent one by which first certain categories of men, later certain peoples, were able mainly by virtue of arms and warfare to establish an exploitative relationship between themselves and women, and other peoples and classes.

Within such a predatory mode of production, which is intrinsically patriarchal, warfare and conquest become the most 'productive' modes of production. The quick accumulation of material wealth – not based on regular subsistence work in one's own community, but on looting and robbery – facilitates the faster development of technology in those societies which are based on conquest and warfare. This technological development, however, again is not oriented principally towards the satisfaction of subsistence needs of the community as a whole, but towards further warfare, conquest and accumulation. The development of arms and transport technology has been a driving force for technological innovation in all patriarchal societies, but particularly in the modern capitalist European one which has conquered and subjected the whole world since the fifteenth century. The concept of 'progress' which emerged in this particular patriarchal civilization is historically unthinkable without the one-sided development of the technology of warfare and conquest. All subsistence technology (for conservation and production of food, clothes and shelter, etc.) henceforth appears to be 'backward' in comparison to the 'wonders' of the modern technology of warfare and conquest (navigation, the compass, gunpowder, etc.).

The predatory patriarchal division of labour is based, from the outset, on a structural *separation* and *subordination* of human beings: men are separated from women, whom they have subordinated, the 'own' people are separated from the 'foreigners' or 'heathens'. Whereas in the old patriarchies this separation could never be total, in the modern 'western' patriarchy this separation has been extended to a separation between MAN and NATURE. In the old patriarchies

(China, India, Arabia), men could not conceive of themselves as totally independent from Mother Earth. Even the conquered and subjected peoples, slaves, pariahs, etc., were still visibly present and were not thought of as lying totally *outside* the *oikos* or the 'economy' (the hierarchically structured social universe which was seen as a living organism (cf. Merchant, 1983)). And women, though they were exploited and subordinated, were crucially important as mothers of sons for all patriarchal societies. Therefore, I think it is correct when B. Ehrenreich and D. English call these pre-modern patriarchies gynocentric. Without the human mother and Mother Earth no patriarchy could exist (Ehrenreich/English, 1979: 7–8). With the rise of capitalism as a world-system, based on large-scale conquest and colonial plunder, and the emergence of the world-market (Wallerstein, 1974), it becomes possible to *externalize* or *exterritorialize* those whom the new patriarchs wanted to exploit. The colonies were no longer seen as part of the economy or society, they were lying outside 'civilized society'. In the same measure as European conquerers and invaders 'penetrated' those 'virgin lands', these lands and their inhabitants were 'naturalized', declared as wild, savage nature, waiting to be exploited and tamed by the male civilizers.

Similarly, the relationship between human beings and external nature or the earth was radically changed. As Carolyn Merchant has convincingly shown, the rise of modern science and technology was based on the violent attack and rape of Mother Earth – hitherto conceived as a living organism. Francis Bacon, the father of modern science, was one of those who advocated the same violent means to rob Mother Nature of her secrets – namely, torture and inquisition – as were used by Church and State to get at the secrets of the witches. The taboos against mining, digging holes in the womb of Mother Earth, were broken by force, because the new patriarchs wanted to get at the precious metals and other 'raw-materials' hidden in the 'womb of the earth'. The rise of modern science, a mechanistic and physical world-view, was based on the killing of nature as a living organism and its transformation into a huge reservoir of 'natural resources' or 'matter', which could be analysed and synthesized by Man into his new machines by which he could make himself independent of Mother Nature.

Only now, the dualism, or rather the polarization, between the patriarchs and nature, and between men and women could develop its full and permanent destructive potential. From now on science and technology became the main 'productive forces' through which men could 'emancipate' themselves from nature, as well as from women.

Carolyn Merchant has shown that the destruction of nature as a living organism – and the rise of modern science and technology, together with the rise of male scientists as the new high priests – had its close parallel in the violent attack on women during the witch hunt which raged through Europe for some four centuries.

Merchant does not extend her analysis to the relation of the New Men to their colonies. Yet an understanding of this relation is absolutely necessary, because we cannot understand the modern developments, including our present problems, unless we include all those who were 'defined into nature' by the modern capitalist patriarchs: Mother Earth, Women and Colonies.

The modern European patriarchs made themselves independent of their *European* Mother Earth, by conquering first the Americas, later Asia and Africa, and by extracting gold and silver from the mines of Bolivia, Mexico and Peru and other 'raw materials' and luxury items from the other lands. They 'emancipated' themselves, on the one hand, from their dependence on European women for the production of labourers by destroying the witches, as well as their knowledge of contraceptives and birth control. On the other hand, by subordinating grown African men and women into slavery, they thus acquired the necessary labour power for their plantations in America and the Caribbean.

Thus, the progress of European Big Men is based on the subordination and exploitation of their own women, on the exploitation and killing of Nature, on the exploitation and subordination of other peoples and their lands. Hence, the law of this 'progress' is always a contradictory and not an evolutionary one: progress for some means retrogression for the other side; 'evolution' for some means 'devolution' for others; 'humanization' for some means 'de-humanization' for others; development of productive forces for some means underdevelopment and retrogression for others. The rise of some means the fall of others. Wealth for some means poverty for others. The reason why there cannot be unilinear progress is the fact that, as was said earlier, the predatory patriarchal mode of production constitutes a non-reciprocal, exploitative relationship. Within such a relationship no general progress for all, no 'trickling down', no development for all is possible.

Engels had attributed this antagonistic relationship between progress and retrogression to the emergence of private property and the exploitation of one class by the other. Thus, he wrote in 1884:

> Since the exploitation of one class by another is the basis of civilization, its whole development moves in a continuous contradiction. Every advance in production is at the same time a retrogression in the condition of the exploited class, that is of the great majority. What is a boon for the one is necessarily a bane for the other; each new emancipation of one class always means a new oppression of another class (Engels, 1976: 333).

Engels speaks only of the relationship between exploiting and exploited classes, he does not include the relationship between men and women, that of colonial masters to their colonies or of Civilized Man in general to Nature. But these relationships constitute, in fact, the hidden foundation of civilized society. He hopes to change this necessarily polarized relationship by extending what is good for the ruling class to all classes: 'What is good for the ruling class should be good for the whole of the society with which the ruling class identifies itself' (Engels, 1976: 333).

But this is precisely the logical flaw in this strategy: in a contradictory and exploitative relationship, the privileges of the exploiters can never become the privileges of all. If the wealth of the metropoles is based on the exploitation of colonies, then the colonies cannot achieve wealth unless they also have colonies. If the emancipation of men is based on the subordination of women, then women cannot achieve 'equal rights' with men, which would necessarily include the right to exploit others.[1]

Hence, a feminist strategy for liberation cannot but aim at the total abolition of all these relationships of retrogressive progress. This means it must aim at an end of all *exploitation* of women by men, of nature by man, of colonies by colonizers, of one class by the other. As long as exploitation of one of these remains the precondition for the advance (development, evolution, progress, humanization, etc.) of one section of people, feminists cannot speak of liberation or 'socialism'.

Subordination of Women, Nature and Colonies:
The underground of capitalist patriarchy or civilized society

In the following, I shall try to trace the contradictory process, briefly sketched out above, by which, in the course of the last four or five centuries women, nature and colonies were externalized, declared to be outside civilized society, pushed down, and thus made invisible as the under-water part of an iceberg is invisible, yet constitute the base of the whole.

Methodologically, I shall try as far as possible to undo the division of those poles of the exploitative relations which are usually analysed as separate entities. Our understanding of scholarly work or research follows exactly the same logic as that of the colonizers and scientists: they cut apart and separate parts which constitute a whole, isolate these parts, analyse them under laboratory conditions and synthesize them again in a new, man-made, artificial model.

I shall not follow this logic. I shall rather try to trace the 'underground connections' that link the processes by which nature was exploited and put under man's domination to the processes by which women in Europe were subordinated, and examine the processes by which these two were linked to the conquest and colonization of other lands and people. Hence, the historical emergence of European science and technology, and its mastery over nature have to be linked to the persecution of the European witches. And both the persecution of the witches and the rise of modern science have to be linked to the slave trade and the destruction of subsistence economies in the colonies.

This cannot be a comprehensive history of this whole period, desirable though this might be. I shall mainly highlight some important connections which were crucial for the construction of capitalist patriarchal production relations. One is the connection between the persecution of the witches in Europe and the rise of the new bourgeoisie and modern science, and the subordination of nature. This has already been dealt with by several researchers (Merchant, 1983; Heinsohn, Knieper, Steiger, 1979; Ehrenreich, English, 1979; Becker *et al*, 1977). The following analysis is based on their work.

The historical connections between these processes and the subordination and exploitation of colonial peoples in general, and of women in the colonies in particular, has not yet been adequately studied. Therefore, I shall deal with this history more extensively.

The Persecution of the Witches and the Rise of Modern Society
Women's productive record at the end of the Middle Ages

Among the Germanic tribes who occupied Europe, the house-father (*pater familias*) had power over everything and everybody in the house. This power, called *munt* (Old High German) (*mundium* = *manus* = hand), implied that he could sell, bill, etc., wife, children, slaves, etc. The *munt* of the man over the woman was established through marriage. The relationship was one of property rights over things, which was founded on occupation (kidnapping of women), or purchase (sale of women). According to Germanic law, the marriage was a sales-contract between the two families. The woman was only the object in this transaction. By acquiring the *munt*-power, the husband acquired the right over the wife's belongings, as she was his property. Women were lifelong under the *munt* of their men – husband, father, son. The origin of this *munt* was to exclude women from the use of arms. With the rise of the cities since the thirteenth century and the emergence of an urban bourgeoisie, the 'whole house' – the earlier Germanic form of the extended family and kinship – began to dissolve. The old *potestas patriae*, the power of the father over sons and daughters, ended when they left the house. Wives were put under the *munt* or guardianship of the husband. However, if unmarried women had property of their own, they were sometimes considered *mündig* (major) before the law. In Cologne, unmarried women who followed some craft were called *selbstmündig* in 1291 (Becker *et al*, 1977: 41). The laws prevailing in the cities, as well as some laws for the countryside, freed women in the crafts from the *munt* or dependence on a father or husband.

The reason for this liberalization of sexual bondage has to be seen in the need to allow women in the cities to carry on their crafts and businesses independently. This was due to several factors:

1. With the extension of trade and commerce the demand for manufactured goods, particularly clothes and other consumer goods, grew. These goods were almost exclusively produced in the household of craftsmen and women. With the growth of money-supply in the hands of the patricians, their consumption of luxury goods also grew. Costly clothes of velvet and silk, lace collars, girdles, etc., became the fashion. In many of these crafts women were predominant.

However, in Germany, married women were not allowed to carry out their business or any property transaction without the consent of their husband, who continued to be their guardian and master. However, craftswomen or business-women could appear before a court as witnesses or complainants, without a guardian. In some cities the businesswomen or market-women were given equal rights with the men. In Munich it was stated that 'a woman who stands in the market, buys and sells, has all rights her husband has'. But she could not sell his property.

The independence of the medieval crafts- and market-women was not unlimited; it was a concession given to them because the rising bourgeoisie needed them. But within the family the husband retained his master role.

2. The second reason for this relative freedom for women in commerce and crafts was a shortage of men at the end of the Middle Ages. In Frankfurt the sex

ratio was 1,100 women for 1,000 men, according to a thirteenth-century census; in Nuremberg (fifteenth century), the sex ratio was 1,000 men to 1,207 women. The number of men had diminished due to the crusades and constant warfare between the feudal states. Moreover, male mortality seems to have been higher than female mortality 'because of the men's intemperance in all sorts of revelries' (Bücher, quoted in Becker *et al*, 1977: 63).

Among the peasants in South Germany, only the eldest son was allowed to marry because otherwise the land would have been divided into holdings too small to be viable. Journeymen were not allowed to marry before they became masters. The serfs of the feudal lords could not marry without the consent of their lords. When the cities opened their doors, many serfs, men and women, ran away to the cities; 'city air makes men free' was the slogan. The poor people in the countryside had to send their daughters away to fend for themselves as maidservants because they could not feed them until they were married.

This all resulted in an increase in the number of unattached, single or widowed women who had to be economically active. The cities, in the twelfth and thirteenth centuries did not exclude women from any craft or business which they wanted to take up. This was necessary as, without their contribution, trade and commerce could not have been expanded. But the attitude towards the economically independent women was always contradictory. In the beginning the crafts' guilds were exclusively men's associations. It seems they had to admit some craftswomen later. In Germany this did not occur before the fourteenth century. Mainly weaver-women and spinsters and women engaged in other branches of textile manufacture were allowed to join guilds. Weaving had been in the hands of the men since the twelfth century, but women did a number of ancillary jobs, and later also female master weavers are mentioned for certain branches like veil-weaving, linen-weaving, silk-weaving, gold-weaving, etc., which were only done by women. In Cologne there were even female guilds from the fourteenth century.

Apart from the crafts, women were mainly engaged in *petty trade* in fruits, chicken, eggs, herrings, flowers, cheese, milk, salt, oil, feathers, jams, etc. Women were very successful as peddlers and hawkers, and constituted a certain challenge to male traders. But they did not engage in foreign trade though they advanced money to merchants who traded with the outside markets.

> The silk-spinners of Cologne often were married to rich merchants who sold the precious products of their wives in far-off markets in Flanders, England, at the North Sea and the Baltic Sea, at the big fairs in Leipzig and Frankfurt (Becker *et al*, 1977: 66–67).

Only one merchant woman is mentioned who herself travelled to England in the fifteenth century: Katherine Ysenmengerde from Danzig (Becker *et al*, 1977: 66–67).

In the fifteenth and sixteenth centuries, however, the old European order collapsed and 'there came to be a European world economy based on the capitalist mode of production' (Wallerstein, 1974: 67). This period is characterized by a tremendous expansion and penetration of the rising bourgeoisie into the 'New Worlds', and by pauperization, wars, epidemics and turbulence within the old core states.

According to Wallerstein this world economy included, by the end of the sixteenth century, north-west Europe, the Christian Mediterranean, Central Europe, the Baltic region, certain regions of America, New Spain, the Antilles, Peru, Chile and Brazil. Excluded at that time were India, the Far East, the Ottoman Empire, Russia and China.

Between 1535 and 1540, *Spain* achieved control over more than half the population of the Western Hemisphere. Between 1670–1680, the area under European control went up from about three million square kilometres to about seven million (Wallerstein, 1974: 68). The expansion made possible the large-scale accumulation of private capital 'which was used to finance the rationalization of agricultural production' (Wallerstein, 1974: 69). 'One of the most obvious characteristics of this sixteenth century European World Economy was a secular inflation, the so-called price revolution' (Wallerstein, 1974: 69). This inflation has been attributed, in one way or the other, to the influx of precious metals, bullion, from Hispano America. Its effect was mainly felt in the supply of foodgrains available at cheaper prices. 'In those countries where industry expanded, it was necessary to turn over a larger proportion of the land to the needs of horses'. Grain then had to be bought in the Baltic at higher prices. At the same time, wages remained stagnant in England and France because of institutional rigidities, and even a decline in real wages took place. This meant greater poverty for the masses.

According to Wallerstein, sixteenth-century Europe had several core areas: northern Europe (Netherlands, England, France) where trade flourished, and where land was used mainly for pastoral purposes, not for grain. Rural wage-labour became the dominant form of labour control. Grain was imported from Eastern Europe and the Baltics – the periphery – where 'secondary serfdom' or 'feudalism' emerged as the main labour control. In northern and central Europe this process led to great pauperization of peasants. There seems to have been population growth in the sixteenth century and the pressure on the towns grew. Wallerstein sees this population pressure as reason for out-migration. 'In Western Europe there was emigration to the towns and a growing vagabondage that was "endemic" ' (Wallerstein, 1974: 117). There was not only the rural exodus due to eviction and the enclosure system (of the yeomen in England), 'there was also the vagabondage "caused by the decline of feudal bodies of retainers and the disbanding of the swollen armies which had flocked to serve the kings against their vassals" ' (Marx, quoted by Wallerstein, 1974: 117).

These wanderers – before they were recruited as labourers into the new industries – lived from hand to mouth. They were the impoverished masses who flocked around the various prophets and heretic sects. Most of the radical and utopian ideas of the time are concerned with these poor masses. Many poor women were among these vagabonds. They earned their living as dancers, tricksters, singers and prostitutes. They flocked to the annual fairs, the church councils, etc. For the Diet of Frankfurt, 1394, 800 women came; for the Council of Constance and Basle, 1500 (Becker *et al*, 1977; 76). These women also followed the armies. They were not only prostitutes for the soldiers but they also had to dig trenches, nurse the sick and wounded, and sell commodities.

These women were not despised in the beginning, they formed part of medieval society. The bigger cities put them into special 'women's houses'. The church tried to control the increasing prostitution, but poverty drove too many poor women into the 'women's houses'. In many cities these prostitutes had their own associations. In Church processions and public feasts they had their own banners and place – even a patron saint, St Magdalene. This shows that up to the fourteenth century prostitution was not considered a bad thing. But at the end of the fourteenth century, the Statues of Meran rule that prostitutes should stay away from public feasts and dances where 'burgers women and other honorable women are'. They should have a yellow ribbon on their shoes so that everyone could distinguish them from the 'decent women' (Becker *et al*, 1977: 79).

The witch-hunt which raged through Europe from the twelfth to the seventeenth century was one of the mechanisms to control and subordinate women, the peasant and artisan, women who in their economic and sexual independence constituted a threat for the emerging bourgeois order.

Recent feminist literature on the witches and their persecution has brought to light that women were not passively giving up their economic and sexual independence, but that they resisted in many forms the onslaught of church, state and capital. One form of resistance were the many heterodox sects in which women either played a prominent role, or which in their ideology propagated freedom and equality for women and a condemnation of sexual repression, property and monogamy. Thus the 'Brethren of the Free Spirit', a sect which existed over several hundred years, established communal living, abolished marriage, and rejected the authority of the church. Many women, some of them extraordinary scholars, belonged to this sect. Several of them were burnt as heretics (Cohn, 1970).

It seems plausible that the whole fury of the witch-hunt was not just a result of the decaying old order in its confrontation with new capitalist forces, or even a manifestation of timeless male sadism, but a reaction of the new male-dominated classes against the *rebellion* of women. The poor women 'freed', that is, expropriated from their means of subsistence and skills, fought back against their expropriators. Some argue that the witches had been an organized sect which met regularly at their 'witches' sabbath', where all poor people gathered and already practised the new free society without masters and serfs. When a woman denied being a witch and having anything to do with all the accusations, she was tortured and finally burnt at the stake. The witch trial, however, followed a meticulously thought-out legal procedure. In protestant countries one finds special secular witch-commissions and witch-commissars. The priests were in constant rapport with the courts and influenced the judges.

One prosecutor, Benedikt Carpzov, first a lawyer in Saxonia, later professor in Leipzig, signed 20,000 death sentences against witches. He was a faithful son of the protestant church (Dross, 1978: 204).

If someone denounced a woman as a witch, a commission was sent to that place to collect evidence. Everything was evidence: good weather or bad weather, if she worked hard or if she was lazy, diseases or healing powers. If under torture the witch named another person, this person was also immediately arrested.

The Subordination and Breaking of the Female Body: Torture

Here are the minutes of the torture of Katherine Lips from Betzlesdorf, 1672:

> After this the judgement was again read to her and she was admonished to speak the truth. But she continued to deny. She then undressed willingly. The hangman bound her hands and hung her up, let her down again. She cried: woe, woe. Again she was pulled up. Again she screamed, woe woe, lord in heaven help me. Her toes were bound . . . her legs were put into Spanish boots – first the left then the right leg was screwed . . . she cried, 'Lord Jesus come and help me . . .' She said she knew nothing, even if they killed her. They pulled her up higher. She became silent, then she said she was no witch. Then they again put the screws on her legs. She again screamed and cried . . . and became silent . . . she continued to say she knew nothing . . . She shouted her mother should come out of the grave and help her . . .
>
> They then led her outside the room and shaved her head to find the stigma. The master came back and said they had found the stigma. He had thrust a needle into it and she had not felt it. Also, no blood had come out. Again they bound her at hand and feet and pulled her up, again she screamed and shouted she knew nothing. They should put her on the floor and kill her, etc., etc., etc. . . . (quoted in Becker *et al*, 1977: 426ff).

In 1631 Friedrich von Spee dared to write an anonymous essay against the tortures and the witch-hunt. He exposed the sadistic character of the tortures and also the use the authorities, the church and the secular authorities made of the witch hysteria to find a scapegoat for all problems and disturbances and the unrest of the poor people, and to divert the wrath of the people from them against some poor women.

> 31 October 1724: Torture of Enneke Fristenares from Coesfeld (Münster)
>
> After the accused had been asked in vain to confess, Dr Gogravius announced the order of torture . . . He asked her to tell the truth, because the painful interrogation would make her confess anyway and double the punishment . . . after this the first degree of torture was applied to her.
>
> Then the judge proceeded to the second degree of torture. She was led to the torture chamber, she was undressed, tied down and interrogated. She denied to have done anything . . . As she remained stubborn they proceeded to the third degree and her thumbs were put into screws. Because she screamed so horribly they put a block into her mouth and continued screwing her thumbs. Fifty minutes this went on, the screws were loosened and tightened alternately. But she pleaded her innocence. She also did not weep but only shouted, 'I am not guilty. O Jesus come and help me.' Then, 'Your Lordship, take me and kill me.' Then they proceeded to the fourth degree, the Spanish Boots . . . As she did not weep Dr Gogravius worried whether the accused might have been made insensitive against pain through sorcery. Therefore he again asked the executioner to undress her and find out whether there was anything suspicious about her body. Whereupon the executioner reported he had examined everything meticulously but had not found anything. Again he was ordered to apply the Spanish Boots. The accused however continued to assert her innocence and screamed 'O Jesus I haven't done it, I haven't done it, Your Lordship kill me. I am not guilty, I am not guilty!' . . .

This order went on for 30 minutes without result.

Then Dr Gogravius ordered the fifth degree:

The accused was hung up and beaten with two rods – up to 30 strokes. She was so exhausted that she said she would confess, but with regard to the specific accusations she continued to deny that she had committed any of the crimes. The executioner had to pull her up till her arms were twisted out of their joints. For six minutes this torture lasted. Then she was beaten up again, and again her thumbs were put into screws and her legs into the Spanish Boots. But the accused continued to deny that she had anything to do with the devil.

As Dr Gogravius came to the conclusion that the torture had been correctly applied, according to the rules, and after the executioner stated the accused would not survive further torturing Dr Gogravius ordered the accused to be taken down and unbound. He ordered the executioner to set her limbs in the right place and nurse her (quoted in Becker *et al*, 1977: 433–435, transl. M.M.).

Burning of Witches, Primitive Accumulation of Capital, and the Rise of Modern Science

The persecution and burning of the midwives as witches was directly connected with the emergence of modern society: the professionalization of medicine, the rise of *medicine* as a 'natural science', the rise of *science* and of *modern economy*. The torture chambers of the witch-hunters were the laboratories where the texture, the anatomy, the resistance of the human body – mainly the female body – was studied. One may say that modern medicine and the male hegemony over this vital field were established on the base of millions of crushed, maimed, torn, disfigured and finally burnt, female bodies.[2]

There was a calculated division of labour between Church and State in organizing the massacres and the terror against the witches. Whereas the church representatives identified witches, gave the theological justification and led the interrogations, the 'secular arm' of the state was used to carry out the tortures and finally execute the witches on the pyre.

The persecution of the witches was a manifestation of the rising modern society and not, as is usually believed, a remnant of the irrational 'dark' Middle Ages. This is most clearly shown by Jean Bodin, the French theoretician of the new mercantilist economic doctrine. Jean Bodin was the founder of the quantitative theory of money, of the modern concept of sovereignty and of mercantilist populationism. He was a staunch defender of modern rationalism, and was at the same time one of the most vocal proponents of state-ordained tortures and massacres of the witches. He held the view that, for the development of new wealth after the medieval agrarian crisis, the *modern state* had to be invested with absolute sovereignty. This state had, moreover, the duty to provide for enough workers for the new economy. In order to do so, he demanded a strong police which above all would fight against witches and midwives who, according to him, were responsible for so many abortions, the infertility of couples, or sexual intercourse without conception. Anyone who prevented the conception or the birth of children he considered as a murderer, who should be persecuted by the state. Bodin worked as a consultant of the French government in the persecution of the witches, and advocated torture and the pyre to eradicate the witches. His tract on witchcraft was one of the most brutal and sadistic of all pamphlets written against witches at that time. Like Institoris and Sprenger in Germany he singled out women for his attack. He set a ratio of 50 women to one man for the witch persecutions (Merchant, 1983: 138). This combination of modern rationality, the propagation of the new state and a direct violent attack on the witches we also find with another great master of the new era of European civilization, namely Francis Bacon (cf. Merchant, 1983: 164–177).

Similarly, there is a direct connection between the witch pogroms and the emergence of the professionalization of *law*. Before that period, the German law followed old Germanic custom; it was people's law or customary law, but not a discipline to be studied. But now Roman law was introduced, most of the universities established a law faculty and several universities, like the university of Frankfurt, consisted in fact only of the law faculty. Some contemporaries complain about the universities:

> They are good for nothing and train only parasites who learn how to confuse the people, how to make good things bad and bad things good, who withhold what is rightful from the poor and give what is not his right to the rich (Jansen, 1903, quoted in Hammes, 1977: 243; transl. M.M.).

The reason why the sons of the rising urban class were flocking to the law faculties was the following: 'In our times jurisprudencia smiles at everybody, so that everyone wants to become a doctor in law. Most are attracted to this field of studies out of greed for money and ambition' (ibid.).

The witch trials provided employment and money for a host of lawyers, advocates, judges, councils, etc. They were able, through their complicated and learned interpretations of the authoritative texts, to prolong the trials so that the costs of the trial would go up. There was a close relationship between the worldly authorities, the church, the rulers of the small feudal states and the lawyers. The latter were responsible for an inflation of fees, and filled their coffers by squeezing money from the poor victims of the witch-hunt. The fleecing of the people was so rampant that even a man like the Elector of Trier (the Archbishop of Trier was one of the seven princes who elected the German Kaiser), Johann von Schoenburg, who had himself had several hundred people executed as witches and sorcerers, had to check the robbing of the widows and orphans by the learned jurists and all others connected with the witch trials. Some of the rulers set up accountants to check what the various officials had done with the money extracted and the fees they had demanded. Among the costs for a trial were the following:

– for the alcohol consumed by the soldiers who pursued a witch;
– for the visit the priest paid to the witch while in prison;
– for the maintenance of the private guard of the executioner.
(Hammes, 1977: 243–257).

According to Canon Law, the property of the witch was to be confiscated, irrespective of whether there were heirs or not. The bulk of the confiscated property, never less than 50 per cent, was appropriated by the government. In many cases, all that was left over after the deduction of the costs for the trial went to the state treasury. This confiscation was illegal, as the 'Constitutio Criminalis' of Emperor Charles V proclaims in 1532. But this law had only paper value.

The fact that the witch-hunt was such a lucrative source of money and wealth led in certain areas to the setting up of special commissions which had the task of denouncing ever more people as witches and sorcerers. When the accused were found guilty, they and their families had to bear all the costs of the trial, beginning with the bills for alcohol and food for the witch commission (their *per diem*), and ending with the costs for the firewood for the stake. Another source of money was the sums paid by the richer families to the learned judges and lawyers in order to free one of their members from the persecution if she was accused as a witch. This is also a reason why we find more poor people among those who were executed.

Manfred Hammes has brought to light yet another dimension of the 'political economy' of the witch-hunt, namely, the raising of funds by the warring European princes to finance their wars, particularly the Thirty-Year War from 1618–1648. From 1618 onwards, the Law of Charles V, prohibiting the confiscation of property of witches and sorcerers, was virtually abandoned and witch-hunts were specifically organised or encouraged by some of the princes in order to be able to confiscate the property of their subjects.

Hammes gives us the example of the city of Cologne and the dispute that arose between the city fathers and the Elector Ferdinand of Bavaria – the ruler of the diocese. The city of Cologne, a rich centre of trading and industries, had remained neutral for a long time during the Thirty-Years War. (In the beginning of the seventeenth century, the city had seen a flourishing trade – mainly in silk and textiles.)[3] Nevertheless, the city had paid considerable sums into the war fund of the Emperor. This was made possible by an increase in taxes. When foreign armies were marauding and looting the villages, many rural people fled into the free and neutral city. The result was a scarcity of food supplies which led to tensions among the people and even to open riots. At the same time the witch trial against Catherine Hernot[4] started, which was followed by an intense witch-hunt. When the first judgements were pronounced, the Elector Ferdinand of Bavaria, who had to pay his armies, presented a bill to the city authorities. In this bill he claimed that all the property of executed witches should be confiscated and go to the exchequer. The city council tried with all means to prevent the implementation of this ordinance. They asked their lawyers to make an expert study of the law. But the Elector and his lawyers finally proclaimed that the bill was an emergency measure. Since the evil of witchcraft had assumed such dimensions in recent times, it would be politically unwise to follow the letter of the law (namely, Constitutio Criminalis of Charles V prohibiting confiscations) word by word. However, the lawyers of the city were not convinced and they suggested a compromise. They said it was fair and just that the persons who had been involved in the witch trial, the lawyers, executioners, etc., would get a fee as compensation 'for their hard work and the time they had spent on the trial'. The Elector, as he could not press money out of the urban witch-hunt, confiscated all the property of the witches executed in the rural areas of the diocese.

But not only the feudal class (particularly the smaller princes who could not compete with the rising bourgeoisie in the cities, or the bigger lords), but also the propertied classes in the cities were using the confiscation of witch-property as a means for capital accumulation.

Thus, in Cologne itself in 1628, ten years after the beginning of the war, the city authorities had introduced the confiscation of witch-property. One of the legitimations forwarded by the lawyers of Cologne was that the witches had received a lot of money from the devil and that it was perfectly in order that this devil's money be confiscated by the authorities to enable them to eradicate the evil breed of sorcerers and witches. In fact, it seems that in some cases the cities and the princes used witch-pogroms and confiscations as a kind of development aid for their ruined economies. The city fathers of Mainz did not make much fuss about legal niceties and simply asked their officials to confiscate all property of the witches. In 1618, the Monastery of St Clare of Hochheim had donated them 2,000 guilders for the 'eradication of witches'.

There is a report of the Bailiff Geiss who wrote to his Lord of Lindheim asking him to allow him to start with the persecution because he needed money for the restoration of a bridge and the church. He noted that most of the people were disturbed about the spreading of the evil of witchcraft:

> If only your Lordship would be willing to start the burning, we would gladly provide the firewood and bear all other costs, and your Lordship would earn so much that the bridge and also the Church could be well repaired.
>
> Moreover, you would get so much that you could pay your servants a better salary in future, because one could confiscate whole houses and particularly the more well-to-do ones (quoted in Hammes, 1977: 254; transl. M.M.).

Apart from the big bloodsuckers – the religious authorities, the worldly governments, the feudal class, the urban authorities, the fraternity of jurists, the executioners – there grew up a whole army of smaller fry who made a living out of the burning witches. Begging monks wandered around and sold pictures of the saints which, if swallowed by the buyers, would prevent them from being afflicted by witchcraft. There were many self-appointed witch-commissars. Since the authorities paid fees for the discovery, the arrest and the interrogation of witches, they accumulated money by wandering from place to place instigating the poor people to see the cause of all their misery in the workings of the witches. Then, when everybody was in the grip of the mass psychosis, the commissar said he would come to eradicate the pest. First, the commissar would send his collector who would go from house to house to collect donations to prove that the peasants themselves had invited him. Then the commissar would come and organize two or three burnings at the stake. If someone was not ready to pay, he was suspected of being a sorcerer or a witch or a sympathizer of the witches. In some cases the villages paid a sum to the commissar in advance, so that he would not visit their village. This happened in the Eifel village of Rheinbach. But five years later the same commissar came back and, since the peasants were not ready to yield a second time to this blackmail, he added more death sentences to the record of 800 he had already achieved.

The hope of financial gains can be seen as one of the main reasons why the witch hysteria spread and why hardly any people were acquitted. The witch-hunt was business. This is clearly spelt out by Friedrich von Spee who finally had the courage, in 1633, to write a book against this sordid practice. He notes:

– the lawyers, inquisitors, etc., use torture because they want to show that they are not superficial but responsible lawyers;
– they need many witches in order to prove that their job is necessary;
– they do not want to lose the remuneration the princes have promised for each witch.

To summarize we can quote Cornelius Loos who said the witch trials 'were a new alchemy which made gold out of human blood' (Hammes, 1977: 257). We could add, out of female blood. The capital accumulated in the process of the witch-hunt by the old ruling classes, as well as by the new rising bourgeois class is nowhere mentioned in the estimates and calculations of the economic historians of that epoch. The blood-money of the witch-hunt was used for the private enrichment of bankrupt princes, of lawyers, doctors, judges and professors, but also for such public affairs as financing wars, building up a bureaucracy, infrastructural measures, and finally the new absolute state. This blood-money fed the original process of capital accumulation, perhaps not to the same extent as the plunder and robbery of the colonies, but certainly to a much greater extent than is known today.

But the persecution and torture of witches was not only motivated by economic considerations. The interrogation of witches also provided the model for the development of the new scientific method of extracting secrets from Mother Nature. Carolyn Merchant has shown that Francis Bacon, the 'father' of modern science, the founder of the inductive method, used the same methods, the same ideology to examine nature which the witch-persecutioners used to extract the secrets from the witches, namely, torture, destruction, violence. He deliberately used the imagery of the witch-hunt to describe his new scientific method: he treated 'nature as a female to be tortured through mechanical inventions' (Merchant, 1983: 168), as the witches were tortured by new machines. He stated that the method by which nature's secrets might be discovered consisted in investigating the secrets of witchcraft by inquisition: 'For you have but to follow and as it were hound out nature in her wanderings, and you will be able when you like to lead and drive her afterward to the same place again . . .' (quoted by Merchant, 1983: 168). He strongly advocated the breaking of all taboos which, in medieval society, forbade the digging of holes into Mother Earth or violating her: 'Neither ought a man to make scruple of entering and penetrating into these holes and corners, when the inquisition of truth is his whole object . . .' (Merchant, 1983: 168). He compared the inquisition of nature to both the interrogation of witches and to that of the courtroom witnesses:

I mean (according to the practice in civil causes) in this great plea or suit granted by the divine favour and providence (whereby the human race seeks to recover its right over nature) to *examine nature herself* and the arts upon interrogatories . . . (Merchant, 1983: 169).

Nature would not yield her secrets unless forcibly violated by the new mechanical devices:

> For like as a man's disposition is never well known or proved till he be crossed, nor Proteus ever changed shapes till he was *straitened* and *held fast*, so nature exhibits herself more clearly under the *trials* and *vexations* of art (mechanical devices) than when left to herself (quoted by Merchant, 1983: 169).

According to Bacon, nature must be 'bound into service', made a 'slave', put 'in constraint', had to be 'dissected'; much as 'woman's womb had symbolically yielded to the forceps, so nature's womb harboured secrets that through technology could be wrested from her grasp for use in the improvement of the human condition' (Merchant, 1983: 169).

Bacon's scientific method, which is still the foundation of modern science, unified knowledge with material power. Many of the technological inventions were in fact related to warfare and conquest, like gunpowder, navigation, the magnet. These 'arts of war' were combined with knowledge – like printing. Violence, therefore, was the key word and key method by which the New Man established his domination over women and nature. These means of coercion 'do not, like the old, merely exert a gentle guidance over nature's course; they have the power to conquer and subdue her, to shake her to the foundations' (Merchant, 1983: 172).

Thus, concludes Carolyn Merchant:

> The interrogation of witches as symbol for the interrogation of nature, the courtroom as model for its inquisition, and torture through mechanical devices as a tool for the subjugation of disorder were fundamental to the scientific *method as power* (emphasis added) (Merchant, 1983: 172).

The class which benefited from this new scientific patriarchal dominance over women and nature was the rising protestant, capitalist class of merchants, mining industrialists, clothier capitalists. For this class, it was necessary that the old autonomy of women over their sexuality and reproductive capacities be destroyed, and that women be forcibly made to breed more workers. Similarly, nature had to be transformed into a vast reservoir of material resources to be exploited and turned into profit by this class.

Hence the church, the state, the new capitalist class and modern scientists collaborated in the violent subjugation of women and nature. The weak Victorian women of the nineteenth century were the products of the terror methods by which this class had moulded and shaped 'female nature' according to its interests (Ehrenreich, English, 1979).

Colonization and Primitive Accumulation of Capital

The period referred to so far has been called the period of *primitive accumulation of capital*. Before the capitalist mode of production could establish and maintain itself as a process of extended reproduction of capital – driven by the motor of surplus value production – enough capital had to be accumulated to start this process. The capital was largely accumulated in the colonies between the sixteenth and seventeenth centuries. Most of this capital was not accumulated through 'honest' trade by merchant capitalists but largely by way of brigandage, piracy, forced and slave labour.

Portuguese, Spanish, Dutch, English merchants went out to break the Venetian monopoly of the spice trade with the East. Most of the Spanish-Portuguese discoveries were inspired by the motive to find an independent sea-route to the Orient. In Europe, the result was a price revolution or inflation due to 1. the technical invention of separating copper from silver; 2. the plundering of Cuzco and the use of slave labour. The cost of precious metal fell. This led to the ruination of the already exhausted feudal class and of the wage earning craftsmen. Mandel concludes:

> The fall in real wages – particularly marked by the substitution of cheap potatoes for bread as the basic food of the people – became one of the main sources of the primitive accumulation of industrial capital between the sixteenth and eighteenth century (Mandel, 1971: 107).

One could say that the *first phase of the Primitive Accumulation* was that of merchant and commercial capital ruthlessly plundering and exploiting the colonies' human and natural wealth. Thus, there had been 'a marked shortage of capital in England' about 1550:

> Within a few years, the pirate expeditions against the Spanish fleet, all of which were organised in the form of joint stock companies, changed the situation . . . Drake's first pirate undertaking in the years 1577–1580 was launched with a capital of £5,000 . . . it brought in about £600,000 profit, half of which went to the Queen. Beard estimates that the pirates introduced some £12 million into England during the reign of Elizabeth (Mandel, 1971: 108).

The story of the Spanish Conquistadores, who depopulated regions like Haiti, Cuba, Nicaragua completely, and exterminated about 15 million Indians is well known. Also, Vasco da Gama's second arrival in India in 1502–1503 was marked by the same trial of blood.

> It was a kind of crusade . . . by merchants of pepper, cloves and cinnamon. It was punctuated by horrible atrocities; everything seemed permissible against the hated Moslems whom the Portuguese were surprised to meet again at the other end of the world . . . (quoted from Hauser in Mandel, 1971: 108).

Commercial expansion from the beginning was based on *monopoly*. The Dutch drove out the Portuguese, the English, the Dutch.

> It is, therefore, not to be wondered that the Dutch merchants, whose profits depended on their monopoly of spices obtained through conquests in the Indonesian archipelago went over to mass destruction of cinnamon trees in the small islands of the Moluccas as soon as prices began to fall in Europe. The 'Hongi Voyages' to destroy these trees and massacre the population which for centuries had drawn their livelihood from growing them, set a sinister mark on the history of Dutch colonization, which had, indeed, begun in the same style. Admiral J.P. Coen did not shrink from the extermination of all the male inhabitants of the Banda islands (Mandel, 1971: 108).

The trading companies – the Oost-Indische Companie, the English East India Company and Hudson Bay Company and the French Compagnie des Indes Orientales – *all combined the spice trade with the slave trade*:

> Between 1636 and 1645 the Dutch West India Company sold 23,000 Negroes for 6.7 million florins in all, or about 300 florins a head, whereas the goods given in exchange for each slave were worth no more than 50 florins. Between 1728 and 1760 ships sailing from Le Havre transported to the Antilles 203,000 slaves bought in Senegal, on the Gold Coast, at Loango, etc. The sale of these slaves brought in 203 million livres. From 1783 to 1793 the slavers of Liverpool sold 300,000 slaves for 15 million, which went into the foundation of industrial enterprises (Mandel, 1971: 110).

Mandel and others, who have analysed this period, do not say much about how the colonizing process affected women in the newly-established Portuguese, Dutch, English and French colonies in Africa, Asia and Latin and Central America. As the merchant capitalists depended mainly on brute force, outright robbery and looting, we can assume that the women were also victims of this process.

The recent work done by feminist scholars has shed more light on to these hidden sides of the 'civilizing process'. Rhoda Reddock's work on women and slavery in the Caribbean shows clearly that the colonizers used a diametrically opposed value system *vis-à-vis* the women of the subjugated peoples as that *vis-à-vis* their 'own' women. Slave women in the Caribbean for long periods were *not* allowed to marry or to have children; it was cheaper to import slaves than to pay for the reproduction of slave labour. At the same time, the bourgeois class domesticated its 'own' women into pure, monogamous breeders of their heirs, excluded them from work outside their house and from property.

The whole brutal onslaught on the peoples in Africa, Asia and America by European merchant capitalists was justified as a *civilizing mission* of the Christian nations. Here we see the connection between the 'civilizing' process by which poor European women were persecuted and 'disciplined' during the witch-hunt, and the 'civilizing' of the 'barbarian' peoples in the colonies. Both are defined as uncontrolled, dangerous, savage 'nature', and both have to be subdued by force and torture to break their resistance to robbery, expropriation and exploitation.

Women under Colonialism

As Rhoda Reddock (1984) has shown, the colonizers' attitude to slavery and slave women in the Caribbean was based clearly on capitalist cost-benefit calculations. This was particularly true with regard to the question whether slave women should be allowed to 'breed' more slaves or not. Throughout the centuries of the modern slave trade and slave economy (from 1655 to 1838), this question was answered not according to the principles of Christian ethics – supposedly applicable in the 'Motherlands' – but according to the accumulation considerations of the capitalist planters. Thus, during the first period, from 1655 to the beginnings of the eighteenth century, when most estates were smallholdings with few slaves, these planters still depended, following the peasant model of reproduction, on the natural reproduction of the slave population. The second period is characterized by the so-called sugar-revolution, the introduction of large-scale sugar production in big plantations. In this period, beginning around 1760 and lasting till about 1800 slave women were actively discouraged from bearing children or forming families. The planters, as good capitalists, held the view that 'it was cheaper to purchase than to breed'. This was the case in all sugar colonies whether they were under catholic (French) or protestant (British, Dutch) dominion. In fact, slave women who were found pregnant were cursed and ill-treated. Moreover, the backbreaking work in the sugar plantations did not allow the slave women to nurse small babies. The reason behind this anti-natalist policy of the planters are expressed in the statement of one Mr G.M. Hall on Cuban planters:

> During and after pregnancy the slave is useless for several months, and her nourishment should be more abundant and better chosen. This loss of work and added expense comes out of the master's pocket. It is he who has to pay for the often lengthy care of the newborn. This expense is so considerable that the negro born on the plantation costs more when he is in condition to work than another of the same age bought at the public market would have cost (G.M. Hall, quoted by Reddock, 1984: 16).

In the French colony of St Dominique the planters calculated that a slave woman's work over a period of 18 months was worth 600 Livres. The 18 months were the time calculated for pregnancy and breast feeding. During such a time the slave woman would be able to do only half her usual work. Thus, her master would lose 300 Livres. 'A fifteen month old slave was not worth this sum' (Hall, quoted by Reddock, 1984: 16). The effect of this policy was, as many observers have found, that the 'fertility' of slave women was extremely low during this period and far into the nineteenth century (Reddock, 1984).

Towards the end of the eighteenth century, it became evident that Western Africa could no longer be counted upon as fertile hunting ground for slaves. Moreover, the British colonizers saw it as more profitable to incorporate Africa itself into their empire as a source of raw material and minerals. Therefore, the more 'progressive' sections of the British bourgeoisie advocated the abolition of the slave trade – which happened in 1807 – and the encouragement of 'local breeding'. The colonial government foresaw a number of incentives in the slave codes of the late eighteenth and nineteenth centuries to encourage local breeding of slaves by slave women on the plantations. This sudden change of policy, however, seems to have had little effect on the slave women. As Rhoda Reddock points out, in the long years of slavery the slave women had internalized an anti-motherhood attitude as a form of resistance to the slave system; they continued a kind of birth strike till about the middle of the nineteenth century. When they became pregnant, they used bitter herbs to produce abortions or, when the children were born, 'many were allowed to die out of the women's natural dislike for bearing them to see them become slaves, destined to toil all their lives for their master's enrichment' (Moreno-Fraginals, 1976, quoted by Reddock, 1984: 17). Rhoda Reddock sees in this anti-motherhood attitude of the slave women an example of 'the way in which the ideology of the ruling classes could, for different though connected material reasons, become the accepted ideology of the oppressed' (Reddock, 1984: 17).

The colonial masters now reaped the fruits – or rather the failures – of treating African women as mere conditions of production for capital accumulation. The problem of labour shortage on the plantations in the Caribbean became so acute, due to the slave women's birth strike, that in Cuba virtual 'stud farms' were established and slave breeding became a regular business (Moreno Fraginals, quoted by Reddock, 1984: 18). Rhoda Reddock summarizes the changing policy of the colonizers regarding slave women's procreative capacities in the following manner:

> As long as Africa was incorporated in the capitalist world economy only as a producer of human labour, there was no need to produce labour locally. Through the use of cost-benefit analysis the planters had taken the most profitable line of action. When this was no longer profitable for them, they were surprised by the resistance shown by the slave women who . . . recognized clearly their position as the property of the plantation owners. The fact is, that for more than 100 years, the majority of slave women in the Caribbean were neither wives nor mothers and by exercising control over their reproductive capabilities were able to deeply affect the plantation economy (Reddock, 1984: 18).

These more than a hundred years that 'slave women in the Caribbean were neither wives nor mothers' were exactly the same period that women of the European bourgeoisie were domesticated and ideologically manipulated into wifehood and motherhood as their 'natural' vocation (Badinter, 1980). While one set of women was treated as pure labour force, a source of energy, the other set of women was treated as 'non-productive' breeders only.

It is, indeed, an irony of history that later in the nineteenth century the colonizers tried desperately to introduce the nuclear family and the monogamous marriage norm into the ex-slave population of the Caribbean. But both women and men saw no benefit for themselves in adopting these norms, and rejected marriage. Now their own double-faced policy boomeranged on the colonizers. In order to be able freely to exploit the slaves, they had for centuries defined them outside humanity and Christianity. In this they were supported by the ethnologists who said that the negroes did not belong to the same 'species' as the Europeans (Caldecott, 1970: 67). Hence, slaves could not become Christians because, according to the Church of England, no Christian could be a slave.

When, around 1780, the new Slave Codes began to encourage marriage among the slaves as a means to encourage local breeding of slaves, the slaves only ridiculed this 'high caste' thing and continued with their 'common law' unions. This meant that each woman could live with a man as long as she pleased; the same also applied to the man. Slave women saw the marriage tie as something that would subject them to the control of one man, who could even beat them. The men wanted more than one wife and therefore rejected marriage. The missionaries and planters who tried to introduce the European middle-class model of the man-woman relationship were exasperated. A church historian, Caldecott, eventually found an explanation for this resistance to the benefits of civilization in the fact that negroes were not able to 'control their fancy' (their sexual desires), and therefore shrank from constancy: 'With them it is the women as much as the men who are thus constituted; there is in the Negro race a nearer approach to equality between the sexes than is found in the European races . . .' (Caldecott, quoted by Reddock, 1984: 47). 'Equality between the sexes', however, was seen as a sign of a primitive, backward race, a notion which was common among nineteenth-century colonizers and ethnologists.

That equality of men and women is a sign of backwardness and that it is part of the 'civilizing mission' of the British colonialialists to destroy the independence of colonized women, and to teach the colonized men the 'virtues' of sexism and militarism are also clearly spelt out by one Mr Fielding Hall in his book, *A People at School*.[5] Mr Hall was Political Officer in the British colonial administration in Burma between 1887–91. He gives a vivid account of the independence of Burmese women, of the equality between the sexes, and of the peace-loving nature of the Burmese people which he ascribes to Buddhism. But, instead of trying to preserve such a happy society, Mr Hall comes to the conclusion that Burma has to be brought by force on the road of progress: 'But today the laws are ours, the power, the authority. We govern for our own subjects and we govern in our own way. Our whole presence here is against their desires.' He suggests the following meaures to civilize the Burmese people:

1. The men must be taught to kill and to fight for the British colonialists: 'I can imagine nothing that could do the Burmese so much good as to have a regiment of their own to distinguish itself in our wars. It would open their eyes to new views of life' (*A People at School*, p. 264).

2. The women must surrender their liberty in the interests of man.

Considering equality of the sexes a sign of backwardness, this colonial administrator warned: 'It must never be forgotten that their civilization is relatively a thousand years behind ours.' To overcome this backwardness, the Burmese men should learn to kill, to make war and to oppress their women. In the words of Mr Hall: 'What the surgeon's knife is to the diseased body that is the soldier's sword to the diseased nations'. And again:

> . . . the gospel of progress, of knowledge, of happiness . . . is taught not by book and sermon but by spear and sword . . . To declare, as Buddhism does, that bravery is of no account; to say to them, as the women did, you are no better and no more than we are, and should have the same code of life; could anything be worse?

He also seeks the help of ethnologists to defend this ideology of Man the Hunter: 'Men and women are not sufficiently differentiated yet in Burma. It is the mark of a young race. Ethnologists tell us that. In the earliest peoples the difference was very slight. As a race grows older the difference increases.' Then Mr Hall describes how Burmese women are eventually 'brought down' to the status of the civilized, dependent housewife. Local home-industries, formerly in the hands of women, are destroyed by the import of commodities from England. Women are also pushed out of trade: 'In Rangoon the large English stores are undermining the

Bazaars where the women used to earn an independent livelihood.'

After their loss of economic independence, Mr Hall considers it of utmost importance that the laws of marriage and inheritance be changed, so that Burma, too, may become a 'progressive' land where men rule. Woman has to understand that her independence stands in the way of progress:

> With her power of independence will disappear her free will and her influence. When she is dependent on her husband she can no longer dictate to him. When he feeds her, she is not longer able to make her voice as loud as his is. It is inevitable that she should retire . . . The nations who succeed are not feminine nations but the masculine. Woman's influence is good provided it does not go too far. Yet it has done so here. It has been bad for the man, bad too for the woman. It has never been good for women to be too independent, it has robbed them of many virtues. It improves a man to have to work for his wife and family, it makes a man of him. It is demoralising for both if the woman can keep herself and, if necessary, her husband too. (*A People at School*, p. 266).

That the African women brought to the Caribbean as slaves were not made slaves because they were 'backward' or less 'civilized' than the colonizers, but on the contrary were *made* 'savages' by slavery itself and those colonizers is now brought to light by historical research on women in Western Africa. George Brooks, for example, shows in his work on the *signares* – the women traders of eighteenth-century Senegal – that these women, particularly of the Wolof tribe, held a high position in the pre-colonial West African societies. Moreover, the first Portuguese and French merchants who came to Senegal in search of merchandise were totally dependent on the cooperation and goodwill of these powerful women, who entered into sexual and trade alliances with these European men. They not only were in possession of great wealth, accumulated through trade with the inferior parts of their regions, but had also developed such a cultured way of life, such a sense for beauty and gracefulness, that the European adventurers who first came into contact with them felt flabbergasted. Brooks quotes one Rev. John Lindsay, chaplain aboard a British ship, as having written:

> As to their women, and in particular the ladies (for so I must call many of those in Senegal), they are in a surprising degree handsome, have very fine features, are wonderfully tractable, remarkably polite both in conversation and manners; and in the point of keeping themselves neat and clean (of which we have generally strange ideas, formed to us by the beastly laziness of the slaves) they far surpass the Europeans in every respect. They bathe twice a day . . . and in this particular have a hearty contempt for all white people, who they imagine must be disagreeable, to our women especially. Nor can even their men from this very notion, be brought to look upon the prettiest of our women, but with the coldest indifference, some of whom there are here, officers' ladies, who dress very showy, and who, even in England would be thought handsome (Brooks, 1976: 24).

The European men – the Portuguese and French who came to West Africa first as merchants or soldiers – came usually alone, without wives or families. Their alliances with the 'ladies' or *signares* (from the Portuguese word *senhoras*) were so attractive to them that they married these women according to the Wolof style, and often simply adopted the African way of life. Their children, the Euroafricans, often rose to high positions in the colonial society, the daughters usually became *signares* again. Obviously, the Portuguese and the French colonizers did not yet have strong racist prejudices against sexual and marriage relationships with West African women, but found these alliances not only profitable, but also humanly satisfying.

With the advent of the British in West Africa, however, this easy-going, catholic attitude towards African women changed. The British soldiers, merchants and administrators no longer entered into marriage alliances with the *signares*, but turned African women into prostitutes. This, then, seems to be the point in history when racism proper enters the picture: the African woman is degraded and made a prostitute for the English colonizers, then theories of the racial superiority of the white male and the 'beastliness' of the African women are propagated. Obviously, British colonial history is as discreet about these aspects as the Dutch. Yet Brooks says that the institution of 'signareship' did not take root in Gambia because it was

> stifled by the influx of new arrivals from Britain, few of whom, whether traders, government officials, or military officers – deviated from 'proper' British behaviour to live openly with Euroafrican or African women, whatever they might do clandestinely. British authors are discreet about such matters, but it can be discerned that in contrast to the family lives of traders and their *signares*, there developed . . . a rootless bachelor community of a type found elsewhere in British areas of West Africa. Open and unrepentant racism was one characteristic of this community; two others were reckless gambling and alcoholism (Brooks, 1976: 43).

These accounts corroborate not only Walter Rodney's general thesis that 'Europe underdeveloped Africa', but also our main argument that the colonial process, as it advanced, brought the women of the colonized people progressively down from a former high position of relative power and independence to that of 'beastly' and degraded 'nature'. This 'naturalization' of colonized women is the counterpart of the 'civilizing' of the European women.

The 'defining back into nature', or the 'naturalization' of African women who were brought as slaves to the Caribbean is perhaps the clearest evidence of the double-faced, hypocritical process of European colonization: while African women were treated as 'savages', the women of the white colonizers in their fatherlands 'rose' to the status of 'ladies'. These two processes did not happen side by side, are not simply historical parallels, but are intrinsically and causally linked within this patriarchal-capitalist mode of production. This creation of 'savage' and 'civilized' women, and the polarization between the two was, and still is, the organizing structural principle also in other parts of the world subjected by capitalist colonialism. There is not yet enough historical research into the effects of the colonizing process on women, but the little evidence we have corroborates this observation. It also explains the shifts in colonial policy towards women – following the fluctuations of the accumulation process – which Rhoda Reddock observed.

Thus, Annie Stoler (1982) has found that, at the other end of the globe in Sumatra in the early 20th century, the Dutch followed a similar double-faced policy regarding women:

At certain junctures in estate expansion, for example, women ostensibly recruited from Java as estate coolies were in large part brought to Sumatra to service the domestic, including sexual, needs of unmarried male workers and management. Prostitution was not only sanctioned but encouraged . . . (Stoler, 1982: 90).

The driving motive for these planters, as was the case with the French or English in the Caribbean, was profit-making, and this motive, as Annie Stoler remarks, explains the fluctuations in Dutch colonial policy *vis-à-vis* women. In the colonial records, the 'issues of marriage contracts, sickness, prostitution, and labour unrest appear as they relate to profit; married workers during the first decade of the century were considered too costly and therefore marriage contracts were difficult to obtain' (Stoler, 1982: 97).

Obviously, to make women prostitutes was cheaper, but then, when almost half of the female workers in North Sumatra were racked with venereal disease, and had to be hospitalized at the company's expense, it became more profitable to encourage marriage among the estate workers. This was between the 1920s and 1930s. Whereas in the first phase, migrant women were good enough to do all hard labour on the plantations, now a process of housewifization took place to exclude resident women from wage-labour on the estates. Annie Stoler writes:

At different economic and political junctures in plantation history, the planters contended that (1) permanent female workers were too costly to maintain, because of the time they took off for child-birth and menstruation, (2) women should not and could not do 'hard' labour, and (3) women were better suited to casual work (Stoler, 1982: 98).

That this introduction of the image of the 'weak woman' was a clear ideological move which served the economic purpose of lowering women's wages and creating a casual female labour force becomes evident from the statistics. Thus, in the Coolie Budget Report of 1903, it is stated that only one per cent of total available working-days were missed because of pregnancy (Stoler, 1982: 98).

Rhoda Reddock also, in the later parts of her study, gives ample evidence of this process – around the same time, in the British Crown Colony of Trinidad – of excluding women from wage-labour proper and of defining them as 'dependents' (Rhoda Reddock, 1984).

Also, in the case of the Dutch colonizers, profit-making was the overall objective, and the contradictory values and policies regarding their own 'civilized' women back home and the 'savage' women in Sumatra constituted the best mechanism to ensure this. The fact that they used two diametrically opposed sets of values to the two sets of women obviously did not give them any pangs of conscience. Prostitution became a public issue only when it was no longer profitable to recruit women as prostitutes. Again here we have to stress that the emergence of the Dutch housewife, the stress on family and homemaking 'back home', was not just a temporal coincidence but was causally linked to the disruption of families and homes among estate workers in the Dutch colonies.

Women under German Colonialism

Whereas the examples of British and Dutch colonial policy regarding women given above mainly focus on the colonial side of the picture, the following example, based on Martha Mamozai's study of the impact of German colonialism on women, includes the effect of this process also on the German women 'back home'. This account will, therefore, help us to perceive more fully the double-faced process of colonization and housewifization.

Germany entered the race for the looting and distribution of the world rather late. The German Colonial Society was founded in 1884, and from then until the beginning of World War I – a direct result of the inter-imperialist scramble for hegemony among the European nations – the government of the German Reich encouraged the establishment of German colonies, particularly in Africa.

Mamozai's study shows that colonization did not affect men and women in the same way, but used the particular capitalist sexual division of labour to bring the labour power of Africans under the command of capital and the White Man. As usually happens with conquerors, invaders and colonizers, the Germans who first came to West Africa as planters around the 1880s came mostly as single men. As had happened with the Portuguese and French men in West Africa, they entered into sexual and matrimonial relations with African women. Many formed regular families with these women. After some time, it became evident that these marriages would eventually lead to a new generation of 'mixed blood' Euroafricans who, following the patriarchal and bourgeois family laws in Germany, would be Germans with full economic and political rights. There were heated debates about the 'colonial question' or the 'native question' in the German Reichstag which centered, on the one hand, on the question of 'mixed marriages' and 'bastards' – hence on the concern for the privileges of the white race – on the other, on the production, subjugation and disciplining of sufficient African labour power for the German estates and projects.

Governor Friedrich von Lindquist expressed the 'bastard-question in South West Africa' in the following manner:

> The considerable preponderance of the white male over the white female population is a sorry state of affairs, which, for the life and the future of the country will be of great significance. This has led to a considerable number of mixed relations, which is particularly regrettable because, apart from the ill-effects of the mixing of races, the white minority in South Africa can preserve its dominance over the coloureds only by keeping its race pure (quoted by Mamozai, 1982: 125; transl. M.M.).

Therefore, in 1905 a law was passed which prohibited marriages between European men and African women. In 1907, even those marriages which had been concluded prior to this law were declared null and void. Those who lived in such unions, including their 'bastards', lost the rights of citizens in 1908, including the voting right. The objective of this law was clearly the preservation of property rights in the hands of the white minority. Had the Afro-Germans had the rights of German citizens and voting rights, they could, in the course of time, have outnumbered the 'pure' whites in the elections. The laws, however, prohibiting marriages between European men and black women did not mean that the Reichstag wanted to put restrictions on the sexual freedom of the colonizing men. On the contrary, the German men were even advised by doctors to recruit African women as concubines or prostitutes. Thus, one Dr Max Bucher, representative of the German Reich wrote:

> Regarding the free intercourse with the daughters of the land – this has to be seen as advantageous rather than as damaging to health. Even under the dark skin the 'Eternal Female' is an excellent fetish against emotional deprivation which so easily occurs in the African loneliness. Apart from these psychological gains there are also practical advantages of personal security. To have an intimate black girl-friend means protection from many dangers (quoted by Mamozai, 1982: 129).

This means black women were good enough to service the white men as prostitutes and concubines, but they should not become proper 'wives' because this would, in the long run, have changed the property relations in Africa. This becomes very clear in a statement of one Dr Karl Oetker who was Health Officer during the construction of the railroad between Dar-es-Salaam and Morogoro:

> It should be a matter of course, but may be stressed again, that every European man who has intercourse with black females has to take care that such a union remains sterile in order to prevent a mixture of races, such a mixture would have the worst effect for our colonies, as this has been amply proved in the West Indies, Brasil and Madagaskar. Such relationships can and should only be considered as surrogates for marriage. Recognition and protection by the state, which marriages among whites enjoy, have to be withheld from such unions (quoted by Mamozai, 1982: 130).

Here the double-standard is very clear: marriage and family were goods to be protected for the whites, the 'Master Men' (Dominant Men). African families could be disrupted, men and women could be forced into labour gangs, women could be made prostitutes.

It is important not to look at this hypocritical colonial policy towards women only from a moralistic point of view. It is essential to understand that the rise and generalization of the 'decent' bourgeois marriage and family as protected institutions are *causally* linked to the disruption of clan and family relations of the 'natives'. The emergence of the masses of German families from 'proletarian misery', as one colonial officer put it, was directly linked to the exploitation of colonies and the subordination of colonial labour power. The development of Germany into a leading industrial nation was dependent, as many saw it in those years, on the possession of colonies. Thus, Paul von Hindenburg, the later Reichskanzler wrote: 'Without colonies no security regarding the acquisition of raw materials, without raw materials no industry, without industry no adequate standard of living and wealth. Therefore, Germans, do we need colonies' (quoted by Mamozai, 1983: 27; transl. M.M.).

The justification for this logic of exploitation was provided by the theory that the 'natives' had 'not yet' evolved to the level of the white master race, and that colonialism was the means to develop the slumbering forces of production in these regions and thus make them contribute to the betterment of mankind. A colonial officer from South West Africa wrote:

A right of the natives, which could only be realised at the expense of the development of the white race, does not exist. The idea is absurd that Bantus, Sudan-negroes, and Hottentots in Africa have the right to live and die as they please, even when by this uncounted people among the civilized peoples of Europe were forced to remain tied to a miserable proletarian existence instead of being able, by the full use of the productive capacities of our colonial possessions to rise to a richer level of existence themselves and also to help construct the whole body of human and national welfare (quoted by Mamozai, 1983: 58; transl. M.M.)

The conviction that the white master men had the god-given mission to 'develop' the productive capacities in the colonies and thus bring the 'savages' into the orbit of civilization was also shared, as we shall see later, by the Social Democrats who likewise believed in the development of productive forces through colonialism.

The refusal of the 'native' women of South West Africa to produce children for the hated colonial masters was, therefore, seen as an attack on this policy of development of productive forces. After the rebellion of the Herero people had been brutally crushed by the German General von Trotha, the Herero women went on a virtual birth-strike. Like the slave women in the Caribbean, they refused to produce forced labour power for the planters and estate owners. Between 1892 and 1909, the Herero population decreased from 80,000 to a mere 19,962. For the German farmers this was a severe problem. One of them wrote:

After the rebellion the native, particularly the Herero, often takes the stand not to produce children. He considers himself a prisoner, which he brings to your notice at every job which he does not like. He does not like to make new labour force for his oppressor, who has deprived him of his golden laziness . . . While the German farmers have been trying for years to remedy this sad state of affairs by offering a premium for each child born on the farm, for instance, a she-goat. But mostly in vain. A section of today's native women has been engaged for too long in prostitution and are spoiled for motherhood. Another part does not want children and gets rid of them, when they are pregnant, through abortion. In such cases the authorities should interfere with all severity. Each case should be investigated thoroughly and severely punished by prison, and if that is not enough by putting the culprit in chains. (quoted by Mamozai, 1982: 52; transl. M.M.).

In a number of cases the farmers took the law into their own hands and brutally punished the recalcitrant women. In the Herero women's stand we see again, as in the case of the slave women, that African women were not just helpless victims in this colonizing process, but understood precisely their relative power within the colonial relations of production, and used that power accordingly. What has to be noted, however, with regard to the comments of the German farmer quoted above, is that although it was the Herero *women* who went on a birth-strike, he refers only to *the Herero* (man). Even in their reporting, the colonizing men denied the subjected women all subjectivity and initiative. All 'natives' were 'savages', wild nature, but the most savage of all were the 'native' women.

White Women in Africa

Martha Mamozai also provides us with interesting material about the 'other side' of the colonizing process, namely, the impact the subordination of Africans, and African women in particular, had on the German women 'back home' and on those who had joined the colonial pioneers in Africa.

As was said before, one of the problems of the white colonialists was the reproduction of the white master race in the colonies itself. This could be achieved only if white women from the 'fatherland' were ready to go to the colonies and marry 'our boys down there', and produce white children. As most planters belonged to that band of 'adventurous bachelors', a special effort had to be made to mobilize women to go to the colonies as brides. The German advocates of white supremacy saw it as a special duty of German women to save the German men in the colonies from the evil influence of the 'Kaffir females' who in the long run would alienate these men from European culture and civilization.

The call was heard by Frau Adda von Liliencron, who founded the 'Women's League of the German Colonial Society'. This association had the objective of giving girls a special training in colonial housekeeping and sending them as brides to Africa. She recruited mainly girls from the peasant or working class, many of whom had worked as maidservants in the cities. In 1898 for the first time 25 single women were sent to South West Africa as a 'Christmas gift' for 'our boys down there'. Martha Mamozai reports how many of these women 'rose' to the level of the white memsahib, the bourgeois lady who saw it as her mission to teach the African women the virtues of civilization: cleanliness, punctuality, obedience and industriousness. It is amazing to observe how soon these women, who not long ago were still among the downtrodden themselves, shared the prejudices against the 'dirty and lazy natives' which were common in colonial society.

But not only did the few European women who went to the colonies as wives and 'breeders for race and nation' rise to the level of proper housewives on the subordination and subjection of the colonized women, so too did the women 'back home'; first those of the bourgeoisie, and later also the women of the proletariat, were gradually domesticated and civilized into proper housewives. For the same period which saw the expansion of colonialism and imperialism also saw the rise of the housewife in Europe and the USA. In the following I shall deal with this side of the story.

Housewifization

1st Stage: Luxuries for the 'Ladies'
The 'other side of the story' of both the violent subordination of European women during the witch persecution, and of African, Asian and Latin American women

during the colonizing process is the creation of the women first of the accumulating classes in Europe, later also in the USA, as consumers and demonstrators of luxury and wealth, and at a later stage as housewives. Let us not forget that practically all the items which were stolen, looted or traded from the colonies were not items necessary for the daily subsistence of the masses, but luxury items. Initially these items were only consumed by the privileged few who had the money to buy them: spices from the Molluccan islands; precious textiles, silk, precious stones and muslin from India; sugar, cacao and spices from the Caribbean; precious metals from Hispano America. Werner Sombart, in his study on *Luxury and Capitalism* (1922), has advanced the thesis that the market for most of these rare colonial luxury goods had been created by a class of women who had risen as mistresses of the absolutist princes and kings of France and England in the seventeenth and eighteenth centuries. According to Sombart, the great cocottes and mistresses were the ones who created new fashions in women's dress, cosmetics, eating habits, and particularly in furnishing the homes of the gentlemen. Neither the war-mongering men of the aristocracy nor the men of the merchant class would have had, if left to themselves, the imagination, the sophistication and the culture to invent such luxuries, almost all centred around women as luxury creatures. It was this class of women, according to Sombart, who created the new luxury 'needs' which gave the decisive impetus to capitalism because, with their access to the money accumulated by the absolutist state, they created the market for early capitalism.

Sombart gives us a detailed account of the development of luxury consumption at the Italian, French and English courts of the sixteenth and seventeenth centuries. He clearly identifies a trend in luxury-spending, particularly during the reign of Louis XIV. Whereas the luxury expenses of the king of France were 2,995,000 Livres in 1542, these had steadily risen and were 28,813,955 in 1680. Sombart attributes this enormous display of luxury and splendour to the love of these feudal lords for their courtesans and mistresses. Thus, the king's fancy for La Vallière prompted Louis XIV to build Versailles. Sombart is also of the opinion that Mme de Pompadour, the representative of the culture of the *ancien régime*, had a bigger budget than any of the European queens ever had had. In 19 years of her reign she spent 36,327,268 Livres. Similarly Comtesse Dubarry, who reigned between 1769–1774, spent 12,481,803 Livres on luxury items (Sombart, 1922: 98–99).

Feminists will not agree with Sombart who attributes this development of luxury which first centred around the European courts and was later imitated by the *nouveaux riches* among the European bourgeoisie, to the great courtesans with their great vanity, their addiction for luxurious clothes, houses, furniture, food, cosmetics. Even if the men of these classes preferred to demonstrate their wealth by spending on their women and turning them into showpieces of their accumulated wealth, it would again mean to make the women the villains of the piece. Would it not amount to saying that it was not the men – who wielded economic and political power – who were the historical 'subjects' (in the Marxist sense), but the women, as the real power behind the scenes who pulled the strings and set the tune according to which the mighty men danced? But, apart from this,

Sombart's thesis that capitalism was born out of luxury consumption and not in order to satisfy growing subsistence needs of the masses has great relevance for our discussion of the relationship between colonization and housewifization. He shows clearly that early merchant capitalism was based practically entirely on trade with luxury items from the colonies which were consumed by the European elites. The items which appear in a trading-list of the Levant trade include: *oriental medicines* (e.g., aloes, balm, ginger, camphor, cardamon, myrobalam, saffron, etc.); *spices* (pepper, cloves, sugar, cinnamon, nutmeg); *perfumes* (benzoin, musk, sandalwood, incense, amber); *dyes for textiles* (e.g., indigo, lac, purple, henna); *raw materials for textiles* (silk, Egyptian flax); *precious metals and jewellery and stones* (corals, pearls, ivory, porcelain, glass, gold and silver); *textiles* (silk, brocade, velvet, fine material of linen, muslin or wool).

In the eighteenth and nineteenth centuries many more items were added to this list, particularly items systematically produced in the new colonial plantations like sugar, coffee, cacao and tea. Sombart gives an account of the rising tea consumption in England. The average tea consumption of an English family was 6.5 pounds in 1906. This level of consumption could be afforded in:

1668 by	3 families
1710 by	2,000 families
1730 by	12,000 families
1760 by	40,000 families
1780 by	140,000 families

(Source: Sombart, 1922: 146)

What did this tremendous deployment of luxury among the European rich, based on the exploitation of the peoples of Africa, Asia and America, mean for the European women? Sombart identifies certain trends in the luxury production, which he, as we have seen, attributes to the passions of a certain class of women. They are the following:

1. *a tendency towards domesticity*: Whereas medieval luxury was public, now it became private. The display of luxury does not take place in the market place or during public festivals, but inside the secluded palaces and houses of the rich.
2. *a tendency towards objectification*: In the Middle Ages wealth was expressed in the number of vassals or men a prince could count upon. Now wealth is expressed in goods and material items, commodities bought by money. Adam Smith would say: 'one moves from "unproductive" to "productive" luxury, because the former personal luxury puts "unproductive" hands to work, whereas the objectified luxury puts "productive" hands to work' (in a capitalist sense, that is, wage-workers in a capitalist enterprise) (Sombart, 1922: 119). Sombart is of the opinion that leisure class women had an interest in the development of objectified luxury (more items and commodities), because they had no use for more soldiers and vassals.

    Similar trends can be observed with regard to sugar and coffee. For most people in Europe in the eighteenth century, sugar had not yet replaced honey. Sugar remained a typical luxury item for the European rich until far into the nineteenth century (Sombart, 1922: 147).

Foreign trade between Europe, America, Africa and the Orient was, until well into the nineteenth century, mainly trade in the above-mentioned luxury goods. Imports from East India to France in 1776 were to the value of 36,241,000 Francs, distributed as follows:

coffee	3,248,000 fr.
pepper and cinnamon	2,449,000 fr.
muslin	12,000,000 fr.
Indian linen	10,000,000 fr.
porcelain	200,000 fr.
silk	1,382,000 fr.
tea	3,399,000 fr.
saltpetre	3,380,000 fr.
Total	*36,241,000 fr.*

(Source: Sombart, 1922: 148)

Sombart also includes the profits made by the slave trade in the figures for luxury production and consumption.[6] The slave trade was totally organized along capitalist lines.

The development of wholesale and retail markets in England followed the same logic from the seventeenth to the nineteenth century. The first big urban shops which came up to replace the local markets were shops dealing with luxury goods.

3. *a tendency towards contraction of time*: Whereas formerly luxury consumption was restricted to certain seasons because the indigenous production of a surplus needed a long time, now luxuries could be consumed at any time during the year and also within the span of an individual life.

Sombart again attributes this tendency – in my opinion, wrongly – to the individualism and the impatience of leisure class women who demanded immediate satisfaction of their desires as a sign of the affection of their lovers.

Of the above tendencies, the tendency towards domestication and privatization certainly had a great impact on the construction of the new image of the 'good woman' in the centres of capitalism in the nineteenth and twentieth centuries, namely, woman as *mother* and *housewife*, and the family as her arena, the privatized arena of consumption and 'love', excluded and sheltered from the arena of production and accumulation, where men reign. In the following, I shall trace how the ideal of the domesticated privatized woman, concerned with 'love' and consumption and dependent on a male 'breadwinner', was generalized, first in the bourgeois class proper, then among the so-called petty-bourgeoisie, and finally in the working class or the proletariat.

2nd Stage: Housewife and Nuclear Family: The 'Colony' of the Little White Men

While the Big White Men – the 'Dominant Men' (Mamozai) – appropriated land, natural resources and people in Africa, Asia and Central and South America in order to be able to extract raw materials, products and labour power which they themselves had not produced, while they disrupted all social relations created by the local people, they began to build up in their fatherlands the patriarchal nuclear family, that is, the monogamous nuclear family as we know it today. This family, which was put under the specific protection of the state, consists of the forced combination of the principles of kinship and cohabitation, and the definition of the man as 'head' of this household and 'breadwinner' for the non-earning legal wife and their children. While in the eighteenth and early nineteenth centuries this marriage and family form were possible only among the propertied classes of the bourgeoisie – among peasants, artisans and workers women had always to share all work – this form was made the norm for all by a number of legal reforms pushed through by the state from the second half of the nineteenth century onwards. In Germany – as in other European countries – there existed a number of marriage restrictions for people without property. These were only abolished in the second half of the nineteenth century, when the state intervened to promote a pro-natalist policy for the propertyless working class (Heinsohn and Knieper, 1976).

Recent family history has revealed that even the concept 'family' became popular only towards the end of the eighteenth century in Europe, particularly in France and England, and it was not before the middle of the nineteenth century that this concept was also adopted for the households of the workers and peasants because, contrary to general opinion, 'family' had a distinct class connotation. Only classes with property could afford to have a 'family'. Propertyless people – like farm servants or urban poor – were not supposed to have a 'family' (Flandrin, 1980; Heinsohn and Knieper, 1976). But 'family' in the sense in which we understand it today – that is, as a combination of co-residence and blood-relationship based on the patriarchal principle – was not even found among the aristocracy. The aristocratic 'family' did not imply co-residence of all family members. Co-residence, particularly of husband and wife and their offspring, became the crucial criterion of the family of the bourgeoisie. Hence our present concept of family is a bourgeois one (Flandrin, 1980; Luz Tangangco, 1982).

It was the bourgeoisie which established the social and sexual division of labour, characteristic of capitalism. The bourgeoisie declared 'family' a private territory in contrast to the 'public' sphere of economic and political activity. The bourgeoisie first withdrew 'their' women from this public sphere and shut them into their cosy 'homes' from where they could not interfere in the war-mongering, moneymaking and the politicking of the men. Even the French Revolution, though fought by thousands of women, ended by excluding women from politics. The bourgeoisie, particularly the puritan English bourgeoisie, created the ideology of romantic love as a compensation for and sublimation of the sexual and economic independence women had had before the rise of this class. Malthus, one of the important theoreticians of the rising bourgeoisie, saw clearly that capitalism needed a different type of woman. The poor should curb their sexual 'instincts', because otherwise they would breed too many poor for the scarce food supply. On the other hand, they should not use contraceptives, a method recommended by Condorcet in France, because that would make them lazy because he saw a close connection between sexual abstinence and readiness to work. Then Malthus paints a rosy picture of a decent bourgeois home in which 'love' does not express itself in sexual activity, but in which the domesticated wife sublimates the sexual 'instinct' in order to create a cosy home for the hard-working breadwinner who has to struggle for money in a competitive and hostile world 'outside' (Malthus, quoted in Heinsohn, Knieper and Steiger, 1979). As Heinsohn, Knieper and Steiger point out, capitalism did not, as Engels and Marx believed, destroy the family; on the contrary, with the help of the state and its police, it *created* the family first among the propertied classes, later in the working class, and with it the housewife as a social category. Also, from the accounts of the composition and condition of the early industrial proletariat, it appears that the family, as we understand it today, was much less the norm than is usually believed.

As we all know, women and children constituted the bulk of the early industrial proletariat. They were the cheapest and most manipulable labour force and could be exploited like no other worker. The capitalists understood well that a woman with children had to accept any wage if she wanted to survive. On the other hand, women were less of a problem for the capitalists than men. Their labour was also cheap because they were no longer organized, unlike the skilled men who had their associations as journeymen and a tradition of organizing from the guilds. Women had been thrown out of these organizations long ago, they had no new organizations and hence no bargaining power. For the capitalists it was, therefore, more profitable and less risky to employ women. With the rise of industrial capitalism and the decline of merchant capitalism (around 1830), the extreme exploitation of women's and child labour became a problem. Women whose health had been destroyed by overwork and appalling work conditions could not produce healthy children who could become strong workers and soldiers – as was realized after several wars later in the century.

Many of these women did not live in proper 'families', but were either unmarried, or had been deserted and lived, worked and moved around with children and young people in gangs (cf. Marx, *Capital*, vol. I). These women had no particular material interest in producing the next generation of miserable workers for the factories. But they constituted a threat to bourgeois morality with its ideal of the domesticated woman. Therefore, it was also necessary to domesticate the proletarian woman. She had to be *made* to breed more workers.

Contrary to what Marx thought, the production of children could not be left to the 'instincts' of the proletariat, because, as Heinsohn and Knieper point out, the propertyless proletariat had no material interest in the production of children, as children were no insurance in old age, unlike the sons of the bourgeoisie. Therefore, the state had to interfere in the production of people and, through legislation, police measures and the ideological campaign of the churches, the sexual energies of the proletariat had to be channelled into the strait-jacket of the bourgeois family. The proletarian woman had to be housewifized too, in spite of the fact that she could not afford to sit at home and wait for the husband to feed her and her children. Heinsohn and Knieper (1976) analyse this process for nineteenth-century Germany. Their main thesis is that the 'family' had to be forced upon the proletariat by police measures, because otherwise the propertyless proletarians would not have produced enough children for the next generation of workers. One of the most important measures – after the criminalization of infanticide which had already taken place – was, therefore, the law which abolished the marriage prohibition for propertyless people. This law was passed by the

North German League in 1868. Now proletarians were allowed to marry and have a 'family', like the bourgeois. But this was not enough. Sexuality had to be curbed in such a way that it took place within the confines of this family. Therefore, sexual intercourse before marriage and outside it was criminalized. The owners of the means of production were given the necessary police power to watch over the morality of their workers. After the Franco-Prussian War in 1870–71, a law was passed which made abortion a crime – a law against which the new women's movement fought, with only small success. The churches, in their cooperation with the state, worked on the souls of the people. What the secular state called a crime, the churches called a sin. The churches had a wider influence than the state because they reached more people, particularly in the countryside (Heinsohn and Knieper, 1976).

In this way the housewifization of women was also forced into the working class. According to Heinsohn and Knieper (1976) and others, the family had never existed among the propertyless farm servants or proletarians; it had to be created by force. This strategy worked because, by that time, women had lost most of their knowledge of contraception and because the state and church had drastically curbed women's autonomy over their bodies.

The housewifization of women, however, had not only the objective of ensuring that there were enough workers and soldiers for capital and the state. The creation of housework and the housewife as an agent of consumption became a very important strategy in the late nineteenth and early twentieth centuries. By that time not only had the household been discovered as an important market for a whole range of new gadgets and items, but also scientific home-management had become a new ideology for the further domestication of women. Not only was the housewife called on to reduce the labour power costs, she was also mobilized to use her energies to create new needs. A virtual war for cleanliness and hygiene – a war against dirt, germs, bacteria, and so on – was started in order to create a market for the new products of the chemical industry. Scientific home-making was also advocated as a means of lowering the men's wage, because the wage would last longer if the housewife used it economically (Ehrenreich and English, 1975).

The process of housewifization of women, however, was not only pushed forward by the bourgeoisie and the state. The working-class movement in the nineteenth and twentieth centuries also made its contribution to this process. The organized working class welcomed the abolition of forced celibacy and marriage restrictions for propertyless workers. One of the demands of the German delegation to the 1863 Congress of the International Workingmen's Association was the 'freedom for workers to form a family'. Heinsohn and Knieper (1976) point out that the German working-class organizations, at that time headed by Lassalle, fought rather for the right to have a family than against the forced celibacy of propertyless people. Thus, the liberation from forced celibacy was historically achieved only by subsuming the whole propertyless class under bourgeois marriage and family laws. As bourgeois marriage and family were considered 'progressive', the accession of the working class to these standards was considered by most leaders of the working class as a progressive move. The struggles of the workers' movement for higher wages were often justified, particularly by the skilled workers who constituted the 'most advanced sections' of the working class, by the argument that the man's wage should be sufficient to maintain a family so that his wife could stay at home and look after children and household.

From 1830–1840 onwards – and practically until the end of the nineteenth century – the attitude of the German male workers, and of those organized in the Social Democratic Party, was characterized by what Thönnessen called 'proletarian anti-feminism' (Thönnessen, 1969: 14). Their proletarian anti-feminism was mainly concerned with the threat the entry of women into industrial production would pose to the men's wages and jobs. Repeatedly, at various congresses of the workers' associations and party congresses, a demand was raised to prohibit women's work in factories. The question of women's work in factories was also discussed at the 1866 Congress of the First International in Geneva. Marx, who had drafted the instructions for the delegates of the General Council to the Geneva Congress, had stated that the tendency of modern industry to draw women and children into production had to be seen as a progressive tendency. The French section and also some of the Germans, however, were strongly opposed to women's work outside the house. The German section had in fact submitted the following memorandum:

> Create conditions under which every grown-up man can take a wife, can found a family, secured by work, and under which none of the miserable creatures will exist any longer who, in isolation and despair, become victims, sin against themselves and against nature and tar by prostitution and trade in human flesh the civilisation . . . To wives and mothers belongs the work in the family and the household. While the man is the representative of the serious public and family duties, the wife and mother should represent the comfort and the poetry of domestic life, she should bring grace and beauty to social manners and raise human enjoyment to a nobler and higher plane (Thönnessen, 1969: 19; transl. M.M.).

In this statement we find all the hypocrisy and bourgeois sentimentalism which Marx and Engels had castigated in the Communist Manifesto, this time, however, presented by male proletarians, who want to keep women in their 'proper' place. But neither did Karl Marx take a clear and unequivocal position regarding the question of women's work. Although in his instructions to the First International he had maintained that women's and children's work in factories be seen as a progressive tendency, he declared at the same time that night work, or work which would harm women's 'delicate physique' should be reduced. Of course, he also considered night work bad for men, but special protection should be given to women. The tendencies of 'proletarian anti-feminism' were most pronounced among the faction of the German Social Democrats led by Lassalle. At a party congress of the *Allgemeiner Deutscher Arbeiter-Verein* (ADAV) in 1866, it was stated:

> The employment of women in the workshops and modern industry is one of the most outrageous abuses of our time. Outrageous, because the material conditions of the working class are not improved but deteriorated thereby. Due particularly to the destruction of the family, the working population ends up in such a miserable condition that they lose even the last trace of cultural and ideal

values they had so far. Therefore, the tendency to further extend the labour market for women has to be condemned. Only the abolition of the rule of capital will remedy the situation, when the wage relation will be abolished through positive and organic institutions and every worker will get the full fruit of his labour (*Social Democrat*, no. 139, 29 November 1867, vol. 3, app. 1; quoted in Niggemann, 1981: 40; transl. M.M.).

But it was not only the 'reformists' in the Social Democratic Party who held the view that the proletarians needed a proper family, the radicals who followed Marx's revolutionary strategy had no other concept of women and the family. August Bebel and Clara Zetkin who belonged to this wing and who, until then, had been, with Engels, considered the most important contributors to a socialist theory of women's emancipation, advocated the maintenance of a proper family with a proper housewife and mother among the working class. Also Bebel wanted to reduce women's employment so that mothers would have more time for the education of their children. He regretted the destruction of the proletarian family:

> The wife of the worker who comes home in the evening, tired and exhausted, again has her hands full of work. She has to rush to attend to the most necessary tasks. The man goes to the pub and finds there the comfort he cannot find at home, he drinks, . . . perhaps he takes to the vice of gambling and loses thereby, even more than by drinking. Meanwhile the wife is sitting at home, grumbling, she has to work like a brute . . . this is how disharmony begins. But if the woman is less responsible she too, after returning home tired, goes out to have her recreation and thus the household goes down the drain and the misery doubles (Bebel, 1964: 157–8; transl. M.M.).

Bebel did not conceive of a change in the sexual division of labour nor a sharing of household tasks by men. He saw woman mainly as a mother, and did not envisage a change in her role in the future.

This is also the main view held by Clara Zetkin. In spite of her struggles against 'proletarian anti-feminism', she saw the proletarian woman as a wife and mother rather than as a worker. In 1896 she gave a speech at the party congress in Gotha where she formulated the following main points of her theory:

1. the struggle for women's emancipation is identical with the struggle of the proletariat against capitalism.
2. nevertheless, working women need special protection at their place of work.
3. improvements in the conditions of working women would enable them to participate more actively in the revolutionary struggle of the whole class.

Together with Marx and Engels, she was of the opinion that capitalism had created equality of exploitation between man and woman. Therefore, the proletarian women cannot fight against men, as bourgeois feminists might do, but must fight against the capitalist class together with men:

> Therefore the liberation struggle of the proletarian woman cannot be a struggle like that of the bourgeois woman against the man of her class; on the contrary, it is a struggle together with the man of her class against the class of capitalists. She need not fight against the men of her class in order to break down the barriers which limit free competition. Capital's need for exploitation and the

development of the modern mode of production have done this for her. On the contrary, what is needed is to erect new barriers against the exploitation of the proletarian woman. What is needed is to give her back her rights as a wife, a mother, and to secure them. The final goal of her struggle is not free competition with man but the establishment of the political rule of the proletariat (quoted in Evans, 1978: 114; transl. M.M.).

What is striking in this statement is the emphasis on women's rights as mother and wife. She made this even more explicit later in the same speech:

By no means should it be the task of the socialist agitation of women to alienate women from their duties as mothers and wives. On the contrary, one has to see to it that she can fulfill these tasks better than hitherto, in the interest of the proletariat. The better the conditions in the family, her effectiveness in the home, the better she will be able to fight. . . . So many mothers, so many wives who inspire their husbands and their children with class consciousness are doing as much as the women comrades whom we see in our meetings (quoted in Evans, 1979: 114–115; transl. M.M.).

These ideas found a very positive echo in the party, which had in any case, as we have seen, a rather bourgeois concept of women's role as mother and wife. This process of creating the bourgeois nuclear family in the working class and of the housewifization of proletarian women also was not restricted to Germany, but can be traced in all industrialized and 'civilized' countries. It was pushed forward not only by the bourgeois class and state, but also by the 'most advanced sections' of the working class, namely the male skilled labour aristocracy in the European countries. Particularly for socialists, this process points to a basic contradiction, which has still not been solved, not even in socialist countries:

If entry into social production is seen as a precondition for women's emancipation or liberation, as all orthodox socialists believe, then it is a contradiction to uphold at the same time the concept of the man as breadwinner and head of the family, of woman as dependent housewife and mother, and of the nuclear family as 'progressive'.

This contradition is, however, the result of a *de facto* class division between working-class men and women. I disagree with Heinsohn and Knieper (1976) when they say that the working class as a whole had no material interest in the creation of the nuclear family and the housewifization of women. Maybe working-class women had nothing to gain, but working-class men had.

Proletarian men do have a material interest in the domestication of their female class companions. This material interest consists, on the one hand, in the man's claim to monopolize available wage-work, on the other, in the claim to have control over all money income in the family. Since money has become the main source and embodiment of power under capitalism, proletarian men fight about money not only with the capitalists, but also with their wives. Their demand for a family wage is an expression of this struggle. Here the point is not whether a proper family wage was ever paid or not (cf. Land, 1980; Barrett and McIntosh, 1980), the point is that the ideological and theoretical consequence of this concept led to the *de facto* acceptance of the bourgeois concept of the family and of women by the proletariat.

Marx's analysis of the value of labour power is also based on this concept, namely, that the worker has a 'non-working' housewife (Mies, 1981). After this all female work is devalued, whether it is wage-work or housework.

The function of housework for the process of capital accumulation has been extensively discussed by feminists in recent years. I shall omit this aspect here. But I would like to point out that housewifization means the externalization, or ex-territorialization of costs which otherwise would have to be covered by the capitalists. This means women's labour is considered a natural resource, freely available like air and water.

Housewifization means at the same time the total atomization and disorganization of these hidden workers. This is not only the reason for the lack of women's political power, but also for their lack of bargaining power. As the housewife is linked to the wage-earning breadwinner, to the 'free' proletarian as a non-free worker, the 'freedom' of the proletarian to sell his labour power is based on the non-freedom of the housewife. Proletarianization of men is based on the house-wifization of women.

Thus, the Little White Man also got his 'colony', namely, the family and a domesticated housewife. This was a sign that, at last, the propertyless proletarian had risen to the 'civilized' status of a citizen, that he had become a full member of a 'culture-nation'. This rise, however, was paid for by the subordination and house-wifization of the women of his class. The extension of bourgeois laws to the working class meant that in the family the propertyless man was also lord and master.

It is my thesis that these two processes of colonization and housewifization are closely and causally interlinked. Without the ongoing exploitation of external colonies – formerly as direct colonies, today within the new international division of labour – the establishment of the 'internal colony', that is, a nuclear family and a woman maintained by a male 'breadwinner', would not have been possible.

Notes

1. The same could be said about the colonial relationship. If colonies want to follow this model of development of the metropoles, they can achieve success only by exploiting some other colonies. This has, indeed, led to the creation of internal colonies in many of the ex-colonial states.

2. The number of witches killed ranges from several hundred thousand to ten million. It is significant that European historians have so far not taken the trouble to count the number of women and men burnt at the stake during these centuries, although these executions were bureaucratically registered. West German feminists estimate that the number of witches burnt equals that of the Jews killed in Nazi Germany, namely six million. The historian Gerhard Schormann said that the killing of the witches was the 'largest mass killing of human beings by other human beings, not caused by warfare' (*Der Spiegel*, no. 43, 1984).

3. The silk spinners and weavers in Cologne were mainly the women of the rich silk merchants who traded their merchandise with England and the Netherlands.

4. Catherine Hernot had been the postmistress of Cologne. The post office had been a business of her family for many generations. When the family of Thurn and Taxis claimed the monopoly over all postal services, Catherine Hernot was accused of witchcraft and eventually burnt at the stake.

5. I found the astounding extracts from Mr Hall's book in a text entitled *Militarism versus Feminism*, published anonymously in London in 1915 by George Allen and Unwin Ltd. The authors, most probably British feminists, had written this most remarkable analysis of the historical antagonism between militarism and feminism as a contribution to the Women's Movement, particularly the International Women's Peace Movement which tried, together with the International Suffrage Alliance, to bring European and American women together in an anti-war effort. Due to the war situation, the authors published their investigation anonymously. They do not give complete references of the books they quote. Thus Mr Fielding Hall's book, *A Nation at School*, is referred to only by its title and page numbers. The whole text, *Militarism versus Feminism*, is available at the Library of Congress, in Washington DC.

6. This is quite logical because the slaves produced luxury items like sugar, cacao, coffee.

4. Housewifization International: Women and the New International Division of Labour

International Capital Rediscovers Third World Women

In the preceding chapter, it was shown that the development of the capitalist world economy was based not only on a particular international division of labour, by which colonies were subjected and exploited, but also on a particular manipulation of the sexual division of labour. The logic governing both divisions is the contradictory relationship between the progress of one pole and the retrogression of the other. From the sixteenth century onwards the world has been divided into regions and areas, in which different yet intrinsically connected forms of labour or production relations have been introduced for different types of production. The accumulation of capital, however, took place in the core-states of Europe, and later also in the USA. The concept of the International Division of Labour (IDL) has been used to describe the structural division, the vertical relationship existing between the colonial powers and their dependent colonies in Africa, Latin America and Asia. The old IDL began in the colonial period and lasted almost up to the seventies of this century.

The old IDL meant that raw materials were produced in the colonies or ex-colonies, that they were transported to the industrialized countries in Europe and the USA, and later also Japan, that they were transformed into industrial products which were then marketed either in the industrialized countries themselves, or exported. In the early phases of this IDL, these machine-made goods, above all machine-made textiles, were also thrown by force into the markets of the colonies. For most of them, this meant the ruin of their own textile industry as the machine-made goods were cheaper. The destruction of the Indian textile industry by English factory-made cloth is the best known example of this process (Dutt, 1970).

The old IDL also meant that labour did not have the same value in the colonies and in the metropoles. In the colonies, labour costs were kept low partly by force (for example, in plantations), by a system of slave labour, by other forms of labour control (for example, indentureship) which prevented the emergence of the free wage-labourer, the prototype of the industrial worker in the West. Hence, the old IDL meant the import of cheap raw materials from the colonies and ex-colonies, produced by cheap labour, and the production of machine-made goods in the metropoles by expensive labour which also had the purchasing power to buy these

112

commodities. Due to their low wages, the purchasing power of the workers in the colonies remained low. This relationship led, as we know, to ever-increasing wealth and growth in the industrialized countries, accompanied by greater wage demands of the workers who were also participating in the growing wealth based on the exploitation of the colonies and their workers. On the part of these workers it led to ever-growing pauperization and underdevelopment.

In the 1970s, however, the managers of the big national and multinational corporations in Europe, the USA and Japan, realized that the boom period which had followed the end of World War II was over, that continuous economic growth, which had been preached to the people in the industrialized countries as a dogma and had thus become for them something they took for granted, had come to an end. This, they feared, could lead to social upheavals if it became clear that the recession was not only a temporary crisis, but might mean the end of a whole epoch of the capitalist world economy. Therefore, the need to change the system of the world economy – or the IDL – in such a way that continuous growth would return to the capitalist countries became paramount. This new model, worked out by the Organization for Economic Cooperation and Development (OECD), the supranational organization of the Western industrial countries, meant labour-intensive – and hence labour-cost-intensive – production processes should be exported to the colonies, now called developing countries, the Third World, etc., that whole industrial plants should be shifted to these countries, and that Third World workers, because of their low wage levels, should now produce the machine-made consumer goods for the masses in the Western countries. At the same time, agriculture in the developing countries should be modernized through new technological inputs so that it, too, could produce products for export to the rich countries (Fröbel *et al*, 1980).

This partial industrialization of Third World countries does not mean that Third World countries obtained much control over the industries established in the Free Trade or Production Zones or World Market Factories. The factories re-located to the Philippines, Malaysia, South Korea, Singapore, Mexico, Sri Lanka and Thailand belong largely to multinational corporations of the USA, Germany and Japan. In particular, such industries were relocated in which the production process was still rather labour-intensive and had not yet been rationalized to a high degree. These were particularly the textile and garment industries, the electronics industry, and the toy industry. The relocation of industries from developed to underdeveloped countries does not mean a genuine industrialization of the latter. It means rather the closing down of a particular factory in Federal Germany, Holland or the USA, and its re-opening in South-East Asia, Africa or Latin America. Thus,

> Trousers for the Federal German market are no longer produced in Mönchengladbach, but in the Tunisian subsidiary of the same Federal German company . . . Injection pumps which were formerly made for the Federal German market by a Federal German company in Stuttgart, are now manufactured partly to the same end by the same company at a site in India. Television sets are produced on the same basis by another company in Taiwan; car radio equipment in Malaysia . . . watches in Hong Kong, electronic components in Singapore and Malaysia all fall into the same category (Fröbel *et al*, 1980: 9–10).

The so-called third technological revolution, the computer 'revolution', based on the development of semi-conductors and microprocessors, was made possible by the relocation of mainly American and Japanese firms to South-East Asia, and by the super-exploitation of Asian women who constituted up to 80 per cent of the workforce in these electronics industries (Grossman, 1979; Fröbel *et al*, 1980).

Some of the consequences of this new IDL are the following:

1. The rising unemployment of workers in industrialized countries. As many of the relocated factories, like those of the textile and electronics industries, had mainly employed women, this unemployment affects more women than men.
2. Developing countries increasingly become areas of production of consumer goods for the rich countries, whereas rich countries increasingly become areas of consumption only. Production and consumption are now divided by the world market to an unprecedented degree.
3. The export-oriented production in developing countries gears most labour time, raw materials, skills, and technical development towards the demand of the markets in the rich countries, not towards the needs of the people in the underdeveloped countries.
4. As the industrialized countries' markets are increasingly saturated with the necessary consumer goods, Third World workers are increasingly forced to produce either luxury items for the rich countries (for example, flowers, handicrafts, luxury food and fruits, entertainment gadgets, etc.), or components for military equipment and other high technology like the microprocessors.
5. As these commodities are produced in countries with an extremely low wage level, they can be sold in the rich countries at rather low prices so that they can become mass consumer goods. Items which were formerly absolute luxury items for a small elite (orchids, for example), can now be bought the whole year round at a low price by ordinary workers. This means that, in spite of rising unemployment and a decrease in real wages, the new IDL guarantees a level of mass consumption in the rich countries which helps to prevent the outbreak of social unrest. However, this is possible only as long as these countries are able to maintain a certain level of mass purchasing power. So far, the Western capitalist states have been able to maintain this level.

The strategy of the new IDL can work only if two conditions are fulfilled:
1. The relocated industries, agro-business and other export-oriented enterprises must be able to find the cheapest, most docile and most manipulable workers in the underdeveloped countries in order to lower production costs as far as possible.
2. These corporations must mobilize the consumers in the rich countries to buy all the items produced in Third World countries. In both strategies the mobilization of women plays an essential role.

Apart from the often analysed integration of women as housewives into the capitalist accumulation process, the integration of Third World women's work into the global market economy takes place in four major sectors:

1. In large-scale manufacturing industries, mostly owned by transnational enterprises in Free Production Zones or World Market Factories. These industries

include mainly electronics, textiles and garments, and toys. Apart from these central units, there are often many small-scale ancillary units, either as small workshops or as cottage industries to which certain production processes are subcontracted (see the Japanese model).

2. In small-scale manufacturing of a variety of consumer goods, ranging from handicrafts, food processing, garment manufacture, to making art objects. This sector, usually referred to as the 'informal sector', is found both in urban slums, as well as in rural areas. The work organization in this sector often follows the putting out system; sometimes women have formed cooperatives in an attempt to avoid the exploitation of the middle men who usually market the products. It is characteristic of this sector that some of the products produced by the women were items traditionally produced for the consumption of the community, that is, they had no exchange value but only a use value. With the integration of such goods into an external market system, these items become commodities and the producers become commodity producers, even if they maintain the same form of production, for example, household production. In recent years, a deliberate effort has been made – known as the strategy to increase income-generating activities among poor Third World women – to link this area of women's work to the world market.

3. The third area where women's work is integrated into the world market is agriculture. It comprises:
   a. large-scale cash crop production for export (for example, strawberries, flowers, vegetables);
   b. women working in plantations (tea, coffee);
   c. women working as unpaid 'family labour' in small peasant units which produce independently or on a contract basis for agro-business firms;
   d. women working as unpaid 'family labour' within cooperatives which produce for export;
   e. women working as casual labour in commercial agriculture (rice, sugar).
   The changes in the sexual division of labour which are taking place under the impact of this new strategy of integrating all Third World countries and areas into a global market system are such that men may gain access to money, new skills, technology, wage-labour, and productive property. Women, on the other hand, are increasingly defined as 'dependents', that is, housewives, irrespective of the fact that in many cases – as, for instance, in Africa – they still play the most crucial role in subsistence production.

4. Women's work in a fourth area has gained increasing importance in recent years: women serving European, American and Japanese men in tourist and sex industries, mainly in Asia and Africa.

Though it would be interesting to make a systematic study of the interplay between the new international division of labour and the manipulation of the sexual division of labour in each of the above-mentioned areas and worldwide, I think for the purpose of this study it will suffice to analyse a few characteristic cases. Thanks to the work done in recent years on the effects of 'development' on Third World women, we today possess sufficient empirical evidence to be able to identify the main trends.[1] But before I come to these more concrete examples, it may be useful to ask ourselves why, all of a sudden, women, and poor Third World women at that, have been rediscovered by international capital. (For they had already been discovered in the early stages of colonialism, as we have seen.) If one were to believe the many official statements on the need 'to integrate women into development' made in the 1970s, particularly following the International Women's Conference in Mexico in 1975, one might think that there was a real change of heart in the centres of capitalist patriarchy. But if we bear in mind the cynicism with which women from the sixteenth century onwards have been treated, we will have to ask for the deeper reasons for the attention given to women in the colonies today.

Why Women?

I propose the following theses to guide us in our quest to find an answer to the above question.

1. Contrary to what is commonly accepted, women, not men, are the optimal labour force for the capitalist (and the socialist) accumulation process on a world scale. Though this has always been the case, in this phase of development of the world economy this fact is openly incorporated into the economic strategies of national and international planners.

2. Women are the optimal labour force because they are now being universally defined as 'housewives', not as workers; this means their work, whether in use value or commodity production, is obscured, does not appear as 'free wage-labour', is defined as an 'income-generating *activity*', and can hence be bought at a much cheaper price than male labour.

3. Moreover, by defining women universally as housewives, it is possible not only to cheapen their labour, but also to gain political and ideological control over them. Housewives are atomized and isolated, their work organization makes the awareness of common interests, of the whole process of production, very difficult. Their horizon remains limited by the family. Trade unions have never taken interest in women as housewives.

4. Due to this interest in women, and particularly in women in the colonies as the optimal labour force, we do not observe a tendency towards the generalization of the 'free' proletarian as the typical labourer, but of the marginalized, housewifized, unfree labourer, most of them women.

5. This tendency is based on an increasing convergence of the sexual and the international division of labour; a division between men and women – men defined as 'free' wage-labourers, women as non-free housewives – and a division between producers (mainly in the colonies and mainly in the country-side) and consumers (mainly in the rich countries or the cities). Within this division there is also the division between women mainly as producers – in the colonies – and as consumers – mainly in the West.

6. The overabundance of commodities in the Western supermarkets is not the result – as is mostly assumed – of the 'productivity' of work and of the workers

in the industrialized countries; this 'productivity' is itself a result of the exploitation and super-exploitation of the colonies, particularly of women there.

The latter is particularly true if we ask who constitutes the labour force in the Third World countries today. Though we do not have statistics covering wide areas of women's work (for example, in the 'informal sector'), we still have enough evidence of the fact that today two-thirds of all labour in the world is done by women (UN Conference on Women, Copenhagen 1980). In the Free Production Zones in South-East Asia, Africa and Latin America, more than 70 per cent of the labour force is female. As Fröbel and his associates have found out, the majority of the women are young women (14–24). They work in the actual production processes on the assembly line, whereas the few men in these industries are mostly supervisors (Fröbel *et al*, 1977: 529–30).

If we add to this number of young women in the Free Production Zones all those women who work in export-oriented agro-business, in the informal sector, in home and cottage industries, we note that a very large proportion of female labour in Third World countries is engaged in production of goods for the market in the rich countries. We must also include in this figure the hundreds of millions of women who do most of the backbreaking work in agriculture in Africa and Asia – both in subsistence, and often also in cash crop production – and of course also in the plantations.

But what is it that makes Third World women more attractive as workers to international capital than men? Rachael Grossman and others (1979) have found out that women in South and South-East Asia are considered to be the most docile, manipulable labour force who, at the same time, show a very high degree of productivity of work. Most governments who want to attract foreign investors advertise their attractive low-paid women with their 'nimble fingers'. Here is a government of Malaysia advertisement:

> The manual dexterity of the oriental female is famous the world over. Her hands are small and she works fast with extreme care. Who, therefore, could be better qualified by nature and inheritance to contribute to the efficiency of a bench-assembly production line than the oriental girl? (Grossman, 1979: 8).

The personnel officer of INTEL Corporation, a US semi-conductor firm in Malaysia, said: 'We hire girls because they have less energy, are more disciplined and are easier to control' (Grossman, 1979: 2). The Third World Investment Bureau of Haiti, trying to attract German investors, published an advertisement showing a beautiful Haitian woman and the text: 'Now you get more labour for your DM. For only 1 US Dollar, she works happily for eight hours for you, and many, many hundreds of her friends will do so, too' (Fröbel *et al*, 1977: 528; transl. M.M.).

The sexist undertones in such ads is quite obvious. One gets the impression that these governments, like pimps, offer their young women to foreign capital. As a matter of fact, prostitution is not only part of the tourist industry, but also of the planning of business enterprises in Third World countries.

It is impossible not to notice the 'prostitution context' within which the new IDL takes place, but if we want to understand whether the new interest in Third

World women is based on a systematic strategy or not, it is useful to look more carefully at the various projects and programmes, devised mainly by international organizations, which are summarily put under the title, *Integrating Women into Development*.

Almost at the same time as this new international division of labour was being worked out and put into practice, the world was made aware of the necessity of 'integrating women into development'. Already in 1970, Esther Boserup had found out that women had not benefited from whatever development had taken place in Third World countries. Her findings were corroborated by the many reports on the status of women prepared by governments for the UN World Conference on Women, held in Mexico in 1975. It was found out that women's status had deteriorated in most Third, and even First World countries in all spheres: in politics, employment, education, health, law. As a consequence, the World Plan of Action presented by this conference demanded that the governments make substantial efforts to remedy the situation and to integrate women into development. After this, the UN organizations, the World Bank, the NGOs, all began to talk of women, and to include a chapter on women and development in their programmes. Can we consider this as a genuine change of heart on the part of the male development planners? Were they now really interested in women's liberation after they had forgotten them throughout all the previous years? And what did they, what *do* they, mean by 'integrating women into development'?

To begin with, let us not forget one thing: women were also integrated into the old strategy of development. Their unpaid or low paid labour as farm workers, as factory workers, as housewives had also been the base of what has been called modernization in developing countries. But this labour had remained invisible; it provided a lot of the subsistence basis on which male wage-labour could emerge. It subsidized the male wage (Deere, 1976). But now something else was meant. 'Integrating women into development' means, in most cases, getting women to work in some so-called *income-generating activities*, that is, to enter market-oriented production. It does *not* mean that women should expand their subsistence production, that they should try to get more control over land and produce more for their own consumption, more food, more clothes, etc., for themselves. Income in this strategy means *money* income. And money income can be generated only if women produce something which can be sold in the market. As purchasing power among poor Third World women is low, they have to produce something for people who have this purchasing power. And such people live in the cities in their own countries, or they live in the Western countries. This means that the strategy of integrating women's work into development also amounts to export- or market-oriented production. Poor Third World women produce not what they need, but what others *can buy*.

Another characteristic of this strategy is that it defines Third World women *not as workers, but as housewives*. What they do is not defined as work, but as an 'activity'. By universalizing the housewife ideology and the model of the nuclear family as signs of progress, it is also possible to define all the work women do – whether in the formal or informal sectors – as *supplementary work*, her income as *supplementary income* to that of the so-called main 'breadwinner', the husband.

The economic logic of this *housewifization* is a tremendous reduction of labour costs. This is one of the reasons why international capital and its spokesmen are now interested in women.

This strategy was first worked out, as we saw, in nineteenth and twentieth century Europe and the USA. Housewifization was the necessary complement to the creation of the 'free' proletarian there. But whereas in Europe and the USA many workers can afford to feed a 'non-working' housewife (due to the exploitation of the colonies), the vast masses of Third World men will never be in a position to have a 'non-working' housewife at home. Therefore, the income-generating strategy for women is based on an image of woman which has no empirical base among the majority of Third World women. In the Caribbean, more than a third of all households are not headed by a male breadwinner (cf. Reddock, 1984). Recent research has shown that the number of households headed and economically supported by women is increasing, particularly in the rural areas of Asia, Africa and Latin America (Youssef/Hetler, 1984). The reasons given are: a turn towards cash crop production for export, the mechanization of agriculture, changes in landholding systems with increased landlessness of the poor. Men have either migrated to the cities in search of wage-work or gone into more remunerative areas like cash crop production, leaving their women and families behind. It is well known by now that men who have migrated to the cities or to other countries not only are away sometimes for 20 years (Obbo, 1980), but that they often partly or totally give up their responsibility as 'provider' for the family. Particularly in Africa, the rural women 'left behind' by the outmigrating men have become

> the major if not the sole supporter of rural households (Mali, Ghana, Brazil, Togo, Liberia, Nigeria, Swaziland and parts of Uganda). Inability to rely on the husband's earnings lead these women to undertake cash cropping or trade in order to pay land taxes and agricultural labour costs (Handwerker, 1974; Carr, 1980; Obbo, 1980; Ahmad and Loutfi, 1981).

> Yoruba women complain that the remittances they receive are insufficient. In Lesotho, only 50 per cent of all women heads of household had access to remittances (Youssef/Hetler, 1984: 44–45).

These findings show that women in Third World countries, particularly in rural areas affected by modernization processes, are increasingly becoming *de facto* breadwinners and heads of household. But this reality has not changed their being defined, both legally and in common ideology, as dependent housewives and their husbands as breadwinners and heads of household. On the contrary, the more the material base for the emergence of the classical capitalist couple – the 'free' wage earner or 'free' owner of means of production and his dependent housewife – is undermined in Third World countries, the more this factual reality is mystified by propagating and universalizing this model. It is, indeed, the structural and ideological core around which development programmes and plans are constructed. The capitalist sexual division of labour, epitomized in this famous couple, is the strategic principle which is responsible for the fact that women in the various income-generating activities, where they produce commodities for the market, are *not* defined and paid as wage-workers, that, on the other hand, in land reform provisions they are *not* given independent and legal ownership of land, that they do *not* get access to other productive property, that in cooperatives they are often mere appendixes to the male members and *cannot* become independent members of a cooperative themselves (v Werlhof, 1983). This mystification that women are basically housewives, is not an accidental side-effect of the new IDL, but a necessary precondition for its smooth functioning: it makes a large part of labour that is exploited and super-exploited for the world market invisible; it justifies low wages; prevents women from organizing; keeps them atomized; gears their attention to a sexist and patriarchal image of women, namely the 'real' housewife, supported by a man, which is not only not realizable for the majority of women, but also destructive from a point of view of women's liberation.

The smaller the chance that most women in the Third World can become 'real' houswives, the greater the ideological offensive today, propagated and spread by all media, to universalize this image as that of 'modern, progressive' women, of 'good' women.

Women as 'Breeders' and Consumers

The 'Bad' Women
This strategy of mobilizing poor, cheap, docile, dexterous, submissive Third World women for export-oriented production is only one side of the global division of labour. As we said before, it is not enough that these commodities are produced as cheaply as possible, they also have to be sold. In the marketing strategies of the Western and Japanese corporations which are thriving on the export-oriented production in Third World countries, Western women play a crucial role, too, but this time not as producers, but as consumers, as housewives, mothers and sex objects.

As producers, women in Europe and the US were the first to be fired as a consequence of this new IDL. They lost their jobs in textile industries and electric industries. When Philipps in Eindhoven in Holland closed its factory there in order to re-open others in Third World countries, thousands of women lost their jobs. They were sent home to their kitchens with the argument that they should show solidarity with Third World women who needed jobs, whereas in Holland the husband's income was so high that a woman could stay at home and use her time to look after her children better. At the same time, the same multinational corporations (MNCs) mobilize women constantly as buyers of their goods. The tremendous expansion of TV and the introduction of cable TV have as their main purpose the expansion of advertising. Most of the advertising is directed towards women as consumers, or the advertisements themselves contain images of women as sex symbols as their most important ingredient. Here we see the new IDL divides the world up into producers and consumers, but it also divides women internationally and class-wise into producers and consumers. This relationship is structured in such a way that Third World women are *objectively* – not *subjectively* – linked to First World women *through the commodities* which the latter buy. This is not only a contradictory relationship, but also one in which the two actors on each side of the globe do not know anything of each other. The women in South and South-East Asia hardly know what they produce or for whom they make the things they make. On the other hand, the Western housewife is totally oblivious of the female labour, the working conditions, the wages, etc., under which the things which she buys are produced. She is only interested in getting these things as cheaply as possible. She, as most others in Western countries, attributes the overabundance in our supermarkets to the 'productivity' of Western workers. We shall have to discuss the question whether this contradictory strategy which divides women worldwide into workers and housewives contributes to women's liberation. It is often argued that this strategy gives jobs to Third World women and cheap consumer goods to Western women/housewives. So both should be happy. But if we look more closely at the consequences of this strategy, we may come to another conclusion, namely, that the enslavement and exploitation of one set of women is the foundation of a qualitatively different type of enslavement of another set of women. One is the condition as well as the consequence of the other.

The division between women as producers, and women as mothers and consumers has yet another dimension which plays an important, if not *the* most important, part in the strategies of the new IDL. Whereas women in the rich industrialized countries are increasingly thrown out of the 'formal sector', are increasingly reminded that the family, their 'reproductive' work for husband and children and consumption work, is their 'natural' destiny, Third World women as consumers and procreators are considered highly undesirable, even expendable. In fact, if one looks at the statements made by Western governments, particularly by the USA, the UN organizations, and also by non-governmental organizations, which have appeared since the end of the sixties, one can see that Third World women as potential 'breeders' and consumers are seen as one of the gravest threats to the world as a whole.

Bonnie Mass (1976) points out that the UN Declaration on Population is continually cited out of context, and is used to convey the notion that over-population is the world's greatest problem today. Thus, quoting the UN, a spokesman of the US State Department already wrote in 1969:

> This is the greatest challenge facing the UN and the world today. This conflict between a rapidly growing, underfed world giving way to despair and violence, and a possible world in which individuals live constructively in dignity and sufficience calls for the greatest effort and dedication of this era (quoted by Mass, 1976: 7).

As Bonnie Mass has shown, the neo-Malthusian strategy of putting the blame for poverty and hunger in the colonized countries on the poor themselves was systematically developed by the pillars of corporate capitalism and imperialism, first by the Rockefeller Foundation, the US State Department and the US Agency for International Development (AID), then by the World Bank, which sold it to a large number of Third World governments and practically to all Western governments.

In 1968 the World Bank stated:

> All such activity [of family planning, M.M.] arises out of the concern of the Bank for the way in which the rapid growth of population has become a major obstacle to social and economic development in many of our member states. Family Planning programs are less costly than conventional development projects and the pattern of expenditure involved is normally very different. At the same time, we are conscious of the fact that successful programs of this kind will yield very high economic returns (E.K. Hawkins, 1968).

Finally, the various UN organizations were successfully convinced that the 'population explosion' was the number one problem in underdeveloped countries, and that family planning programmes had to be added to their other activities. Even the International Labour Office began to introduce family planning into its policy for underdeveloped countries. From 1970 to 1979, the annual expenditure of the ILO for population activities (financed by the United Nations Fund for Population Activities (UNFPA)) rose from US$60,217 to US$4,500,000 (ILO Governing Body statement, GB 211/OP/31 1979). It is quite revealing that an organization which had restricted its focus to the 'productive sphere' where people appear as 'labour power' began to take an interest in the 'family' and women as 'producers of labour powers', only when population control became a priority area, and not out of a concern for women as human beings. Although this whole policy was euphemistically camouflaged as 'family planning' or even 'family welfare', it made women, right from the beginning, its main target group for research and policy measures.

After the UN Conference on Population in Bucharest in 1974, and particularly after the UN World Conference on Women in Mexico in 1975, this focus on women and their 'status' became quite explicit in a number of policy statements. In 1975, the World Bank concluded:

> The need to recognize and support the role of women in development is an issue which the World Bank considers of great importance for itself and its member governments. The Bank expects to participate to an increasing extent in the efforts of those governments to extend the benefits of development to all of their population, women as well as men, and thus ensure that so large a proportion of the world's human resources is not underutilized (World Bank, 1975).

The World Bank put pressure on governments asking for loans to take specific social and economic action to reduce fertility and to raise the status of women, socially, economically and politically (McNamara, 1977). 'Raising the status of women', however, when spelled out in concrete policy measures, amounts mainly to educating women in order to increase their productivity, and to increasing their knowledge of contraceptives and their readiness to accept birth control measures.

These two goals are not contradictory, though it may appear so, but are part and parcel of the same strategy to 'integrate poor women's supposedly under-utilized' productivity into the global capital accumulation process. This strategy is interested in poor Third World women only as producers, not as consumers and 'breeders'.

Through the provision of credits, their work is tied to the requirements of the

World Market, not to the satisfaction of their own needs. To repay these credits – which they obtained through various development programmes – they are forced to sell the items they produce which might be necessary for their own consumption (Bennholdt-Thomsen, 1980: 36), or they are forced to produce items which are of no use value to themselves, but are often luxury items for an international market.

As none of the programmes aimed at integrating women into development is interested in augmenting the consumption fund of the poor, but only in increasing the marketable output, *reduction of the numbers of poor consumers* becomes the necessary 'other side' of this strategy.

Whereas the subordination of poor women's productive work under capital accumulation is *obscured* by defining it as income-generating activity, that is, by defining it as the supplementary work of 'housewives', their 'generative behaviour' is pushed into the limelight of the whole world. The rhetoric on integrating Third World women into development means precisely this: obfuscating women's work as producers for capital by defining them as housewives and not as workers (Mies, 1982), and by emphasizing their behaviour as 'breeders' of unwanted consumers.

Therefore, a comparison of the amounts spent on population research and population control measures in Asia, Latin America and Africa, and those spent on the promotion of income-generating activities for Third World women would probably show that the former by far surpass the latter. In fact, within the modernization strategy of the new IDL, Third World women have become, as the Indian demographer Ashok Mitra writes,

> [an] expendable commodity as consumers and procreators: In the last thirty years after Independence Indian women have increasingly become an expendable commodity, expendable both in the demographic and in the economic sense. Demographically woman is more and more reduced to her reproductive functions, and when these are fulfilled she is expendable. Economically she is relentlessly pushed out of the productive sphere and reduced to a unit of consumption which therefore is undesired (Mitra, 1977).

What Mitra does not see, however, is the fact that 'being pushed out of the productive sphere' does not mean that now women's work is not used productively for capital accumulation. It is precisely this pushing women out as 'workers', and turning them into so-called 'small entrepreneurs' and 'housewives' in the so-called informal sector which makes unrestricted exploitation and superexploitation possible. If, in the course of this process of superexploitation, they themselves and their children are destroyed, there is no great regret, for as breeders and consumers these women are seen as a threat to the global system. And even with regard to the strategy of using their 'underutilized capacity productively' (World Bank, 1975), one may no longer need as many as there are, particularly since High Tech is making more and more human labour redundant.

Is this too harsh a conclusion?

If one looks at the strategies, tactics and technology used in countries like India, Bangladesh, China, Singapore under the guise of 'family planning', one cannot help but recognize a virtual trend towards gynocide. Not only have Third World women, particularly in India and Bangladesh, unhesitatingly been used as guinea pigs by the multinational pharmaceutical industries to test dangerous contraceptives and methods, like amniocentesis,[2] but contraceptives like Depoprovera, which were banned in the USA because of their carcinogenic qualities, have been massively dumped in many Third World countries.[3] The government of Bangladesh was forced not only to allow all kinds of scientific experiments to be carried out on its territory, but also to buy huge amounts of contraceptives from the Western pharmaceutical industry (Minkin, 1979). In all this, some of the scientific lieutenants in the international war against population growth not only advocated compulsory measures, but also the open use and strengthening of patriarchal or sexist attitudes. Already in 1968 William McElroy, in a controversy with Kinglsey Davis who advocated compulsion, said: 'In most societies male babies are more desirable than females and if the male were the first offspring, the motivation for having additional offspring would be reduced' (McElroy, 1968, quoted in Mass, 1975: 22). In 1973, the biologist Postgate goes a step further in deliberately advocating sex selection as a method of population control. Vimal Balasubrahmanyan refers to the Male Utopia thus propagated by people like Postgate:

> Postgate argues that birth control 'does not work' in the countries that 'need it most' and 'alternative methods of population control such as war, disease, legalised infanticide and euthanasia are rejected as they are not selective, acceptable, quickly effective or permanent enough'. He suggest that 'breeding male is the only solution which meets all the above criteria'. Countless millions of people would leap at the opportunity to breed male (particularly in the third world) and no compulsion or even propaganda would be needed to encourage its use, only evidence of success by example (Balasubrahmanyan, 1982: 1725).

Meanwhile, with the advance of sex-preselection technology, amniocentesis and the ultrasound scanner, the prospect of 'breeding male' has become practice, not only in India but, with even more far-reaching consequences, in China. In India, the practice of aborting female foetuses, after sex determination by amniocentesis, became a public issue only after it became known that some clever doctors in Amritsar had made a flourishing business out of Indian parents' preference for male offspring. They advertised to do both sex-preselection and abortion of female foetuses. After the protests by many women's groups in India, the practice will, as Vimal Balasubrahmanyan fears, simply continue in a more discreet way, particularly when ultrasound scanning becomes widely available.

During a visit to India in summer 1984 I learned that sex-preselection and the abortion of female foetuses were already practised by many low caste and poor people in the countryside of Maharashtra.

The case of China is even more horrifying since here the whole mighty state and party apparatus is mobilized to implement the one-child policy which constitutes part of the modernization strategy of China after Mao. 'Breeding male' may not be a deliberate strategy of the Chinese government, but is, as Elisabeth Croll and other have shown, the inevitable result of the contradictions between furthering small peasants' private landownership, the continuation of patrilocal marriage and family patterns, and the one-child policy of the state. Peasants who still largely have to depend on their children for old-age security want sons, since the sons inherit the family plot and remain in the village. Daughters are married to some other family and village, as is the case in India. Daughters, therefore, are not wanted. This situation is aggravated by the policy of the government to reward those who follow the one-child norm: they get more private land, if they are peasants, and they get more room, more school and health facilities, more modern equipment, if they live in the cities.

Thus, those who get most land have least family labour to work on it. This contradiction combined with the compulsory measures of the government, the interplay of incentives and discentives under the total control of the party, and growing neo-patriarchal attitudes and relations put women under pressure from all sides, so much so that female foeticide has risen to alarming dimensions (Croll, 1983: 100).

When the developments were first reported in the Western media, a cry of indignation could be heard from many corners. But often the people who now condemn China for its anti-woman policy are the same who have for years subscribed to the argument that population growth was the cause of poverty in Third World countries, and have advocated stricter measures to bring the birth-rate down.

We still have to analyse in more depth later why a country, after a revolution which had adopted a socialist path of development, eventually ends up with this blatantly anti-woman policy. Suffice it to say here that in the Peoples Republic of China, too, women are today obscured as workers and highlighted as breeders and consumers, and as such are unwanted.

The 'Good' Women

The dialectics of obscuring and highlighting have yet another dimension which, so far, has been totally excluded from the discourse on women and development. This dimension is the role housewives play in the overdeveloped countries and classes.

Here again women are highlighted as mothers and consumers, and obscured as producers. But, whereas this is considered highly undesirable in Third World countries, all policies in the accumulating countries and classes see this as highly desirable for 'their' women. First World women must by all means be made to breed more (white) children than they are doing at present, and they must be made by all means to buy more goods and commodities for their families, their children, the household, and for themselves as sex objects.

The logic behind this contradictory valuation of 'their' women and 'our' women is the same which we have observed in the earlier phases of colonialism. Capital needs women in the colonies as cheapest producers, therefore, they cannot be defined as 'free workers'. But, in order to market the commodities thus produced, it needs women in the metropoles as specialists in consumption because without consumption or purchase of commodities, no realization of capital! To mobilize women to fulfil their duty as consumers has become one of the main strategies of capital in the industrialized countries. 'Consumption work' (Bridges and Weinbaum, 1978) is, therefore, increasing tremendously in the rich countries, and is using more and more of the 'free' time of wage-working and non-wage-working women. As most of the people in the overdeveloped countries are tied to the market for the satisfaction of their basic needs, they are forced to do this consumption work if they want to survive. With the massive replacement of human labour by computers and robots, this consumption work will increase even further. Whereas some years ago the housewife had to run through the supermarkets to select the commodities, compare prices, pay the bill at the cash counter, carry the commodities home, unpack everything, store everything, remove the packing, etc., she is now already forced also to put the commodities into a bag herself, weigh them, put the price into the computer, and put the price tag on her merchandise, before she can pay at the counter. In such supermarkets hardly any service personnel is left. All the work necessary is done by the consumers themselves, except for the person who has to collect the money from the customer at the check-out desk. But even this may become expendable when everyone is forced to buy by credit cards, or via home computer.

As we noted earlier, international capital not only rediscovered women – mainly in the underdeveloped countries – to lower the production costs, it also rediscovered women in the centres of capitalism to lower the costs of producing an adequate demand for its commodities. Increasingly, the socialized services (in health, education, information, transport) which in many countries were paid for by the welfare state, are again being privatized. This privatization means that women's work as housewives will increase tremendously in the future. As Jaques Attali has said, the production of the adequate consumer increasingly becomes the work of the consumers themselves. The new commodities require a particular type of consumer, and the new technologies, particularly micro-electronics, are such that they, in fact, manipulate and produce this new consumer (Attali, 1979). The more this technology finds its way into private households, the tighter the grip of capital over the indvidual consumers, particularly women. In future, women who have 'been pushed out of the productive sphere' in factories and offices will find themselves in front of a home computer where they will be engaged in electronic homeworking, along the traditional lines of the putting out system, for the same firms or others which have pushed them out. Thus, more and more 'free wage-labour' is being transformed into non-free housewifized labour, and the 'free' consumer is increasingly forced into a coercive structure which makes her/him not only buy the commodiites, but also do more consumption work than before if she/he wants to survive.

The housewife is the optimal labour force for capital at this juncture and not the 'free proletarian', both in the underdeveloped and overdeveloped countries (v. Werlhof, 1983). Whereas the consumer-housewife in the West has to do more and more unpaid work in order to lower the costs for the realization of capital, the producer-housewife in the colonies has to do more and more unpaid work in order to lower the production costs. Both categories of women are increasingly subjected not only to a manipulative ideology of what a 'modern', that is, 'good' woman should be, but even more to direct measures of coercion, as was already clearly visible in the Third World as far as birth control is concerned.

The new strategy of obscuring women's productive work for capital is propagated under the slogan of 'flexibilization of labour'. Not only are women pushed out of the formal sector – as happened some time ago to Indian women – they are reintegrated into capitalist development in a whole range of informal, non-organized, non-protected production relations, ranging from part-time work, through contract work, to homeworking, to unpaid neighbourhood work. Increasingly, the dual model according to which Third World labour has been segmented is re-introduced into the industrialized countries. Thus, we can say that the way in which Third World women are at present integrated into capitalist development is the model also for the reorganization of labour in the centres of capitalism.

Ideologically, however, increasingly open racist arguments are used to camouflage the *de facto* structured similarity between the two sets of women. Whereas the Western consumer-housewives are encouraged to consume more and to breed more whites, the colonial producer-'housewives' are encouraged to produce more and cheaper, and to stop breeding more blacks. The new wave of racism which we encounter today in the West has its deepest roots in this contradiction, and in the growing fear of an increasing number of marginalized people in the rich countries that they might all become as expendable as women in Third World countries.

Linkages: Some Examples

The general pattern of the interplay of the sexual division of labour with the new international division of labour may be clear. What is less clear, however, are the *de facto* linkages which exist between consumer-housewives and producer-housewives. This lack of clarity is due to the mystification created by commodity production and the division between consumption and production. Once the commodity reaches its consumer, the latter is no longer able to know what production relations have been incorporated in the commodity. In the following, therefore, a few examples of the *de facto* linkages which exist between First World and Third World women are analysed. I restrict myself at present to this relationship, although we should not forget that a similar relationship prevails between women of different classes within Third World and First World countries. Of the many possible examples, I choose only some where these linkages are less blurred than is the case in most others:

a. Women in agriculture and dairying;
b. Women in handicrafts production;
c. Women in the electronics industry;
d. Women in prostitution/tourism.

One could add a number of examples like women producing flowers in Columbia, or the garment industry in South Asia (India, Sri Lanka), or women in food and fish production. But the relationships and structures will be more or less the same. I base this discussion on the findings of several empirical studies carried out in recent years (Mies, 1982, 1984; Risseuw, 1981; Grossman, 1979; Phongpaichit, 1982; v. Werlhof, 1983; Mitra, 1984).

a. Women in Agriculture

When feminists began to discover and analyse the function of housework for capital accumulation, some of us, as early as 1978, pointed to the structural similarity between the production relations of the Western housewife and those of the poor peasant producer in Asia, Africa or Latin America (cf. v. Werlhof, 1978; Bennholdt-Thomsen, 1981; Mies, 1980).

The production relations of both are usually considered to be 'outside' capitalism proper. They are sometimes characterized as 'pre-capitalist', 'semi-feudal', 'petty-bourgeois', etc., by orthodox Marxists. A closer analysis, however, revealed that these subsistence producers, as we called them, still constitute the hidden, non-waged base for extended reproduction of capital (see Bennholdt-Thomsen, 1981).

Initially, however, we thought, following Carmen Diana Deere's analysis (1978), that subsistence peasant producers only subsidize the wage of the men who have migrated to the cities, or to the industrial centres of the West. With the Small Peasants Strategy of the World Bank, it became clear, however, that this dimension – namely, lowering the wage costs of the 'real' proletarians – constitutes only one of the various production relations by which poor peasants in general, and peasant women in particular, are integrated into the process of capital accumulation. In the following, I shall describe two examples of how this integration of women in agriculture may take place. One is about typical women agricultural labourers and marginal peasants in India (Mies, 1984; Mitra, 1984), the other is about women in a model cooperative in Venezuela which produces sugar cane for agro-business (v. Werlhof, 1983).

The study on women agricultural labourers and marginal peasants took place in Nalgonda District, in the state of Andhra Pradesh in south India. Its aim was to find out how far market-oriented production had affected the work and living conditions of typical agricultural labourer women, who do most of the work in the rice-producing areas of South India. The fieldwork carried out by Lalitha, Krishna Kumari and myself, took place in three villages and covered the whole range of women's work, their work in and around their huts (cleaning, food processing and preparation, water- and fuel-collection, tending the buffaloes, etc.), as well as in the fields, which included rice transplantation, weeding and harvesting, transplantation, weeding and processing of cash crops like tobacco, chillies, oil-seeds, etc.

Although the *form* of this work as well as the overt production relations had not undergone any dramatic change – the women were still mainly hired as casual labourers or 'coolies' by landowning middle and rich farmers, who from time immemorial had cultivated their land with the help of coolies, usually people from the untouchable communities – the actual *essence* of these production relations had undergone significant changes.

The relationship between the landlords and the coolie-castes was no longer the traditional one in which the coolies had a *right* to do certain jobs (for example, removing dead bodies, watering the fields, making shoes, women doing all transplantation and weeding work in the fields, etc.), and were entitled to get a fixed amount of remuneration, usually in kind. Now the landlords no longer felt responsible for these people. Due to the constant indebtedness of the poor, they were able to keep many of the *men* of these communities as *bonded labourers*. The women, however, were still hired as casual labour during the agricultural season. But they were neither treated in the traditional manner as coolies, with a right to do certain jobs, nor as 'free' wage-labourers who had contractual rights to sell their labour freely, as real proletarians do. They were *de facto* treated as dependent 'housewives', whose work was considered supplementary to that of the 'breadwinner'. In reality, however, these women did not only do all housework, they also did most of the work in agriculture: about 80 per cent of the agricultural operations were performed by them. They constituted the bulk of the rural workforce. Moreover, in many cases, they were the real breadwinners of their families because the men were either jobless or had migrated to the city and did not send money back. In recent years, much has been written in India on the trend of pushing women out of 'productive' work or gainful employment. Most of these studies are based on census data and other statistical sources which all define housework as non-work.[4] As all women *also* do housework, apart from the other work they may do, a lot of their other work disappears from the statistics and, therefore, from public perception. Our findings, however, suggest that rural women in India do not work less than before, but rather work more. In fact, men seem to do less, but they do the better paid, more prestigious modern jobs (for example, on the new machines). Modernization and capitalist development have only deprived women workers of their traditional rights, without giving them the new rights of a 'proletarian'. But since they are forced to produce their own survival and that of their children, they mostly have to accept wages which are below the minimum wage and to do all kinds of work in order to make a living. Thus, women were not only getting poorer in absolute terms, they were also getting poorer in relative terms, namely in comparison to the men.

Since part of the agricultural production process, even in this poor area, was geared towards cash crop and market production and had undergone a certain degree of modernization, the women of the traditional coolie-classes were marginalized and pauperized. Due to the introduction of electric pumps and other machinery, their men had lost work; many had left the villages and others were just idle, and often the women had to make ends meet for the families. Moreover, as the traditional artisan castes in the villages had also largely lost their occupations, due to the introduction of factory-made goods, their women also joined the mass of agricultural labourers, competing with the traditional coolie-women for the scarce jobs, and thus lowering their wages.

In this situation of growing poverty, programmes for small farmer development were introduced and also extended, by the help of a voluntary organization, to the poor women. They included, among other objectives,[5] income-generating activities based on small bank loans for getting a buffalo, some goats, starting a small shop, etc. The buffalo scheme was the most important item in the package. It not only involved the largest loan amount, but was also more directly integrated into the capitalist market mechanism and was, therefore, under total control and supervision. The buffalo scheme in these villages was part of the dairy development scheme, called Operation Flood, through which milk production in India was stepped up in recent years.[6] This programme was also extended to small, and even marginal, farmers. The 'beneficiaries' got a bank loan for the purchase of a high-breed buffalo. They were at the same time made members of the dairy cooperative society. They were supposed to deliver all milk to the milk centre, which transported it to the dairy in the city. The repayment of the loan was secured in such a way that the bank would deduct 50 per cent from the milk money directly from the milk centre. Thus, the actual producers did not get direct control over the milk money till the loan was repaid.

Most of the work in the maintenance of the buffalo was women's work. Women had to collect the grass for the animal and carry it home; they had to feed, clean and milk the buffalo. But the milk money was collected by the men. For marginal peasants and landless labourers to feed a buffalo meant that women had to walk for miles to find grass and fodder at the edges of the fields or on uncultivated land. Formerly, this had been the common property of all. The landowners had always allowed their coolies to collect fodder on their fields. After the introduction of the dairy scheme, however, the landlords claimed all grass growing on or around their fields as their private property, which they either wanted for their own cattle or wanted to sell as a commodity. The poor women who continued to collect grass in the traditional way were accused of stealing the grass, and were often beaten and harassed by the landowners.

The following account of one woman may illustrate what the integration of poor women into this type of commodity production means: Abamma had got a buffalo two years previously. For two months she gave five litres of milk, for two months four litres, and for two months only two litres. Then she stopped giving milk because she had conceived. The calf died. For almost a year she gave no milk. Her husband took the milk to the milk centre and collected the milk money. They got Rs(Rupees)1.50 on average per litre, according to the fat content. In all, they had got Rs990 as milk money. Of this, 50 per cent was deducted for the repayment of the loan. Thus, they received Rs445. Abamma had bought feed-mix for Rs76, to feed the buffalo during the lactation period. After she delivered, she stopped giving her the feed-mix because she could not afford to pay for it. Since they had hardly any land of their own, they had to take a loan for grass. She repaid Rs150 of that loan. Since her husband was working as a porter in the nearby market town and she had to go for coolie work, they had to employ someone to take the buffalo grazing. The main problem was the maintenance of the buffalo during the summer months, March, April, May, June, when everything is dry and parched. During these months the buffaloes don't give milk, but they have to be fed. Poor people like Abamma, however, have no money to buy fodder for the animal when they don't get milk. So they either neglect the animal during these months or they have to borrow more money to keep it alive until the monsoon starts. The local breed of buffaloes is used to living on little fodder during these months without falling ill, but the expensive hybrid type which the poor peasants had to buy often do not survive these months. Abamma could not take another loan to feed her buffalo during the summer months.

What has Abamma gained through her extra work with the buffalo which was supposed to supplement her meagre income from wage-labour? The buffalo gave milk for six months in two years. After deduction of 50 per cent for the repayment of the loan, Abamma was left with Rs445. Out of this amount she had to pay Rs76 for feed-mix, and Rs150 for the repayment of the loan for grass. The boy who took the buffalo for grazing had also to be paid, but she did not say what she gave him. At an estimate he got Rs40. Hence, the net income from the dairy scheme for Abamma was Rs445 − Rs266 = Rs179. In the course of two years Abamma had earned Rs179. The milk she had produced during these two years, however, was sold in the city for Rs2.50 per litre; this amounts to Rs2,475 for 990 litres.

If we now compare this income with the labour-time spent on the maintenance of the buffalo and the milk production, we shall be able to see how this scheme, which is supposed to help the poor, compares with the exploitation of the women as agricultural labourers. The profits made by the sale of the milk in the city are not distributed to the actual producers but are appropriated in this case mainly by the state-owned Andhra Pradesh Dairy Corporation and by the various private firms selling milk products in the city. As an agricultural labourer she received Rs2.50 per day. As she worked eight hours per day, this amounts to Rs0.31 per hour. The exploitation of Abamma as a commodity producer is hence more than double that of her as a wage-labourer (Mies, 1984: 176–7).

In a more recent and broad-based study on the effects of the Operation Flood on poor and marginal peasant women in Andhra Pradesh, Manoshi Mitra corroborates these findings. She found that the introduction of dairying among landless and poor peasants has increased women's workload without giving them adequate access to the fruits of their labour or to new avenues of participation and management of dairy cooperatives. Not only were all paid jobs in the cooperatives occupied by men, but men also controlled the income from dairying. Moreover, women from landless and poor peasant families producing milk hardly consumed any milk themselves. The little milk these women kept for their families was consumed by the men or the male children, girl children hardly got any. She also found that with the new cash income from milk, many men, who usually controlled this income, had stopped going for agricultural work and hung around on the pretext of looking after the animals (Mitra, 1984).

These findings corroborate Veronika Bennholdt-Thomsen's thesis about the profitability of the 'investment in the poor' (Bennholdt-Thomsen, 1980), the control capital gets over housewifized producers, through the extension of credit, and about the actual 'trickling up' effect, which takes place due to such development programmes ostensibly meant to help poor women. They also show clearly that these programmes enhance the inequality between men and women, women doing more work and getting a smaller share of the pudding. Thus they aggravate the polarization between the sexes.

The other side:

The analysis of this process of 'draining' poor and landless peasant women in India of their work and their milk – a process called 'Operation Flood' (OF) in the Orwellian newspeak tradition ('flooded' are the cities, 'drained' are the villages and the women) – would be incomplete without at least a brief analysis of the connections between the superexploitation of poor women in India integrated into capitalist milk production, and the overproduction of milk in the European Common Market. What has the British or Dutch or German or French housewife, who can choose from hundreds of varieties of cheese, yoghurt, milk-products, cream, etc., to do with women like Abamma? The ordinary Western consumer-housewife hardly knows that *before* 'Operation Flood', the milk which was produced in the villages in India was also consumed in the villages. Now it is exported to the cities. She will also not know what Abamma's exploitation has to do with the milk-sea and the butter-mountains of the European Common Market. And yet this is why 'Operation Flood' (OF) was started.

When the European Economic Commission was looking around in 1968 for a place to dump their surplus milk and butter-oil, they discovered India. Initially, they offered their surplus to Indian dairying organizations as gifts. These should reconstitute skimmed milk power (SMP) into milk and milk products to sell to the urban markets, and thus earn the capital necessary to invest in the modernization of the dairy industry in India. The Indian government then approached the Food and Agriculture Organization (FAO) to obtain butter-oil and milk powder donations from the EEC.

With an initial investment of Rs954 million (revised estimate, Rs1,164 million), OF was the largest dairy development programme ever launched in the world. It promised to create a 'white revolution' by copying the model of the Kaira District Cooperative Milk Producers Union Ltd., at Anand in Gujerat, and to 'flood' the cities with rurally produced milk. It was hoped this 'flooding' would be achieved, among others, through the extension of dairies, the installation of rural milk collection and chilling centres, the development of improved milk animals, and the organization of milk producers in cooperatives. The cities would get more milk and the milk producers more income. It was hoped that in this way the poor would also eventually get more milk. That this expectation was not fulfilled is now admitted by many. The four big cities – Bombay, Delhi, Madras and Calcutta – do, however, get more milk. But since the majority of poor urban people cannot afford to buy milk at the price of Rs2, the dairies convert milk into other luxury items like ice-cream, sweets or baby food. Thus, it is mainly the middle-class housewives who benefit from the OF and who have access to expensive milk products, not the rural or urban poor.

In Europe, however, the Indian OF as recipient of surplus milk has played an important role in maintaining the continuous overproduction of milk, based on the import of cattle feed from Third World countries and the USA, and on state-subsidized prices. European dairy farmers, European food multinationals and European governments all had a vital interest in keeping the OF going and growing, since it helped them solve the problems of the overproduction of milk which otherwise might have led to political unrest. At the same time, the over-abundance of milk has led to a tremendous proliferation of industrially-produced milk products which all compete for the attention of the European housewife. The multinational food concerns, who control the market, constantly mobilize the European housewife through TV and other advertisements to buy more milk products. They have a vital interest in further propagating the image of the housewife as mother, consumer and sex-object.

The integration of poor and landless peasant women into the OF has created an objective link between the poor women as producers who cannot afford to consume milk, and middle-class housewives in the Indian cities and in Europe who are supposed to buy ever more and more sophisticated milk products. Unrecognized between the two sets of women are the big multinational food and cattle feed concerns, the governments, and a whole host of firms which profit from this arrangement.

Women Working for Agro-business:

The housewife model is not only of strategic importance in the informal sector in rural areas, but also in the most modern sectors in agro-business. Claudia von Werlhof (1983) has shown that in Venezuela women's labour is not only exploited in the form of the unpaid family labour of the small peasants, but also in the big modern sugar cane cooperatives, which were established by the state after land reform and which, on contract and credit basis, produce directly for agro-business. In the model cooperative of Cumaripa in the province of Yaracuy, men could only become members of the cooperative if they had a family, that means, if they could substitute their own labour with that of their wives and children. If they were ill, their wife or their son had to work in their stead. But women could not become members of the cooperative. They could enter the cooperative only through marriage. That means they were defined as housewives, attached to a male family head. A woman, therefore, had to be ready and able to do all the work her husband had to do, but without his rights and even without any right to monetary income. Therefore, women's economic position was worst in this most modern type of cooperative. According to Claudia von Werlhof, women were defined as housewives in this cooperative because they were thus made an ever-ready and available labour reserve, which did not even need to be paid at all. This model, promoted by the state, ensured that not only could the men in the cooperative use their women's productive labour for their own benefit, but also the cooperative as a whole, and finally the agro-industry for which the cooperative worked.

Apart from this invisible integration of women's work into the production of commercial crops, however, these women were also mobilizd as housewives proper – with the help of rural social workers and through the promotion of 'housewives' credits' – to change their food habits and to learn new skills (for example, to make dolls), in order to use their so-called leisure time productively, enter commodity production directly and supplement the breadwinner's income. Thus, these women's labour was totally subsumed under commodity production and capital accumulation, but it still appeared as the subsistence production of housewives. Claudia von Werlhof concludes: 'To be a housewife does not mean not to be a commodity producer, but rather to figure as a subsistence producer in spite of being a commodity producer' (v. Werlhof, 1983: 148; transl. M.M.). It is this mystification which makes the housewife model so profitable for capital.

The model cooperative Cumaripa produced sugar-cane for agro-business on a contract basis. It is not known how and in which forms this sugar eventually entered the world market, nor what were the end products which may have reached the consumers in the rich countries or cities of the Third World. I am not, therefore, in a position to trace the direct links that may exist between housewives in the USA or Europe and the unpaid housewife-producers in Venezuela. This difficulty in tracing the path of the product from the primary producer to the final consumer is typical for many of the products which enter the world market via agro-business. Whereas in the case of exotic fruits and vegetables, it may still be easy, the picture becomes totally blurred in the case of cash crops like manioc, tapioca, palm oil, sugar, groundnuts, etc., which are used as raw material for the production of either animal feed or food items. We can only state in general terms that the fact that women's unpaid labour is tapped for the production of these commodities has to be seen as one of the reasons why there is an overabundance of commodities in Western markets.

Thus, unpaid housewifized labour in Third World countries is not only tapped for the production of commodities which can be directly consumed by housewives in the rich countries, but also for the production of commodities which may be used as raw material for a variety of other production processes, including the production of arms. The transformation of sugar into alcohol as a substitute for petrol may serve as an illustration.

b. Women in Handicrafts Production (Lace and Coir Mats)

The production of handicrafts has long been propagated as a strategy for poor rural and urban women in Third World countries to 'supplement' their meagre incomes. This strategy is based on home- or cottage-industries. Women do this work in their 'leisure' time at home. They consider themselves as housewives and not as workers. The work is usually organized through the putting out system. The women get piecework rates which are far below the minimum wage of agricultural labourers. In our study on the lace-makers of Narsapur, who were already engaged in this industry in the nineteenth century, the daily wage rate was about Rs0.58 for eight hours of work. More than one hundred thousand women were engaged in this industry, but they were nowhere found in the statistics as workers. Their work was defined as a leisure-time activity of housewives.

All the lace was exported to the USA, Europe, Australia and South Africa. The women themselves had absolutely no use in their huts for the lace goods they made. They were not even aware of the use that was made of these goods, as the division of labour was such that a single woman would not make a whole piece but only a component, or a 'flower', as they called it. This industry was introduced by missionaries in the nineteenth century; in the course of time, a number of big export houses have emerged in the area and have made millions of rupees from the exploitation of these women (Mies, 1982).

The other side of the coin are the importers in the industrialized countries, today mostly supermarket chains which have included Third World handicrafts in their selection of goods. In a supermarket in Cologne I found handmade lace from Narsapur side by side with handmade lace from China, both at a rather low price. This means that today women of the working class also can afford to give their homes a sophisticated bourgeois look by adding some handmade lace to their furniture, a luxury formerly not found in such homes. Thus, the working-class women in our countries can afford a lifestyle formerly only possible for bourgeois women because poor rural women in India make these things for a wage below their own subsistence level. This relationship thrives on the definition of women as housewives at both ends of the globe.

A similar case was studied by Carla Risseeuw in Sri Lanka (Risseeuw, 1981) where women were encouraged to make coir mats for export. Whereas lace-making was introduced already in the nineteenth century, the skill of making attractive mats of coir was introduced by a Dutch development project for women. The organization of the work was similar to that of the Narsapur lace-makers, but the Sri Lankan mat-makers had set up a small workshop where they worked together. This can be seen as an improvement with regard to the atomization of the lace-makers. On the other hand, the fierce competition which is bound to emerge among these atomized producers was perhaps even more pronounced in Sri Lanka than in Narsapur. Carla Risseeuw emphasizes in her study the difficulty in getting such women workers organized. Another difficulty she mentions is the fact that, in spite of all the well-meant efforts supported by Dutch women to organize an alternative marketing system for the sale of these mats in Holland and in Europe, the end result was that the big marketing corporations began marketing these mats. With them the small Third World shops could not compete. The conclusion is that this project created a new commodity – again, another luxury item for Western homes – which was then integrated into the variety of goods proffered by the big supermarket chains. For the women producers this project did bring more money income, but it also made them dependent on the whims and the fluctuations of the Western market. I would not be surprised if all the women in Third World countries who have been mobilized in recent years to start some export-oriented handicraft production were severely affected by the economic crisis affecting the industrialized countries today. What will the coir-makers of Sri Lanka or the lace-makers of India do when the women in Holland or Germany have no more money to buy coir mats, or simply stop buying because they are fed up with coir mats or lace?

c. Women in the Electronics Industry

Whereas the above examples illustrate the effects of subsuming women's labour under capital through house-industries, the women working in the Free Production Zones in Indonesia, Malaysia, Singapore, Hong Kong, Thailand, El Salvador, Mexico, the Philippines, etc., are working in real factories. It might be added here that the house-industry and the putting out system are not only restricted to handicrafts or to Third World countries. With the so-called third technological revolution, the same atomized work organization will be used for highly sophisticated production processes. Already US firms are putting home computers out to American housewives who then do parts of the work for them in the same way as the Narsapur lace-workers are making lace components. This 'technological revolution', based on the microchip, is, however, based on the work of over a million women working in the electronic industries in South-East Asia. Whereas everybody today talks of the effects of this microchip revolution on the Western labour market – the possibility of throwing millions out of work through automation and computerization – hardly anybody mentions the 'nimble-fingered, dexterous, docile Asian women' who have made this all possible. Rachael Grossman has studied the conditions under which these women work and the mechanisms by which they are manipulated.

Asian women in the electronics industry are placed on a global assembly line that reaches from Silicon Valley in the USA to South-East Asia. On this assembly line the Asian women do the most monotonous, time-consuming, stress-producing, unhealthy jobs. They have to weld together under a microscope the hair-thin wires which hold the tiny chips together to make them an integrated circuit. These electronic components are the actual 'brains' by which the new computers and automats are directed. The American and Japanese firms have worked out a subtle system of labour control which combines methods of direct compulsion with methods of psychological manipulation. It goes without saying that trade union activity is prohibited in these factories. In Malaysia, if women are found to belong to some trade union, they are fired.

The firms employ only young women between 14 and 25. When they marry, they usually lose their job. Hence, the firms save maternity benefits and always have young, inexperienced women who get some quick on-the-job training. The women have to complete a certain quota of chips per day. A woman from a semi-conductor plant in Penang, Malaysia, said that every woman worker had to complete 700 chips per day, that they were not allowed to speak during work, that they were not allowed to move away from the workplace, that there were no breaks. The supervisors constantly criticized the workers. Eight hours of work at the microscopes would lead to eye-pains and nervousness (Fröbel *et al*, 1977: 593). Every woman had a table by her side where she had to mark her daily quota of work. The women in the individual plants are constantly set against each other in productivity competitions to increase their quota. A woman who cannot meet the daily target is fired or has to work overtime. The woman quoted earlier said: 'They treat us like garbage'. At the same time, the firms manipulate women in a very obnoxious way as sex-symbols. At the weekends they not only organize cosmetics bazaars where the women are encouraged to spend their hard-earned money on lip-sticks, make-up, creams, etc., to emulate the glamorous women of the West projected by the media and in films, but they also organize beauty contests in their firms where the women compete with each other for the title of the beauty queen of their company. After one such beauty contest, the company magazine published the following statement: 'Our last winner of the company beauty contest spent 40 dollars on her evening gown, but she made so many slits to show her legs that she can't wear the dress anymore' (Grossman, 1979).

The companies organize singing and sewing competitions and the photos of the competition winners are published in their magazines. Thus, the workers are not only totally in the grip of the company in their work hours but also during their leisure time. The company presents itself as a big family with the white or Japanese male manager as the father figure who kisses the winner of the beauty contest. Here patriarchal structures and attitudes are not simply used and strengthened, the 'submissiveness of the Asian female' not only used to lure Western or Japanese capital to these countries, whatever the traditional form of patriarchy may have been, the new patriarchy has clearly capitalist aims and objectives, as well as forms of expression. The Asian women in the Free Production Zones are *not* seen primarily as workers, but as women. In contrast to the women in the house-industries, they are this time primarily defined as sex-symbols. This shows how closely this whole mobilization of Asian women for production for the world market is linked to what I call the prostitution nexus.

The other side:
The other side of the IDL in this case means not only that millions of women (and men) in the West who are already losing – and will increasingly lose – their jobs in the mechanical and electronics industries, and even more so in the tertiary sector due to the introduction of computers, automats, text composers, etc., but also that women will be mobilized as housewives, consumers and sex-symbols in the marketing strategy for the sale of all these things. It is one of the hopes of the economic and political planners today that the crisis in the economy will again be mastered and a new accumulation cycle started by these new technologies which, it is hoped, will be bought by every second household in the West in coming years. It is expected that every second household will have a home computer by 1990, that housewives will have computerized ovens, do their shopping via a computer, send their letters by telex, etc. One of the biggest expectations is with regard to the video industry. It is expected that video films and gadgets will replace the old TV to a large extent, so that, as was recently said, every husband is the programme director for his family. What does this mean for women in the West? In West Germany a recent TV discussion on the new video wave revealed that 40 per cent of all video films are horror and war films, 30 per cent are so-called action films, in which cars smash other cars, etc., 12 per cent are pornographic films, and the rest is on education, culture, etc. If one adds the horror films to the pornographic films – because women, and increasingly 'black', women are the victims of sexist and sadistic violence in both types – one can imagine the extent of violence against women which is already, and will increasingly be, the result of this integration of women into capitalist development. Violence against women itself becomes a new commodity. At this stage, it must also become clear to women in the West that this kind of development, this kind of technological progress, this kind of promised wealth is not and can never be in the interest of women. For women are being used here in the most cynical and sadistic way to create new 'needs' for the already frustrated men in our societies, and in order to keep the already saturated market going.

d. Sex-Tourism and the International of Pimps
The most blatant manifestation of the combination of the new IDL with the neo-patriarchal or sexist division of labour is sex-tourism. Tourism to Third World countries, particularly in Asia, became a growth industry in the 1970s and continues to be propagated as a development strategy by international aid agencies. In fact, this industry was first planned and supported by the World Bank, the IMF and US AID. Between 1960 and 1979, tourist arrivals in South-East Asia increased 25-fold and the countries of the region which had opened their gates to tourists, mainly from the West and Japan, 'took in over four billion tourist dollars in 1979' (Wood

in *South-East Asia Chronicle*, no. 78). But not only Hong Kong, Thailand, Malaysia, the Philippines, and Singapore have made tourism one of their main areas of export production, but many other Third World countries have followed, for example, Kenya, Tunisia, Mexico, countries of the Caribbean, Sri Lanka, Peru, etc. The main export product which, perhaps more than sunny beaches, has attracted streams of male tourists from Japan, the USA and Europe, are Asian, African and Latin American women. Particularly the Thai and Philippino governments are offering their women as part of the tourism package. Thus, the Deputy Prime Minister of Thailand urged the provincial governors in October 1980 to contribute to the national tourism effort by developing scenic spots in their provinces while encouraging 'certain entertainment activities which some of you may find disgusting and embarrassing because they are related to sexual pleasures' (Santi Mingmonkol in *South-East Asia Chronicle*, no. 78: 24). According to Pasuk Phongpaichit, about 200,000 to 300,000 women are working in the sex industry in Bangkok, camouflaged as massage parlours, tea-shops and hotels (Phongpaichit, 1982). Officially, prostitution has been prohibited in Thailand since 1960. According to another estimate, about 10 per cent of Bangkok's women are working in this industry (Santi Mingmonkol in *South-East Asia Chronicle*, no. 78). In Manila the number of prostitutes is said to be 100,000.

Prostitution is also legally prohibited in Kenya. But the government is keen to attract Western tourists and closes its eyes to what is happening on the famous beaches. Rare protests, like that of a member of parliament who accused the Germans and the Swiss in particular of having made the coastal provinces their neo-colonial sex province, have not led to any consequences regarding tourism. Too much money is involved of which the governing elite also gets its share (*Tourismus Prostitution Entwicklung*, 1983: 52).

The close collusion between the tourist industry and the sex industry and the government is even more blatant in the Philippines, where the relatives and business partners of president Marcos and his wife Imelda are among the main beneficiaries of the tourist bonanza (Linda Richter: *South-East Asia Chronicle*, no. 78: 27–32).

As is well known, South-East Asian women were first turned into prostitutes on a mass scale in the context of the Vietnam war and the establishment of American air and navy bases in the Pacific region. The three countries which at present form the centres of South-East Asian sex-tourism, Thailand, the Philippines and South Korea, have experienced a massive presence of American soldiers from the middle of the 1960s onwards. Not only Vietnamese women were made prostitutes for the US army; the American military bases in Thailand were surrounded by bars, brothels, night clubs and massage parlours where thousands of women worked in the 'Rest and Recreation Industry' for American soldiers. Most of the American military establishments were in northern Thailand, and many girls were recruited from the small peasants of the region. When the American troops withdrew in 1976, most of these women went to Bangkok, and continued to work in the sauna 'service-sector', but now for European, Japanese and American tourists.

A similar development took place in the Philippines where the American Subic Bay Naval Base in Olongapo and the Clark Air Force Base in Angeles gave rise to a quick expansion of the R&R industry, to such an extent that the economy of these towns experienced a tremendous boom betwen 1964 and 1973. The end of the Vietnam war meant a certain slowing down of growth in the R&R industry, but the military base of Subic Bay also became a growth area for industrial development proper. The 'National Economic Development Authority' invited foreign capital to invest in this area. The Japanese firm Kawasaki established a dockyard here. Thus, imperialist industrial capital follows the imperialist military, both, however, strengthen the sex industry. Planners of the city development authority estimate that the R&R industry will remain the biggest industrial complex in the area, even after the US marines leave Subic Bay in about 20 years (Moselina, 1981).

The close links between capital, the military and the sexploitation of Asian women is also illustrated by the following personal account of a Peruvian engineer, working for an American firm at a military construction site in Saudi Arabia. Due to security requirements, the workers were completely cordoned off from the surroundings. Every fortnight they were flown to Bangkok where the Thai women working in massage parlours and bars had to serve them sexually and emotionally. This man was enthusiastic about the Thai women who, according to him, were not simply prostitutes who sold sex for money, but gave men what they could hardly find any longer in the West, namely *love*. He did not ask *why* these women were selling 'love' to men like himself or to male tourists from West Germany, Switzerland, the USA or Japan. Most of them are daughters of poor peasants who got into debt or lost their land in the course of the modernization drive of the national planners. Many of the indebted fathers give their daughters – often still children – to some agent against a certain amount of money. These agents bring the girls to some establishment where they have to work virtually as bonded labourers, for this agent or the owner till the loan has been repaid. Usually they do not even know when this is the case. Most of the so-called masseuses of Bangkok send most of their money back to their families (Phongpaichit, 1982). The customers of the South-East Asian, African – and increasingly also Latin American – women who work in this growth industry are not only the businessmen and bureaucrats from Europe, the USA and Japan, and the Asian elites. Many Western sex-tourists are ordinary Western workers who consider it their right to spend their holidays and their hard currency on the sunny beaches of Third World countries and to buy themselves exotic women. Of the two million tourists who visited Thailand between 1970 and 1980 71.1 per cent were men.

A Vietnamese woman, who flew to Bangkok, described the strange situation in the plane, where she sat amongst German men – some workers, some business people – who spoke broken English with a Thai accent which they must have picked up in the bars of Thailand.

Another dimension of this industry is the marriage market of Asian or Latin American women, established by private firms, mainly in West Germany. These firms openly advertise 'submissive, non-emancipated, docile' Asian women in their prospectuses and even in the matrimonial columns of respectable newspapers. The German Karl-Heinz Kretschmann, who maintains a German-Filipina Kontakt Club advertises the Filipinas as not only sexy but also cheap: 'A housemaid costs no more than 30 Marks and her food per month. Why then buy an expensive washing machine?' All 'marriage' or 'partner' institutes assure their male customers that with Asian women the man can be sure of remaining the lord and master. He can 'keep his trousers on'. One customer wrote: 'After two broken marriages with German women I am fed up with our German *emanzen*' (slang word for 'emancipated woman') (Schergel, 1983).

Apart from their submissiveness, the German men are attracted by the family orientation and non-demanding character of the Filipinas. One customer wrote:

> Many German men want a Filipina because the German women are more interested in their job and career than in the family. The Filipinas put the family above everything else and they are not as hopelessly materialistic as the German women (Schergel, 1983; transl. M.M.).

An ordinary German man – even if he is jobless – can order one of these Asian women per catalogue. If he is satisfied with her, he can keep her, if not he can send her back or send her to the brothels in Frankfurt, Hamburg or Berlin. In a village near Hamburg an unemployed mason ordered two Asian women for DM9,000. His 'investment' has brought him rich dividends because he forced both of them into prostitution. In a small town in the Ruhr district a bowling club ordered one Asian woman, who was formally married to one of the men, but had to serve all of them sexually. Many German men also arrange marriages in Thailand or the Philippines directly. The German ambassador in Bangkok stated that a large number of German men who had come to Bangkok as tourists had married Thai women. He declared that the only purpose of these marriages was to take these women to Germany and force them into prostitution (Ohse, 1981). What is remarkable in this statement is the fact that the German embassy in Bangkok obviously does not create great problems for German men if they want to 'marry' a Thai woman. According to a personal communication, Thai women married to German men get visas without any great difficulty. This is in absolute contrast to the rules and the practice followed when German women marry Asian or Turkish or African men who may have come to Germany in search of political asylum, who want jobs or whom they may have met in their countries. In their case it is usually first assumed that these are fake marriages. The couple has to undergo long investigations and the man is often denied a residence permit or a visa. Because exotic men as workers are *not* wanted in Germany, but exotic women are obviously in great demand in the sex industry which constitutes one of the growth sectors in the Western countries. Therefore, the West German state also applies a double standard with regard to the flesh trade from Third World countries.

The other side:

The other side of this story is the fact that the men in the rich industrialized countries, even at the time of an economic crisis, still have enough money at their disposal – particularly if they spend it in soft currency countries – to afford a holiday in Third World countries and to buy themselves exotic women as a commodity. The fixation of Western men, particularly German men, on cars and their exotic sex holidays is so strong that the governments do all they can to supply these two most important mass consumer goods at a fairly low price. A government which deprived German workers of their cars and vacations would soon be toppled.

Thus, in the 'International of Pimps', governments not only in Third World countries, but also in the rich countries, play an important role. The most important, yet mostly invisible, role in this export industry is, however, played by multinational tourist enterprises (like Neckermann or TUI in West Germany), the hotel chains (Hilton International, Holiday Inn, Intercontinental Hotel Corporation, Sheraton, Hyatt, etc.), airlines, and a whole range of related industries and services. It is significant that hardly any hard figures are available about the profits these companies derive from sex-tourism and the flesh trade. They preserve their appearance as 'decent' and 'clean' enterprises; however, it cannot be denied that there are not only close direct links between the different branches of this sector – for example, Intercontinental Hotel Corporation is a subsidiary of Pan Am (Wood in *South East Asia Chronicle*, no. 78) – but also that most of the profits gained by sex-tourism do not remain in the Third World countries, but go to the countries where these multinational enterprises are located (*Tourismus Prostitution Entwicklung*, 1983: 47–49). With the new trends towards production of 'non-material commodities' – because our markets are already overflowing with material goods – it can be expected that the flesh trade of Third World women to industrialized countries will increase. What will also increase are the more open sexist, racist and sadistic tendencies in this market. Racism has always been part and parcel of this business, from early colonialism up to the present. Increasingly 'black' or 'brown' women are not only wanted because of their exotic sex appeal, but because they can be turned into objects of sadism and violence. The video industry thrives on violence against women, many of whom are women of colour. The taboos against torture and violence against women were first broken with regard to coloured women. Now white women are also increasingly 'given free' for the satisfaction of the apparently irresistible appetite of white men for sexual cruelty.

In the International of Pimps, made up of international and national capital, the local and Western governments, the military and smaller men, one should not forget the role played by so-called 'avant-garde or alternative' tourists, those who do not want to stay in big hotels but open up with their 'rucksack tourism' new areas and new fields for sexploitation. Often it was these avant-garde tourists and alternative travel guides who dared to break local and Western taboos first, for example, by bathing naked on the beaches of Goa or by giving tips to tourists where to find still 'unpolluted, virgin land' for their hunger for sex and adventure. Whereas some years ago the authors of alternative travel guides to Asia would still admonish their customers to show respect for the culture of the local people and treat the women as human beings, many of them are now offering tips, usually received from globetrotters, as to where to find the youngest and cheapest women in Asia. Their clients are the 'alternative' tourists, mostly young and with little money. But they are often the ones who create new needs and fashions (*Frankfurter Rundschau*, 24 November 1984).

Many women's organizations have begun to protest against the sexploitation of Third World women by Western and Japanese men. But with all the moral indignation some of them have expressed, particularly Church organizations, they do not attack the root cause of this most blatant manifestation of the new IDL. In the documentation issued by the Centre for Development-Oriented Education, an organization sponsored by the Protestant church (*Tourismus Prostitution Entwicklung*, 1983), a number of actions are proposed to fight against sex-tourism. But Third World tourism as a strategy of capital accumulation is not exposed and criticized. Neither is the International Division of Labour rejected which has integrated the racist, sexist and sadistic exploitation of Third World women into its development strategy, nor the capitalist sexual division of labour by which women are universally defined as 'dependent' housewives and sex objects. It is precisely the objective interplay and manipulation of these two divisions of labour which constitute the basis of sexploitation. As long as women in the West and in Third World countries are only upset *morally* by the blatant and inhuman use of poor Third World women by men from rich countries and classes without openly attacking the national and international capitalist growth model, they objectively subscribe to the justifications advanced by the American pioneers of the R&R industry in Olongapo military base in the Philippines: 'Instead of exposing our decent women to the possible danger of being raped or to other forms of sexual abuse, it is better to provide a safety valve for the sexual drive of the marine and at the same time to make money' (Moselina, 1983: 78, transl. M.M.).

As long as the 'decency' of the American, or European or Japanese or Thai, or Filipino middle-class housewife is based on the 'abuse' of poor women in Asia or in their own countries, as long as women world-wide do not reject this concept of decency which, as has often been said, implies prostitution, capital will be able to use this sexual and international division of women 'to make money'.

Conclusion

If we look at the new international division of labour from the point of view of women, of women's liberation, we can now say that it is always necessary to look at both sides of the coin, to understand how women at both ends of the globe are divided and yet factually linked to each other by the world market, and by international and national capital. In this division, the manipulation of women as invisible producers in the Third World and as atomized, visible yet dependent consumers (housewives) plays a crucial role. The whole strategy is based on a patriarchal, sexist and racist ideology of women which defines women basically as housewives and sex objects. Without this ideological manipulation combined with the structural division of women by class and colonialism, this strategy would not be profitable for capital. We can also observe that increasingly women as sex objects are used for the expansion of otherwise stagnating markets in the in-dustrialized countries. In this strategy men play a decisive role as 'agents of capital' (Mies, 1982). This role, however, has to be differentiated according to class, as well as to race and the location in the international division of labour. Not only do the BIG WHITE MEN or Mr CAPITAL profit from the exploitation of their own women and of Third World women, so also do the small white men, the workers.

Not only do the Big Brown or Black Men profit from the exploitation of 'their' women, but also the small black or brown men. And the big and small white women also share in the profit from the exploitation of both small brown and black men and women in the colonies. So do the big brown or black women in the colonies who aspire to the status of the real Western housewife as a symbol of progress and who have been discovered as promoters of Third World capitalism.

But in contrast to the men, the women – whether white or black – are increasingly made to pay openly with their human dignity and their life for the 'honour' of being either prostitute or housewife. Thus, I think women in the rich countries have no objective interest in the maintenance of this integrated system of exploitation called the New International Order in which poor Third World women (poor peasant and marginalized urban women) constitute the bottom, because it is these women who are the 'image of the future' (v. Werlhof, 1983) also for women in the industrialized countries. This future has already begun for many women in the USA and Europe who are 'integrated into development' in the same manner and by the same methods which were applied to their Third World sisters, namely, to work 'invisibly' in the new informal sector, and to prostitute themselves in a variety of ways in order to make a living.

Notes

1. The series of working papers and publications on Third World women and their work, sponsored by the World Employment Programme of the ILO, contains a wealth of empirical information on the situation of poor women in underdeveloped countries.

2. Thus amniocentesis was tested on Indian women some years ago. Meanwhile, amniocentesis is being used in India mainly as a sex-determinating test, and a number of private clinics are now offering their services to abort female foetuses after such tests (cf. Balasubrahmanyan, 1982; Patel, 1984).

3. Feminist protest against the dumping of Depoprovera in underdeveloped countries has not been able to stop the sale of this contraceptive, but it has given the US firm, Upjohn Co., a bad name. Meanwhile, a new injectable, hormonal contraceptive, NET-EN (Norethisterone Enanthate), developed by the German firm, Schering, in West Berlin, is being propagated as a contraceptive in India. Whereas the German Federal Health Office has restricted the use of injectable contraceptives, German Remedies, the Indian subsidiary of Schering, is seeking a licence from the Indian Drug Control Board to produce NET-EN on a mass scale in India (cf. Mona Daswani, 1985).

Moreover, as Mona Daswani observed, NET-EN and other dangerous contraceptives are tested on Indian women by the researchers of the Indian Council of Medical Research. In many instances, these women do not even know that they are being used as guinea-pigs for research. The WHO seems to be the main force behind the research on hormonal contraceptives. The research funds of the Indian Council of Medical Research stem largely from the WHO. Indian feminist groups have started a campaign to ban injectable contraceptives, particularly NET-EN, because of their unknown side-effects and because they reduce women's control over their bodies even further (Daswani, 1985).

4. The Census of India of 1971 defines 'work' in the following way: *Work implies* 'participation in any economically productive work by physical or mental activity'; *non-work* is defined in the following manner: 'A man or woman who is engaged primarily in household duties such as cooking for own household or performing one's own household duties or a boy or a girl who is primarily a student attending an institution, even if such a person helps in the family economic activity but not as a full-time worker, should not be treated as a worker for the main activity' (Census of India, 1971, pp. 240–242. Source: Ashok Mitra, Lalit Pathak, Shekhar Mukherji: *The Status of Women, Shifts in Occupational Participation 1961–1971*, New Delhi, 1980).

5. The voluntary organization (CROSS) which organized the poor peasants and landless labourers in the Bhongir area, where the study was conducted, saw one of its main objectives in the conscientization of the people. In this they used night-schools and adapted Paulo Freire's method to the Indian context. This organization had also taken the pioneering step of organizing poor rural women in separate women's associations, called *Sanghams*.

6. For a discussion and critique of the Operation Flood, see: *Operation Flood: Development or Dependence?*, Research Team, Centre of Education and Documentation, 4 Battery Street, Bombay 400 039, India, 1982.

5. Violence Against Women and the Ongoing Primitive Accumulation of Capital

Whatever the differences between the various production relations through which women are 'integrated into development', or rather subordinated under the global process of capital accumulation, one thing is clear: this integration does *not* mean that they become 'free' wage-labourers or proletarians. They also do not become 'free' entrepreneurs, in spite of all the rhetoric used by development agencies. Nor do they become 'real' housewives. On the contrary. The common feature of all the production and labour relations described above is *the use of structural or direct violence and coercion by which women are exploited and superexploited.*

The women in India doing casual agricultural labour see that the traditional village norms which guaranteed their work and income are breaking down under the impact of capitalist farming, and they are increasingly subjected to direct violence if they demand the legally guaranteed minimum wage.

Marginal peasant women are being raped, their huts are burnt, their husbands beaten if they try to cultivate the land allotted to them legally by land reform provisions. The men are increasingly turned into bonded labourers instead of becoming 'free' proletarians. In the dairy cooperatives in India we saw that poor rural women are forced to do all the work necessary in the production of milk without having any access to the income from dairying. The repayment of bank credits was secured by automatically deducting 50 per cent from the milk money. The labour of these women was, therefore, already pawned to the banks and the state-owned Dairy Development Corporation before they saw any money. Their own husbands appropriated the rest of the milk money. Women's labour could, therefore, be tapped almost free of costs for the accumulating agencies.

The extraction of female labour was guaranteed by the violence inherent in the patriarchal men-women – as well as in the existing class – relations. The poor women involved in dairy production met with the direct violence of the land-owners when they tried to exercise their traditional right to collect grass on the fields. The superexploitation of women in the modern model cooperative of Cumaripa was based on the introduction of the housewife-producer. This example also reveals that poor peasant women in Third World countries do not voluntarily embrace the housewife model, but have to be put under considerable economic and ideological pressure to give up subsistence production proper and accept commodity production. One of the constant fears of the development planners is the threat that small-scale producers, who have been introduced to the credit-induced commodity production and who still control some means of production, could use the credits for their own consumption instead of producing the required commodities for export. This fear also exists with regard to the housewife-producers (cf. Mies, 1982). Therefore, the production processes are organized in such a way that the producers are no longer free not to work for commodity production, nor free to get control over the product. The model cooperative of Cumaripa was thus organized as a quasi-total institution, with a bureaucratic hierarchy, where everybody had to sign a bond that he/she would only work for the cooperative, where people could not leave the cooperative when they wanted but had to be present all the time. These *de facto* forced labour relations had the effect, as Claudia von Werlhof (1983) notes, that the members of the cooperative behaved like the inmates of a garrison, a prison or forced labour camp.

The features of a total institution with quasi-forced labour relations under quasi-military control can also be observed in the most modern Free Production Zones or World Market Factories. Not only are trade unions usually not allowed in these factories, but most of the labour laws are not implemented or are circumvented by a clever manipulation of the 'woman the housewife' model. Only young unmarried women are recruited; on marriage they are dismissed. Moral and direct pressure is used to make women work faster and more.

The violence and brutality against women who work in the sex-industry in the Third World and First World countries need no special emphasis. They constitute the very milieu in which this production relation thrives. It is slave labour in its crudest and most inhuman form.

In all these production relations, based on violence and coercion, we can observe an interplay between men (fathers, brothers, husbands, pimps, sons), the patriarchal family, the state and capitalist enterprises.

Looking at these examples and at the fact that violence and coercion seem to be present in all female work relations, the question arises as to whether this is necessarily so, or whether this violence has to be explained by other, more accidental reasons. Before answering this question I want to present some more examples of violence against women which, in recent years, have been brought into the open by feminists in Third World countries. I shall concentrate on the situation in India, where feminist groups have since the end of the seventies started campaigns against particular manifestations of violence against women, above all against excessive dowry demands and the murder of brides who did not bring enough dowry, against sex-preselection methods and female foeticide, and above all against the increase of rapes and sexual assaults and brutalities.

Dowry-Murders

The modernization process in rural India has not only sharpened the class conflict between the rural rich and the rural poor, but has also, since the end of the 1960s, led to violence against women on an unprecedented scale. The standard pattern of how the ruling landowning classes taught the poor and landless peasants a lesson was by burning their huts, beating and killing the men, and raping their women (Mies, 1983).

From 1972 onwards, I have collected Indian newspaper clippings about so-called 'atrocities against weaker sections' which, in many cases, included the rape and abuse of poor women. These brief news items hardly evoked any protests from the urban educated middle class. For the left organizations, the rape of women was part of the feudal or semi-feudal production relations which, according to them, still prevailed in rural India. Also, the women's wings of the Communist Party of India (CPI) and the Communist Party of India (Marxist) (CPI(M)) had not made rape and violence against women an important issue at that time.

Between 1978 and 1980, however, this situation changed. Small women's groups in the big cities of Bombay, Delhi, Hyderabad and Bangalore, who were inspired by the new women's movement,[1] began a campaign against rape as well as against the murder of young brides who had not brought enough dowry to their husbands' families. Around that time it became increasingly obvious that violence against women was not restricted to remote rural areas, but was becoming a common feature in the big cities. What was more, the educated middle-class women now also had to realize that they, too, had become potential victims of rape, molestation, and particularly of sexual harassment and eventually murder because of ever-growing dowry demands.

The argument often heard from 'progressive' middle-class women and men, that women's liberation was useful only for poor rural and urban women, but that middle-class women had no problem, could no longer be upheld.

The dowry murders in India all follow more or less the same pattern: marriages are arranged by the families of bridegroom and bride, who often know each other only from an exchange of photographs. During the marriage negotiations the groom's family demands a certain amount of 'dowry'. The bride's family has no right to demand anything, but has to try its best to meet the demands of the groom's side. The dowry demands have risen in recent years to astronomical figures. In well-to-do middle-class families, dowries are demanded to the tune of Rs500,000 or more in cash, plus demands for prestigious items like refrigerators, scooters, TV sets, gold, radios, watches, cars and travel. Ordinary middle-class families still demand and receive dowries ranging from Rs5,000 to Rs30,000 (Krishnakumari & Geetha, 1983). The bride's family is eager to 'marry off' their daughter because an unmarried woman still has neither place nor status in patri-archal India. Therefore, brides' parents eventually give in to the dowry demands of the 'other side'. If they don't have the money to hand, they take up loans. In a survey of 105 families in Bangalore it was found that 66 per cent of the families had incurred debts in order to marry off their daughters. Or they promise to pay more after the marriage. After the marriage the bride has to go to her in-laws' house because most families are patrilocal. Often the harassment starts immediately. Either the husband or his mother or other in-laws of the bride begin to harass her to extract more dowry from her father or brothers. Apart from these demands, she is often subjected to all kinds of humiliations and brutalities. If she cannot bring more dowry, one day – as in many of the dowry cases – she is found dead. The in-laws usually inform the public that the woman either committed suicide by burning herself, or that an accident occurred while she was cooking. By the method of burning the women to death all evidence is usually destroyed so that hardly any of the dowry-death cases is taken up by the police and the law courts. These cases are reported in the newspapers only under the three-line news items, like: 'Woman commits suicide' or 'Woman burnt to death in cooking accident'. Here are a few case histories, taken from various regions and a cross-section of Indian society, which were published in feminist and other journals after the anti-dowry murder campaign was started by some women and the feminist group, *Stri Sangarsh*, in Delhi in June 1979 (cf. *Manushi*, no. 4, 1980).

Delhi: Abha is a graduate in zoology from Daulat Ram College, a school teacher and mother of a five-month-old daughter. It is reported by her parents that, after her marriage to Dr Hari Shankar Goar, Scientific Research Officer, (Class I) at IARI, Pusa, New Delhi, she was being tortured for more dowry. A refrigerator was demanded which was given by her parents four months before her murder. On July 7, 1979, her husband beat her and injured her on the forehead so that the wound required four stitches. Her husband wanted to go to West Germany and it is suspected that he wished to remarry for more dowry. On October 1, Abha went to her parents to celebrate Dussehra. When she returned home at night, her brother and younger sister, too, noticed that her husband seemed angry. The next day, an unknown person came and informed her parents that Abha was seriously ill and was in hospital. When they rushed there, a nurse informed them that Abha had died of poisoning. The parents have registered a case of murder against her husband and father-in-law. No arrests have been made so far (from *Manushi*, Dec. 1979 – Jan. 1980).

Delhi: Two months after Prem Kumari of Delhi got married, she died due to severe burns on May this year (1980).
   'Ever since she got married her husband and her in-laws kept complaining that we had given an insufficient dowry', Padmavati Khanna, Prem Kumari's mother told me. 'They complained that we had not given a fridge, a television set, a fan and various other things . . . After that (the marriage ceremony M.M.) we were not allowed to talk to her or meet her. It was only when her health became very bad that she was allowed to come over to our house. She told us how badly they treated her and how they beat her because we had given insufficient dowry. The next time we saw her was when she was burnt' (from *Sunday*, 27 July 1980).

Agra: The Tajganj police have arrested four members of a family including a woman for alleged cruelty to Mrs Rajni Sharma, daughter-in-law of the family, and cutting off her breasts in one of the most brutal dowry cases in the history of this city.
   According to police, Mrs Rajni Sharma was married to Hari Shankar of the Tajganj locality a few months ago.
   Hari Shankar and his family members had been allegedly pressing the girl to bring Rs10,000 to buy a scooter.
   On her refusal to do so, Hari Shankar allegedly bit off both breasts of his wife. He was allegedly encouraged in this torture by members of his family (from *Indian Express*, 10 December 1980).

Bangalore: Phyllis belonged to a Protestant Christian family of five daughters. Her father is an estate superintendent. Her marriage was arranged with Mr Thomas, working in the post and telegraphs department, Bangalore. Mr Thomas's brother demanded Rs10,000 in cash, 15 sovereigns in gold, and a share in the immovable property. The family fulfilled the first two demands but did not give a share in the property. The marriage took place in September 1981. Mr Thomas started torturing Phyllis both physically and mentally, and demanded Rs50,000 more in cash as he claimed he had debts to repay. She was made to go without food and water for many days and became very weak. Seeing her condition, her mother asked the couple to come and stay with her till Christmas. Both of them agreed to this, but on December 15, Thomas sent Phyllis to her mother's house and took her back to his house the same night, promising to bring her again next day. On December 17 Thomas informed Phyllis's mother that Phyllis had burnt herself to death. Her family strongly suspects foul play. They say Phyllis did not want to get divorced because she had three unmarried sisters. They allege that though the post mortem shows the girl died of suffocation and brain congestion, no action has been taken due to the unhelpful attitude of the authorities. Thus ended the life of a bride within 88 days of her marriage (from *Manushi*, June–July 1983).

Chandigarh: Manorama, 25, was burnt to death last August in the house of her in-laws, 72-B Rani-ka-Bagh, Amritsar. She died apparently because her brothers, who had since her marriage given money to her in-laws, refused to comply with further demands for dowry.

Manorama was married to Kailash Chand three years ago and had a son and a daughter. According to neighbours, Manorama was constantly harassed by her mother-in-law Savitri Devi. Manorama's in-laws had always taunted her for bringing insufficient dowry and their demands became more persistent when their neighbour's son got a car in dowry. Two days before Manorama met her gruesome death, there was a violent quarrel between her in-laws and her brothers. Manorama and her brothers were brutally beaten up.

The girl's bhabi (sister-in-law) implored her to return with them to her brothers' home. Her bhabi expected the worst from Manorama's in-laws because they had burnt their youngest daughter-in-law barely ten months before in their ancestral village of Fatehgarchhurian. The youngest daughter-in-law's parents were poor, moreover her stepmother was unconcerned, so the case was not pursued. Another reason why her in-laws got away with the heinous crime was that they had managed to force the poor girl into signing a statement saying she had committed suicide (from *Manushi*, Dec. 1979 – Jan. 1980).

Also, a policewoman, Veena Sharma, was burnt to death by her husband in Delhi in 1980. These are extracts from the report from *Manushi*:

Delhi: She was in the kitchen, cooking for her husband, when he poured some highly inflammable material on her and set her ablaze. He then ran out screaming that the gas cylinder had burst. However, this was found not to be so, and the four-year-old son testified that his father had set fire to his mother.

Veena was a sub-inspector of Delhi police . . .

Veena had married Nagrathe (her husband) against the wishes of her parents. She was an MA in Hindi literature from Delhi University, while he had barely passed the seventh standard, was physically handicapped and had never had a regular job. Veena was the primary breadwinner of the family. Though Nagrathe had no regular income, and wasted much money drinking and gambling, yet he resented Veena's independent income, was madly suspicious of her, forbade her to mix with colleagues and friends and refused to help with housework or childcare . . . (from *Manushi*, July–August 1980).

After the anti-dowry murder campaign was started, many more cases of young brides killed by husbands and relatives, or driven to suicide, appeared in the press. Women's groups and organizations put pressure on the government for more stringent legal action against the culprits, for a reform of the Dowry Prohibition Act of 1961 which was just another paper bill, not even followed by the politicians themselves, and for more investigation into the circumstances under which young brides died in India, and the number of such deaths. 'Atrocities against Women' were discussed in Parliament on 10 June 1980. It was revealed by the Delhi police that in 1979, a total of 69 women had died from burns, while by July 1980 there were already 65 women who had lost their lives due to burning. During the 1975 International Women's Year, 350 girls and women were suspected of having been burned because of dowry demands. According to the Home Minister, 2,670 women died of burns in India in 1976, and 2,917 in 1977. These were only the cases registered by the police (*Sunday*, 27 July 1980).

In spite of the growing movement against dowry murders and other atrocities against women, the number of young women killed by husbands and/or in-laws rose rapidly after 1980. In 1983, the Supreme Court for the first time imposed the death penalty on the husband, the mother-in-law and the brother-in-law of a 20-year-old woman, Sudha, who had been in the ninth month of pregnancy. They had poured kerosene on her and set her on fire because she did not bring enough dowry. Even his harsh judgement did not have the expected deterrent effect, however. In the same week, ten more dowry murders were registered.

In 1981, in the state of Uttar Pradesh alone, 1,053 women reportedly committed suicide (*Maitreyi*, no. 4, Oct.–Nov. 1982). At a conference in Madras on 6 November 1982, Dr K. Janaki, Professor of Forensic Medicine, said that the pattern of social relationships had changed drastically in the last few years. 'The number of women dying of burns has trebled and those ending their lives by hanging have doubled since 1977 . . .' Quoting hospital statistics, she said that in South Madras alone the number of women dying of burns every year had gone up from 52 to 178 in the previous five years, and the number of those dying by hanging had gone up from 70 to 146 (quoted from the daily *Hindu*, 4 November 1982, in *Maitreyi*, no. 4, 1982).

According to another press statement from the state of Madhya Pradesh, on average, every day at least one woman is admitted to the biggest hospital of Madhya Pradesh with burns. Most of them are young. The reasons given by their husbands are mainly the explosion of gas bottles or accidental fires while cooking. Every third of these women succumbs to her injuries (quoted from *Sunday*, 4 October 1982, in *Maitreyi*, no. 4, 1982).

Amniocentesis and 'Femicide'

The declining sex-ratio in India since 1911,[2] the extortionate dowry demands of recent years, the spread of dowry to communities and sections of the poor which formerly did not know this custom but followed the practice of bride-price (Epstein, 1973; Mies, 1984; Rajaraman, 1983), the fact that excessive dowry demands are a decisive factor in the growing indebtedness of the poor (Sambrani & Sambrani, 1983; Krishnakumari & Geetha, 1983) are sufficient evidence of the fact that women are not wanted in India; in fact, that they are increasingly *less* wanted than men. Before we come to analyse the causes of this new trend of neo-patriarchy, it is necessary to give a brief account of the latest developments of this trend. These are the possibilities opened up by the new technology of sex-preselection through amniocentesis and ultra-sound scanning, combined with population control policies and the strengthening of patriarchal institutions and attitudes of male dominance.

Several years ago, a news item appeared in an Indian newspaper under the heading: *'Doctor, kill it if it is a girl.'* This sentence was quoted from pregnant women who had been used as test-persons in an Indian clinic in sex-preselection experiments. A fair number of the women on whom the tests were tried out told the doctors to abort the foetus if it was female.

When this item appeared in the press, there was no reaction from the public. People are so used to anti-women attitudes that they take it for granted when women as mothers do not want to give birth to other women. When I read this little news item I wondered what would have happened if pregnant women had told the doctor: 'Doctor, kill it if it is a boy.'

As it has become socially accepted that the birth of a daughter is a disaster, it is not surprising that some years later, in July 1982, some clever doctors in Amritsar saw the chance of their lives to make a business out of the anti-women and pro-male bias of patriarchal Indian society. They advertised and sold amniocentesis as a method of sex-preselection, followed by the abortion of female foetuses. As happened with the anti-dowry and anti-rape campaigns, the press began to report on the extent and the circumstances of female foeticide only after women's groups had started agitating against a threatening tendency towards the extermination of women. Popular magazines published reports on investigations about the use of amniocentesis and the abortion of female foetuses. About the subsequent controversy, Vibhuti Patel writes:

> One estimate that shocked everyone, right from the planners and policy makers to the academicians and activists was: Betwen 1978 and 1983 around 78,000 female foetuses were aborted after sex determination tests in our country.
> The government and private practitioners involved in this lucrative trade, justify the sex determination test as a measure for population control (Patel, 1984: 70).

In spite of the protests from the women's movement, sex-determination tests and female foeticide are carried out in both private and government hospitals in cities like Bombay, Delhi, Amritsar, Chandigarh, Baroda, Kanpur, Ahmedabad and Meerut. A research team of the Women's Centre in Bombay found out in their survey of six hospitals that ten women per day undergo the test. One of the prestigious 'non-vegetarian', 'anti-abortion' hospitals conducts the tests and recommends the pregnant women to other clinics for the 'dirty job' of the abortion. They ask the women to bring back the aborted female foetuses for further research (Abraham & Sonal, 1983, quoted in Patel, 1984: 69).

The cost of amniocentesis plus abortion of female foetuses is rather low. It ranges between Rs80 to Rs500. This means that it is not only well-to-do middle-class families who can afford to 'breed male' (Postgate), but also poor families in the rural areas. Meanwhile, the money-minded medical professionals and clinics have also organized services for out-patients. Women living away from the big clinics where the test is conducted get the result by mail, which takes at least a week. 'By the time they decide to abort the foetus it is over 18 weeks old. Abortion at such a late stage is quite harmful for the mother,' writes Vibhuti Patel (*op. cit* : 69).

Meanwhile, sex-determination tests and the abortion of female foetuses have also spread to rural areas in Maharashtra.[3] A survey of slums in Bombay has revealed that many poor women undergo this treatment and pay the money for the test and an abortion of female foetuses because they argue that it is better to spend Rs80 or even Rs800 now, than to spend thousands of rupees on the girl at the time of her marriage (Patel, 1984: 69).

The controversy about amniocentesis was sparked off, according to Vimal Balasubrahmanyan, not so much by the fact that these methods constitute a threat to the female sex as a whole, but due to 'the mistake (of the Amritsar doctors, M.M.) of hard-sell advertising and sales promotion' (Balasubrahmanyan, 1982: 1725). She is of the opinion that, with more sophisticated methods like ultra-sound scanning becoming widely accepted, and a more discreet way for doctors and clinics to sell this technology, female foeticide would become much more widespread than it is now. She blames not only the patriarchal preference for male offspring for these femicidal tendencies, but more so the 'international philosophy that inspires much of the elitist thinking of the scientists who today dabble in foetal research, embryo transfer and the vast tricky field of genetic engineering' (Balasubrahmanyan, 1982: 1725).

Abortion of female foetuses was advocated as early as 1974 by one of the key persons in the Indian population control establishment, namely Dr D.N. Pai (Balasubrahmanyan, 1982: 1725). But not only male doctors and scientists advocate female foeticide as the best way of solving India's 'population problem'. There are also women like Dharma Kumar who tries to apply the capitalist logic of supply and demand to the valuation of women in society. In response to the economist Bardhan, who like so many others sees the anti-women tendencies in India as a direct result of the changing economic participation of women in agriculture (Bardhan, 1983), she writes:

> But why not see this economic logic through? Sex selection at conception will reduce the supply of women, they will become more valuable and female

children will be better cared for and will live longer. We have here a good instrument for balancing the supply and demand for women, and for equating their price all over India (since caste, regional, religious and other barriers prevent the movement of women). So in course of time one should expect dowries to fall in the North (Kumar, 1983: 63).

She even advocates amniocentesis and female foeticide as a more humane solution than female infanticide: 'Is not female foeticide better than female infanticide or even the ill-treatment of little girls? What are the alternative policies of improving the treatment of women?' (Kumar, 1983: 64).

I do not think that one can find a starker expression of the woman-hatred of patriarchal-capitalist society, internalized by women themselves and turned against their own sex, than this advice by Dharma Kumar. Patriarchal and sexist social relations are not even mentioned and no change of these is advocated; rather the extermination of women themselves is suggested as a solution. This reminds me of the logic of the population control establishment which suggests eliminating poverty by annihilating the poor. But this case is even worse since it is a woman who is suggesting this femicidal final solution.

Rape

Around the time when women's groups and organizations launched a movement against dowry murders in India, another campaign was started against the increase in rape and other brutalities against women. The anti-rape campaign was again started by small feminist groups in Bombay and Delhi.

As was the case with dowry murders, rape had for a long time been taken as a normal affair, a feature of the 'backward' or feudal relations apparently prevailing in rural India. After a number of incidents which took place in the big cities, it became clear that rapists were also found among the educated middle class. Moreover, rape cases seemed to be on the increase in the cities. But what eventually horrified and angered the small feminist groups more than anything else was the fact that, after 1978, women were not only raped by all kinds of men, but increasingly by the police, the custodians of law and order. Most of these rapes took place within the police-stations themselves and the victims were mostly gang-raped.

The first ghastly story of this genre happened in Hyderabad on 30 March 1978. A young Muslim woman from the countryside, Rameeza Bee, had come to Hyderabad with her husband to visit their relatives. When the couple were returning from a late cinema show, Rameeza Bee was picked up by the city police and dragged into a police-station. There she was detained the whole night, beaten and raped by at least three policemen. After that her husband was also brought to the police-station. The police extracted Rs400 from him. When he learnt that Rameeza Bee had been beaten and raped by the policemen, he protested. Then he, too, was beaten so badly by the police that he died the same day (Muktadar Commission Report, 1978).

The case was investigated by the Muktadar Commission and the policemen were found guilty. When Justice Muktadar demanded strong action against the guilty policemen, however, the police took their revenge. A film producer from Hyderabad asked Rameeza Bee, who had meanwhile returned to her home town, to come to Hyderabad because he wanted to make a film about her. When she was returning from the house of the film producer in Hyderabad, three girls approached her and talked to her. All of a sudden, two policemen appeared and asked what she had to do with these girls. The girls said that Rameeza Bee had taken them for prostitution. Rameeza Bee was then arrested on the charge of being a procuress for prostitution. She was declared a prostitute and sentenced to two years' imprisonment. The police spread all kinds of slander about her. When the trial of the rapists was to start in October 1980, the police requested a transfer of the case to a different – and distant – state. The Supreme Court agreed on the grounds that the accused might not get a 'fair trial' in Hyderabad. In February the accused police officers were acquitted of the charges of rape, murder and extortion. Only two constables were declared guilty for 'wrongful confinement' (*Manushi*, no. 7, 1981).

The Rameeza Bee case was followed by mass protest, particularly by Muslim youth, in Hyderabad city. There was also protest in the feminist magazine, *Manushi*, and by some women's organizations. This feminist protest became more articulate when, a year after the events in Hyderabad, a woman called Shakila near Hyderabad experienced similar brutal treatment by the police in the small town of Bhongir. This woman was imprisoned by the police in a room near the police-station. She had to cook for the policemen during the day, and at night it is alleged that several policemen raped her. Her husband was arrested on a charge of theft and kept in police custody. On 10 October 1979, she and her husband were admitted by the police as unidentified persons to hospital, where Shakila died the same day. Her husband told a fact-finding commission that she had been raped several times during the night, that he had been beaten and forced to swallow sleeping pills. The body of Shakila was hurriedly buried by the police before a post-mortem could take place.

This case led to state-wide agitation in which a number of women's organizations also participated. Thousands of women came out to protest against police atrocities against women (Farooqui, no date).

The case which sparked off a nationwide campaign against rape, however, was that of Mathura. Mathura was not even sixteen years old. She was raped by two constables in a police-station. This is how Chhaya Datar describes the events:

> Mathura was a landless labourer residing under the Desaiganj police-station in Chandrapur district in the state of Maharashtra. Two constables of the Chandrapur police-station had been accused of having raped her at the time of interrogation, carried on with respect to some other complaint inside the police station. The prosecution went on for eight years. The accused were acquitted by the Lower Court. In the appeal to the High Court, they were found guilty and convicted. Finally in the Supreme Court the High Court judgement was reversed and the constables were freed of guilt. The case was closed (Datar, 1981).

The policemen were acquitted because the Supreme Court accepted the statement of the constables that the rape took place with the consent of Mathura.

When this judgement appeared in the press in 1979, a small group of women in Bombay, which later started the Forum Against Rape (FAR), supported an open letter initiated by four law professors, requesting the reopening of the Mathura case, on the accusation that the Supreme Court judgement was based on male-biased views. This letter and the demand to reopen the Mathura case became the rallying point for a nation-wide women's campaign against rape. It was begun by small feminist groups in Bombay and Delhi, but supported by the women's organizations of the left parties and by a large number of other women's organiza-tions. In the years 1979, 1980 and 1981, numerous rape cases were reported in the Indian press, and the women's movement, which by now had not only gained in number and momentum, but also in a clearer focus on violence against women, came up with one case after the other and demanded a change in the law, stricter punishment for the guilty and, generally, a change in the patriarchal and sexist social values, norms and institutions.

I shall not dwell here on the development of this broad movement which rallied women from all classes, all regions of India and from all political affiliations around the one issue of violence against women.[4] But I want to point out that the anti-rape and anti-dowry-murder campaigns marked a change in the new Indian women's movement in the sense that it now became clear that feminism was not only an imported Western ideology, but that its struggle against patriarchal and sexist man-woman relations had relevance also for Indian women. What also became clear in the course of these campaigns was the stark fact that violence against women was also threatening middle-class women. Thus, the standard explanation of the Indian left that rape and atrocities against women were only part and parcel of feudal and/or capitalist class relations could no longer be upheld. Not only landless labourer and poor tribal women were among the rape victims, but also respected and educated middle-class women, as the case of Maya Tyagi shows:

Maya, a 23-year-old woman from a well-to-do farmers' family, was travelling with her husband by car to attend the wedding of her niece. Maya was pregnant. When one of the tyres got a puncture, they stopped near a police-station at Baghpat. A policeman in civilian dress came up to the car and started to molest Maya. Her husband then gave him a beating. The man went to the police-station and came back with a whole police force which started firing at them. They tried to escape from the police, but two people inside the car, including Maya's husband, were shot dead. Another man was also shot dead. After this, Maya was dragged out of the car, beaten, robbed of her ornaments, stripped naked and paraded through the market place. She was then brought to the police-station where she was raped by seven policemen, and arrested. They also offered her their urine to drink.

The police alleged in their report that it was not a rape case, but that the men killed were robbers and that Maya was the 'mistress' of one of them (*Economic and Political Weekly*, 26 July 1980; *Manushi*, August 1980).

This case, more than any of the others, caused mass protests, an uproar in parliament, protest meetings of many women's organizations and the demand to punish the guilty. The government, however, was reluctant to take strong action against the police, because it feared that its own legitimacy and that of those who are supposed to protect 'law and order' would be undermined. The Home Minister saw Maya Tyagi, but advised a fact-finding committee also to take Maya to the Prime Minister, Mrs Indira Gandhi. This is what the fact-finding committee wrote:

> Realising that her (Indira Gandhi's) approval was necessary even to do justice in a case where a woman had been barbarously treated, we asked for an appointment with the Prime Minister and went to her with Maya. The Prime Minister listened to us and then merely remarked in English: 'Well, there are different points of view.' She wished to talk to Maya herself. We learnt later that she had asked Maya only two questions: First, how much gold was she carrying with her and did she have a list of the ornaments? And second, under whose advice was she brought to Delhi? (*Economic and Political Weekly*, 26 July 1980)

I have quoted this reaction of the Indian government at length, because it reveals that for politicians, including the woman prime minister, this ghastly case was just something to be used in their political manoeuvres. The opposition parties used it to demonstrate that Indira Gandhi's government was not able to 'protect' the 'honour' of women in India.

In the wake of these events, there was a whole spate of news items in the press about rapes and other atrocities against women. It became clear that not only policemen raped women, although these gang rapes by the police seemed to be increasing, but that rapists were found among ordinary men. Among them were priests, *sadhus*, postmen, brothers-in-law, teenage boys, the woman's employers, workers, landlords, etc., etc. Gang rapes seemed to have become a fashion throughout the country. Moreover, rape cases occurred in all communities, among Hindus, Muslims and Christians. Not only women of the 'other' communities were raped, but also the women of the community of the rapists. Rameeza Bee was raped by several Muslim policemen. It had eventually to be admitted that rape occurred in all classes, and that it was on the increase in recent years. Thus the Home Minister had to state openly that, in the years from 1972 to 1978, the following number of rape cases had been officially registered:

1972	2,562 cases	1976	3,611 cases
1973	2,861 cases	1977	3,821 cases
1974	2,862 cases	1978	3,781 cases
1975	3,283 cases		

(*Sunday*, 27 July 1980)

These figures are certainly on the low side but they show the trend towards an increase in rape. Peter Layton from the Marie Stopes Society said that two million women were victims of rape every year (*Sunday*, 27 July 1980). And the chief minister of the state of Karnataka said that a woman was raped every 15.3 hours; a woman was kidnapped every 34 hours (*Maitreyi*, June–July 1982).

Analysis

That violence against women is increasing in India can no longer be denied. Not only the women's movement but also the press, the politicians and some of the academics have begun to ask for the causes of the growing 'atrocities against women'. Demographers in India are worried about the shrinking female population in India, but do not know how to explain it.[5] For the educated middle class, it was a kind of shock to admit that India was far from the Gandhian ideal of a peaceful society. Hence, the movements against dowry-murders and rape were accompanied by reflexions by women's organizations, the press, and eventually also some scholars about the reasons why women in India were increasingly becoming victims of male violence, or why they were unwanted. The classical left explanation is that women are not economically equal to men in capitalist countries and that they, therefore, are subjected to male violence. Or that laws are passed, but not executed and that the government is responsible for the degeneration of the law-and-order situation (Gita Mukherjee, 1980). Another explanation from the left is given by Vimla Farooqui. She writes:

> In the last three decades there has been an alarming degeneration in our social values, because our rulers are pursuing a path of capitalist development while keeping intact the feudal value system which offers the weaker sections no protection at all. Women being the weakest among the weaker sections naturally suffer the most. This is a situation which calls for serious consideration by the women's organizations, political parties and everyone working for the welfare and advance of the Nation (Farooqui, 1980).

That atrocities against women, particularly dowry demands and murders, are part of India's 'feudal past' is also expressed in the following statement of a liberal paper:

> But the increase in the number of such complaints and the notice they have attracted through the zeal of organizations like Stree Sangarsh Samiti, Nari Raksha Samiti, Mahila Dakshata Samiti, has created the quite erroneous impression . . . that Indian bridegrooms are becoming more extortionate. The social system has always encouraged them to strike the best conceivable bargain: the richer and better placed the groom, the higher his demands. This is one situation where the educated affluent urban society *zealously preserves the values of village India* (Editorial, *Sunday Statesmen*, Delhi, 10 August 1980; author's emphasis).

It is characteristic of many explanations found in the Indian discourse on violence against women that most of them look at the manifestations of patriarchal and capitalist social relations from a narrow perspective of *economic determinism*. Thus, Indira Rajaraman explains the spread of dowry among the poorer sections of Indian society, who hitherto had practised bride-price, as a result of the decline in the female rural labour force. This decline was caused, according to her, by the increased productivity of modern agriculture. In her article, 'Economics of Bride Price and Dowry' (*Economic and Political Weekly*, 19 February 1983), she applies simplistic capitalist cost benefit calculations to bride-price and dowry. As she totally ignores the different historical and cultural roots of either bride-price or dowry, she can define them both as a kind of value equivalent for the woman, which may be positive (bride-price), or negative (dowry). For her, dowry is a kind of 'negative bride-price', which comes into existence when the economic or productive contribution of the woman, namely her housework, her childbearing capacity and her participation in income-earning work is outweighed by the consumptive costs of feeding and clothing her. This situation has arisen, according to Rajaraman, when women have been thrown out of productive jobs in the 'informal sector' classes. Dowry is thus defined as 'value of the cost of supporting a woman over a lifetime if female earnings drop to zero, and something less if female earnings drop below the cost of subsistence but not all the way to zero' (Rajaraman, 1983: 276).

As her whole argument is based on the erroneous assumption that dowry is meant to compensate 'in part or in full for the lifetime subsistence of a woman', she can also advance the argument, often heard in India, that dowry is basically a rotating fund: it is assumed that families have an equal number of sons and daughters. What they pay as dowries for their daughters, they get back when their sons marry. This assumption of the circulatory character of bride-price and dowry – based most probably on Levi-Strauss's theory of the equation of brides and marriage goods which move in such circles – does not only ignore Indian reality, but also the basically asymmetric, non-reciprocal and hypergamous relationship between bride-giving and bride-receiving families in India (Ehrenfels, 1942; Dumont, 1966).

Due to the narrow economistic argumentation, Rajaraman is not able to explain the existing situation, namely that now *all* families with female children are punished due to the dowry system, not only those who have more daughters than boys. Because of the assumption that there is an *exchange of value equivalents* between the bride-giving and bride-receiving families, she believes that the bride-giving family has some bargaining power *vis-à-vis* the bride-receiving family. The reality, however, is that the groom's family can almost totally determine the amount of the dowry. The qualities of the groom – his education, caste, family wealth, employment situation, etc. – are the measure for the dowry. The bride's beauty, education, employment, family wealth, etc., cannot be used in the bargain to *lower* the dowry demands of the groom's family. The demands come only from one side, the other side has to supply the goods *on top* of the woman.

But Rajaraman tries to construct an abstract economic model in the face of a reality which has nothing to do with it. Therefore, she can argue that bride-price and dowry are basically the same, that the transition from bride-price to dowry in the poorer sections of the society need not have any more negative effect than bride-price:

> Whatever the cause of the transition (from bride-price to dowry, M.M.), it is clear that the resulting system of dowry payment will have no more extensive punitive impact than the bride-price system it replaces, as long as it retains a purely compensatory rotating character (Rajaraman, 1983: 278).

It is not surprising that the policy implications which follow from this argumentation do not demand structural changes of patriarchal and capitalist social relations, do not demand a change in the man-woman relationship, do not demand a different valuation of women's contribution, but only a *reduction* of expenses, combined with more income-generating activities of women.

The economist Bardhan, in his review of Barbara Miller's book on the neglect of female children in North India (Miller, 1981), also explains the declining survival chances of female children in North India by the same economistic logic: as women in the South are still employed in large numbers in wet-rice cultivation, the sex-ratio in these regions is better than in the North, particularly in the wheat-growing areas of Punjab and Haryana, where women do not participate much in fieldwork. For him too, more employment for women is the best remedy against Indian anti-women tendencies. According to his analysis:

> the differential survival chances of the female child improve with higher female employment rate or with a lower male-female earning differential per day. If there is any validity to this, this means that expanding employment opportunities for women or lowering the male-female differential in rural India is not just a 'feminist' cause: it may actually save the lives of many little girls in rural households (Bardhan, 1982: 1450).

The problem with explanations like the ones mentioned above is that they are all based on an essentially narrow capitalist concept of 'economy', irrespective of whether they are advanced by Marxists or non-Marxists. This concept *excludes* per definition housework and childbearing and childrearing from the category of 'productive labour', and thus reduces women to a unit of consumption. Thus, at the centre of this argumentation is the concept of woman as a 'non-productive', dependent housewife. All violence against women, dowry murders, female foeticide, rape, neglect of baby girls, etc., is, in the last analysis, attributed to this theoretical assumption that women are a liability, a burden because they are economically 'non-productive' entities. The anti-women tendencies can only be remedied, according to these theoreticians, if the female sex, following Engels's famous statement, is '*re*-introduced into social production', that is, if women are 'gainfully employed'.

This logic, however, does not even suffice to explain the existing reality anywhere in the world, let alone in India. It is now known that violence against women is increasing in the West, where at least 40 per cent of the women are engaged in 'socially productive' work outside the household. Wife-beating and violence against women occur in all classes and affect women who are 'mere' houewives as well as women who are gainfully employed. Violence against women is also found in the Soviet Union (cf. *Women in Russia*, Almanac, 1981), in China (cf. Croll, 1983) and in Zimbabwe (where prostitutes are persecuted), and other socialist countries like Yugoslavia.[6]

Also in India it is more than evident that women are beaten in all classes, irrespective of whether they are 'economically independent' or not. Among the women who were murdered for more dowry were many who were highly educated, held a good job and were indeed income earners for the family. How do Bardhan, Rajaraman and others account for the murder of such 'economically productive' women? Moreover, I know several unmarried Indian women who seek employment in order to save the income to get a dowry together for themselves because their fathers are too poor or have too many girls. I would suspect that more and more 'earning women' will be asked by their own families to earn the dowry herself which is necessary for her to be delivered from the odium of spinsterhood. We have also learnt from Manoshi Mitra that men give up work altogether as soon as their wives are getting some money from income-generating activities. This brief look at reality may suffice to give up that simplistic economistic argument that women's introduction into socially productive labour will liberate them from patriarchal oppression, exploitation and violence.

The stark reality of existing and growing violence against women all over the world is not only a historical criticism of Engels's famous utopia but also of the *concept of capitalism* that still prevails unbroken, both with Marxists and non-Marxists. The case of dowry makes it sufficiently clear that the capitalist law of the *exchange of equivalents* does not function or is not applied when women's contribution to the economy is concerned, irrespective of whether this contribution is housework, childbearing and rearing, or wage-work or other gainful employment. This is not just an oversight or a relic from 'backward', 'feudal', 'village India', but a genuine precondition for 'modernization and development'.

In fact, the law of exchange of equivalents *must not* be applied when it comes to women's work. Therefore, this work is separated out of the (capitalist) economy and obscured. Women do not stop working in the houses, in the fields, in the factories, they do not stop giving birth to children and bringing them up but this work *is no longer considered* socially productive work, it is *made* invisible.

Therefore, dowry cannot be a compensation for women's lifelong subsistence, because she herself is *de facto* the main subsistence worker for the family, often even in middle-class families. If we no longer accept the capitalist separation between 'productive' and 'non-productive' work, we will see that, in fact, more men depend on women's work than do women on a male 'breadwinner'.

Dowry as tribute

Historically and structurally, dowry has nothing to do with compensation for providing the bride with her lifelong subsistence. It is, indeed, a kind of *tribute* from the bride-giving family to the bride-receiving family. The tribute is commanded from one side for the 'honour' the man and his family bestow upon the woman for making her a 'wife', and for incorporating her into his family. This is the original meaning of dowry. It cannot be understood unless one studies it in the context of the Indian patriarchal system, the caste system and capitalism. Dowry was developed and legitimized by the Brahmins in their theories of patriarchal marriage and family. According to the Brahmanic marriage concept, the daughter is 'given away' by her father. And 'he who gives has always to give'. The relationship between the bride-giving and the bride-receiving families is never an egalitarian one. The bride-receiving groom's family has, per definition, a higher status. The relationship between the two families is always an asymmetric, non-reciprocal one (Kapadia, 1968). As he who gives has always to give, as is the case with a tribute, it is strictly prohibited that the giving side also dare to demand something. In Rajasthan, for example, the bride's family in some communities is not even allowed to visit their daughter's in-laws and accept food from them until she has 'given' a son to her family of procreation.

Dowry, therefore, is a clear manifestation of a structurally hypergamous, non-reciprocal, asymmetric and extractive relationship between a) bride-giving and bride-receiving families, and b) between men and women. In this social relation, one side commands (the woman, goods, money, services, offspring), and the other side has to supply these goods. All the giving side 'receives' is the 'honour' of having 'given' a daughter to such and such a man, and such and such a family.

The Brahmins had a vital interest in the establishment of this non-reciprocal tributary relationship, because this caste of priests neither lived by the work of their hands, as did the other castes, nor from warfare, as did the Kshatriyas. They lived by the gifts given to them by the wealthy and the poor. The givers were only promised spiritual gains for their gifts. This is precisely the relationship between man and woman according to the patriarchal Bramanical conception (Mies, 1980). The woman gives her body, her work, her children, on top of that money and other goods, to her husband, and she 'receives' the honour of being a wife. If there is an exchange, it is one between material and 'spiritual' goods. Due to the high prestige Brahmins and other high castes of the Great Tradition[7] have in India, even now, the dowry-giving families are considered to be of a higher social status than the bride-price giving families. This status has even been further raised due to modernization and westernization. As Srinivas pointed out in 1966, sanscritization[8] processes go along with westernization processes. But whereas he found that economic prosperity was usually preceding a process of sanscritization of a community, the spreading of dowry among bride-price giving castes is rather indicative of a trend to *use* sanscritic – which means Brahmanical patriarchal customs – to *achieve* economic prosperity and westernization (Srinivas, 1966).

To equate bride-price with dowry totally mystifies the basic character of the social relationships which are expressed in these transactions. Whereas bride-price, which stems from an originally matrilineal tradition, constitutes indeed a compensation for the loss of women's contribution to the subsistence of her family, the dowry system is a one-sided tribute, in which only the groom's qualities count. Thus, there are differential dowry rates for doctors, officers of the Indian Administrative Service (IAS) and foreign-returned PhDs from the USA or England, which are among the highest dowry commanders, not 'bidders'.

Under the bride-price system, woman's value as subsistence producer is still acknowledged and positively valued. Under the dowry system, this contribution is de-valued and obscured. Analysts who apply capitalist supply and demand logics to these transactions contribute further to the obscuring of women's contribution.

Looking at concrete historical reality can also help to explode another myth which is generally advanced to explain violence against women, particularly in India. This is the argument that dowry and 'atrocities against women' are manifestations of still 'backward', 'feudal' or semi-feudal production relations which would disappear with modern, capitalist or socialist production relations. The opposite is in fact the case.

Dowries are most exorbitant in the big cities, among the most 'advanced' men:

IAS officers,[9] doctors, engineers, dentists, businessmen and 'progressive' capitalist farmers. Rape and the molestation of women do not only occur in rural India, but increasingly in the big cities. The most modern technology is used to exterminate the female sex in sex-selection tests and abortion. Hence, it is not 'village India' that is holding back the 'civilizing process' among the urban, educated middle class, *but it is capital-patriarchal civilization itself which is the 'father of barbarism'*. Atrocities against women are also not alien to capitalism but are manifestations of its basically *predatory* character, which it has never lost in the course of its history.

The case of dowry and the business made by doctors in sex-preselection tests can help to understand this character. Dowries are increasingly *not* appropriated by the bride-receiving family – as is often assumed – but by the bridegroom himself. This is particularly the case with the category of high dowry-fetchers. According to a survey of 105 families in the South Indian city of Bangalore, the dowry was handed over to the son-in-law himself in 57 per cent of the cases (Krishnakumari & Geetha, 1983). These men may demand high dowries in cash and kind as a compensation for the money spent on their education, but in many cases they use it for an initial investment to start a business, a lawyer's office, a private practitioner's clinic, an engineering office, etc. The dowry demands also increasingly include expensive and prestigious modern consumer items like a car, a TV set, a scooter, a video set, which are appropriated by the young man himself. Only some of these items are for the whole family, like refrigerators or furniture. Among the poorer sections, these modern commodities may be a western suit, a radio, a wrist watch, western shirts. The instution of dowry can thus be seen as a source of wealth which is accumulated not by means of the man's own work or by investing his own capital, but by *extraction, blackmail and direct violence*. The command over dowry gives all men the chance to get hold of money which they have not earned and to have access to modern consumer items which they might otherwise not be able to buy. The dowry creates a market for such goods, even among people who have to take up consumption loans in order to secure their survival. It paves the way for the spread of market-values and market-commodities, even among the poor.

Are men rapists by nature?

Whereas mainly economistic reasons have been forwarded to explain the increase of dowry and dowry-murders, the rapid spread of rape, police rape, gang rape, and other sexual assaults on women is mostly explained by the biologistic argument that men's sexuality is basically aggressive and based on irresistible drives, and that that of women is basically passive and masochistic.

The women's groups who demanded a revision of the definition of consent in the paragraph on rape in the Indian Penal Code have pointed out that it is practically impossible for a woman to prove that she has not consented to sexual intercourse, because resistance to the assault is recognized as non-consent only under fear of death or grave injury. This means that, unless a woman is able to forward evidence that she has been half killed, it is assumed that she has consented to intercourse. This definition has been amended meanwhile under the pressure of public protest by women, but the ideology which is expressed in the rape law in India, as in most other countries, is still very much there. This ideology consists of a number of male myths about women and sex. These myths are found in most male-dominated societies and it is the institutions and social relations they are meant to prop up which determine people's behaviour, and not the written laws. It is useful to look at some of the myths about rape put forward by men in all patriarchal societies, also in India.

1. Rape does not exist, because no woman can be raped against her will. Women like to be raped.
2. Women are masochists by nature; they do not enjoy sex unless they are forced to have intercourse. They want to be beaten and subordinated by force.
   (In the refuges for battered women which feminists organized in Germany and other parts of Europe, many women say that their men used to beat them and then force them to have intercourse with them.)
3. A woman who is raped has provoked the man by her behaviour, that is, she is behaving like a prostitute.
   (Most women all over the world have first to prove in court that they are not prostitutes. They are considered the guilty party, not the man. The Rameeza Bee case gives glaring evidence of this.)
4. It is a woman's fault if she is raped. Why does she wear clothes which provoke men, or walk alone after a certain time in the evening? Why does she go without male protection, etc?
   But the Indian cases, as well as many others, prove that the 'protectors' (for example, the police or male relatives) are the rapists themselves.
5. Rape takes place only outside marriage. Intercourse within marriage is, according to the definition of law, based on mutual consent.
   We all know that as much – or even more – sexual violence takes place within marriage as outside it. Wife-beating is often connected with the refusal of women to have intercourse.
6. Rape occurs mainly in the poorer and less educated sections of society. Hence, it is a manifestation of poverty and backwardness.
   (We have seen that rape, or more generally, sexual violence, is increasing in the urban centres and also among the so-called advanced sections, particularly if one includes sexual violence by family members and husbands in this category.)
7. Rape is a feature of feudal or semi-feudal production relations, that is, it is mainly a class issue. The feudal lords and their sons rape the women of the poor peasants. There is harmony between the poor peasant and his wife. These feudal forms of sexual violence will disappear with a change of property relations.
   This myth is usually put forward by the left. It is not able to explain the increase in sexual violence in the urban centres, in areas which have seen more capitalist development, or the increase in violence against women in the poorer sections of the society by the men of these sections.

Most of these myths blame the woman, that is, the victim. These myths also say something about men and their relation to sex. They imply that a man, if provoked, cannot resist and has to assault a woman. This means his sex-urge – or, as most people put it, his sexual instinct – needs immediate satisfaction. As women are seen as basically masochistic and mute, sub-human beings, men are seen as aggressive, if not sadistic, by nature. This nature can only be controlled by severe laws, by strict social taboos on certain categories of women (mothers, sisters), and by the women themselves who are expected to behave in such a way that the aggressive, sadistic sex 'instinct' of men does not get out of control.

I wonder whether law-makers and male scholars have ever thought about the caricature of a human being they have made of themselves by subscribing to such ideas. But it is not only these popular myths which have influenced the common ideology on women, men and sex. What is more consequential is the fact that most of these myths have been propped up, scientifically elaborated, and 'proved' by a number of highly respected scholars and their theories. Whole libraries have been filled with books which try to prove that men's sexual drives are basically aggressive and uncontrollable, and that women either have no sexuality of their own or that it is their biological destiny to satisfy the aggressive needs of men. To mention only the most famous among these scholars and their schools, Darwin held that evolution was based on control over the aggressive and disruptive instincts of the males in their competition for sexual control over the females.

The neo-Darwinists, social Darwinists, and the whole school of behavioural sciences which dominates American social sciences – and particularly the social biologists – basically subscribe to this concept of man. In particular, scholars like Konrad Lorenz, Lionel Tiger and Robert Fox have popularized this concept in the last twenty years, epitomized, as we saw, in the 'Man-the-Hunter model'. Therefore, aggressiveness is part of men's nature and cannot be changed through social reform or revolution. I am sure that there are many male (and female) social scientists who are against rape for moral reasons, but who nevertheless subscribe to these concepts and theories. If they had a more critical attitude to the hidden biases in scientific thought, they would be able to see that these so-called value-free sciences are based on certain myths which serve to legitimize oppression, exploitation and subordination of other human beings: women, low castes, classes, peoples and nations. They would for instance see that biology or nature does not compel any males to rape. Rape does not exist in the animal world. It is an invention of the human male.

'The survival of the fittest' – the strong MEN – means that the conquerors, the victors, are always right. This is precisely the ideology behind the rape laws and rape myths. Are we unable to see that those who subscribe to this sort of science also subscribe to fascism and imperialism?

Even Sigmund Freud, the founder of the psychoanalytic school and the discoverer of the subconscious, was influenced by these myths and their 'scientific' legitimation by the evolutionists. He also believed that culture was based on the repression and sublimation of these violent male sex drives. His theory of the Oedipus complex is basically a theory of male sexual competition, between fathers and sons, for one sex-object, the mother. Also, Freud subscribes to the theory that male sexuality is active, aggressive – in its neurotic forms, sometimes sadistic. And female sexuality is considered to be passive and even masochistic. Woman, according to Freud, can reach her full, adult sexuality only by accepting her 'natural' female role, that is, by giving up her 'immature' clitoral sexuality and switching over to vaginal sexuality which is necessary for the man to satisfy his sex drive. It is surprising that a serious scholar like Freud consolidates the theory of vaginal orgasm as the 'mature' form of female sexuality, although he must have known that the vagina does not contain nerve ends and hence does not 'produce' an orgasm. He knew that the clitoris is the active sexual organ of women which can produce a female orgasm without penetration of the vagina. But in his preoccupation with male sexuality, he defined women as incomplete or castrated men, the clitoris as a small penis, and the attempt of women to change their subordinate role in society a result of penis-envy.

Scholars would do well to take a very critical look at these theories before adopting them as their theoretical framework, because they imply that both male and female sexuality are only biologically determined. These theories do not explain why certain parts of the male and female bodies were given prominence at a particular time in history, and others not. It needed, for instance, the feminist movement in the West to rediscover the clitoris as an independent female sex organ. In many parts of Africa, the clitoris is removed by circumcision when girls are nine to twelve years old. But the women in Europe and in other parts of the world, too, have been psychologically circumcized so that they no longer knew their bodies and did not know what an orgasm was.

One cannot talk about men without talking about women. The ideology on rape and male sexuality criticized above had its complementary features in the self-concepts of women all over the world.

No aggressor can maintain permanent control over those he has conquered and subordinated unless the subordinated are made to accept this state of affairs as nature-imposed or, what amounts to the same, as God-given. The inventors of the patriarchal ideology on men have also invented a fitting ideology for women. That is the ideology of the eternal victim, the ideology of self-sacrifice (in the modern Western version, it is the ideology of female masochism). Hindu religion and popular belief idealize the self-sacrificing woman in the role of the mother and the Pativrata. [10] Woman has no identity of her own, she is born to serve others, mainly husbands and sons. She has no autonomy over her own life, her own body, her own sexuality. She is a means, an object, not a subject. The figures of Sati, Sita, and other self-sacrificing women of the Hindu religion are advanced as models for girls even now. They are widely popularized by text-books, films and novels. No wonder that rape victims, rather than hit back or defend themselves, commit suicide because their 'honour' as a 'good' woman is destroyed. In the self-perception of most women are feelings that they are weak, that they need male protection, that they cannot fight back – or should not fight back; 'self-immolation', either *de facto* or symbolically, is the act through which they try to regain their humanity.

As in the case of men, women mostly do not recognize how they are subscribing to the ideology of the rapists by clinging to this self-sacrificing ideal of womanhood.

The men, particularly those who make money propagating this ideology of the weak woman, cynically put the blame on women, like the film-maker Dinesh Thakur, who said in a discussion on rape: 'Why do women glamourize and idolize a woman who makes sacrifices?' (*The Times of India*, 15 June 1980). But he denies that by having rape scenes and also the self-sacrificing women in his films that he contributes to this ideology for the sake of profit. This is another classic case of putting the blame on the victim while profiting from the attitudes criticized. It is just not enough to say that women want to be victims and idolize self-sacrifice. It is necessary to say that this ideology was invented and is maintained in the interest of men who rule over women. But what is more important, this ideology is the outcome of thousands of years of direct and structural violence against women, first practised in some patriarchal societies, but universalized today by capitalism. Those who are constantly oppressed directly – and women have no autonomy over their lives even now – have no other psychological choice but to interpret what they are forced to do into voluntariness if they do not want to lose all self-respect as a human being. This is the deepest reason why women also share in the ideology of their oppressors, and subscribe to the notion that their 'honour', their family's honour, is violated when they are raped. This is the reason why Maya Tyagi's mother could say that she wished her daughter was dead because, as a result of the rape, she had diminished her family's honour. As long as the rape victims themselves, the mothers and sisters, believe in this concept of 'honour' which they cherish more than the autonomy of a woman over her body and life, they are in tacit complicity with the rapists. Therefore, it is important that women's groups, like Stree Sangarsh in Delhi, attack the notion that rape is a matter of 'dishonouring women', of 'humiliating' women. This group states: 'For us rape is an act of hatred and contempt – it is a denial of ourselves as women, as human beings – it is the ultimate assertion of male power'.[11]

If men were rapists by nature, then we should not witness an increase of rape cases in India and in the rest of the world. The most urgent issue for men and women today is to understand the reasons for this increase in sexual violence. What are the factors that contribute to it? As the man-the-hunter concept offers no explanation for this increase, there must be reasons which do not lie in the male nature, in his genetic infrastructure, but are social, economic and historical – as they have always been.

What we can witness today is a general brutalization of life, a merciless struggle of the strong against the weak, the rich against the poor, men against women. This, of course, is the manifestation of the contradictions of a society, and a concept of man based on the man-the-hunter model and a predatory and dominance relationship between man and nature, a concept that emerged, as we saw, with capitalism. But why do these contradictions manifest themselves more now than earlier? Sexual violence has been part and parcel of the patriarchal man-woman relationship. But why are dowry-deaths increasing, why are rapes increasing? Why are the so-called advanced sections of society – the urban middle class – affected by these contradictions?

What seems to be happening is the following: the traditional controls and checks of repressive patriarchal morality are breaking down in India and other Third World countries, but not through liberalization of sexual morality but by the peculiar way in which capitalism penetrates these societies. The breakdown of the traditional morality is faster in the classes which have made a lot of money in recent years. The men of these classes 'liberate' themselves of many checks and obligations they formerly had *vis-à-vis* women of the lower classes and of their own class. They imitate the Big White Men in the West who are their model of a modern man. That is why they adopt Western dress, go abroad for education, accept Western science; they import blue films, but they do not want 'their' women to be emancipated. Capitalism gives them the means to move up and share in the new international (male) culture, but they want their women to remain the repositories of what they consider to be their 'traditional' culture. The women are supposed to follow the 'traditional' ideals of womanhood.

This contradiction between an increasingly international male culture of the educated middle class of men in underdeveloped countries, and the jealousy with which they preserve the so-called traditional culture of their women as the main symbol of their national identity is leading to an increased polarization between men and women in these countries. The most well-known example is Iran and Muslim fundamentalism in this respect. The Iranian women are made to wear the veil, but the men do not go back to their traditional dress.

This dimension of the relationship of men of colonized countries to men of colonizing countries, I would like to call the BIG MEN-little men syndrome. The 'little men' imitate the BIG MEN. Those who have enough money can buy all those things the BIG MEN have, including women. Those who do not have enough money still have the same dreams.

It is on this contradiction that the Indian film industry thrives. The men are depicted as modern, fashionable, Westernized heroes, the women represent traditional India. And there always has to be rape in these films, but kissing is not allowed by the censors.

The maintenance of this contradiction is not only a moral issue, but is closely related to the specific type of capitalist development in India. Films and sex are growth industries in India. The surplus generated through the exploitation of rural labour, for example, in the Green Revolution areas, is not invested productively to give people work and better wages; it is rather exported to the cities and invested in cinemas, the factories of dreams and illusions (Mies, 1982). There is a clear connection between the profit interests of a capitalist class and the propagation of sexual violence and rape in films. The 'little men', who don't have jobs and opportunities and will not go abroad like the film heroes, and the men of the urban rich, are the main audience of these films, and bring the big money to the BIG MEN. To compensate for all their frustrations in real life, the film-makers offer them a rape scene so that they can identify with the aggressor, in a way which does not endanger class domination. As targets for their aggressive tendencies, they are offered women, but not the BIG MEN. However, when we analyse concretely the reports on rape cases in India, we find very little or nothing of a need to satisfy an irresistible sexual urge. If any 'urge' appears in these scenes, it is the desire to humiliate, violate, torture, to show that man is the master. We find that rape is in many cases used as an instrument of one class of men to punish or humiliate another class of men. This is most clearly manifest in many rape cases which are taking place in rural areas. Whenever poor peasants and agricultural labourers try to get their legal rights, for example, minimum wages, or the land that has been promised to them, 'they are taught a lesson', they are 'put in their place'. But this invariably involves raping their women. Why? What is the connection between raping some women and their men's claims to land? This shows clearly the link in the minds of the ruling classes between control over means of production (land), and the workers' control over women. If people demand land, they are punished by raping the women of this class. Rape is thus an instrument to maintain both existing class and existing men-women relations. The struggle which takes place is, in fact, a struggle between BIG MEN and small men; the women are used in this struggle as objects to prove the *manhood* of the BIG MEN, their power. This power does not only consist in money or control over more property, it is also power stemming from control over arms and the use of direct violence. This becomes particularly clear in the case of police or army rape. The power of the police exists neither in money nor property, but the police have arms. And control over arms gives them a chance to imitate the BIG MEN. Of course, in recent years the police in India have been so often set against the people, against the weak and for the protection of the economically strong, that they simply take what they can get by virtue of their arms. I do not think that one can say that they rape because they want sexual satisfaction. Rape and sexual torture have so often been used by police that, most probably, sadistic motives are stronger than the need to satisfy their sexual desires. The police rapes are perhaps the clearest manifestation of the outcome of a basically repressive patriarchal system. Those who are supposed to keep bourgeois law and order are *de facto* beyond any law because they control arms. To call for more police, even if they are female, to check the increase in rape is, therefore, self-defeating. Police rapes also show the interconnection between the economic motive of 'getting rich quickly' by using direct violence and black-mail, and violence against women.

Conclusion

The discussion of violence against women has focussed mainly on the situation in India, with which I am more familiar. But it would not be difficult to find other examples of direct and structural violence as an integral part of sex and class relations, as well as of the international division of labour. The Western feminist movement has, since its inception, highlighted this aspect in the 'advanced' capitalist countries. The discussion on clitoridectomy and its modernization in Africa has revealed another dimension of violence against women (Hosken, 1980; Dualeh Abdalla, 1982). The almanac 'Women in Russia', produced as a *samisdat* by a group of feminists in the Soviet Union, gives evidence of the brutalization of the man-woman relationship also in this fatherland of the socialist revolution. And the reports which have recently appeared from China about female foeticide and anti-women tendencies in the wake of the population control policies of the state are evidence of the fact that 'modernization' policies go along with neo-patriarchal tendencies, even in a socialist country.

Violence against women, therefore, seems the main common denominator that epitomizes women's exploitation and oppression, irrespective of class, nation, caste, race, capitalist or socialist systems, Third World or First World.

If this is so, what theoretical and practical conclusions are we to draw from this recognition? After the above discussion, we are now in a better position to answer the question whether violence and coercion are *necessarily* part of all production relations women are involved in, or whether they are peripheral to them.

From our discussion, it should be clear that violence against women can neither be adequately explained by narrow economistic arguments, basically inherent in capitalist supply and demand calculations, nor by biologistic arguments about an inherently sadistic male 'nature'.

All our examples give evidence of the fact that violence against women is a historically produced phenomenon that is closely related to exploitative men-women, class and international relations. All these relations are today more or less integrated into systems of accumulation. These systems of accumulation are either capitalist or market-oriented, or they are centrally planned or socialist. Irrespective of their ideological differences, the accumulation of capital in both systems is based on the expropriation of subsistence producers from their means of production. In the centres of the capitalist market economies, the expropriated *men* were turned into the new class of 'free' wage-earners, who own nothing but their labour power. But as *owners* of their labour power, they formally belong to the category of bourgeois 'free' citizens, who are defined as those who *own property*, and who can thus enter into contractual relationships with each other on the basis of the principle of exchange of value equivalents. Therefore, the proletarian *men* could be seen as historical subjects, as free persons, also by the theoreticians of a socialist transformation.

The women, however, have never been defined as free historical subjects in a bourgeois sense. Neither the women of the class of owners of means of production, nor the women of the class of proletarians were owners of their own person. They themselves, their whole person, their labour, their emotionality, their children, their body, their sexuality were not their own but belonged to their husband. They *were* property; therefore, following the formal logic of capitalism, they could not be owners of property. If they are formally not included into the category of property-owners – which the male proletarians are, in the sense that they are owners of their labour power, of their bodies – they also cannot become 'free' citizens, or historical subjects. This means that the civil liberties of the bourgeois revolution are not meant for them. This, I think, is the deeper reason why voting rights were given so late to women and why rape in marriage is not considered as a crime.

If women, according to the bourgeois logic, cannot be free subjects because they *are* property and not owners of property, objects themselves, then it is also not possible to enter into a contract with them, as it is possible with the 'free' proletarian who is, at least formally, owner of his labour power which he can sell to whomever he wants. The labour contract between capitalist and proletarian is based on the assumption that two free subjects enter into a relationship of an exchange of equivalents. Such a contract is not possible with women. If one wants to extract anything in terms of labour or services from them, it is necessary to apply violence and coercion because, although women are not defined as free subjects, they nevertheless have their own will which has to be subordinated by force under the will of the 'free' subjects of civilized society, the men, as well as under the law of capital accumulation.

This violent subordination of women under men and the process of capital accumulation was first acted out on a mass scale during the witch hunt in Europe. But it has ever since constituted the infrastructure upon which so-called capitalist production relations could be established, namely the contractual relationship between owners of labour power and owners of means of production. Without this infrastructure of non-free, coerced female or colonial labour in the broadest sense, the non-coerced, contractual labour relations of the free proletarians would not be possible. Women and colonial peoples were defined as property, as nature, not as free subjects, who could enter a contract. Both had to be subordinated by force and direct violence.

Economically this violence is always necessary when people still have some access to means of production. For example, peasants do not voluntarily begin to produce commodities for an external market. They first have to be forced to produce things which they do not consume themselves. Or they are evicted by force from their fields, or tribes are driven by force from their territory and re-settled in strategic villages.

Women's first and last 'means of production' is their own body. The worldwide increase in violence against women is basically concentrated on this 'territory', over which the BIG MEN have not yet been able to establish their firm and lasting dominance. This dominance is not only based on narrowly-defined economic considerations, although these play an important role, but the economic motives are intrinsically interwoven with political ones, with questions of power and control. Without violence and coercion, neither the modern men nor the modern states would be able to follow their model of progress and development which is based on dominance over nature.

Within the capitalist market economies, violence against women can, therefore, be explained by the necessity for 'ongoing primitive accumulation' which, according to André Gunder Frank, constitutes the precondition for the so-called 'capitalist' accumulation process. In a Third World country like India, the people who have become 'free' subjects in the sense described above is rather small. The fact that civil rights are enshrined in the Indian Constitution does not affect the *de facto* production relations which are, to a large extent, based on violence and coercion. We have seen that violence against women as an intrinsic element of the 'ongoing primitive accumulation of capital' constitutes the fastest and most 'productive' method if a man wants to join the brotherhood of the 'free' subjects of owners of private property.

Violence against women and extracting women's labour through coercive labour relations are, therefore, part and parcel of capitalism. They are necessary for the capitalist accumulation process and not peripheral to it. In other words, capitalism has to use, to strengthen, or even to invent, patriarchal men-women relations if it wants to maintain its accumulation model. If all women in the world had become 'free' wage-earners, 'free' subjects, the extraction of surplus would, to say the least, be severely hampered. This is what women as housewives, workers, peasants, prostitutes, from Third World and First World countries, have in common.

Notes

1. For a first account of the new women's movement in India, see Gail Omvedt, *We Will Smash This Prison*, Zed Press, London, 1980. See also K. Lalitha, 'Origin and Growth of POW, First ever Militant Women's Movement in Andhra Pradesh', in *HOW*, vol. 2, no. 4, 1979. Since 1979, the feminist magazine *Manushi* has been covering the main events in the new Indian women's movement.

2. In India, the ratio of female to male population has been declining since 1911. The steepest decline was, however, registered between 1961 and 1971, when for 1,000 men only 930 women were counted, whereas in 1921 the ratio was still 1,000 men to 955 women (cf. Mies, 'Capitalist Development and Subsistence Reproduction: Rural Women in India', in *Bulletin of Concerned Asian Scholars*, vol. 12, no. 1, 1980).

3. Personal communication to me in August 1984.

4. A documentation and analysis of the Anti-Rape Campaign in Bombay was carried out by Chhaya Datar in 1981. To my knowledge, this is the only attempt so far to document the development of this important feminist campaign in India. The following leaflet was published by the Forum Against Rape on 23 February 1980:

Isn't it time we looked rape in the face?

Not rape, the Supreme Court said, it was only intercourse. Mathura, a 14 to 16 year old farm labourer in a village in Maharashtra, 'willingly submitted' to sexual intercourse with Ganpat, a policeman she had never seen before. While another constable, Tukaram, watched – too drunk to stop his friend, but not too drunk also to molest her.

This was on March 26, 1972. In the middle of the night. Near a police station latrine. Where the door was bolted and the lights put out. The 'stiff-resistance' Mathura put up was false, the Supreme Court declared, a 'tissue of lies'. 'The alleged intercourse was a peaceful affair.' 'Her cries of alarm are of course a concoction on her part', and she said she'd been raped to prove she was virtuous. The Supreme Court ruled that there was 'no reasonable evidence of guilt on the part of the policemen'. The semen on Ganpat's pyjamas and on Mathura's body and clothes proved nothing. Since the girl was not a virgin, ran the implication, she could have slept with someone else between her alleged rape and the medical examination the following morning. Needless to say, he could have done the same.

And so the Supreme Court dispensed justice as it saw fit – reversing the Bombay High Court judgement which sentenced Ganpat to five years and Tukaram to one year. The two policemen went scot free. Once again, like in most rape cases, the prosecutor had become the defendant, the accusor the accused. And the case forgotten, consigned to the musty pages of a law journal.

One year later. September '79. Four lawyers – Upendra Baxi, Lotika Sarkar, Raghunath Kelkar and Vasudha Dhagamwar – came across the judgement and were utterly astounded by the 'cold blooded legalism' of the verdict. They wrote an open letter to the Chief Justice of India asking for a reopening of the case and condemning the judgement which 'snuffs out all aspirations for the protection of human rights of millions of Mathuras'.

What does this signify? Mathura's case is only one such instance. To single it out would be to question all rape case judgements, to question the rape law, to begin to wonder why, with unfailing frequency, the convictions are so few, to realise that under the Indian Penal Code it is virtually impossible to prove rape. It would draw too much attention to something which for too long we have pretended doesn't really exist. Isn't it time we looked rape in the face?

Isn't it time we accepted that it does occur, all the time, everywhere? Accepted that all women are potential victims – be they young or old, attractive or plain, 'nice' or 'not nice', rich or poor? Only, if you're not Mathura, an illiterate farm labourer, the chances are less. The Mathuras of the country are doubly oppressed, they are women and they belong to an already oppressed section in a nation where justice is the privilege of a few. And then women don't face the terror of rape as individuals – but as a category. Mass rape, often used as a weapon to demonstrate power. You don't have to look far for examples. Have you forgotten what happened to the wives of railway workers during the '74 railway strike? To the wives of mine workers at Baila Dilla in 1977? To Dalit women at Chandigarh, Bhojpur and Agra? Or Muslim women at Jamshedpur, Aligarh and in almost all communal riots? To Mizo and Nepali women at the hands of the Indian army?

But you don't have to be raped to realise what you're up against. Don't you know it already? Doesn't every woman know it? Watching a film, where the graphic rape scene and the encouraging hoots and whistles from the audience turns your stomach. Walking down the road, travelling in a bus or a train, trying to ignore remarks, taunts, someone's hand feeling you up, brushing against you. Did you ask for it? Invite it?

And if tomorrow you're raped, what will you do? And if you're a man and your sister or daughter or mother is raped, what will *you* do? After your carefully cherished myths disintegrate around you and it dawns on you that rape occurs without women 'asking for it'. Will you be one of the 800 cases reported in Bombay in one year and have the courage to say 'I was raped'? Or will you be one of the 8,000 others, for to every reported rape there are 10–12 unreported ones.

Yes, there is safety in number. And strength. So let's change the balance. Join us. Let's look rape in the face and demand:
1) **An immediate reopening of the case**
2) **Amendment of the rape law.**
Things can change, once we get down to it.

★ At Bhatinda, Punjab, The Association of Democratic Rights, Punjab, did just that. When Lakshmi Devi, a lame beggar was raped repeatedly by three-four policemen, and left bleeding profusely in a deserted area of the town, some workers of this organisation admitted her to hospital and doggedly pursued the case until the culprits were arrested.

★ In Maharashtra, when an adivasi woman was raped by a landlord, the women of the village got together, held a trial presided over by the people. The culprit was paraded through the village and thus publicly humiliated.

★ At Hyderabad, a spontaneous popular outburst followed the raping of Rameeza Bee.

★ At Dombivli, Bombay, several weeks ago, when news of a rape incident spread, more than 500 people gathered around the house of the rapist and demanded that he be punished.

We appeal to all trade unions, women's organisations, democratic rights organisations, student organisations, lawyers, teachers, journalists, dalit groups and others to come and join us in a

PUBLIC MEETING ON FEBRUARY 23, 1980, AT 3 P.M., AT CAMA HALL (OPPOSITE LION GATE), FORT

INTERNATIONAL WOMEN'S DAY DEMONSTRATION ON MARCH 7, 1980, AT 3 P.M., FROM AZAD MAIDAN TO HUTATMA CHOWK.

FORUM AGAINST RAPE

Ms Meera, c/o Flat No. 3, Carol Mansion, Sitladevi Temple Road, Mahim, Bombay 400 016.

Published by Ms Meera, Forum Against Rape, c/o Flat No. 3, Carol Mansion, Sitladevi Temple Road, Mahim, Bombay 400 016 and printed by her at New Age Printing Press, 85 Sayani Road, Prabhadevi, Bombay 400 025.

5. In a newspaper report on the shrinking female population in India since 1950, Indian demographers admit 'that they have no explanation' for this trend. As one of them said, neglect of women and the bad status of women could not fully explain the situation:

'If that were the only factor, then the improvement in the status of women in recent years would have led to a corresponding improvement in the woman-man ratio, but the situation is just the opposite. While the status of women has improved considerably in recent years, their number has also at the same time declined. This shows that there is more to the problem than meets the eye. We are really puzzled' ('Shrinking Population of Women', in *The Statesman*, 14 August 1980).

6. According to a personal communication from a Yugoslav friend, wife-beating is quite prevalent in Yugoslavia. But there is no women's movement which could take up this issue. Wife-beating is considered to be part of the national culture, according to this friend.

For information on the anti-prostitute drive in Zimbabwe, and the women's reaction to it, see *Women of Zimbabwe Speak Out: Report of the Women's Action Group*, Workshop Harare, May 1984.

7. The concepts 'Great' and 'Little' traditions were first applied to India by McKim Mariott. The Great Tradition is more or less identical with the Brahmanical-sanscritic culture. It is characterized by the recognition of the sanctity of the vedas, by vegetarianism, Brahmanical ritual, belief in Brahmanical theological concepts, belief in the caste system and the subordination of women under patriarchal institutions and norms (cf. McKim Mariott: 'Little Communities in an Indigenous Civilization', in *Village India, Studies in the Little Community*, McKim Mariott (ed.), *The American Anthropologist*, vol. 57(3) 1955: 181).

8. The concept 'sanscritization' was developed by M. N. Srinivas. It describes the process by which low castes, who have become economically prosperous, try to imitate the values, norms, institutions of the sanscritic (Brahmanical) castes, and eventually claim a higher caste status. Today these sanscritization processes go along with Westernization processes (M. N. Srinivas: 'A Note on Sanscritization and Westernization', *The Far Eastern Quarterly*, vol. XV, November 1955 – August 1956: 492–536).

9. Officers of the Indian Administrative Service, together with doctors, engineers, and executives belong to the most prestigious dowry-commanders, as the following matrimonial advertisement illustrates:

Marriage proposals invited
From well employed, highly educated, smart gentlemen or their parents for rich, beautiful, highly educated, modest Nair girl, 21, talented in Arts, rank holder, award winner, daughter of Senior Govt. Officer, IAS Officers, Bank Officers, Engineers, Post-Graduate Doctors, Executive preferred.
BOX No. 2136-CN, c/o INDIAN EXPRESS, COCHIN-682001.

10. The Pativrata – the wife who worships her husband and makes sacrifices to him as her first god – is the ideal of womanhood in the classical Hindu scriptures (see Mies, 1980).

11. The following is the leaflet brought out by the feminist group Stree Sangarsh in Delhi on 8 March 1980:

'Were there more rapes during the Janata regime or Cong-I?'
That is Not the Question!

The Baghpat incident has triggered off the strange phenomenon of politicians of various hues falling over themselves to 'protect the honour of our women'. Parliament echoes with their strident calls to flog, stone, and hang rapists. The same Charan Singh under whose administration circulars were issued banning women IAS officers from serving in his state, is today beating his chest about atrocities against women. The Janata Party which hushed up incidents of mass rape in the Santhal Parganas today condemns the 'humiliation' of women. Raj Narian has been heard saying that a 'wave of rapes' has swept the country since Mrs Gandhi came to power, and is demanding her resignation.

Has he forgotten Narianpura? And Basti?

For the Congress-I of course all this talk about rape has blown the issue out of proportion – their history does not record Telengana, Bailadilla, the 1974 railway strike rapes . . . the Goonda incident . . .

Rape Is Not Only a Matter of Honour

The vocabulary of Indian politicians has always been limited. From the BJP to the Cong-I, key terms in their sound and fury are 'honour and humiliation'. They say the 'dishonouring of women' is the 'dishonour of our country' – they say the 'honour of our women is the honour of our country'. Yet it is in *this* country that women are forced into prostitution, sold as slave labour, killed for dowry and raped by their husbands, brothers-in-law and fathers-in-law. Recently a man committed suicide because his wife had been raped. Two months ago a woman killed herself instead of telling her husband she had been raped. Families have thrown out their sisters, daughters, and daughters-in-law for having been raped. How can your honour be taken away when you yourself have committed no crime? It is in *this* country that the State itself allows mass rape by its Police, CRPF, and BSF. If these are honourable actions, then we spit on honour.

For us rape is an act of hatred and contempt – it is a denial of ourselves as women, as human beings – it is the ultimate assertion of male power.

Rape Is Not a Law and Order Problem

The Opposition says that the law and order situation has worsened under the Cong-I. The Cong-I says that 'mischievous elements' are using rape to 'demoralise the police'. Both agree that it is a party political problem. Both imply that they can solve the problem of police rape.

Yet for women in Bailadilla and the Santhal Parganas, for Rameeza Bee, Mathura and Maya Tyagi it is not a question of who is in power – Congress-I or Janata. For them the sight of a policeman implies fear, intimidation and sexual violence. The authority that a man acquires when he puts on a police/CRPF/BSF uniform and picks up his lathi/gun itself allows him to beat, to torture and to rape. It is an authority given by the State, and in most cases torture, arson and rape are the weapons of his authority. It is the defender of law and order who commits rape in working class houses and peasant villages, law and order means police atrocities.

For decades our history has endlessly repeated this truth – we cannot fight it by pretending, as the politicians do, that this is false. If today we allow them to turn our truth into their lie we will have lost what few gains we fought for on March 8th.

STREE SANGARSH

New Age Printing Press, Rani Jhansi Road, New Delhi-55

6. National Liberation and Women's Liberation

When one points out the necessary interrelation between capitalist development and women's exploitation and oppression, analysed in the preceding chapters, one is often asked: But what about socialism? Depending on the political orientation of the questioner, socialism is either seen as *the* solution to the 'women's question'; or 'actually existing' socialist countries are also criticized because women there also seem to be far from being liberated from patriarchal men-women relations.

For many Third World women, the issue of women's liberation was and is closely connected with the issue of national liberation from colonial and/or neo-colonial dependency, and with the perspective of building up a socialist society. And even many feminists in the West looked at the combination of an anti-imperialist struggle with an anti-patriarchalist struggle with great hope, at least in the early 1970s. As had happened with the students' movement, also large sections of the feminist movement in the West expected the real feminist break-through to come from the women's movements in Third World countries which were fighting an anti-imperialist liberation struggle.

I remember a poster hanging over my desk during the Vietnam war. On a red background there were three women with guns in their hands. Under them was written: Cambodia, Laos, Vietnam, Victoire! The women symbolized the national liberation struggles of these peoples. We all know such posters; they are being sold at solidarity meetings for national liberation movements in Asia, Africa and Latin America. The woman with the gun in one hand and a baby on her back is the standard image by which the unity between national liberation and women's liberation is symbolized. Many of us have been inspired for many years by this image without questioning why national liberation movements always choose women to symbolize a free nation, or whether there was indeed this supposedly logical connection between national liberation and women's liberation.

Today such posters rather evoke in me a feeling of sadness. If we ask what has happened to women's liberation after victory in a national liberation war, we are today faced with growing evidence of the persistence – or even a renewed introduc-tion – of sexist and patriarchal attitudes and institutions in such countries (Row-botham, 1974; Weinbaum, 1976; Urdang, 1979; Reddock, 1982). Recent reports about female infanticide and foeticide in China and about the campaign launched by the Zimbabwean government against prostitutes have destroyed the illusion that there would be a direct path from national liberation to women's liberation.

Faced by these developments, some Western feminists who drew inspiration from women's participation in liberation struggles in Asia, Latin America or Africa are now turning away from asking why women's liberation did not follow national liberation. They give up their former internationalist orientation with the arguments that we Western feminists have no right to criticize these countries, that we do not know enough about what is happening there, that culturally and historically these societies are so different from Western societies that our criticism would amount to yet another manifestation of paternalism or euro-centric cultural imperialism. As many are afraid of being accused of 'feminist racism' by Third World men and women, they rather avoid the issue altogether and concentrate on what is happening in their own society. Others, who are still active in solidarity groups and believe in some kind of socialist internationalism, often argue that women in socialist countries have made great steps towards their liberation, that emancipation is not achieved at a stroke, that these societies are in a phase of transition from capitalism/imperialism to socialism and communism, and that they are in any case better equipped to bring about full liberation for women than capitalist societies.

I do not think that either of the two positions is very helpful for furthering our understanding of what is happening in the world, and for furthering women's liberation. Moreover, events in the USA and Europe force Western feminists to develop a somewhat clearer position regarding the question of the relationship between national liberation and women's liberation because, at present, women are again being reminded in many Western countries of their 'national duties' to bring forth children for 'race and nation' (Women and Fascism Study Group, 1982), and/or to be ready to join the military forces for the defence of the fatherland, as is happening in West Germany today. Also, these policies are based on the assumption that women's interests are identical with national interests. And there are even some feminists who think that women's participation in military service could further equality between men and women.[1]

The majority of European feminists, however, do not believe in this equality brought about by the 'brotherhood in arms'. Many have joined the peace movement in the years 1982 and 1983, because they felt that the threat of an atomic holocaust, brought about by the stationing of SS 20 and Cruise missiles and Pershing II, by the two superpowers was the immediate cause to fight against. But also in the peace movement feminists could not escape the issue of national liberation and women's liberation. Many of them were against the use of arms altogether, sometimes on the basis of a more or less implicit assumption that women, because of their capacity to give life, could not also be on the side of those who destroy life. This has also basically been the position of the old left women's peace movement and its follow-up organizations.[2]

But these women face a dilemma when it comes to the question of women's participation in national liberation struggles. Many acknowledge the necessity of an anti-imperialist struggle and sometimes also support national liberation movements. But they do not know how to harmonize their implicit or explicit understanding of a basically pacifist or non-violent female 'nature' with the reality that all national liberation movements are also drawing women into the actual fight with arms. If the image of the woman with the baby and the gun has no positive meaning for them in their own situation, how can they then support it in the case of women in national liberation struggles? Or is it sufficient to say that there is a basic difference between a war a nation or a people fights for its liberation from imperialist and colonial dependency, and an inter-imperialist war?

Third World women, involved in a liberation struggle or in nation-building after such a struggle, may find these moral dilemmas of Western feminists a luxury they may have no time to indulge in. But even they cannot escape the question eventually, if they do not deliberately close their eyes to reality. The moment will come when they have to ask, like the woman in Zimbabwe who was picked up by the police in the anti-prostitution drive last year, whether this was the state or the society her brothers died for (*Sunday Mail*, Harare, 27 November 1983).[3]

Not only for feminists from imperialist countries, but also for feminists from colonies and ex-colonies the relationship between national liberation and women's liberation is far from clear. A clarification of this question, however, is more than ever necessary today, since not only women from overdeveloped and under-developed market economies are linked to each other and integrated into the world market by the international division of labour, but also women from centrally planned socialist economies. A discussion of the relationship between national liberation and women's liberation will, therefore, have to take cognisance of the existing international division of labour and its relation to a particular sexual division of labour.

The questions to be clarified are not only whether women, after a national liberation struggle, have more access to political power than before, but also whether the socialist goal of a classless society was achieved and an abolition of an exploitative and oppressive sexual division of labour took place. An answer to these questions will depend, in the last analysis, on the concept of society and the model of development that is pursued during and after the liberation struggle. In this, the concept of the *nation-state* plays an important role, because the post-liberation nation-states are the political subjects which determine the further destiny of people, also of women.

Before we come to this discussion, it may be useful to have a brief look at some of the post-liberation socialist states and ask what happened to women's liberation after the victory was won. This analysis cannot attempt to be comprehensive and do justice to the complex historical reality that emerged during and after the liberation wars and/or the revolution in these societies. I shall concentrate on some societies which followed a socialist perspective, and combined the trans-formation of production relations from private property to collective or state property with a claim to bring about women's emancipation from 'feudal', or patriarchal male dominance. The most prominent of these are the Soviet Union, which provided the initial model of a socialist society, and China and Vietnam. Developments in other socialist countries which underwent a national liberation struggle, like Yugoslavia, Cuba, Mozambique, Angola, Guinea Bissau, Algeria, etc., would show variations from patterns observed in the three cases mentioned above, but there will also be fundamental similarities regarding the strategy of women's liberation because in all these states, the strategy followed for women's liberation was/is based on the theoretical foundations worked out by Marx and Engels.

The theoretical foundations for the assumed interrelation between women's liberation and national liberation struggles – and the ensuing building up of socialist production relations were laid down by Marx, and, more particularly, Engels, who emphasized the necessity for women's 're-entry' into 'socially productive labour' as a precondition for their liberation from patriarchal bondage. Following the bourgeois political economy, which defines housework as non-productive and private (see chapter 2), and the sphere of commodity production and surplus generation as productive and public, Engels saw a direct correlation between women's participation in wage-labour and an improvement of their economic, as well as their human and political, status. As Marx and Engels saw the 'free' wage-labourer as the subject of history, women could become historical subjects only by entering the wage-labour force. August Bebel, Clara Zetkin, and later on Lenin, elaborated this theory of women's emancipation a bit further, but did not add any substantially new elements to it. Where the leaders of revolutionary national liberation struggles adopted scientific socialism, developed by Marx, Engels and Lenin, as their theoretical and strategic framework, they also included their ideas on women's liberation into their revolutionary project.

The main strategic points derived from this general theory can be summarized in the following manner:

– The 'woman question is part of the social question' (that is, the question of production relations, property and class relations) and will be solved in the course of the overthrow of capitalism.

– Women have, therefore, to enter social production (that is, waged labour outside the household) in order to gain a material base for their economic independence and emancipation.

– As capitalism has eliminated the differences between men and women, because all are made propertyless wage-workers (Zetkin), there is no longer a material base for women's oppression among proletarians, and hence no need for a special women's movement in the working class.

– Working-class women should, therefore, participate in the general struggle against the class enemy, together with their male class companions, and thus create the precondition for their emancipation.

– Women as women may be oppressed or subordinated, but they are not exploited. If they are wage-workers, they are exploited in the same way as male workers are exploited. This exploitation they can fight, together with the men, in a struggle for a change of production relations (class struggle).

– The struggle against their specific oppression as women has to take place on an ideological plane (through legal action, education, propaganda, exhortation and persuasion), not at the level of basic production relations, where the problem of exploitation is tackled.

– This struggle is, in any case, secondary to the class struggle, which is primary. Therefore, women should not form separate and autonomous organizations. Their organizations should be under the direction of the (revolutionary) party. Separate women's organizations would be divisive for the unity of the oppressed class. So also would be too much emphasis on particular women's grievances.

– After a revolutionary change of basic production relations and women's entry into social production or wage-labour, there must also be a collectivization (social-ization) of private domestic labour and child-care. This will enable women to participate not only in wage-labour, but also in political activity.

– On the level of man-woman relations or the family, efforts have to be made to achieve true equality or democracy between man and woman. This is possible through ideological struggle since the family has lost its economic meaning.

In the following, I shall give a brief overview of some of the main countries which have gone through a revolution or national liberation struggle, and have followed the above principles of women's liberation, combined with a strategy of socialist development. The leading questions will be whether women, who in most cases participated in large numbers in the actual liberation wars, have been able to achieve liberation from patriarchal relations as well.

Elisabeth Croll (1979) has analysed the experiences of rural women in 'produc-tion and reproduction' in four countries which have undergone a socialist trans-formation of production relations, some of which after a revolutionary struggle, namely the Soviet Union, China, Cuba and Tanzania. As her findings are very relevant to our question, I shall briefly summarize them.

All four countries have undertaken programmes of collectivization in the agricultural sector in order to change the production relations from privately-held property in land to socialized forms of ownership: state farms, communes, co-operatives. It was expected that this collectivization would liberate rural women from the patriarchal control of the male head of household, since they could become individual members and wage-earners in these collectives. '. . . their labour should become visible, individually remunerated and a source of economic independence' (Croll, 1979: 2). But, apart from these collectivized units, all four have maintained, or even re-established, as is happening in China today, privately-owned plots.

In all four countries great efforts were made to mobilize women to 'enter social production', that is, to participate in collective agricultural production because, following the general Marxist theory on women, they were seen as housewives and hence involved in private production.

In Russia and Tanzania, however, women had always participated in large numbers in agricultural production. In Tanzania, they even constitute the main agricultural labour force. In China their participation differed between the north and the rice-producing south. Whereas women in the north hardly did any field work, women in the south did. In Cuba women were drawn in large numbers into agricultural wage labour only in the 1970s.

Women in the 'Dual Economy'

In all four countries today women not only participate in large numbers in the collectivized sector of agriculture, but they are also the main labour force in the private sector which still remained, or was re-created. Let us consider the examples of the Soviet Union, China and Vietnam for illustration.

The Soviet Union

Due to its policy of rapid industrial growth which drew many men from agriculture to the urban industrial centres, peasant women in the Soviet Union had to shoulder a large proportion of agricultural production. They make up 56.7 per cent of the labour force on collective farms, 41.0 per cent on state farms, 65.2 per cent on individual peasant farms and 90.7 per cent on private subsidiary farms (Dodge, 1966, 1967, 1971, quoted in Croll, 1979: 15–16). Yet, the number of days per year which women have to work on collective farms is lower than that of men. This is mainly due to their involvement in the private subsidiary sector which provides between 75–90 per cent of the subsistence food for the rural households. Also, mainly older women work on these private plots. Thus, women's labour in agriculture in the Soviet Union is divided up between an informal sector of privately-owned plots with subsistence production, and a formal sector of state-owned collectivized farms. They constitute by far the bulk of the subsistence producers and still make up about 50 per cent of the labour force on the state farms. On top of this double workload they are responsible for all the household work. Men do not generally share housework in the Soviet Union and the socialization of housework in the form of crêches, kindergartens, public dining rooms etc., has not been adequately developed. Apart from a short period of radical reforms and experiments immediately following the 1917 revolution, the provision of public services was not of primary concern to the government. Crêche and nursery facilities remained largely concentrated in the cities, where 37 per cent of the pre-school children go to a crêche or nursery. Also, the few public canteens which still remain are in the cities.

On the state farms women usually perform the unskilled, non-specialized tasks which involve physical labour and not machines. They have less education and training than the men, and thus their proportion in the managerial and supervisory jobs is low. They are rarely heads of farms, brigades, or dairy departments, or farm managers.

Due to their heavy workload, and the unchanged sexual division of labour in the household, women's political participation in the Soviet Union is generally low, particularly in rural areas. As political gatherings take place outside working hours, that is, mainly in the evening, women who have to do the shopping, cooking, and housekeeping after their work on farms or in factories are not able to attend such meetings. All reports admit that, due to the burden of household responsibilities, women cannot compete with men over hours and commitment in political activities. The consequence is that they are even more under-represented among political decision-making bodies (Croll, 1979: 17–18).

The high rate of employment of women in the socialized and so-called subsidary sectors, the limited availability of public services and communal facilities, the lack of modern household gadgets and appliances, and the refusal of men to share housework mean that women have much less leisure time than men and are constantly overburdened.

The resentment of Russian women at this situation, particularly at the persistent and reinforced patriarchal and sexist attitudes of men, who fill their leisure time with drinking and TV-watching without bothering in the least how the housework is done, also found vivid and bitter expression in the almanac *Women in Russia*, brought out as a *samisdat* by a group of Russian feminists in 1980.[4] This is a phenomenon which could be observed in all four societies: '. . . a new division of labour seems to have been established: not between skilled and unskilled or lighter or heavier jobs within agriculture, as before, but between agricultural and non-agricultural jobs' (Croll, 1979: 5). Typically, the non-agricultural jobs are mainly in the hands of men, a situation which we already know from both over- and underdeveloped market economies.

Women in the Soviet Union tried to lower their double or triple burden of work by refusing to bear more children. As the state treated them mainly as workers, without including housework and childrearing in the category of productive labour, without providing sufficient collective services because these appeared too costly, without any change in the sexual division of labour, the women answered with a kind of 'birth-strike'. This led to a downward trend in the birthrate which caused great concern to government circles who feared the negative effects of this trend on the economy as well as on political and military power. As is happening in capitalist industrialized countries (for example, West Germany), the government has offered financial incentives to married – and for a time also to unmarried – women to bear more children: 'Motherhood has been extolled as a patriotic duty and those who had many children were honoured accordingly' (Croll, 1979: 19).

Yet, as nothing else had changed in the patriarchal set-up, in the definition of productive and non-productive work, women resisted complying with the dual demands of the government to enter 'productive labour' and to bear many children. As one woman doctor observed, all theories about improving the status of women were made by men who had no interest in that neglected area, re-production, which filled women's lives (Croll, 1979: 20).

China

The People's Republic of China also followed the socialist principles of women's emancipation spelt out above. But due to the prolonged national liberation struggle, in which women participated to a large extent, combined with a revolutionary transformation and Mao Tse Tung's priority to rural development instead of to rapid industrialization, the changes that took place in women's life appeared to be more dramatic than those in the Soviet Union. Moreover, Mao Tse Tung had specifically included the patriarchal power of men over women into one of the four powers which held the Chinese people down and which had to be toppled by revolution. The heroic stories of women who participated in the revolutionary struggle, both as combatants and in maintaining the economy are well known. One of the structural changes necessitated by the liberation war was the taking over of field-work by women which, according to a survey of 1937, had been traditionally a men's domain in China.

After the revolution, a number of legal changes were introduced which tried to combine the abolition of patriarchal husband-power with the introduction of women into 'social production'. Thus, the new Marriage Code of 1950 was combined with the Law on Land Reform. The Chinese leadership took the decision to distribute land not to families, which would have meant to male heads of households, but to those who *de facto* worked on the land. Thus, also women who worked on the land were given land titles. Even when families as a unit were given the land rights, a special clause provided that women had the same rights as men, even the right to sell the land, which was a truly revolutionary measure because it rooted the emancipatory demands in the change of the basic production relations between men and women. Women and men could become owners of land. As land reform was combined with marriage reform which provided for easy divorce for women, the consequence was a spate of applications for divorce, most of them from women. As Delia Davin reported, many rural women immediately grasped the significance of this combined reform, and said that they would ask for a divorce when they would get their land title, then their husbands could not oppress them any longer (Davin, 1976: 46). Meijer estimates the number of divorces that occurred in the first four years after the marriage reform at 800,000 (Meijer, 1971: 120). The conflicts that arose in the countryside due to these changes were such that, after a period in which women were encouraged to grasp their new rights *vis-à-vis* husbands and in-laws, the cadres of the mass organizations were advised to go slow with implementation of the marriage reform and try to solve marital conflicts by persuasion rather than by divorce. In the course of time, the radical marriage reforms of the early revolutionary and post-revolutionary phases were again changed in the direction of more conservative and patriarchal family relations. According to Delia Davin (1976) and Batya Weinbaum (1976), the official policy regarding women in China fluctuated several times after the revolution, following the general economic and political priorities spelt out by the communist leadership. This policy put either more stress on women, as productive workers or as reproductive housewives and consumers.

After the establishment of the People's Republic of China, it was necessary to mobilize all people for the reconstruction of the economy and an increase in production. In the early 1950s, women were encouraged to enter social production both in agriculture and in industry. By their participation in labour outside the home, they increased their income, but they had to neglect their domestic responsibility. This contradiction was partly solved by the mobilization of older women, such as grandmothers, to take care of small children. Where women had no such help, they had to reduce their wage-labour, and thus had to accept lower work-points. In some areas women achieved only half of the workpoints of men (Davin, 1976: 149). Childcare and other domestic services were not yet collectivized to a great extent.

There was a brief period of renewed glorification of housework as the true domain of women in 1955, under the influence of Liu Shaogi, during which women were demanded to do more half-paid or unpaid work in 'dependents' organizations' in the cities in order to make room for men in the expanding socialized sector, particularly industry (Davin, 1976: 66).

This policy was changed again with the Great Leap Forward and the establishment of communes in 1958. The campaign aimed to draw all members of the household into social production. This meant that domestic services also had to be socialized to a certain degree to free women for work in the fields. Nurseries, kindergartens, community dining rooms, grain mills, etc., were set up. According to an estimate in 1959, 4,980,000 nurseries were set up in rural areas and 3,600,000 public dining rooms (Croll, 1979: 25). But much of this collectivization was done along the same sexual division of labour as before: men used to go into the more capital-intensive, collectivized or state-owned sectors of industry and agriculture, whereas women had to build up the so-called risk-sector in collectivized services, in education and health and in small-scale production of basic consumer goods, in street factories and workshops. This sector is characterized by a low level of technological development, low capital outlay, production of subsistence consumer goods and low income. In 1958, 83 per cent of the workers in state-owned production units were male, whereas in the street factories 85 per cent of the workers were female between 1959 and 1960 (Weinbaum, 1976). Thus, the sexual division of labour coincided with a sectoral division of the economy into the well-known structure of a formal and an informal sector where women constituted the bulk of the labour force in the informal sector.

The efforts at collectivization of domestic services, however, did not last long. After 1960, most of the rural childcare facilities were closed down again because of the shortage of trained personnel and because 'private' grandmothers were cheaper. Also, community dining halls proved to be more expensive than private domestic labour performed by women free of cost (Croll, 1979: 25). Since this experiment in the late 1950s there has been no particular effort to socialize housework. During the cultural revolution, and particularly during the anti-Confucius campaign, the patriarchal or – as official parlance went, the 'feudal' – attitudes of men were criticized; they were asked to share in household tasks, but these efforts remained typically on the cultural, that is, the ideological level, and did not touch the social relations of production and reproduction.

Due to their continuing responsibility for 'reproduction' and for the labour intensive, low remunerated, informal sector, women usually achieved fewer workpoints than men. This was also due to the fact that the criteria for the measurement of work were based on physical energy expended. Thus, men's work was supposed to be 'heavy' work and they, therefore, got more workpoints than women, whose work was considered to be light work (Davin, 1976: 145–146).

As in the Soviet Union, the participation of women in political activities, and particularly in decision-making processes, is not proportionate to their participation in the economic process as a whole. In the 1970s, women represented one-third to two-fifths of the members of the Communist Party (Croll, 1979: 23). Their representation in revolutionary committees where the main decisions were made regarding the implementation of government policy was far from satisfactory. Even where the majority of workers are women, the managing committees are often made up of a majority of men. In particular, women's representation in the higher echelons of economic and political power continues to be low, even today. And in spite of a considerable exhortation that women should come forward for leadership in political organizations, their participation in these bodies is in no way representative of their number and their importance for the society. Their participation in the National People's Congresses between 1954–1978 rose initially from 11.9 per cent, to 22.6 per cent in 1975, but then dropped again to 21.1 per cent in 1978 (Croll, 1983: 119).

As Elisabeth Croll remarks, this lack of political participation cannot be attributed only to die-hard feudal attitudes, but has to be explained by the structural necessities of the development model followed in China.

It can be expected that the shift towards modernization, rapid growth and industrialization will aggravate the dilemmas which Chinese women already had to face, namely, the contradiction of being ideologically mobilized to enter social production, but in fact being pushed back into the sphere of the privatized household and the informal sector. This is so because the maintenance or reconstitution of a patriarchal sexual division of labour with women responsible for household and subsistence production still provides the cheapest means not only for the reproduction of labour power, but also for lowering the production costs of marketable consumer commodities. Thus, a policy of rapid modernization will, of necessity, lead to the reconstitution of the housewife model, as we know it from other Third World and First World societies.

In fact, analyses of the effect of the new policies of the Chinese government after Mao on women (Croll, 1983; Andors, 1981), reveal that, as in India and other parts of the underdeveloped world, women in China are no longer defined mainly as producers or workers, but increasingly as 'dependents', consumers and 'breeders'. Whereas in the 1960s and early 1970s, the contradiction between a socialist strategy for women's emancipation and the *de facto* policy of making women, not men, responsible for unpaid and low paid household and subsistence production (gardening, private plots, handicrafts, childcare, health services) was still camouflaged behind a lot of revolutionary rhetoric which emphasized women's contribution to the revolution, this rhetoric seems to have been given up, together with the socialist strategy to liberate women.

From People to Population
I shall limit the discussion to that aspect of the new policy on women which shows more clearly than others the shift towards housewifization in China, namely the new population policy.

Before Mao's death, the 'masses', the 'people', were mainly seen as producers, capable of solving their problems themselves. But the new government is emphasizing the consumptive costs of a growing population. Since 1979, it has launched a campaign for the promotion of one-child families. It has calculated the costs of educating and employing the young generation, the costs of providing basic needs for a billion nation and has shown that, with more than one child in each family, there would be few resources left for accumulation, investment, modernization and an increasing standard of living for urban as well as rural households. It would also be difficult to provide employment for a growing population (Croll, 1983: 91).

The emphasis on people as consumers is part and parcel of the policy of the 'four modernizations' because consumers are not only a cost-factor, but constitute also the necessary market for the consumer goods and gadgets which are considered indicators of a modern standard of living.

The present Chinese government sees the large and growing population as one of the main obstacles in its effort to reach the goal of modernization. Before 1979, family planning was part of general health work and work with women, where the decision to limit the number of children was left to the couple or the women. Now the control of people's generative behaviour has become a direct state affair. The decision of a couple to have or not to have another child has become a question of responsibility for the nation's welfare. This responsibility is mainly put on the shoulders of women. They are the main target group for family planning measures. We have, thus, the peculiar situation that the state in the Soviet Union has declared that it is women's 'patriotic duty' to bear more children, whereas the state in China makes it women's 'patriotic duty' to reduce the number of their children to one child. In both cases, women have had practically no say in the formulation of these policies. It is the state which regulates and controls their childbearing capacity.

In China, the state is using an elaborate system of coercion, of punishments and rewards to get this capacity under control. This system of coercion, first designed by the scientific advisors of the population control establishment in the USA (Mass, 1976), then applied in countries like Singapore and India, means that economic rewards or punishments are used to force couples to lower the number of their children to the number targetted by the government.

The Chinese government has set itself the population growth targets of 1 per cent by the end of 1979, 0.5 per cent by the end of 1985, and zero population growth by the end of the century (Croll, 1983: 89). This means that families cannot have more than one child.

The punitive economic sanctions used against families who do not, on their own, fulfil the patriotic duty of adhering to the one-child norm include an 'excess child levy' as economic compensation to the state for the cost another child means for the community. The total income of such couples is reduced from 5–10 per cent over a period of 10–16 years after birth. Sometimes the levy for a third or fourth child is 15–20 per cent of the couple's income. 'The wages of couples may be directly debited by their units of employment, or in the rural areas a production team may retain an equivalent portion of their distributed income' (Croll, 1983: 89). The mother with more than one child is excluded from free maternity care. The couple has to bear all expenses for medical care and education of the extra child. The child gets no priority in admission to kindergarten, school or medical institutions. In the countryside, the grain ration for the 'surplus' child is either reduced or available at a higher price. In the cities, the families with more than one child do not get additional housing space; in the rural areas they do not get additional land for private plots and the right to collective grain in times of flood and drought. Commune members are punished by losing three to five work-days per month. Parents do not get promotion for four years or may be demoted, or their salaries reduced (Andors, 1981: 52; Croll, 1983: 90). The one-child families, on the other hand, get economic rewards and privileges. They include a cash subsidy for health or welfare paid to the couple monthly or annually until the child is 14 years old. In rural areas the parents are entitled to additional private plots from the commune; in the cities, to extra housing space. The single child is entitled to free education, free health services, and gets priority in admission to nurseries, schools and hospitals. It also gets an adult grain ration. The parents of such a child get an additional subsidy to their old age pension (Croll, 1983: 89).

The state is using the organizational machinery set up in the cities and the countryside in the course of the collectivization programme to implement this population policy. The policy itself has been formulated by family planning committees which work under the control of party committees. There are hardly any women in these decision-making bodies. But the actual implementation of population control measures has to be carried out by local units of the women's organization, by barefoot doctors and health workers, who are mainly women (Andors, 1981: 52).

The fact that each person is a member of some kind of organization makes an almost total control of women's generative capacity possible. Each family is visited individually by members of the family planning committee of the neighbourhood, the factory, the rural production team, etc. Women and men are put under pressure to comply with the one-child norm. The women are given a one-child certificate which entitles them to a number of privileges. Each woman is allotted a particular year in which she should have a baby (Andors, 1981: 52).

This massive state control of women's reproductive activity has met with resistance, particularly in the rural areas. There the percentage of one-child families is lower than in the cities and the birth-rate was, in 1981, even rising instead of falling (Croll, 1983: 96). The reasons given by Elisabeth Croll for the peasants' resistance to the state intervention in their decisions to have children point to the basic dilemma of the government's policy of modernization:

> At the same time as the value of the labour resources of the peasant family is maximised by the new economic policies, so the single-child family policy attempted to radically restrict the birth of potential labourers. The conflicting demands on the peasant household by the Chinese state as both a unit of production and reproduction have probably never been greater (Croll, 1983: 96).

Single-child families are allotted more private land and have a reduced output quota to be handed over to the collective. But more private land also means increased need for more family labour which, on the other hand, is being curtailed by this policy. Single-child families in the countryside can solve this basic contradiction only by working more and longer hours. As no changes have occurred in the sexual division of labour, it can only mean that women who comply with the government policies will have to work more on the private plots. The contradictory policy has its roots in the new conception of women mainly as breeders and consumers, and of children mainly as cost-factors. But for the peasant households everywhere, children and women are mainly producers and not only consumers, as may be the case for the urban middle classes and workers.

In the wake of the state's population control measures, another conflict has arisen which, in the last analysis, is capable of undoing whatever emancipatory progress had been made by women in China. The single-child family constitutes a threat to the old-age security system in the rural areas. As old parents have to be looked after by their children in their old age, women in the countryside still prefer three or more children (Croll, 1983: 97–98); and their preference is mainly for boys, because old parents usually live with their sons.

This is a direct result of the unchanged patrilineal and patrilocal marriage and kin-patterns. Whereas the reform of the marriage law foresaw a number of changes for the women, viz., easier divorce, free choice of partner, it left intact the traditional patrilocal and patrilineal structure of the families. This means a woman moves to her husband's residence and village at the time of marriage, gets incorporated into his line, loses the base she had in her parental village and is supposed to bring forth sons who would look after the old parents and continue the male kinship line.

Thus, even after the collectivization of land, the men in the villages remained in their kinship and family relations, whereas the women were all brought in as outsiders. Lanny Thompson has shown that these patriarchal structures were even deliberately used in the collectivization drive to break the resistance of peasants against collectivization. The brigade was equivalent to a village, the production team to a patrilineal kin-group:

> Together as a team, a group of male kinsmen held usage rights over socialized land, water and equipment. Many of the small teams were referred to by family name, and in the village members of one family may have held the most prominent position (Thompson, 1984: 195; Diamond, 1975).

And the local cadres are also mostly drawn from these male lineage groups. As women in this system are an economic loss to the parental families, the parents do not invest much in their education and training.

By the new economic policy of re-privatization of parts of the land, these patriarchal structures are strengthened. But the combination of economic policies, the population policy and patriarchal structures is detrimental to women. The party puts enormous moral and economic pressure on the woman to have only one child. The patrilocal and patrilineal kin-group demands that this child should be male and that she should have more sons.

As has been reported by the press, the consequences of this policy range from the killing of female children to female foeticide, where sex-preselection technology is available, to forced termination of pregnancy, even at a late date, and to forced sterilization.

As in India under the emergency rule from 1975 to 1977, cadres get financial rewards of up to Y100 for meeting certain sterilization or abortion quotas, or they get penalized by Y10 if they do not meet these quotas. Thus, force is used by cadres in China, as it was in India, to meet the targets set by the government. The use of force and indirect coercion is not an outcome of inherently aggressive or 'feudal' remnants, but of the structural contradictions, particularly in the rural economy, as well as in the modernization model followed by the state as a whole. The state is not in a position to achieve its modernization goal unless it squeezes more 'surplus' out of the countryside. On the other hand, the state cannot provide for adequate food, shelter, old-age care, health-care and education for all its rural citizens. In this situation, it is not surprising that peasants in China resist the government policy of population control by saying: 'We cultivate our own land, eat our own grain and bring up all our children on our own. We have taken responsibility for the land; there is no need for you (the state, M.M.) to bother about our childbirth' (quoted by Croll, 1983: 97).

The Women's Federation of China seems utterly helpless in its effort to criticize the anti-woman tendencies which have come to the surface recently. It had always been an instrument for the implementation of party politics designed mainly by male leaders. Thus, it was also instrumental in bringing the new government's policies to the women masses (Andors, 1981: 45–46). Following the official socialist theory and strategy of women's liberation, the anti-woman tendencies are seen as ideological survivals of 'feudalism'. The women's organization is not capable of identifying these tendencies as part and parcel of the new production relations. But these are not just a reconstruction of 'feudal-patriarchal' ones, but are structurally the same as those we find in other underdeveloped countries which are being integrated into the capitalist system. By defining women as housewives and breeders, it is possible to obfuscate the fact that they are subsidizing, as unpaid family workers and as low paid production workers, the modernization process. And as in other such, apparently dual, economies, violence here is also the last word to ensure socialist ongoing primitive accumulation of capital.

Vietnam

In Vietnam, too, the Communist Party had made women's emancipation one of the ten principal tasks of the revolutionary struggle against colonialism and capitalism. It seems the Marxist leaders saw the tactical necessity of mobilizing women for the anti-colonial and class struggle right from the beginning. They tried to bring a Marxist perspective to the already existing women's movement. According to Truong Than Dam, male revolutionaries even published books on the woman's question under a female pseudonym and proposed strategies to bring bourgeois and Marxist women together in a united front to fight against the common colonial enemy (Truong Than Dam, 1984). In so doing, the Communist Party followed the well-known strategy of denouncing feminist ideas about equality as 'bourgeois ideologies', and subordinating women's struggles for emancipation to the task of national liberation:

The Party must liberate women from bourgeois ideologies, eradicate the illusion of 'sexual equality' advocated by bourgeois theories. At the same time it must make women participate in the revolutionary struggle of workers and peasants: this is the essential task. Because if women do not participate in these struggles, never will they be able to emancipate themselves. To achieve this, it is necessary to combat feudal or religious customs and superstition, give female workers and peasants a serious political education, raise their class consciousness and make them participate in working class organisations (Mai Thi Tu and Le Thi Nham Tuyet, 1978: 103–4, quoted by Truong Than Dam, 1984).

The mobilization of women for the national liberation struggle was crucial. Theoretically and strategically, the Communist Party followed the principles laid down about the woman's question by Marx, Engels and Lenin. This means, above all, women's entry into 'social production' was seen as a precondition for their liberation. But this classical Marxist-Leninist assumption, that women in pre-revolutionary societies are not involved in public social production is simply not based on a concrete analysis of Vietnamese reality. Because, as Christine White remarks, the masses of peasant women in Vietnam were not cloistered or limited to working in the house, but worked in the fields, in rice cultivation, travelled all over the country as traders, and thus played a crucial role in social production (White, 1980: 7).[5]

The leaders of the Communist Party understood that it was absolutely necessary to mobilize women for the *continuation* of this social production (not for a re-entry) if they wanted to wage a national liberation war. The heroic performance of women during the anti-colonial wars against French and American imperialism is well known. They made up 80 per cent of the rural and 48 per cent of the industrial labour force during the war against the USA. They were active in the fields of administration, education, and health, and also participated as combatants in the guerrilla struggle. Most important, however, was their role in keeping the economy going while most of the men were at war. And after the victory in 1975, women's participation in all sectors of the economy was high. According to 1979 statistics, the participation of women in all sectors of social production was 65 per cent, 62.3 per cent in light industry, 85 per cent in agriculture, 63 per cent in state trading, 61 per cent in health, 69 per cent in education (Mai Thu Van, 1983: 329; quoted by Truong Than Dam, 1984: 22).

But after the war, many women who had held leadership positions during the liberation struggle were replaced by men. Prominent women were sent to the provinces. The promotion of women to management positions does not reflect their high rate of work participation. The percentage of female cooperatives' presidents rose only from 3 per cent in 1966 to 5.1 per cent in 1981. It was higher in handicrafts' cooperatives where the bulk of the workers are women (Eisen, 1984: 248). It seems that Vietnamese men not only resent women in leadership positions, but also belittle or ridicule women's objective contributions to society and economy (Eisen, 1984: 248–254; White, 1980; Truong Than Dam, 1984).

In spite of all their heroism during the liberation war, women's participation in political organizations after the victory does not at all reflect their economic contribution. There are no women in the politbureau of the Communist Party. In other leading political positions also their number is small. The number of women ministers or vice-ministers rose from five in 1975 to 23 in 1981. Madame Binh, who was foreign minister during the war, took over the ministry of education, a typical 'women's' ministry. The percentage of women representatives in the National Assembly rose sharply during the war years from 18.2 per cent in 1965, to 32.3 per cent in 1975, but then declined again to 26.8 per cent in 1976 and 21.8 per cent in 1981 (Eisen, 1984: 244).

The same declining trend could be observed in the People's Councils, which are the next echelon under the National Assembly in the government structure. At all three levels, the provincial, district and village level, the percentage of women representatives declined from 1975 to 1981: in the Provincial Councils from 33 per cent to 23, in the District Councils from 38 per cent to 22, in the Village Councils from 41 per cent to 23 (Eisen, 1984: 246).

This declining trend is explained by spokespersons of the party or the Women's Union either by the fact that, after the reunification of Vietnam in 1976, the most 'backward' South was also represented in these statistics, or that this trend is a manifestation of die-hard 'feudal' attitudes. Arlene Eisen quotes a vice-president of the Women's Union who said:

> The heritage of Confucianism, feudalism and capitalism runs deep. No genera-
> tion could have changed as much as we have. We have been pushed by history.
> But we still do not have full equality. We have one of the most progressive
> wonderful constitutions in the world; but we cannot liberate women by the
> stroke of a pen. It is much harder to fight against obsolete customs than against
> the enemy . . . (Eisen, 1984: 248).

'Feudal survivals' are mainly blamed for any manifestation of inequality between the sexes or for outright anti-women tendencies which can be observed when women compete with men for leadership positions, particularly in executive and political positions (Eisen, 1984: 242). This means the problem is seen as an ideological and not a structural one. One is reminded that people's attitudes and consciousness change much slower than production relations, that it may take 'generations' to root out 'feudalism', that this is a slow, gradual process which needs patience and a continual ideological struggle. Thus, an author like Arlene Eisen, who has observed the negative trends in the women's movement in Vietnam after the liberation, feels it is 'too soon' to pass judgement, or that Western feminists should rather look at the achievements of Vietnamese women instead of working into the hands of Vietnam's enemies by criticizing these trends, and that 'a closer look at the cultural aspects of women's struggle is imperative' if the persistence of feudal patriarchal ideology is considered the most formidable obstacle of women's liberation (Eisen, 1984: 65, 254).

As already remarked with regard to China, the ideological and cultural explana-
tions of these trends contribute little to an understanding of the situation. In Vietnam, as in China and the Soviet Union, the reconstruction of the economy eventually followed the model of the so-called dual economy, consisting of a 'modern', formal, socialized or state-owned sector, particularly in industry and in collectivized agriculture, and an informal sector, called subsidiary sector, consisting

of household production, private plots, handicrafts' cooperatives and subcontracting of work in socialized agriculture. As in other parts of the world, the capital intensive, technologically more advanced and socialized sector with better incomes is mainly a domain of men, whereas the bulk of the labour power in the informal sector is female.

As Jayne Werner has analysed in Vietnam, this pattern was introduced after a period of collectivization which, however, resulted in a grave crisis of the economy. Obviously, the post-liberation Vietnamese government faced the same problem which many governments have to face in post-revolutionary agrarian societies, namely that the peasants, who had supported the war effort, were satisfied by producing for themselves, but resisted producing more 'surplus' for the state. This resistance was partly due to the fact that the state was not able to give them better prices, or provide them cheap inputs to increase productivity. When in this situation the aid from China and the Soviet Union was drastically cut, the people faced a grave agricultural crisis, with its peak in 1977–1978. In the sixth plenum of the fourth party congress, the Party proposed a number of reforms, known as the 'Sixth Plenum Reforms'.

The main items in this new policy were: the decentralization of production, the strengthening of the system of private family plots and, above all, the system of subcontracting of agricultural tasks on cooperatives and state farms. Particularly the latter has proved to be very successful. Production in some co-ops which subcontracted labour rose by 30 per cent in the course of one year (Werner, 1984: 49). Subcontracting means that the state enters into a system of dual contracts with peasant producers: 'These contractors oblige the peasants to deliver a negotiated amount of grain to the state in exchange for the state's obligation to supply fertilizer, seeds and certain kinds of equipment at a reasonable price to the peasants (Werner, 1984: 49).

In 1981, this subcontracting system was supplemented by subcontracting specific agricultural tasks to private family labour, mainly women. The tasks subcontracted to family labour are transplanting, weeding and some harvesting, tasks which, since time immemorial, have been women's jobs in Vietnam and in other rice-cultivating areas. Men's jobs, on the other hand, like ploughing, water control, pest control and also some harvesting jobs, remained part of collectivized labour on cooperatives. It would be interesting to know whether women are signing these labour contracts with the state themselves or whether the 'head of the family', usually a male, signs this contract and then allocates the work to various household members. As this labour is defined as 'family labour', this might be the case.[6]

The private plots which make up 5 per cent of the total collective land are also worked by 'family labour'. The contract system, based on family labour, is also used for pig and fish production. Pigs and fish produced over and above the government quota can be consumed or sold by the family. Handicrafts production, too, is done on contract basis. The contract system, combined with the family economy of private plots, has proved to be quite successful as far as increasing production is concerned. Agricultural co-ops which used subcontracted labour were able to raise their production considerably, and the family economy supplies 90 per cent of the pork and chicken and more than 90 per cent of the fruit of Vietnam. Jayne Werner remarks that, although the family economy is highly productive, it is still considered a 'subsidiary economy' or a 'supplementary economy', because workers and administrators can have a 'family economy' too (Werner, 1984: 50). This reveals that the concept 'family economy' is based on the well-known capitalist, social and sexual division of labour between the 'non-productive' private or family sphere, and the 'productive' public, socialized and industrialized sphere. As these divisions have not been abolished in socialist countries, the 'family economy' or, as I call it, subsistence production, subsidizes the socialized modern sector.

It is also not surprising, therefore, that the contract system is interpreted as a means of using the 'leisure time' of peasants, particularly of peasant women, productively (Werner, 1984: 50).[7]

As the formal, collectivized sector is not capable of generating enough wage-employment throughout the year, the 'subsidiary' family economy also comes in handy to relieve the labour market of too much pressure. It is typically men who are given employment in the socialized sector whereas women are typically called upon to perform the tasks in the 'subsidiary family economy'. The 'family economy' comprises 40–60 per cent of total peasant income. According to an estimate, 90 per cent of the subcontracted tasks in agriculture are performed by women. They also perform most of the work in the private family economy. Together with the tasks still performed by women in the collective sector, this means that women have to work harder and longer hours, that they have less time for leisure, education or political activity, because they actually work as 'housewives', not as workers with fixed labour time and wages. The workload of women is also enhanced by the fact that there are not many socialized services for childcare. The shift to the strengthening of the family as a unit of production means not only a double, but a triple burden for women: housework including childcare, subsistence production for their own family, and 'subsidiary' or contract work for the state. This housewifized labour is particularly cheap for the state as it need not be as visibly and equitably remunerated as women's work in collectives, where women receive individual wages in cash or kind. This may be the secret behind the success of this new policy.

This is even more apparent in the handicrafts sector where 85 per cent of the labour force are female. Handicrafts production is obviously seen in Vietnam, as in other underdeveloped market economies, as *the* solution for all the problems of agricultural development, but also of the economy as a whole. Handicrafts are mainly produced for export. They thus earn for the state foreign exchange which is badly needed for the import of modern technology and equipment. Handicrafts production, on the other hand, does not require much investment capital because much of it is done as house-industry or in co-ops which do not require much machinery. Handicraft work also produces more income for the producers, as craft prices are dependent on the market, whereas rice prices are fixed by the state. Women in the handicrafts' sector produce carpets, mats, embroideries, knitted and other apparel, ceramics, glassware, furniture, and lacquerwork. These items are mainly exported to the Soviet Union and other Comecon states. But craft cooperatives also produce items for the home market like spare parts, tools, bicycles, bricks and small machines (Werner, 1984: 53). The handicrafts sector expanded rapidly, particularly the export-oriented production. This has led to decollectivization of a lot of women's work, and a shift from production of basic requirements for local consumption to the production of luxury items for a foreign market. One cannot avoid the impression that the same strategy of housewifization is used in Vietnam which is proposed by capitalist agencies in other Third World countries to integrate women into development through 'income-generating activities', handicrafts and small-scale production of luxury items for Western or urban consumers (Mies, 1982). The strategy is supported by the argument that handicrafts production, subcontracting and the family economy are 'soaking up surplus labour' in the rural areas. Jayne Werner questions the definition of 'surplus labour' used here. The concept does not account for the houswork and other labour women already have. Moreover, the labour that is subcontracted to them is the same work they formerly did as collective wage-work. Thus, she concludes, the family economy and contract labour rather increase women's work-hours than take up idle hours (Werner, 1984: 54).

It is interesting that also the capitalist manufacturers, who exported hand-made lace from India to the West, said that by 'giving work' to a hundred thousand and more poor rural women they were simply using the idle 'leisure time' of these women productively (Mies, 1982).

In both cases, women's housework is seen as 'leisure time'. In conclusion, we can say that the new economic policies in Vietnam with the emphasis on family labour, private plots, subcontracting and handicrafts' production for women are defining women rather as dependent housewives than as economically independent workers. This enables the state to tap women's labour for its socialist accumulation process in at least four to five production relations: 1. in unpaid housework, 2. in work for the market which is paid for by the product, 3. unpaid family subsistence production on the private plot, 4. contract labour paid by the task and 5. wage-labour proper. Analytically, one can say that Vietnamese women's subsumption under the accumulation process of capital has taken the forms of housewife-subsumption, formal subsumption, market subsumption, marginal subsumption and real subsumption (Bennholdt-Thomsen, 1979: 120–124).

As this strategy is based on the nuclear family with the man as its 'natural' head and assumed breadwinner, it is not surprising that men in general have an interest in tying women down to family labour and the family economy. This is not only profitable for the socialist state, but also for the men. It removes women's competition for scarce and more lucrative jobs in the formal sector, it subsidizes men's wages by securing a solid base of subsistence, it ties women down to a never-ending work-day, and thus frees the men for the political activity which is not only prestigious, but also gives economic privileges (Eisen, 1984: 152). Finally, it gives the man control over his wife's labour. These seem to me to be the material reasons why Vietnamese men make light of women's contributions, why they resent their rise to positions of authority, and why they have no interest in egalitarian family relations.

The patriarchal tendencies criticized by the Vietnamese women (see Eisen, 1984: 248ff) are not feudal, but are manifestations of the international neo-patriarchy described in the other chapters. No amount of ideological struggle for the establishment of the 'new democratic family' (see Eisen, 1984: 180–200) will be able to change these production relations to egalitarian and liberated ones, because the nuclear family is the institution *par excellence* through which women's labour is exploited.

The analysis of the situation of women in the three socialist nations has shown that, in spite of the changes that occurred in the status of women during the liberation struggle and afterwards, the economic policies adopted by the governments in these countries had a similar effect for women. Notwithstanding the political differences between these socialist states, their policies of integrating women into socialist development are quite similar. They are all more or less based on the sexual division of labour which relegates women to the family and/or to non-wage work. This family, however, is not a 'feudal' family, but a modern nuclear one. The problems arising for women in these societies are closely linked to the creation or reconstitution of this family model which, according to Engels and Marx, was to disappear with private property. Developments in other countries which have undergone a socialist transformation of relations of production are similar to those described above.

What is striking in the account of women's position in socialist countries is the similarity with women's problems in market economies.

Before we can determine whether socialism has created better preconditions for women's liberation than capitalism, it is necessary to ask two questions:

1. Why are women mobilized at all to participate in national liberation or revolutionary struggles with a socialist perspective?
2. Why are women 'pushed back' after the victory is won?

Why are women mobilized for the national liberation struggle?

By its very nature, a national liberation struggle is the struggle of a broad front of people who live in a particular territory, have a certain common history and culture, a certain community of interests, and understand themselves as a nation. The enemy is usually an imperialist or colonial external power and/or its representatives within the country. Sometimes, as is the case with many African countries, the concept of 'nation' did not exist prior to the liberation struggle, the political and economic entities created artificially by the colonial powers cut across historically grown tribal and territorial boundaries. In these cases one could say that the national liberation struggle itself created something like a national identity which hitherto did not exist. As the struggle of a whole people or nation against a militarily and economically superior colonial oppressor, it is necessary that all sections of the people are mobilized in the struggle if it is to be successful. It is, indeed, a people's uprising and not a war fought by a professional army. Women's contribution to such a people's war is important for two main reasons: 1. As the producers of the next generation, they are the guarantors of the future of this nation. This is particularly important in liberation wars which often demand heavy sacrifices from the living for a better, happier future. 2. As the adult males are at the front, either as regular soldiers or in the guerrilla force, the women at the 'home front' have to maintain the economy. Apart from their unpaid housework, they have to keep agricultural and industrial production going and thus provide the requirements of the people at home and the men at war. Without women's responsibility for the continuation of the economy, no successful liberation war can be fought.

Apart from this, in many cases women also join the army or the guerrilla forces directly as combatants. This is also necessary, particularly in cases of long drawn-out struggles and when the number of men is not sufficient. The women also perform a number of services for the liberation fighters: they work as nurses, messengers, health workers, administrators, etc.

Many have seen this direct participation of women in the guerrilla struggle as a direct contribution to women's liberation. Their reasoning is that women with a gun in their hand would no longer accept male oppression and exploitation. But the history of the national liberation wars, as well as other wars, has taught us another lesson.

The need to mobilize large masses, if not all women, of a 'nation' for these patriotic tasks requires the foundation of national women's organizations. These organizations appear necessary to overcome the localized, individualized form of existence of most women who are not members of larger social groups than their families, kin-groups or the village. Women would be unable to carry out the programmes worked out for them by the revolutionary party unless they are organized.

Apart from the efforts to draw as many women as possible into the women's organization which, as a mass organization, is always under the authority and direction of the revolutionary party, the leaders of the liberation struggle have to bring about a number of structural and ideological changes in order to make sure that women are able to fulfil the necessary economic and military tasks. For example, in most cases a number of patriarchal institutions and relations have to be changed. The traditional sexual division of labour has to be abandoned: women are required to do men's jobs, men are required to do women's jobs. In China, for example, women in the liberated zones in the North who were not used to working in the fields had to learn how to cultivate land, to work with a plough, and to carry on agricultural and crafts-production. To do so, they had to move out of the house, form work teams, and learn new skills. In Vietnam, women not only carried on agricultural production, in which they always played a crucial role, but also produced other consumer goods and war material.

In guerrilla warfare, men also have to do women's jobs like cooking or nursing the sick. A woman ex-guerrilla from Zimbabwe reported that women who had joined the guerrillas first looked after the sick and wounded, but then also became combatants. When these women wanted to participate in the political meetings, some could not because they had to look after the babies born there. They criticized the men and demanded that crèches should be established and that the fathers of the babies share the work with the mothers. During the actual guerrilla fighting the men also shared the work at the crèches.[8]

The fact that women organize in a nationwide organization represents a change in the *status quo* which has wider consequences. In some cases, as in Nicaragua, Somalia, Vietnam and China, women's organizations had been formed by women committed to women's liberation prior to the national liberation struggle. When the revolutionary party, particularly a party following Marxist-Leninist principles, takes over the leadership of the struggle, these women's organizations are usually subordinated to the party and 'purged' of so-called 'bourgeois feminist' tendencies (Truong Than Dam, 1984). After the revolution, these organizations lose whatever autonomy they may have had and become instruments for the implementation of party policies.

We see changes in the sexual division of labour were possible, the organization of women was possible. In fact, remarkable steps in the direction of women's liberation were possible because they were *necessary* for the general struggle. These successes, however, cannot be interpreted as the result of a profound subjective and objective change in men-women relations. We should remember that during the imperialist wars also the sexual division of labour was changed, and women did men's work in farm and factory. But after these wars, the old order was immediately restored. The fact is that these wars are seen as exceptional situations which demand extraordinary measures. They do not necessarily bring about a profound change of consciousness. After the war, people go back to what they consider the 'normal' state of affairs in man-woman relations. Men's attitude in post-liberation Vietnam is a telling example.

This leads us to the second question:

Why are women 'pushed back' again after the liberation struggle?

An answer to this question has to take into consideration the objective conditions prevailing after a liberation war, as well as the subjective consciousness of men and women. Both levels are interrelated.

One of the biggest problems after a successful anti-colonial liberation war or a revolution is the reorganization of the economy. All energy has to be mobilized for the reconstruction of the country which may have been extensively devastated by the war, as was the case in Vietnam. The first aim is to provide enough food, clothing, shelter and health-care for the people. This is sometimes even beyond the capacity of the new government, not only because factories, the transport system, equipment, housing, and also the fields have been destroyed by bombing, but also because many of the colonized peoples had produced cash crops mainly for export to the industrialized countries and hardly had any industry of their own.

In situations where the whole economy was tied to the colonial powers or to the international division of labour, it is particularly difficult for the new government to build up an independent economy in the service of the people. One of the biggest problems is the unemployment of the ex-soldiers and ex-*guerrilleros*. In Zimbabwe, for example, the government could not provide enough wage-labour jobs to the ex-*guerrilleros* who had fought for them. In this situation it decided to give the scarce paid jobs in industry or government services to men rather than to women. Mao Tse Tung tried to solve this problem by mobilizing all people for an increase in agricultural and industrial production. But in China, too, as well as in Vietnam, the socialist aim of transforming all workers into free wage-workers or proletarians conflicted with the pressing need to increase production in agriculture, and even more so with the aim of socialist accumulation of capital for further industrial development. It is usually argued that, due to the low level of development of productive forces, the surplus generated in agriculture and industry was too low to pay every worker an adequate wage, or even to define all workers as wage-labourers. We have seen that the way out sought by most post-revolutionary governments is a kind of splitting up of the economy following the model known from other underdeveloped countries, namely, into a modern, capital-intensive, socialized, 'formal' sector with waged labour as the dominant production relation, and a 'subsidiary' labour-intensive, non-socialized ('private'), technologically backward 'informal' sector, where not only the bulk of the subsistence for the masses, but also commodities for export to capitalist or socialist countries are produced. This sector produces these goods at much lower costs than would have been the case if all the producers had to be remunerated as free wage-labourers. Here, as in the capitalist countries, the free wage-labourer, the proletarian, the hero from whom the Marxists expected the revolutionary transformation, is, as Claudia von Werlhof has put it, far too expensive, he works far too little, is not flexible enough and cannot easily be 'squeezed' for the generation of more surplus because he is better organized than peasants, and particularly women who, as we saw, are the ones who provide the bulk of the labour force in the 'subsidiary' sector (v. Werlhof, 1984). Thus women, or rather women defined as housewives and not as workers, are the optimal labour force for socialist as well as for capitalist development, not proletarians. The economic difficulties of post-liberation governments are not only to be explained by the objective national and international conditions within which the liberated nations find themselves, but they are also a result of the fact that the new governments want to build up a modern national economy. The model most of them are following is that of the industrialized countries. Even where priority is given to agriculture, as was the case in China under Mao, the basic development model is based on the growth model of industrialized societies. The investment capital in this model either has to come from outside – through aid – or it has to be generated indigenously by exploiting some sections of the society for the construction of a modern national industry. The strata and groups who are usually exploited for this purpose are women and peasants. As in this development model, the concept of labour is the same as under capitalism; the social division between the sphere of public, 'productive' labour and private, 'non-productive' or reproductive labour and the sexual division of labour cannot be abolished because these divisions guarantee that women's and peasants' subsistence and commodity production remain socially invisible. Their labour can thus be tapped in a process of ongoing primitive accumulation of capital which can then be fed into the building up of a modern economy and state. This is the main reason why women have to be 'pushed back'.

The subjective side of the problem, namely, that there may have been *de facto* changes in the sexual division of labour during the liberation struggle, but that neither men's nor women's consciousness had undergone a radical change, is of course also there. Such a change could only have been brought about if an independent women's movement had waged a struggle against patriarchal man-woman relations during and after the liberation war. It was precisely an independent anti-patriarchal struggle of this kind, however, that was prevented by the Marxist-Leninist parties which led the liberation wars, because all contradictions among the people, including the man-woman contradiction, were subordinated to the main contradiction between the nation and the imperialist power. Marxist-Leninists usually consider the independent mobilization and organization of women around the man-woman contradiction a threat to the unity of the oppressed, the unity of the united front, and as inherently counter-revolutionary. In their concept of revolution, the 'woman's question' constitutes a secondary contradiction which has to be tackled, ideologically, after the primary contradiction of imperialist and class relations have been solved.[9]

This is the reason why feminists who did not want to subordinate the struggle against patriarchy to other 'general' struggles were isolated and 'forgotten', like Ding Ling in China and Alexandra Kollontai in the Soviet Union. But the experience of anti-women tendencies in China, and the Vietnamese Women's Union's complaints about the 'die-hard feudal' attitudes of men are evidence that people's consciousness cannot be changed by cultural revolutions or ideological struggle alone, as had been tried, more than anywhere else, in China.

In spite of progressive constitutions and legal equality between men and women, and in spite of women's enormous contribution to the war effort and to the reconstruction of the economy, women are nowhere adequately represented on the political decision-making bodies and are, moreover, sent back to the family and the 'subsidiary economy', whereas the men move up. This confirms that the change of consciousness, which may have taken place during the actual struggle here and there, did not last.

I want to propose the thesis that such a change of consciousness could not take place because there was little change in the material production relations, of which the patriarchal man-woman relation is part and parcel. In the 'dual economy' established after the revolution, the maintenance or creation of patriarchal man-woman relations, as well as their institutionalization in the nuclear family are absolutely crucial for the building up of a 'modern economy', based on the growth model. The fact that, after the liberation, a national government has captured state power and that certain sectors of the economy have been socialized or are state-owned does not yet mean that all production relations have been revolutionized so that some sections of the people are not exploited for the benefit of other sections of the people.

But the model of development followed by most post-liberation governments necessitates the continuation of this exploitation. It is usually justified by the argument that the surplus thus accumulated by the state will be of benefit eventually also to those who have been 'exploited' most, peasants and women. But those who have control over political and state power can decide what should happen with the 'surplus'; they can also decide that they themselves should get a bigger share of it than others. This may lead to the emergence of a new *state-class* which lives by the fact that it monopolizes politics. In a situation where little 'surplus' is generated through 'productive' labour proper, it is plausible that after the victory the competition for such lucrative state-jobs is particularly fierce. This, I suspect, is the main reason behind the low representation of women in all political decision-making bodies in post-revolutionary states. The men, particularly those who were in the revolutionary party, have monopolized state power.

Women, however, are relegated to the family and the private or informal 'subsidiary' economy. This model ensures that the 'big men' are not challenged in their monopoly over state power. Women are excluded from this sphere and the 'little' men are 'bought over' by the relative power they are given in their families.

This process is also reflected in the shift that is taking place from emphasis on the *nation* to the *state*. Whereas during the liberation struggle the whole nation represented the psychological and historical commonality, after the liberation the state and its organs claim to represent the common good. Building up a modern economy is therefore usually identical with building up a strong state. In this phase, the female image of the nation, found on the revolutionary posters mentioned above, is replaced by the images of the founding-fathers: Marx, Engels, Lenin, Stalin, Mao, Ho Chi Minh, Castro, Mugabe, to name only a few. Typically, among this gallery of socialist patriarchs, there are no women. They are, indeed, the fathers of the socialist *states*, not of the nations. As in other patriarchies, the role of women in the whole process of nation-building is obscured by idealizing the founding fathers of the socialist state.[10]

Theoretical blind-alleys

Christine White has attributed the blindness of many Third World Marxist-Leninists regarding the concrete historical reality in their own countries to the uncritical adoption of the analytical framework developed by Marx, Engels and Lenin in their analysis of nineteenth-century European society (White, 1980). This is particularly evident in the concept 'feudalism', used to describe non-capitalist relations in these countries. We could say the same of the use of the words 'working class', 'labour', 'productive labour', 'surplus' and others.

The problem, however, is not only that this theoretical framework was developed for nineteenth-century Europe, and that conditions in the colonies in Africa, Asia and Latin America may not fit into this framework. The question is also whether this framework was and is adequate for the analysis of even the European or American situation. The recent feminist critique of the Marxist analysis (or rather the absence of an analysis) of housework has already pointed to one of the 'blind spots' in this theory (v. Werlhof, 1978, 1979). But that is not all. The Marxist-Leninist theory of society and revolution was developed for a fundamental change within capitalist societies. But the woman's question and the colonial question were analytically excluded from this theory, although they constituted a central and integral part of the social reality shaped by capitalism. According to Marxist theory, the contradiction between wage-labour and capital, and the extended reproduction of capital through the ongoing exploitation of the surplus labour of propertyless proletarians constituted the driving force of this historical epoch. In its greed for ever-growing accumulation, capital would develop the forces of production to such an extent – and thereby produce such an abundance of commodities – that eventually the contradiction between the production relations (property-relations) and the productive forces (technological progress) would lead to the disruption of the production relations through a revolution of the propertyless proletariat. This then would lead to a new socialist society.

Yet, we have already seen that the exploitation of colonies, as well as that of women and other non-wage workers, is absolutely crucial to the capitalist accumulation process, and not only accidental or peripheral. Without the exploitation of non-wage labour, wage-labour exploitation would not be possible (see Chapter 1). To leave these two main areas of 'super-surplus' extraction outside of the analysis has led into a blind alley not only the working class of Europe, but also the peoples who have undergone liberation struggles.

This becomes evident if one looks at the history of the German Social Democrats, the first European socialist party which adopted Marxism or Scientific Socialism as its theoretical base. With the exception of the radicals around Rosa Luxemburg, the German Social Democrats were not against colonial expansion. Efforts at gaining control over colonies were criticized only when they were accompanied by violence and inhuman brutality.

> Where the expansion could be expected to be peaceful, the party usually saw no reason to raise objections. When, for example, the leasing contract of the Chinese province Kiautschu was discussed in the German Reichstag, the social-democratic delegates condemned the *violence* which accompanied the operation, but not the leasing contract as such (Mandelbaum, 1974: 17).

In the Party organ, *Der Vorwärts*, this contract was even justified on the grounds that the 'opening of China' was a historical necessity.

Following Marx's analysis, the German Social Democrats expected the overthrow of capitalism and the victory of socialism – which they interpreted mainly as the state taking over the means of production – from a rapid development of productive forces, viz., technology and industry in the 'most advanced' industrial countries. Therefore, they considered colonial expansion, as one of them (David) said, as an 'integral part of the universal cultural mission of socialism', because it would further the growth of capital in the metropoles and remove the obstacles to increased production in the 'barbarian countries' (Mandelbaum, 1974: 19). In this respect, the social democrats shared the cultural chauvinism of the German bourgeois class. They referred to the capitalist industrial nations always as the *Kulturnationen* (civilized nations), in contrast to the colonies, which were referred to as the 'savage' or 'wild' *Naturvölker* (native or nature-peoples). The social democrat Quessel even argued that the colonial policies of the European nations could bring all productive forces on earth into the service of the European *Kulturmenschen* (civilized people), and at the same time develop the 'native peoples' through a kind of 'welfare despotism'. This welfare despotism would teach the coloured peoples the work discipline which was necessary if they were to produce more than they needed for their own immediate subsistence. In this work discipline, he saw a particular ethical value (Mandelbaum, 1978: 17–18).

Also Bernstein, one of the theoreticians of the 'right' faction of the party, wrote: 'We shall condemn certain methods by which the savages are subjected, but we shall not condemn that savages *are* subjected and that we claim the right of the superior civilization with regard to them' (quoted by Mamozai, 1982: 212; transl. M.M). The material core of such chauvinistic ideas was the fact that the proletarian masses in the so-called *Kulturnationen* (civilized nations) could not expect a quick development of the productive forces, as well as of their own living conditions, unless the industrial nations had established their 'right' to exploit freely the labour power of the colonies, to extract their raw materials at the lowest possible price and to use the colonies as markets for the realization of capital (Luxemburg, 1923). In this, the material survival interests as well as the autonomy of the peoples in these colonies were of secondary importance.

In this respect, there was not much difference between the German, French or British working class who all supported not only the colonial efforts of their states, but also the imperialist war.

One may try to dismiss this 'proletarian pro-colonialism' of the German Social Democrats as a manifestation of 'revisionism', but it is difficult not to find its deeper theoretical foundations in Marxist theory on the development of productive forces. Marx himself saw colonialism, in spite of all its brutality, as a kind of midwife that would 'open up' the hitherto closed, stagnating, 'virgin' lands of Asia and Africa and throw them into the capitalist modernization process. The great hopes with which he accompanied the 'opening up' of India through the construction of the railroads by the British colonial power are well known.

It was precisely through the existence of external and internal colonies (the housewife) that European capitalism was able to avoid the revolutionary disruption of the production relations, which Marx had expected to take place.

Lenin was one of those who condemned the revisionism of the German Social Democrats. In his writings on the national and the colonial questions, he argues for proletarian internationalism. He supports the colonial peoples in their struggle for national independence and calls upon the European working classes and the communist parties in the 'advanced West-European countries' to also support the national liberation struggles in the colonies. But he had already observed that this solidarity of the European workers could not be taken for granted. The British workers were not prepared to fight against the colonial policy of their government. But Lenin only condemns this attitude as a manifestation of the corruption of the labour aristocracies in Western Europe (Lenin, 1917). He did not address himself to the theoretical problems inherent in the Marxist theory of society and revolution. Like all scientific socialists, he expected the socialist transformation from the 'most advanced sections of the proletariat', that is, the industrial workers. Their progress, however, is based, as we saw, on the free access to cheap raw materials, labour and markets in the colonies. Also, Lenin's model of a future society was that of an industrial nation with the highest development of productive forces. For such a model, however, internal and external colonies are *necessary*. To ask the worker aristocracies in the colonizing countries to fight against colonialism means, in the last analysis, to ask them to put the very social model into question which has made them into a 'workers' aristocracy'.[11]

As the governments in the newly-liberated nations are mostly committed to the same model of development and progress, they are faced with a serious dilemma. During the liberation struggle they had to mobilize all sections of the people for the anti-colonial struggle. They did this with the promise of equality, an end to exploitation and oppression, and the vision of a socialist society. But, in their economic policies, they often want to follow the growth model and induce a rapid development of productive forces.

According to the principles of scientific socialism, only this would bring about an end to poverty, improved standards of living, and the abundance of commodities and goods which, under capitalist relations, are produced through the exploitation of the workers. We have seen, however, that this 'progress' of the capitalist societies is not only based on the exploitation of the 'free' wage-labourers in these countries, but also on the exploitation of non-wage labourers there, typically housewives, as well as on the plunder and exploitation of colonial and underdeveloped peoples. If the governments in the liberated nations want to follow this model, they cannot, in the last analysis, do without exploitation or treat all people as equals in the process of accumulation. In the absence of external colonies, they saw a way out in the division of the economy into a collectivized modern state sector and a 'subsidiary' private sector. This social division, however, is almost congruent with the classical capitalist sexual division of labour: men, defined as wage-labourers and 'breadwinners', dominate the socialized priority sector and women, defined as housewives, are relegated to the subordinated, family-based, 'subsidiary' sector. This division has, indeed, increased production, improved the living standards of the producers, including rural women, and acclerated the accumulation process. But it has also led to an increased load of labour for women, their increased de-collectivization and privatization, their retreat or eviction from the political decision-making process which is increasingly dominated by men, particularly the male state class. This division then has also resulted in the fact that the goal of women's liberation is treated as a matter of the superstructure, of ideology and culture, as is the case in most capitalist countries, and not of the basic economic structures. But this division is itself contradictory. While on the level of the superstructure the revolutionary rhetoric about women's emancipation under socialism is still maintained, manifestly on the 8 March celebrations, on the level of the political-economic base their situation is getting closer to that of women under capitalist relations in developed and underdeveloped countries. They constitute the 'last colony' also for the socialist accumulation process (v. Werlhof, Mies, Bennholdt-Thomsen, 1983).

Notes

1. During the 2nd Interdisciplinary Congress on Women's Studies in 1984 in Groningen (Holland), there were several workshops on 'Women in the Military'. In some of them, the participation of women in the armed forces was discussed as a means of 'empowering' women and achieving equality with men. Also, in West

Germany, well-known feminists like Alice Schwarzer had a somewhat ambivalent position regarding the question of whether women should be recruited into the army. The argument of such feminists is usually that they are, in principle, against war and the army, but 'as long as things are as they are', women could also join the army as equals with men.

2. This notion that women are pacifist 'by nature' is reflected in many publications of the women's peace movement, particularly also from the socialist countries. It is also the basic premise of the otherwise excellent study of 1915 on *Militarism Versus Feminism*, mentioned earlier.

3. This is what this woman wrote when she was arrested:

I was growing food and looking after my father's cattle in Chibi when I was 15 years old and I don't need a man, police or not, to tell me what to do. Is this the independence and freedom my two young brothers died in the bush for, and for which my older brother lost his right leg from the hip?

We do not need committees to waste time inquiring why there is prostitution. We all know why – because uneducated girls cannot find work and must have money for food in the drought for their families.

Don't pay more civil servants to waste our countries' time and money. Give these girls some employment. No woman wants to sell her body to strange men (Patricia A.C. Chamisa, *Sunday Mail*, Harare, 27 November 1983).

4. This almanac *Women in Russia* was the first feminist document which gave information on the situation of the man-woman relationship in the Soviet Union. It was, in fact, women's outcry of anger, bitterness and disgust about the callousness and brutality of patriarchal relations (*Almanac: Women in Russia*, no. 1, 1980).

5. Christine White quotes a statement of Le Duan, Secretary-General of the Vietnamese Communist Party, in which he says that women under the feudal regime were cloistered and completely isolated, that for 'thousands of years women's activities had been confined to the narrow circle of their family', that women 'must have a clear class position, take part in public activities and think more collectively . . .' On this statement, Christine White comments:

This statement is simply not true; only in the upper classes did the Confucian theory that 'men live outside, women inside the family' apply. Ordinary Vietnamese peasant women, the overwhelming majority of the population, were neither cloistered nor limited to working in the house. Not only did they work in the fields, either for their own families or as hired labourers, but often they worked in groups as rice transplanters or harvesters.

The women were traders, travelled over the country, and worked in groups (White, 1980: 6–7).

6. This situation resembles that of the co-operatives in Venezuela, which C. von Werlhof has described, where only the male head of household could be a member of a co-operative and sign contracts, but where his wife and children had to work without remuneration when he could not work (see v. Werlhof, 'New Agricultural Co-operatives on the Basis of Sexual Polarization Induced by the State: The Model Co-operative "Cumaripa", Venezuela', in: *Boletin de Estudios Latino-americanos y del Caribe*, no. 35, Amsterdam, December 1983).

7. 'It was explained that peasants now enjoy the system because they can use additional labor to advantage. That is, leisure hours spent for the co-operative are

remunerated – once the quota is met, the surplus belongs to the producer' (Werner, 1984: 50).

8. Cf. M. Mies and R. Reddock (eds.): *National Liberation and Women's Liberation*. Institute of Social Studies, The Hague, 1982: 123–124.

9. With regard to socialist governments' attitudes to separate women's organizations, Elisabeth Croll observes:

> Government statements on the establishment of separate women's organisations in all four societies have suggested that while their presence is a matter of practical revolutionary expediency, they should eventually become unnecessary in any socialist society where levels of consciousness are such that policies affecting women are not a separate but an integral part of the strategies of development (Croll, 1979: 13).

10. I had the opportunity of witnessing the creation of such a socialist-patriarchal genealogy on 8 March 1982 in Grenada. The late Prime Minister Morris Bishop, in a speech to the assembled women of Grenada, praised their contribution to the economic construction of the country, and their struggle against US imperialism. But then he concluded:

> You are the daughters of Fidel Castro.
> You are the daughters of Che Guevara.
> You are the daughters of Rupert Bishop.

Rupert Bishop was the father of Morris Bishop. He had been killed by the police of the erstwhile Premier Gary. What struck me in this speech was that Morris Bishop not only degraded working women and 'mothers' to 'daughters', but that he did not even mention the mothers of Fidel Castro, Che Guevara or his own mother. This degradation of 'mothers' to 'daughters' of revolutionary patriarchal founder-fathers means a loss of power for women and the legitimation of a new 'rule of the fathers', this time socialist ones. This patriarchal, socialist genealogy is as idealistic as other patriarchal genealogies, because women, the real creators of people, have no place in it.

11. This was already recognized by Kim Chow, a Korean delegate at the First Congress of the Toilers of the Far East, in 1922 in Moscow. This delegate saw a parallel between the Indian, the Irish and the Korean masses who were oppressed by British and Japanese imperialism. He also saw that the British and Japanese working masses profited from this exploitation. He said:

> . . . the working masses in England have been brought up with the idea that their own conditions may be bettered, but the toiling masses of India and other colonies must really be used to effect this improvement . . . Now the same thing is quite true of the Japanese working masses in general, if not more so . . . The Japanese working class is one of the oppressors of the Korean working masses. Although they work side by side, they look upon their Korean brother workers with contempt and they also help the imperialist and capitalist Japanese Government to oppress them (*1st Congress of the Toilers of the Far East*, Reports, Moscow, 1922).

7. Towards a Feminist Perspective of a New Society

After the analysis of the interplay of the sexual and international division of labour within the framework of capital accumulation, and the effect this has on women's life and humanity, the most burning question now is, how do we get out of this situation? And what would a society be like in which women, nature and colonies were not exploited in the name of the accumulation of ever more wealth and money? Before I try to answer these questions, I would like to clarify my position with regard to the potentialities of the international feminist movement.

The case for a middle-class feminist movement

The Western feminist movement is often accused by leftists, particularly in Third World countries, of being only a movement of educated, middle-class women, and of having been unable to build up a base among working-class women. Middle-class women in underdeveloped countries are admonished to go rather to the slums of the big cities or to the villages, and help the poor women to escape from the clutches of misery and exploitation. I have heard many urban middle-class women in India saying that they themselves were privileged, that they were not oppressed, and that work for women's liberation should start by making poor women conscious of their rights. Those middle-class women, who had begun to discuss women's oppression amongst themselves, were often accused of being self-centred and elitist. And often these women reacted with feelings of acute guilt for belonging to the class of 'privileged' women.

The reasoning behind this critique of so-called middle-class feminism is based on the assumption that women who have to fight to secure their survival from day to day cannot afford to indulge in such luxuries as fighting for 'women's liberation' or for 'human dignity'. It is said that poor women need 'bread' first, before they can think of liberation. On the other hand, women who, due to their class status, have access to modern education and employment, are considered to be already emancipated, particularly if they live in a liberal family atmosphere. It is obvious that such a concept of women's emancipation excludes precisely those sensitive dimensions of the patriarchal man-woman relation around which the new women's movement mobilized, particularly the aspect of violence against women.

But we have seen that an increase in violence against women was the issue in

India and other parts of the world which sparked off genuine feminist movements in many countries. The increase in India of dowry-murder, rape, wife-beating and other anti-women tendencies brought home to urban middle-class women that their so-called privileged class position did not protect them against sexual violence, not even from the men of their own class or family, nor from other men, nor even from the protectors of law and order, the police. In spite of all these experiences in recent years, one can still hear the argument that there is no need for women's liberation among educated urban middle-class women, because these are supposed to be already liberated or to have the means to liberate themselves. This argumentation is an example of the kind of blindness to reality which is often found among middle-class people, also in Third World countries. It is also an example of the economistic equation of liberation with wealth. Contrary to this position, *I consider a feminist middle-class movement, both in the over- and in the underdeveloped countries, as an absolute historical necessity.*

There are a number of reasons to support this position, the most obvious being the already-mentioned fact that patriarchal oppression and exploitation, that sexual harassment and violence are as rampant in the middle classes everywhere as they are among workers or peasants. One could even say that they are more prevalent among this class than among peasants where old sexual taboos still function better. The second reason is that the very privileges middle-class women so often refer to as distinguishing them favourably from poor women do, in fact, expose them more to this kind of violence. They are supposed to be 'protected' women, protected by the men of their family. Therefore, they have not learned to move about freely or/and to defend themselves when they are attacked. Moreover, they are 'privileged' housewives; that means they are isolated in their homes, have hardly any social network of other women or men around them to support them. They are so self-sufficient in everything that they do not have to borrow from friends and neighbours. All this makes them much more vulnerable to patriarchal oppression than working-class or rural women who usually still live and work within a collective context, at least in Third World countries.

In addition, the education middle-class women have received has hardly equipped them to fight against male oppression. The virtues taught to girls in all educational institutions, including the family, are such that the girl loses all self-reliance, all courage and independence of thought and action. As marriage and family are still seen as the natural destiny of women, education means that girls are prepared for this role of housewife and mother.

This preparation for domesticity may have been supplemented by some kind of professional training, but has not been changed fundamentally.

The ideology that woman is basically a housewife is upheld and spread by this class. Home Economics is taught to girls of this class to give this ideology a scientific perspective. All the media, particularly the cinema, foster an image of women based on this ideology. Part of this image is also the idea of romantic love, which more than anything else has fettered women in the West emotionally to patriarchal and sexist man-woman relations.[1] All this, combined with the fact that the middle-class woman as an ideal type is economically dependent on a husband as breadwinner, is enough to allow us to conclude that to be a middle-class woman or housewife is not a privilege, but a disaster.[2]

In most underdeveloped countries, however, the image of the middle-class woman, the housewife, is still upheld consciously or subconsciously and propagated as *the symbol of progress*. This is done not only by explicitly 'bourgeois' agencies and organizations like conservative women's organizations, but also by the scientific community, by politicians and administrators, and particularly by the development planners, nationally and internationally, and above all, by the business community. What is more, left organizations, too, which want to spread class consciousness among workers and peasants, have basically no other image of woman in their mind when they work among women. Not only are their cadres mainly middle-class men and women, but also the issues they consider as specific women's issues (childcare, health, family planning, housework) are related to this image. We have seen that, even in socialist countries which underwent revolutionary changes in the property relations, the middle-class image of woman as a (dependent) housewife has been at the core of the new economic policies of creating a subsidiary or informal sector.

The 'privileges' of middle-class women are not only that they are domesticated, isolated, dependent on a man, emotionally fettered and weakened, and tied down to an ideology that totally objectifies them. All this is combined with the fact that they, as housewives, have to spend the money their husbands earn. They have become – at least in the urban areas – the main agents of domestic consumption, who provide the necessary market for the commodities produced. It is this class of women which, to a large extent, are the subjects and objects of consumerism. In the West it is a common phenomenon that women compensate for their many frustrations by going on a shopping spree. But also middle-class women in poor countries follow the same pattern. African, Asian or Latin-American urban middle-class women follow more or less the same lifestyle and model of consumption. A look at African or Indian women's magazines suffices to show how middle-class women are mobilized as consumers.

National and international capitalists have a keen interest in upholding and spreading this image of woman, and the model of consumption that goes along with it, as the symbol of progress. Where would the national and multinational corporations sell their cosmetics, detergents, soaps, synthetic fibres, plastics, fast food, baby food, milk-powder, pills, etc., if middle-class women would not provide the market?

Therefore, it is the middle-class woman as housewife, mother and sex-symbol who is constantly mobilized to follow all fashions and fads, who is one of the main items in the advertising strategy of all marketing agencies. As Elisabeth Croll has remarked, the image of this woman has also made its appearance on the billboards of Peking where woman as the 'model worker' has been replaced by 'woman the consumer' of cosmetics, television, washing machines, toothpaste, watches, modern cooking pots. The new Chinese woman on these posters is curling her straight hair, using lipsticks, and beautifying her eyes. The protests of the Women's Federation against this kind of advertising had little effect, because this image of woman is intimately bound up with the growing commercial interests and connections the Chinese government is establishing with the West (Croll, 1983: 105). Thus, the Western middle-class woman as consumer appears as the symbol of progress also in the People's Republic of China. Western feminists are challenging this image of woman and the social reality behind it, not only because they have realized the gigantic bluff behind this image of the 'happy woman' in the face of so much direct and indirect brutality against women, but also because many are realizing that consumerism is the drug by which women and men are made to accept otherwise inhuman, and increasingly destructive, conditions of life. The new 'needs', created by industry in its desperate effort to keep the growth model going are all of the type of *addictions*. The satisfaction of these addictions is no longer contributing to more happiness and human fulfilment, but to more destruction of the human essence.

In the early 1970s, the women's movement together with other protest movements may still have believed that now, since 'we have enough of everything' the woman's question could be solved by a process of simple redistribution and the eventual realization of the promises of the bourgeois revolutions. But now it is evident that it is the very over-abundance of commodities and the paradigm behind this over-production which destroy the environment, as well as human life and happiness. Moreover, the sadistic, cynical woman-hatred of the whole capitalist-patriarchal civilization is so openly demonstrated today that feminists can no longer have the illusion that women's liberation will be possible within the context of this social paradigm.

This realization is not yet very widespread among middle-class feminists in underdeveloped countries. But I think they, too, have grounds enough not to feel apologetic about the existing and growing feminist movement in their class. Such a movement is, indeed, necessary if urban women are to defend themselves against the growing anti-woman tendencies we can observe worldwide. But it is also necessary that middle-class women themselves begin to destroy the myths, the images, the social values, which make them a false symbol of progress. If middle-class women in India, for instance, begin to question such patriarchal values as virginity, or the ideals of self-sacrificing womanhood propagated by mythology, like Sita or Savitri, or the modern housewife ideology, then they do not only contribute to their own liberation, but also to the liberation of working-class and peasant women. Because as symbols of progress, these images of women, these myths and values, are now brought to all Indian villages by the media, the cinema, the education system, as well as by developmentalists, activists and social workers. With the spread of the middle-class housewife ideology into the rural and slum areas, the problem is not only its intrinsic devaluation of the woman, but also that for most poor rural and urban women, these images will never become *reality*. And yet these images exert a great fascination on them, and many may try desperately to come up to the standard of these modern middle-class women. With TV also being available in many rural areas, American TV productions (like Dallas), or local ones imitating them, will reach all corners. It is, therefore, necessary that urban middle-class women, particularly those who want to work among poor rural and urban women in Third World countries, begin to criticize the ideology and reality of middle-class womanhood. The existence of a strong middle-class feminist movement with a clear perspective is a safeguard against the further propagation of the false image of woman the housewife and consumer as a model for women's liberation and progress. Without such a movement and without the feminist critique of the middle-class woman as the bearer of a happier future, women activists who work among poor women will subconsciously transport this image to women who have no use for it.

There is yet another aspect. Without a radical feminist critique of the middle-class ideal of womanhood – with its specific national and cultural manifestations – there is the danger that middle-class women, even if they are genuinely committed to women's liberation and to liberation of all oppressed and exploited, will remain blind to the truly progressive and human elements to be found among the so-called 'backward' classes and communities with regard to women. These may be elements of a tradition which has not yet been totally subsumed under patriarchy, remnants of matriarchal or matrilineal traditions, or there may be pockets of women's power which these may derive from their still communal and collective way of living and working, or even from their long tradition of resistance to male, class and colonial oppression (Mies, 1983; Chaki-Sircar, 1984; Yamben, 1976; van Allen, 1972).

As Christine White has observed with regard to the Vietnamese communist leaders, their blindness regarding the matriarchal traditions in Vietnam, and the almost exclusive concentration on feudal and Confucian traditions is a manifestation of the male middle-class preoccupation with patriarchal civilization (White, 1980: 3–6). As the European bourgeoisie tried to emulate the lifestyle of the aristocracy, the working classes have imitated the bourgeoisie. The same process of emulation and imitating is taking place between Third World and First World countries. In this whole process, all national and local traditions whereby women had or still have some kind of autonomy and strength are defined as 'backward', 'primitive', 'savage'. It cannot be in women's interest to contribute to this destruction of women's history. A feminist middle-class movement could draw strength, inspiration and guidance from the history and the culture of these 'backward' women.

This is all the more urgent and necessary since the myth of 'man the breadwinner', the sun around which the middle-class women move like a planet, is rapidly being exploded. Increasing evidence is emerging that marriage and family are no longer an economic life insurance for women, that increasing numbers of men are shunning the responsibility for women and children, among the educated middle classes as well. Therefore, middle-class women would do well to go to their poorer sisters, and to learn from them how to survive under these circumstances. And how to survive with dignity.

Basic Principles and Concepts

It is easier to know what one does not want than to know what one wants. To formulate a feminist perspective for a future society is a formidable task which no single individual can accomplish. Furthermore, there is no ideological or theoretical centre in the women's movement which could assume the task of formulating a consistent theory, strategy and tactics. The international feminist movement is a truly anarchic movement in which any woman who feels committed and has something to say can contribute to the formulation of the vision of the future society. Some consider this as a weakness of the movement, others as its strength. But whatever position one may take, the fact remains that the feminist movement does not work otherwise. This is true at least for all the groups, organizations and individual women who do not subordinate the woman's question to any other, supposedly more general, question, who, in other words, want to maintain the autonomy of the movement.

The following thoughts have, therefore, to be understood as one such contribution to our common effort to work out a concrete feminist utopia of a new society. The perspective I want to present does not claim to be comprehensive, although I shall try to start from a consideration of the totality of the social reality in which we live. Nor is it all new and original; many ideas have been expressed already by others. But I shall try to draw some conclusions from our struggles, and the experiences, studies, reflections, and quarrels of the recent past, as well as from the history of the first women's movement. It is an effort to learn from our history. I feel that, unless we do this now, the roll-back tendencies observable everywhere today may succeed in again destroying the history of our struggles and ideas. What is more, they threaten to destroy the very essence of what so far has been understood as 'human'.

To develop a new perspective requires first that we step back, pause, and take a panoramic view of the reality that surrounds us. That means we have to start from a world-view that attempts, as far as possible, to comprise the totality of our reality.

Our analysis has shown that the capitalist-patriarchal paradigm of man-the-hunter which has shaped our present reality is characterized at all levels by dualistic and hierarchically structured divisions which are the basis of exploitative polarizations between parts of the whole: between humans and nature, man and woman, different classes, and different peoples, but also between different parts of the human body, for example, between 'head' and 'the rest', rationality and emotionality. On the level of ideas, these dualistic divisions are found in the hierarchical evaluation and polarization of the concepts of nature and culture, mind and matter, progress and retrogression, leisure and labour, etc. I call these divisions *colonizing divisions*. According to this paradigm, the totality is not only divided up in this manner, but, as was said before, the relationship established between the two sides is a dynamic, hierarchical and exploitative one, in which one side progresses at the expense of the other.

This cannot be otherwise, since the world is *finite*, at least the world in which we all live. However, the White Man, the incarnation of the capitalist patriarch, does not accept the finiteness of reality; he wants to be like God: almighty, eternal, omniscient. So he has invented the idea of infinite progress and of infinite evolution from the lower, more primitive, to ever higher and more complex levels of being. This idea, of course, is rooted materially in the historical experiences of conquest of patriarchal nomadic peoples, mainly the Jews and the Arians. Judaic and Christian theologies have given the necessary religious sanction to the idea of the right to dominate and subordinate nature and to unlimited expansion. The scientific revolution in Europe in the 15th and 16th centuries only secularized this religious idea (cf. Merchant, 1983).

Since the finiteness of human beings and of the earth, however, could not be thought or speculated away, and since the principles of equality and freedom were formulated with a claim to universal applicability, the retrogression of the 'other side', pushed into the dark, could not be simply interpreted as God-ordained. It was interpreted as a 'lagging behind', as a 'lower stage' of evolution. In fact, the idea of evolutionary change became the centrepiece in the idea of progress of the 'advanced' peoples of the West. They became the symbol of progress for all 'backward' peoples, in the same way as men became the symbol of progress for women.

We have seen, however, that evolutionary progress for the colonized, namely, their accession to the level of the oppressors, is a logical impossibility within a finite world. Yet the illusion that they will eventually make it is held up by the 'ever progressing', 'advanced' side. This progress, however, is more than ever based on the progressive destruction of the foundations of life, of nature, of human nature, of human relationships, and particularly, of women. It is indeed a production of death. This is particularly true of the latest technological inventions of the White Man: atomic energy, micro-electronics and, above all, genetic engineering, bio-technology and space research. None of these so-called technological revolutions will be able to solve any of the big social problems based on exploitation. They will rather contribute to the further destruction of nature and the human essence.

In recent years, feminists and many others have begun to articulate their radical rejection of the paradigm of the White Man or Man-the-Hunter (Daly, 1978; Fergusson, 1980; Merchant, 1983; Griffin, 1980; Singh, 1976; Capra, 1982). In this they reject particularly the dualistic divisions within this model, and search to constitute a holistic approach, first to our bodies, then to reality at large. Many feminists, in their search for a new holistic paradigm, limit their analysis and their new perspective to the 'cultural' or ideological phenomena, or the sphere of the world-view or religion. Important though this may be, it is not sufficient to come to a realistic and politically concrete concept of a new society, a concept which would include the material life of the majority of the people in the world. To do so means not only to reject the colonial divisions in the realm of ideas, but those which exist in material reality, which shape our everyday life and the world at large.

Thus, a feminist perspective has to start with some basic *principles*, which can guide political action at all levels. The following seem to me the most basic:

1. Rejection and abolition of the principle of *colonizing dualistic divisions* (between men and women, different peoples and classes, man and nature, spirit and matter) based on exploitation for the sake of ever-expanding commodity production and capital accumulation.
2. This implies the creation of non-exploitative, non-hierarchical, reciprocal relationships between parts of our body; people and nature; women and men; different sections and classes of one society; different peoples.

3. A necessary consequence of non-exploitative relations with ourselves, nature, other human beings and other peoples or nations will be the regaining of *autonomy over our bodies and our lives*. This autonomy means, first and foremost, that we cannot be blackmailed, or forced to do things which are against human dignity in exchange for the means of our subsistence or our life. Autonomy in this sense should not be understood individualistically and ideal-istically – as it often is by feminists – because no single woman in our atomized society is able to preserve her autonomy. Indeed, it is the antithesis of autonomy if it is understood in this narrow egoistic sense. Because the enslavement of the consumers under capitalist conditions of generalized commodity production is brought about precisely by the illusion that each individual *can buy* her or his independence from other human beings and social relations by the purchase of commodities.[3]

Autonomy understood as freedom from coercion and blackmail regarding our lives and bodies, can be brought about only by collective effort in a decentralized, non-hierarchical way.

4. A rejection of the idea of infinite progress and acceptance of the idea that our *human* universe is finite, our body is finite, the earth is finite.

5. The aim of all work and human endeavour is not a never-ending expansion of wealth and commodities, but *human happiness* (as the early socialists had seen it), or the *production of life itself*.

If one tries to translate these more or less abstract principles into historical and everyday practice, one perceives immediately that the basic concepts, around which everyday life is organized, are formidable obstacles in the realization of these principles. The concept which, more than any others, has shaped life in capitalist patriarchy is the *concept of labour*. For a feminist perspective the concept of labour, prevalent in *all* capitalist and socialist societies, has to be changed radically. From this changed concept will follow a change of work, of work organization, of the sexual division of labour, of the products, of the relation between work and non-work, of the division between manual and mental work, of the relation between human beings and nature, of the relation to our bodies.

With regard to the concept of labour prevalent in our societies, there is no qualitative difference between capitalist societies and socialist societies. In both, labour is considered a *necessary burden*, which has to be reduced, as far as possible, by the development of productive forces or technology. Freedom, human happiness, the realization of our creative capacities, friendly unalienated relations to other human beings, the enjoyment of nature, of children's play, etc., all these are *excluded* from the realm of work and are possible only in the realm of non-work, that is, in leisure time. As *necessary labour* is defined as that labour which is required for the satisfaction of basic human needs – food, clothing, shelter – a reduction of this labour by machines is then the aim. It is assumed that the other 'higher' needs mentioned above (freedom, human happiness, 'culture', etc.), cannot be satisfied at the same time as one performs the labour necessary for the basic maintenance of one's life. 'Progress' is defined as a progressive reduction of necessary labour time and an increase of leisure time, when people can at last fulfil their 'higher needs'. The capitalist, as well as the socialist, utopia, is one in which *machines* (computers, automats, artificially cloned work slaves?) do *all* necessary labour, and in which *people* can indulge in consumptive and creative activities.

Before attempting to specify a feminist concept of labour, it may be useful to have yet another look at the Marxist concept of labour because, in contradistinction to the capitalists, labour for socialists is not only the necessary curse or burden, but also the motor that leads mankind to the transition to the true communist society. Let us see whether the concept of labour used by Marx is adequate to fulfil these promises.

In *Capital*, Marx writes:

> In fact, the realm of freedom actually begins only where labour which is determined by necessity and mundane considerations ceases; thus in the very nature of things it lies beyond the sphere of actual material production. Just as the savage must wrestle with nature to satisfy his wants, to maintain and reproduce life, so must civilized man, and he must do so in all possible modes of production. With his development this realm of physical necessity expands as a result of his wants, but at the same time, the forces of production which satisfy these wants also increase. Freedom in this field can only consist in socialized men, the associated producers rationally regulating their interchange with nature, bringing it under their common control, instead of being ruled by it as by the blind forces of nature; and achieving this with the least expenditure of energy and under conditions most favourable to, and worthy of their human nature. But it nonetheless still remains a realm of necessity. *Beyond it* begins that development of human energy *which is an end in itself, the true realm of freedom*, which, however, can blossom forth only with this realm of necessity as its basis. *The shortening of the working day is its basic prerequisite* (Marx, *Capital*, vol. III: 799–800; emphasis added).

The most important idea in this passage is that the 'realm of freedom' will not come before 'labour which is determined by necessity . . . ceases'. Therefore, the goal of all economic, scientific and political endeavour is the 'shortening of the working day as the prerequisite of the advent of the realm of freedom', or as Alfred Schmidt writes: 'The problem of human freedom is reduced by Marx to the problem of *free time*' (Schmidt, 1973: 142; emphasis in the original). Shortening of the time necessary for the production of the basic requirements to maintain our physical existence will still remain a main social goal when private property and commodity production have been abolished. Marx writes about this in *Grundrisse*:

> If we presuppose production in common, temporal determination naturally remains essential. The less time society needs to produce wheat, cattle, etc., the more time is gained for other kinds of production, material and intellectual. Just as in the case of the single individual, whose all-round development, enjoyment and activity depend on the amount of time saved. *All economics ultimately reduces itself to economy in time* (*Grundrisse*: 89; emphasis added).

The reduction of 'socially necessary labour time' and the jump to the realm of freedom are brought about by two processes: (1) the ever-increasing development of the forces of production, of science and technology, (2) the abolition of private

213

property, of class society, the socialization of means of production and the socialization or assocation of the producers. The first process will not only lead to a reduction in necessary labour time, but also to the *rationalization* of the associated producers themselves, whose domination over the 'blind forces of nature' is thus immensely increased. This 'rationalization' not only means domination and control over external nature, but even more importantly, suppression of one's 'instincts', of mere 'nature' or 'blind' 'animal nature' in man. The colonization of this 'lower' nature in man is both a prerequisite for and a consequence of the expanding development of science and technology, or as Marxists put it, the forces of production. Whereas for Engels the jump to the realm of freedom is achieved with the abolition of private property and continuing development of science (Engels, 1936: 311–12), Marx is more sceptical, because he does not expect that, in spite of the socialization of the means of production and the highest degree of technological progress, labour (also as a 'burden') can be totally abolished, even in communism. Because, as we saw in chapter 2, labour, according to Marx, is not only a burden, the weight of which is historically determined by the development of productive forces, but also, independent of history, a *human interaction with nature*, the 'everlasting nature-imposed condition of human existence and therefore [it] is independent of every social form of that existence or rather is common to every such form' (*Capital*, vol. I: 183–4).

In this respect, Marx was more of a realist and materialist than Engels, but both men were optimistic and idealistic with regard to the potentiality of science and technology to transform society, particularly to abolish the divisions of labour which they considered in their early writings the main cause of man's alienation from himself: the social division of labour by class society, the division of labour in the (capitalist) work process and the alienation of the worker from his product, and the division of labour between head and hand.

The communist utopia is one in which socially necessary labour has been reduced to almost zero, where *man* has abundant leisure time for his self-realization and the human development of his rich individuality.

In *German Ideology*, they write:

> For as soon as the distribution of labour comes into being, each man has a particular, exclusive sphere of activity, which is forced upon him and from which he cannot escape. He is a hunter, a fisherman, a shepherd or a critical critic, and must remain so if he does not want to lose his means of livelihood. While in communist society, where nobody has one exclusive sphere of activity, but each can become accomplished in any branch he wishes, society regulates the general production and thus makes it possible for me to do one thing today and another tomorrow, to hunt in the morning, fish in the afternoon, rear cattle in the evening, criticize after dinner, just as I have a mind without ever becoming hunter, fisherman, shepherd or critic (Marx, Engels, vol. 5, 1976: 47).

Marx and Engels expected the realization of this utopian vision of a communist society (in which women seem to be absent, by the way) from the development of the forces of production, the abolition of private property and the socialization of production. In Marx's later works, however, the idyllic picture of how communist man passes his day becomes blurred.

As Alfred Schmidt observes, according to Marx the process of replacement of human labour by machines and automats will be relatively independent of social organization. Under communism, this process will rather be accelerated than slowed down or stopped:

> Marx emphasized in *Grundrisse* that the ceaseless transformation of nature in industry also proceeds under socialist conditions. The unity of knowledge and transformation of nature, realized on a large scale in industry, should in future become a still more determining feature of processes of production. He had in mind the *total automation (Verwissenschaftlichung)* of industry, which would change the worker's role more and more into that of the technical *'overseer and regulator'* (Schmidt, 1973: 147; emphasis in the original).

The total permeation of the industrialized labour process by science, the increased shortening of labour time, the development of automation eventually result in making the worker as the main agent of production obsolete:

> He stands beside the process of production, instead of being its main agent. In this metamorphosis, it is neither direct labour, done by man himself, nor the time he takes over it, but *rather the appropriation of his own general productive powers, his understanding of nature*, and *his mastery of the latter* through the agency of his existence as a member of society – in one phrase, the development of the social individual – which now appears as the great foundation of *production and wealth* (*Grundrisse*: 592 *et seq*.; emphasis added).

I have elaborated on the Marxist concept of labour, the Marxist views on technological progress and the communist vision of a true society because these ideas are shared by most socialists, as well as by many feminist socialists. Particularly the view that unlimited progress of science and technology is a kind of 'law of nature' or history, and will be the main force to transform human society and social relations has become a new faith with many people. Even people who are seriously looking for an alternative to destructive capitalism still base their blueprint of a new society on the wonders of technological innovation.

Thus, for André Gorz the time has now come for a straight march into the Marxist paradise because, with micro-electronics, computers and automation, necessary labour can almost be reduced to zero (Gorz, 1983). For Gorz, the only problem remaining is to distribute the rest of this labour among the people and to move forward to the realization of the Marxist paradise, in which people's main problem will be to fill their leisure time with creative activities. What Gorz and others systematically exclude is the underside of paradise, or 'hell'. This paradise of the Brave New World is based on continued imperialist exploitation of external colonies and of women, the internal colony of White Man. These will be the people who still produce *life*, and to a large extent in unfree, housewifized forms of labour in the so-called informal sector. Because in spite of complete automation and computerization, people still have bodies which need food and human care, etc., and this does not come from machines. As Claudia von Werlhof has pointed out, this paradise is not for women, but it is based on women's ongoing exploitation on a worldwide basis. It is the last desperate effort of White Man to realize his technocratic utopia, based on domination of nature, women and colonies (v. Werlhof, 1984).

The conflict which Alfred Schmidt observes with regard to Marx's optimism about the quantitative development of a rich human individuality as the main aim of communism has been solved by modern left and alternative theoreticians in this way, that the colonies (nature, women, exotic peoples) are kept in bondage by Homo Oeconomicus and Homo Scientificus so that he is not totally cut off from nature, the earth, his sensuality, the ever-lasting condition of all human existence *and* happiness. As long as *this base* is secured, *he can go on with his unlimited development of productive forces, for the unlimited satisfaction of his unlimited wants (or rather addictions)*. For this man, the realm of freedom is indeed round the corner, but at the expense of the slavery of women and the Third World.

Towards a feminist concept of labour

It is obvious from our above discussion that the development of a feminist concept of labour has to begin with a rejection of the distinction between socially necessary labour and leisure, and the Marxist view that self-realization, human happiness, freedom, autonomy – the realm of freedom – can be achieved only *outside* the sphere of necessity and of necessary labour, and by a reduction (or abolition) of the latter.

1. If we take as our model of a 'worker' not the white male industrial wage-worker (irrespective of whether he works under capitalist or socialist conditions), but a *mother*, we can immediately see that her work does not fit into the Marxian concept. For her, work is always both: a burden as well as a source of enjoyment, self-fulfilment, and happiness. Children may give her a lot of work and trouble, but this work is never totally alienated or dead. Even when children turn out to be a disappointment for the mother, when they eventually leave her or feel contempt for her – as in fact many do in our society – the pain she suffers at all this is still more human than the cold indifference of the industrial worker or engineer *vis-à-vis* his products, the commodities he produces and consumes.

The same unity of work as a burden *and* work as enjoyment can be found among peasants whose production is not yet totally subsumed under commodity production and the compulsions of the market. The peasants who have to work from dawn to dusk during the harvesting season, for instance, feel the burden of work more than anybody else in their bodies and in their muscles. But in spite of the hardship of this work, it is never only 'a curse'. I remember the times of haymaking or harvesting on our small subsistence farm in my childhood as times of extreme labour intensity for everybody – mother, children, father – and as times of the greatest excitement, enjoyment, social interaction. I found the same phenomenon among poor peasant and agricultural labourer women in India during the season of rice transplantation. Although in this case the work had to be done for an exploiting landlord, the combination of work and enjoyment, of labour and leisure was still there. Moreover, this time of intense work was also the time of the most pronounced cultural activity of the women. During the collective work-processes in the fields, they sang an endless number of ballads which helped them to bear the burden of work more easily. And in the evening, after the evening meal, they danced and sang together till late (Mies, 1984). Anyone who has had an opportunity to observe the work-process of people involved in non-market oriented subsistence production will have found this interplay of work as necessity and burden, and work as a basic source of enjoyment and self-expression.[4]

The same is true for the work of the artisan or in handicrafts production, as long as this work is not yet fully subsumed under the compulsions of the market.

The main characteristics of the work-processes described above is that they are all connected with the *direct production of life* or of use values. A feminist concept of labour has to be oriented towards the *production of life* as the goal of work and not the production of *things and of wealth* (see the quotation from Marx above), of which the production of life is then a secondary derivative. The *production of immediate life* in all its aspects must be the core concept for the development of a feminist concept of work.

2. Apart from the unity of labour as a burden and labour as expression of our human nature and as enjoyment, a feminist concept of labour cannot be based on the Marxist (and capitalist) *economics of time*. The shortening of the daily labour time or of the labour time within a life span cannot be a method for the realization of a feminist utopia. Women have by now realized that the reduction of time spent in commodity production does not lead to more freedom for women, but rather to more housework, more non-wage work in household production, more relationship or emotional work, more consumption work. The vision of a society *in which almost all time is leisure time* and labour time is reduced to a minimum is for women in many respects a vision of horror, not only because housework and non-wage work have never been included in the labour that is supposed to be reduced by machines, but also because it *will be women* who have to restore to the then idle men a sense of reality, meaning and life.

A feminist concept of labour has, therefore, to be oriented towards *a different concept of time*, in which time is not segregated into portions of burdensome labour and portions of supposed pleasure and leisure, but in which times of work and times of rest and enjoyment are alternating and interspersed. If such a concept and such an organization of time prevail, the length of the working-day is no longer very relevant. Thus, a long working-day and even a lifetime full of work, will not then be felt as a curse but as a source of human fulfilment and happiness.

Such a new concept of time cannot, of course, be brought about unless the existing sexual division of labour is abolished. Such a change, however, will not come, as some women expect, by a reduction of the working-day or week through rationalization and automation. The men whose weekly or daily or life labour time has already been shortened through modern technology do not share more of the housework, but rather indulge in more drinking, more TV-watching, or in other male leisure time activities (like watching videofilms or playing computer games).[5] The whole reduction of the work-day since the times of Marx and Engels has nowhere resulted in a change in the sexual division of labour, has not resulted in men feeling more responsible for housework, children, or the production of life.

3. The third element which has to be stressed in a feminist concept of labour is the maintenance of work as a *direct and sensual interaction with nature, with organic matter and living organisms*. In the Marxist concept of labour, this sensual, bodily interaction with nature – human nature as well as external nature – is largely eliminated because more and more machines are inserted between the human body and nature. These machines are, of course, supposed to give man dominance and power over 'wild' 'blind' nature, but at the same time they reduce his own sensuality. With the elimination of labour as necessity and burden, the potential of the human body for enjoyment, for sensuality and for erotic and sexual satisfaction, is also eliminated. As our body will ever be the base for our enjoyment and happiness, the destruction of sensuality, resulting from the interaction with machines rather than with living organisms, will only result in a pathological search for an idealized 'nature'. In a desperate effort to restore this lost sensuality to the (male) body, the female body is mystified as both 'pure or base nature' and as the goal of fulfilment of all desires.[6] The expropriation and eventual destruction of human sensuality by modern machinery is nowhere more pronounced than in the cult of the computer which at present can be observed everywhere. It is a typical male cult and meant for men whose sensuality has already been largely destroyed by the fact that technological progress has placed them 'beside the process of production instead of being its main agent' (Marx, see quotation above). Far from leading to man's 'appropriation of his own general productive powers, his understanding of nature, his mastery of the latter' (Marx, see quotation above), computer technology is, indeed, destroying all productive human powers, all understanding of nature and, in particular, all capacity for sensual enjoyment. I consider this one of the reasons *why violence against women is increasing* in industrialized societies. Men who no longer *feel* their body in the work process itself try to regain some bodily and emotional feeling by *attacking* women. This is also the reason why horror and hard porn films are among the best sellers of the video industry. Their main consumers are men, many of them unemployed, or in computerized or service jobs in industry.

4. Direct and sensual interaction with nature in the work process is not yet sufficient, however. This could also be realized through some sport or hobby. And, indeed, the architects of modern society are visualizing an increase of such physical activities as a kind of *therapy* for people who have been made redundant as workers through automation. But how long will hobbies and sports provide a sense of purpose and meaning to people, even if their daily requirements are provided for by the welfare state?

A feminist concept of labour has to maintain that work *retains its sense of purpose, its character of being useful and necessary* for the people who do it and those around them. This also means that the *products* of this labour are *useful and necessary*, and not just some luxuries or superfluous trash as are most of the handicrafts made today by women in 'income-generating activities' in Third World countries.

5. This sense of usefulness, necessity and purpose with regard to work and its products, however, can only be restored as the division and the distance between production and consumption are gradually abolished. Today, the division and

alienation are, as we have seen, global. Third World women produce what they do not know, and First World women consume what they do not know.

Within a feminist perspective, *production of life* is the main goal of human activity. This necessitates that the processes of production of necessary things and processes of consumption are again brought together. Because only by *consuming* the things which we produce can we judge whether they are useful, meaningful and wholesome, whether they are necessary or superfluous. And only by *producing* what we consume can we know how much time is really necessary for the things we want to consume, what skills are necessary, what knowledge is necessary and what technology is necessary.

The abolition of the wide division between production and consumption, does not mean, of course, that every individual, or even every small community, must produce all they need and have to find everything in their ecological surroundings. But it does imply that the production of life is based on a certain autarkic relation of a certain community of people of a specific region, the size of which has to be determined on the basis of the principles spelt out at the beginning of this section. Goods and services imported into such a region should be the result of non-exploitative relations to nature, women and other peoples. The tendential bringing together of production and consumption will drastically reduce the possibilities for this exploitation, and largely increase the potential for resistance to economic and political blackmail and coercion.

An alternative economy

It is obvious that such a concept of work transcends the framework of an economy based on ever-expanding growth of monetary revenue, and of ever-expanding forces of production in terms of high technology development. As this paradigm has led to the overdevelopment of some nations and to the underdevelopment of women, nature and colonies, a concept of work oriented towards the production of life requires a reversal and a transcendence of this framework.

We may not yet be in a position to present a fully worked out alternative framework for an economy not based on the exploitation of nature, women and colonies, but there are already quite a number of important features of such a society, spelled out in recent years by people who understood that overdevelopment is not only damaging for people in Asia, Latin America and Africa, but is also destroying the very essence of human life in the centres of overdevelopment itself (Caldwell, 1977; Singh, 1976, 1980).

The first basic requirement of an alternative economy is a change over, both in the overdeveloped and in the underdeveloped societies, from dependency for their basic subsistence needs – food, clothing, shelter – from economies *outside* their national boundaries towards greater *autarky*. Only societies which are to a large extent self-sufficient in the production of these basic necessities can maintain themselves free from political blackmail and hunger. In this, self-sufficiency in *food* is the first requirement.

Malcolm Caldwell has shown that such self-sufficiency in food, as well as in energy would be quite possible in Britain, with the available cultivable land and its present population. It would equally be possible in any other of the overdeveloped countries of Europe or North America (Caldwell, 1977: 178). But what is more, if the governments of these overdeveloped countries had not bribed their working people by importing cheap food, cheap clothes, cheap raw materials, etc., from so-called cheap labour countries, these countries in Asia, Africa and Latin America could all be self-sufficient in food, clothing, shelter, etc. It is strange that people in the West have already forgotten that all the underdeveloped countries are not only rich in natural and human resources, but were also all self-sufficient societies before the conquest of White Man. If the protein food imported to Europe from Third World countries in the form of animal feed to produce milk seas, butter mountains, etc., was used to feed the local people, there would be no hunger in any of these regions (Collins & Lappé, 1977). In 1977, 90 per cent of the protein concentrates British farmers fed to their livestock was imported from underdeveloped countries. It is also well known that the energy efficiency (the ratio between the energy used to produce food and the energy gained by the consumption of this food) is lowest in the overdeveloped countries with their food mainly produced by agro-industry. Thus, the energy efficiency of greenhouse lettuce is only 0.0023, of white sliced bread 0.525, whereas local Mexican corn grown without the use of machinery has an energy efficiency factor of 30.60 (Caldwell, 1977: 179–180).

A largely[7] autarkic economy would necessarily lead towards a change in the existing exploitative and non-reciprocal international division of labour, a contraction of world trade and of export-oriented production, both in the overdeveloped countries (whose economies are dependent on the export of industrial products) and the underdeveloped countries who have to pay back their credits by exports of mainly primary goods.

A further consequence of a more or less self-sufficient economy would be a drastic reduction of all non-productive work, in the sense I use the term, particularly in the tertiary sector, a change in the composition of the workforce with a movement away from employment in industries towards employment in agriculture. If people of a given region want to live mainly by the natural and labour resources available in that region, then it follows that many more people will have to do necessary manual labour in food production. Within such a finite region, people would also be careful not to destroy the very ecology on whose balance the survival of all depends by use of too much agricultural chemical products and too much machinery, which again uses up too much energy. Therefore, as Malcolm Caldwell says, with reduced inputs of inanimate energy an increase in production could only come from an increase in muscle power (Caldwell, 1977: 180). Instead of capital intensive farming there would be labour intensive farming. It would be not concentrated in big agri-business farm factories, but in decentralized small farms. With such a change of the international division of labour, the division of labour between agriculture and industry, with agriculture oriented towards food self-sufficiency, many of the elements specified with regard to a changed feminist concept of labour would already be fulfilled; for example, the restoration of labour as necessary and meaningful, of its direct contact with nature or living organisms, possibly also a different notion of labour time, the narrowing down of the gap between production and consumption and more autonomy of producers-consumers over what they produce and consume. Within such an economy there would be no room and no use for the production of unnecessary things and sheer waste, as is the case within the growth model. Because production decisions would be based on a realistic assessment of natural, ecological and human resources as well as on peoples' true needs for a human life. It would lead away from the creation and feeding of ever more destructive *addictions*, which at the present juncture are the only way by which capital can still hope to expand its markets in the overdeveloped regions. It would give people back more autonomy over their lives and the production of life. As Caldwell points out, this radical restructuring of the economy is not only a beautiful dream or a case of exhortatory politics, but will increasingly become a necessity, particularly for workers who have been made redundant for good by the rapid development of high tech and automation. He reminds us that already in 1976 massive unemployment in Italy led to a big movement of workers back to the land. About 100,000 workers returned to farming (Caldwell, 1977: 181). A similar movement back to the land took place two years ago in India during the strike of the textile workers in Bombay which lasted almost a year.

Although at present the movement back to the land may still appear as an option mainly open to the frustrated urban middle classes, growing poverty in the metropolitan centres, particularly among foreign workers, the youth and above all, among women, will transform the romanticism of many alternative land freaks into a necessary survival strategy. Such people may be the first to realize that one cannot eat money and that food does not grow out of computers.

Most ecologists and people who are searching for a radical alternative to the destructive society we live in would agree with the above ideas. So also would many feminists. But they would discover that the brief description of an alternative economy spelt out by Caldwell is again silent about the non-reciprocal, exploitative *division of labour between the sexes*. The perspective of a relative autarkic economy based on non-exploitative relations to the ecology, other peoples, people within a region, on small, decentralized units of production and consumption is, for feminists, not broad enough if it does not *start* with a radical change of the sexual division of labour. In most ecological writings, however, the 'woman question' is either not mentioned at all, or it is simply added on to a long list of other more urgent, more 'general' issues. I have already said, in the first chapter, that this 'adding on' will no longer do if we want to change the existing inhuman man-woman relation. The conception of an alternative economy is, therefore, not only incomplete without the goal of transcending the patriarchal sexual division of labour, it will rather be based on the *illusion* of change and therefore will not be able truly to transcend the *status quo*.

A feminist conception of an alternative economy will include all that has previously been said about autarky and decentralization. But it will place the transformation of the existing sexual division of labour (based on the breadwinner-housewife model) *at the centre* of the whole restructuring process. This is not mere narcissistic self-indulgence of women, but the result of our historical research as

221

well as our analysis of the functioning of capitalist patriarchy. Feminists do not start with the external ecology, economy and politics, but with the social ecology, the centre of which is the relation between men and women. *Autonomy over our bodies and lives* is, therefore, the first and most fundamental demand of the international feminist movement. Any search for ecological, economic and political autarky must start with the respect for the autonomy of women's bodies, their productive capacity to create new life, their productive capacity to maintain life through work, their sexuality. A change in the existing sexual division of labour would imply first and foremost that the *violence* that characterizes capitalist-patriarchal man-woman relations worldwide will be abolished not by women, but *by men*. Men have to refuse to define themselves any longer as Man-the-Hunter. *Men* have to start movements against violence against women if they want to preserve the essence of their own humanity.[8]

This demand for autonomy with regard to women's bodies also implies that any *state control* over women's fertility has to be rejected. Women have to be freed of their status of being a natural resource for individual men, as well as for the state as the Total Patriarch. True women's liberation will be the cheapest and most efficient method of restoring the balance between population growth and food production. This is, indeed, the main flaw in Caldwell's otherwise excellent exposé of an alternative, homeostatic society. 'Population control' is still considered the responsibility of the state; it is not in the hands of women. They are not considered as fully responsible human subjects as long as men or the state still try to exert control over their fertility.

Secondly, in an alternative economy men have to share the responsibility for the immediate production of life, for childcare, housework, the care of the sick and the old, the relationship work, all work so far subsumed under the term 'housework'. Where this work would have been socialized to some extent – which may be useful – men have to share this work on equal terms with women. In a community keen to preserve its autarky and to follow a non-exploitative path of human development, this 'housework' could not be paid. It would have to be free work for the community. But each man, each woman, and also children, would have to share this most important work. Nobody, particularly no man, should be able to *buy* himself free from this work in the production of immediate life. This would then immediately have the effect that men would have to spend more time with children, cooking, cleaning, taking care of the sick, etc., and would have less time for their destructive production in industry, less time for their destructive research, less time for their destructive leisure time activities, less time for their wars. Positively put, they would regain the autonomy and the *wholeness* of their own bodies and minds, they would re-experience work as both a burden and enjoyment, and finally also develop a different scale of values altogether with regard to work. Only by *doing* this life-producing and life-preserving work *themselves* will they be able to develop a concept of work which transcends the exploitative capitalist patriarchal concept.

A change in the sexual division of labour would have the same effect on the level of the individuals which the change in the international division of labour would have on the level of whole regions or nations. A political decision in the overdeveloped countries, to de-link their economies from the exploitative world-market system and to establish self-sufficiency in the main areas, will pave the way for autarkic economic development in the underdeveloped countries. Similarly, a conscious decision on the part of the 'overdeveloped' men to forego building up their ego and identity on the exploitation and violent subordination of women, and to accept their share of the unpaid work for the creation and preservation of life will make it easier for women to establish autonomy over their lives and bodies and to come to a new definition of what woman's identity is.

These processes of liberation are interrelated. It is not possible for women in our societies to break out of the cages of patriarchal relations, unless the men begin a movement in the same direction. A men's movement against patriarchy should not be motivated by benevolent paternalism, but by the desire to restore to themselves a sense of human dignity and respect. How can men respect themselves if they have no respect for women? In the same way, the overdeveloped peoples have to start rejecting and transcending the economic paradigm of ever-increasing commodity production and consumption as a model of progress for the under-developed economies.

Yet, the change in the exploitative international division of labour cannot come within a short time. Similarly, the establishment of ecologically balanced, autarkic economies will take time and demand an immense intellectual, moral and physical effort. But the change in the sexual division of labour could be started immediately. Each man and woman could start at his/her individual level; groups of women and men could develop different models; larger political movements like the peace movement, the ecology movement, national liberation movements could immediately experiment with a changed sexual division of labour and develop their alternative ideas about a better society from these central experiences. If this happened, feminists would lose their scepticism regarding many of these movements, because time and again we have seen that women's mobilization for such movements ended up with the old or a new patriarchal division of labour.

There is still another reason why feminists must insist on the centrality of the change in the sexual division of labour. Our analysis of the socialist countries has shown that the maintenance, or the creation, of the bourgeois, patriarchal, sexual division of labour and of the nuclear family is the apparently insignificant gate through which reactionary forces can again find entry into a society which tried to free itself from the clutches of imperialism and capitalism. As long as the sexual division of labour is not changed within the context of an alternative economy, capitalism will not be abolished. For the time being, however, feminists in the underdeveloped and the overdeveloped societies do well to keep their scepticism and critical sense. They must insist, again and again, that there will be no liberation for women unless there is also an end to the exploitation of nature and other peoples. On the other hand, they must also insist that there will be no true national liberation unless there is women's liberation and an end to the destruction of nature, or that there cannot be a true ecological society without a change in the sexual and international division of labour.

It is precisely by putting *one* of these contradictions into the limelight and by pushing the others into the darkness that capitalist patriarchy has been able to build up and maintain its dominance. This strategy is at present followed by a number of people in the ecology and alternative movement. Following the old Marxist-Leninist strategy of primary and secondary contradictions, they have put the ecology crisis into the centre now. But they no longer talk of capitalist exploitation of Third World countries. Yet we know that the governments in Europe and the USA will try to solve the ecological and economic crises in their countries by dumping their dangerous factories and products into underdeveloped countries. And the cheap food, cheap clothes, cheap sexual services, etc., will be provided for this class of white *rentiers* by further exploitation of Third World countries and peoples. Of course, there are also white women who will belong to that international class of non-producing *rentiers* who are maintained and alimented by increased exploitation of Third and Second World countries, but by and large, women in the overdeveloped countries will increasingly share the destiny of the underdeveloped countries. By their invisible, low-paid or unpaid work, they will provide the base upon which the international male white class will march into the 'post-industrial' paradise.

Intermediate steps

In discussions about alternatives to the existing destructive 'order', the question immediately arises: 'How does one get from here to there? How do such beautiful utopias help us to change reality in the direction we want? Are the powers that stand against us not overwhelming: internationally operating capital, the big transnational corporations, the ever-increasing interplay between the scientific, the economic, the military and the political establishments, the rivalry of the two superpowers and their never-ending spiral of producing ever more destructive arms, the extension of these destructive weapons into outer space, etc., etc.?' *Vis-à-vis* this formidable threat to all human life and to life as such, many women and men in the West feel utterly helpless and tend to close their eyes and wait in a defeatist manner for the unavoidable holocaust.

I think feminists cannot afford such defeatism, not only because it would be suicidal, but also because it is *unrealistic*. As long as class society exists, the collapse of a ruling class has been projected as the collapse of the universe. This is also the case today with the threat of collapse for the capitalist-patriarchal growth model. But our analysis has shown that women worldwide have nothing to gain in their human development from the growth of this gigantic parasite. On the contrary, therefore, we should here and now begin to refuse our allegiance to and our complicity with this system, because women are not only victims of capitalist patriarchy, they are also, in varying degrees and qualitatively different forms, collaborators with this system. This is particularly true for middle-class women worldwide, and for the white women in industrialized countries. If we want to regain autonomy over our bodies and over life in general, we must start by renouncing this complicity with patriarchy. How can that be done?

I think the strategy could be the same for women in overdeveloped and underdeveloped countries, but the tactical steps might be different. In the following, I shall discuss some concrete steps that could be taken in the direction of freeing ourselves from the clutches of the anti-human and anti-women capitalist patriarchy. I shall begin with what could be done by Western feminists.

Autonomy over consumption

An area which has been almost totally left out for political struggle in the West has been the area of *consumption*. Trade unions, political opposition groups, as well as the women's movement have addressed their protests and demands either to the bosses of the economy or to the state, or to men in general. Rarely have they discussed their own role in the exploitative system. And yet, it is common sense knowledge that capitalism cannot function unless it is able to create and expand the market for its ever-growing amount of material and non-material commodities. This market is partly provided by us, the buyers of these commodities. It is mainly provided by the masses in the overdeveloped countries who have the purchasing power, due to the exploitative, international and sexual division of labour. It is also provided, to a lesser degree, by the urban middle classes in the underdeveloped countries. And it is provided to a large extent by the states and their monopolies over huge areas of the economy, for example, education, health, the postal system, defence.

We may not be able to influence the whole marketing system. But a *consumer liberation movement*, started by feminists among women who, as housewives, are important agents of consumption and crucial pillars of the market, could go a long way towards undermining the capitalist-patriarchal system. Such a movement has a number of advantages in contrast to other social movements:

— It can be started immediately by each and every woman on an individual basis. The decision what to buy and what not to buy is not totally predetermined by our needs and by what is offered in the market. Perhaps more than 50 per cent of what is bought and consumed in households in overdeveloped countries and overdeveloped classes is not only superfluous, but also harmful. This includes the consumption of alcohol, tobacco, drugs, a lot of luxury foods, fruits, flowers, but also most of what is produced today by the electronic industry: computers, video-sets, other media, music, TV. Particularly the products of the new growth-industries are no longer meant for the satisfaction of basic human needs, but for the creation and expansion of new addictions of *passive* consumers. We cannot say that we have no choice in buying or not buying these things; otherwise, we hand over the last bit of our subjective individual freedom to Mr Capital and agree to become mere puppets of consumption. Thus, the individual refusal to buy superfluous, and basically harmful, luxury items would enlarge the area of freedom within each individual woman.

— Apart from a boycott of luxury commodities, feminists, if they want to be true to their political goals, must boycott all items which reinforce a sexist image of woman, or anti-woman tendencies in our society. Thus, the new wave of 'beautifying women', created by the garment and cosmetics industries as a kind of counter-attack against the feminist refusal to shape their bodies and appearance according to the standardized model of an 'attractive and sexy' woman, can be successfully disturbed if women openly boycott cosmetics and new sexy fashion fads.[9]

— Similarly, the manipulation of women as housewives and mothers, carried out by the multinational food and pharmaceutical industries and others, can be thwarted if women consciously refuse, as far as possible, to buy certain items, like, for example, the chocolate milk products, fast foods, drugs, etc., produced by such multinationals as Nestle or Unilever, Bayer or Hoechst. Of course, the enslavement of Western housewives to Mr Capital has already reached such an extent that a consistent boycott of *all* such items would lead to immediate starvation. Therefore, the boycott of items which reinforce the tendencies to define women as sex-objects and super-mothers can only be selective.

— A further essential criterion for the selection of commodities to be boycotted is the degree of exploitation of Third World producers, particularly of Third World women, incoporated and materialized in the commodities. Thus, women who buy lipsticks made by Unilever, or any of his 'daughter'-firms can be sure that they, too, are contributing to the further exploitation and expropriation of poor tribal women in India.[10] They, too, are responsible for the destruction of the autonomy these women had over their life-production. A boycott of such items would, therefore, mean both the liberation of women in the overdeveloped countries from a sexist image of woman, and increased autonomy of poor Third World women over their environment and subsistence production.

— Lipstick and cosmetics provide a good example of another criterion in the selection of articles to be boycotted by women: namely, the degree to which, in the production of these commodities, living organisms are being subjected to brutal violence, and how far the ecological balance of the producing areas and countries has been upset. In short, the destruction of nature which is inherent in commodity production must also be a criterion for refusing the purchase of certain commodities. This aspect has mobilized the friends of animals, for example, the animal protection associations, to campaign for a prohibition on experiments on living animals by the cosmetics industry. Feminists could certainly support such a campaign. But if they want not only to feel for the 'humanity' of the animals who are tortured as guinea-pigs in the production of cosmetics, but also to be aware of their own humanity, they must extend this campaign to a boycott of the cosmetics produced by these firms.

But how do we know about the various exploitative relations which are materialized in the commodities we buy and consume? How do we know that the lipstick I buy contains the starvation of women in Bihar as well as the torture of thousands of guinea-pigs and mice in the laboratories of the MNCs? Indeed, capitalist commodity production, with the almost total division between producers and consumers in an international, social and sexist division of labour, has been able to mystify almost totally the exploitative relations incorporated in the commodities. Blind consumers are linked to blind producers!

A feminist consumer liberation movement, therefore, has to start with the lifting of this blindness, with a de-mystification of the commodities, a re-discovery of the exploitation of women, nature, colonies, inherent in these commodities, and an effort to transform the market relations which link us *de facto* to women, men, animals, plants, the earth, etc., into *true human relations*. This means to re-discover concrete people behind the abstract commodities. This can happen if we try to trace the path a certain commodity has travelled until it reached our tables or our bodies. At the end of this journey, we would meet in many cases poor women and men in the underdeveloped countries, and learn about how they produce certain items for the world market, what they get for their work, how this has changed their autonomy over their life production, what they feel about this, and how they struggle to maintain or regain their humanity.

A consumer liberation movement would, therefore, also imply a new and fascinating learning process, a *conscientization* different from that of the early feminist consciousness-raising groups, which would, indeed, clarify our minds about the really existing relations within which we live and work, both as objects *and* as subjects. The revival of social awareness of all the exploitative relations inherent in the commodities would extend the area of subjective freedom *within* people much more than any amount of book-knowledge accumulated by so-called experts. It would increase our autonomy over the *knowledge* about nature, foreign peoples and their lives and struggles, and enable us to decide what we need and what we do not need.

Concretely, this means that feminist groups in the overdeveloped and under-developed countries could begin to make such concrete studies of certain products, selected according to the criteria spelt out above, publish their results and feed them into the international networks of women's groups and organizations who would be ready to join such a consumer liberation movement.

This last point brings us to the question of the *politics* of such a movement. Although it can and should be started by each individual woman in her immediate surroundings, where she has a certain amount of power and freedom of choice, it is clear that individual acts of renunciation or boycott will not have the desired impact on the big capitalist corporations. Only a social and political boycott movement could have a major effect. This means women's groups or organizations must *publicly announce* their boycott campaign, accompany their actions with information and analysis about the exploitative relations in the product they have selected as target of their campaign and create as wide a publicity for this movement as is possible without betraying its basic principles. The formation of such action-and-reflection-groups would by itself have another liberating effect: It would liberate women in the affluent societies, particularly housewives, from their atomized, isolated existence within their tiny cages called households, liberate them from their depressions, drug addictions, the housewife-syndrome and their need for compensatory consumption. It would bring them back into the public sphere and make them aware of their place in the worldwide network of social relations.

The politics of a feminist consumer liberation movement would include, but go beyond, the strategies of the critical consumer movements started in the USA and Europe by people like Ralph Nader or Hans A. Pestalozzi. Whereas in most of the movements, the self-interest of the consumer in having clean, healthy, chemically unpolluted and unadulterated products is linked to the ecological consideration of preserving scarce energy resources and maintaining an ecological balance, the aspect of women's exploitation and of underdeveloped countries is mostly excluded. Thus, Pestalozzi is a spokesman of a critical consumer movement in Switzerland, but he believes that critical and ecologically conscious consumers would not endanger 'our system of a free society and economy'. He pleads for new marketing strategies to be adopted by the managers of capitalist corporations (Pestalozzi, 1979: 31 *et seq.*).

Feminists cannot be satisfied if international capital uses our consumer boycott of certain items only to develop a new marketing strategy to make us consume so-called health food, produced perhaps in alternative self-help enterprises which may work on a contract basis for the multinational food corporations, as we have already seen happening in the underdeveloped countries. We know by now that any such partial liberation, if it takes place *within* the framework of internationally operating capital, will be compensated for by the further exploitation and subjection of some other categories of people and of nature elsewhere.

A feminist consumer liberation movement could certainly subscribe to the slogan coined by the French organization, *Terre des Hommes – Frères des Hommes*: 'Ici vivre mieux/La-bas vaincre la faim' (To live better here and to fight hunger there). It would have to keep in mind, however, that 'to live better here' cannot mean an extension of the principle of egotistic self-interest, but has to be given a new content by creating non-exploitative, reciprocal relations to our bodies, between men and women, our natural environment, and people in the underdeveloped world. On the other hand, this slogan expresses the desire that the definition of what the 'good life' or human happiness is should no longer be left to the lieutenants of transnational capital, but that we ourselves begin to define it. Women should never forget that it is *we* who produce life, not capital.

Autonomy over production

A feminist consumer boycott movement would be *one* step in the direction of our liberation. Another, equally necessary step, which would follow from the first, would be a movement to regain control over the production processes as such. This, of course, ultimately implies that women and producers in general regain control over the means of production. But before this can be achieved, control over the *production decisions* could become a goal for trade unions and other working-class organizations. It is absolutely absurd that the Western working classes accept the production decisions – for example, the automation of production, arms production, the production of dangerous chemicals, and of luxury items – all in the *name of preserving their jobs* and of an abstract idea of progress. Meanwhile, it is obvious that they will neither save their jobs by this strategy, nor avoid this destructive production. But the male workers often advance the argument that they have no choice because they have to 'feed a family'. This argument is partly a pretext, because women are as much the breadwinners of their families as the men. But women who are serious about our liberation could go a long way to regain a greater measure of autonomy over production. This could start by producing more of the things we need ourselves. It could also mean that urban people could think of ways and means to grow food in the cities.

It could further mean to establish new local markets between small, ecologically-oriented peasant producers and urban women, where a direct link between production and consumption would be re-established. Through such a link, it would not be difficult for urban women and children to go to the country-side in their holidays, not as idle tourists, but as farm workers who would work on the farms of such small peasants for an exchange of the products thus commonly produced. This would come near Caldwell's vision of diverting industrial labour to labour intensive agriculture, but, in contrast to his vision, it would not be the state but producer-consumers themselves who would organize such a system of labour exchange between city and village.

It would be important, however, to make sure that such a system of production-consumption would not degenerate into the well-known 'informal' sector which then, in a dual economy, would only serve to feed the formal sector. This sector would go on as before to produce its destructive high tech and other useless commodities, and the informal sector production would again mainly subsidize wages in the formal sector. Therefore, autonomy over production must also eventually become a demand of the trade unions, of men and women in the trade unions and in other movements, like the ecology and alternative movements. A broad consumer liberation movement could be a direct challenge to the classical wage-workers' self-image that they are the necessary 'breadwinners' of their families. With more and more people returning to some new form of subsistence production, the myth of capital and wage-workers as *the* producers of life would have to disappear.

Struggles for human dignity

It would be contrary to the principles of the autonomous women's movement if I tried to present a catalogue of what feminists in Africa, Asia and Latin America should do. Since the emergence of a feminist movement in many underdeveloped countries, the discussion on the analysis of their situation, on possible strategic and tactical steps, on necessary actions is carried out by Third World women among themselves. But since, according to our analysis, women in overdeveloped and underdeveloped countries are linked to each other by the world market, it would be unrealistic to pretend that we can concentrate only on our respective situations and movements and close our eyes to what is happening in other parts of the world. In particular, since the rebellion of Third World women against patriarchal exploitation and oppression was sparked off by similar issues, for example, the issue of violence against women, we can identify several points on which Third World and First World women could be united. This is above all the case in the area of *body politics*, whereby women worldwide demand *autonomy over their lives and bodies*.

The following is not a full-fledged strategy for joint actions of feminists in overdeveloped and underdeveloped countries. I only want to point out certain areas where united struggles could take place and reflect on some experiences of such struggles.

Body politics implies a struggle against all forms of direct violence against women (rape, woman-beating, clitoridectomy, dowry-killings, the molestation of women), and against all forms of indirect or structural violence against women embedded in other exploitative and oppressive relations, like class and imperialist relations, as well as in patriarchal institutions like the family, medicine, and the educational systems. Within this sphere of *body politics*, there is unity among women about the central goal of their struggles. This is ultimately the insistence on the human essence of women, on their dignity, integrity and inviolability as human beings, and a rejection of their being made into *objects* or into natural resources for others.

I think that, if this deepest dimension and motive force of the above-mentioned struggles were recognized, it would no longer be possible for one exploited and oppressed group to expect its 'humanization' at the expense of another exploited and oppressed group, class or people. For instance, white women could not expect their humanization or liberation at the expense of black men and women; oppressed First and Third World middle-class women at the expense of poor rural and urban women, oppressed men (black *or* white workers and peasants) at the expense of 'their' women. The struggle for the human essence, for human dignity, cannot be divided and cannot be won unless *all* these colonizing divisions, created by patriarchy and capitalism, are rejected and transcended.

If we study the brief history of the new women's movement in underdeveloped and in overdeveloped countries, we can identify a number of struggles which started with the aim of preserving the human integrity and dignity of women, in the context of which these colonizing divisions were transcended, at least tendentially, and the prospect of a new solidarity emerged. This solidarity is not based on the narrow self-interest of the respective groups, but on the recognition that capitalist patriarchy destroys the human essence, not only in the oppressed, but also, and perhaps even more so, in those who apparently profit from this oppression.

Thus, the feminist struggles against male violence, against rape, wife-beating, the molestation and humiliation of women, have been a rallying point for women in First and Third World countries. The literature on these issues has been translated and read in many countries. Women can identify with 'the other woman' across class, racial and imperialist barriers, if they have begun themselves to struggle against male violence. Thus, in India, the struggle against rape and dowry-killings transcended the barriers created by caste and class. There was genuine solidarity among women on these issues, although these divisions did not disappear.

The barriers between women and men can also be transcended if women and men courageously begin to struggle against male violence. In traditional left organizations, the issues of rape, wife-beating, and the molestation of women are played down by the leaders. It is assumed that a campaign around such issues would be divisive for the unity of the oppressed class (the workers, the peasants). Thus, women in these organizations are told to subordinate their grievances about such 'private' matters to the general aim of class struggle, the anti-colonial struggle, the land struggle, etc. Third World, middle-class women are particularly susceptible to this line of thinking, and often ready to postpone the struggles around the man-woman relation to some distant future.

It has been my experience, however, that poor peasant women in India were not ready to accept this 'subsumptionist' strategy. They have shown that a determined struggle against male violence did not undermine the unity of the poor peasant class *vis-à-vis* the oppressive landlords, but that it rather doubled their unity and strength.[11]

One example of how the division between Third World and First World women can be successfully overcome was/is the combined international struggle of Western feminists in Holland and West Germany, and that of feminists in Thailand and the Philippines, who have launched a campaign against sex and prostitution tourism to Third World countries. One such joint action was organized by a group of Third and First World women in 1982, both at the airport at Schiphol (Holland) and in Bangkok. At Schiphol airport, the women informed the passengers on a flight to Bangkok about the inhuman exploitation of young women and girls in Thailand by the European sex tourist industry. At Bangkok airport a similar group greeted the European men, who had been flown in for a sex tour, with posters telling them that Thai women were not their prostitutes. This action was so embarrassing to the Minister of Tourism that he was compelled to make a statement, saying that the government welcomed tourists but that it did not want Thai women to be used as prostitutes by foreigners. A further outcome of this joint campaign is the creation of a centre for Asian women in Frankfurt, the entry point to Europe for many women from Asia who are brought there as 'wives' by German men and who, in most cases, end up in the brothels of Frankfurt or Hamburg.

Though this campaign started with the spontaneous rebellion of women against this cynical form of neo-patriarchy, it inevitably led them to recognize the joint commercial interests of the tourist industry and of men.

Similar joint campaigns and actions of Third World and First World women have been started around the issues of family planning, fertility control, genetic and reproductive engineering.[12] Here, too, the principle of autonomy over our lives and bodies has been the starting point. Whereas feminists in the West have been struggling for years against the state, which demands more white children from them, Third World women are beginning to realize that they are subjected to coercion and even femicidal tendencies because they are *not* supposed to breed more children. In such joint campaigns and actions, feminists are not only in a position to expose the policy of fascist 'selection and annihilation', but also to identify clearly the corporate interests and the people behind them who manipulate women worldwide in their greed for ever-growing accumulation.

The case of Depoprovera, prohibited in the USA because of its cancerogenous qualities, but dumped in Third World countries, is perhaps the best-known example of how Third World and Western feminists can work together to expose these tactics. With the new developments in reproductive and genetic engineering, the combination of the experiences, analyses and the information of Third World and First World women will be absolutely crucial for any movement of resistance (cf. Corea, 1984).

All these struggles were/are taking place in the sphere of *body politics*. A combination of struggles and actions on the part of feminists in overdeveloped and underdeveloped countries can expose and undermine the double-faced policy of international capital towards women. Third World and First World feminists can overcome the colonial divisions by fighting jointly against the dehumanizing and anti-women tendencies of capitalist patriarchy.

It is more difficult to discover commonalities between women in overdeveloped and underdeveloped countries in the sphere of economics or economic struggles, because this sphere is, as we have seen, almost fully controlled by the international and sexual division of labour. Within this framework, Third World women producers are related to First World women consumers in a contradictory, even antagonistic way. If world market factories, producing garments and underwear for Western consumers, strike for better wages and work conditions, the companies can demand higher prices for their products from Western consumers. Even if Western women were made aware that such higher prices were the result of strikes in one of the re-located factories, it is not certain that such higher prices would reach the actual producers. On the one hand, if feminists were to start a boycott of such products in support of the striking women in these factories, the women there might not be able to understand such an action because, within the given structures, their immediate interest in keeping a job and getting a wage is intimately tied up with the interest of capital in selling its products.

On the other hand, women in Europe who worked in textile industries, which were relocated to Asia or Africa, lost their jobs to badly paid Asian or African women. And between these two categories of women workers, there is no material base for solidarity. If one set of women tries to better its material conditions as *wage-workers*, or *consumers*, not as human beings, capital will try to offset its possible losses by squeezing another set of women. Thus, within the given framework of the international division of labour and of the wage-workers' interests closely bound up with those of capital, there is little scope for true solidarity between Third World and First World women, at least not the type of solidarity which can go beyond paternalistic rhetoric and charity.

But if women are *ready to transcend* the boundaries set by the international and sexual division of labour, and by commodity production and marketing, *both* in the overdeveloped and underdeveloped worlds; if they accept the principles of a self-sufficient, more or less autarkic, economy; if they are ready, in Third World countries, to replace export-oriented production by production for the needs of the people, then it will be possible to combine women's struggles at both ends of the globe in such a way that the victory of one group of women will not be the defeat of another group of women. This could happen, for instance, if the struggle of Third World women for the control over their own land and their subsistence production – often fought against the combined interests of international or national corporations and of their own men – was supported by a consumer boycott in the overdeveloped countries.

A feminist-led consumer liberation movement in the overdeveloped countries could prepare the ground, in many respects, for a women's production liberation movement in underdeveloped countries. This would be a movement of people to use the land and the human and material resources available in a given region for the production of those things which they need first: food, clothing, shelter, health, and education. At the same time, their economy would be partly de-linked from the world market, particularly from the international credit trap. The combination of a consumer liberation movement in the West with a production liberation movement in Asia, Africa and Latin America would not leave much incentive for the MNCs to further colonize these countries through the unjust international division of labour. Many of them would close down their sites and move back to their fatherlands. The local industries would then have to produce for a home market, and not for the already overflowing markets in the affluent societies. In the West, the drying up of cheap imports from Third World countries would lead to higher prices of all basic consumer goods, would force the economies to return to their own agricultural base, and would put an end to hypertrophic, wasteful and destructive production. It would be a logical consequence of such movements that the models of man-the-breadwinner, woman-the-housewife had to be given up. For, without the exploitative international division of labour, there would be very few men in the erstwhile overdeveloped countries who would be in a position to 'feed' and maintain a 'non-working' housewife. All would have to work for the production of life or for their subsistence. And the women would have to demand that men, too, accept their share in this life-production. The bourgeois model of the housewife would eventually lose its attraction as a symbol of progress.

Notes

1. While working with battered women in Cologne, we found that it was not economic dependency on a male 'breadwinner' which fettered these women to men who abused and tortured them, sometimes over many years, but their self-concept of a woman. They were not able to have an identity of their own unless they were 'loved' by a man. The beatings of the man were often interpreted as signs of love. This is why a number of the women went back to their men. In our society, a woman who is not 'loved' by a man is a nobody.

2. This can be said as an analogy to what Marx wrote about the 'productive worker', the classical proletarian. In *Capital* he writes: 'To be a productive worker is, therefore, not a good thing but a bad thing' (my translation, *Das Kapital*, vol. I: 532).

3. I consider this individualism, which ultimately is based on the 'freedom' of private owners of property and their purchasing power, Western feminism's most serious handicap. Instead of seeking a social solution to some of the problems afflicting women, the market and technology offer them an individual solution in the form of a commodity, at least to those who have money. Thus, women who can afford to buy a car are much less exposed to male violence in the streets than those who cannot.

4. I noticed the same unity of work as enjoyment and as a burden among tribal people in Andhra Pradesh in India.

5. I have read that, in England, a new category of 'widows' has been identified by women sociologists. After the 'football-widow', it is now the 'computer-widow' who has lost her husband, this time to the machine.

6. This seems to be a kind of law in capitalist patriarchy. It applies to women, nature and colonies. Capitalist patriarchy and science have first to destroy woman or nature or other peoples as autarkic *subjects*. And then they are adored and phantasied as goals of all male desires. This is the basis of all romantic love, of romanticizing nature, of romanticizing exotic peoples or 'natives'.

7. In all discussions about an alternative economy, it is necessary to stress that the concept 'autarkic' does not imply *total* self-sufficiency. A totally self-sufficent economy or society is an abstraction, but a largely self-sufficent economy is possible.

8. There are a few hopeful signs that some men are beginning to understand this. In Hamburg, men have created a new initiative called 'Men against Male Violence against Women'.

9. Many women, including feminists, often argue that women have a need to beautify themselves. This may be, as it may be true for men, but this does not mean that we have to accept the standards of beauty set by the garment and cosmetics industries.

10. Unilever, with its Indian counterpart, Hindustan Lever, have developed a method to extract the oil from the seeds of the sal trees which grow wild in the jungle areas of Bihar in India. Formerly, these seeds were collected by the women of the Santhal tribe to make oil for their own use. Now the tribal women collect the sal seeds for the agents of Hindustan Lever for a paltry sum. The sal-oil derivatives are used as a substitute for cocoa-butter and for the production of cosmetics of all sorts. Due to its characteristic melting capacity, it is particularly useful for the production of lipstick. Thus, the production of lipstick or chocolate by Unilever deprives the tribal women of Bihar of control over their oil production (cf. Mies: 'Geschlechtliche und internationale Arbeitsteilung', in Heckmann & Winter, 1983: 34ff).

11. This struggle took place in the years 1980–81 in Nalgonda district, Andhra Pradesh, among poor peasant and agricultural women who, together with their men, had been organized in village and women's associations. The fact that they had separate women's organizations, not under the leadership of the men, gave them the courage to wage a struggle against wife-beating. The case of one of the women, who was regularly beaten by her husband when she attended the women's meetings, was the point which sparked off this struggle. It led to protracted discussions among poor peasant women in all the villages of the area. In these discussions, most of the women decided that, where women were regularly beaten by the husband and the two could no longer get along, the husband must leave the house, 'Because the house belongs to the woman'. This decision was then discussed

among the organizers and the men. It was recognized by them that if they treated their own women in the same way as the landlords treated them, they could never expect to escape from oppression and exploitation. The women had made wife-beating a public issue and they had suggested social sanctions against such men. In a later struggle against the landlords, the men realized that the women, who had not subordinated their 'women's struggle' to 'class struggle', were much more militant, courageous and persevering than the men. They also showed more commitment to the 'general cause' than many of the men, who could easily be bribed or corrupted by the landlords. This was understood by at least some of the men (Mies, 1983).

12. See the international congress, 'Women against Genetic Engineering and Reproductive Technology', which took place from 19 to 22 April 1985 in Bonn, and the Feminist International Network of Resistance against Reproductive and Genetic Engineering (FINRRAGE).

Bibliography

Ahmad, Z. & M. Loutfi. *Women Workers in Rural Development* (ILO, Geneva, 1982).

Allen van, J. 'Sitting on a Man: Colonialism and the Lost Political Institutions of Igbo Women', *Canadian Journal of African Studies*, vol. IV, no. 2, 1972.

Amos, V. & P. Parmar. 'Challenging Imperial Feminism', *Feminist Review*, no. 17, July 1984.

Andors, P. ' "The Four Modernizations" and Chinese Policy on Women', *Bulletin of Concerned Asian Scholars*, vol. 13, no. 2, 1981, pp. 44–56.

Arditti, R., Duelli-Klein, R. & S. Minden (eds). *Test-Tube Women: The Future of Motherhood* (Pandora Press, Boston & London, 1984).

Ardrey, R. *The Territorial Imperative* (Atheneum, New York, 1976).

———— *The Hunting Hypothesis* (Atheneum, New York, 1976).

Atkinson, T.G. 'Die Frauenbewegung hat versagt' (The failure of the women's movement), *Courage*, 9 September 1982.

Attali, J. *L'Ordre Cannibale* (Paris, 1979).

Aziz, Abdul. 'Economics of Bride Price and Dowry', *Economic and Political Weekly*, 9 April 1983.

Badinter, E. *L'amour en plus* (Flammarion, Paris, 1980).

Balasubrahmanyan, V. 'Medicine and the Male Utopia', *Economic and Political Weekly*, vol. XVII, no. 43, 23 October 1982.

Bandarage, A. 'Towards International Feminism', *Brandeis Review*, vol. 3, no. 3, Summer 1983.

Bardhan, P. 'Little Girls and Death in India', *Economic and Political Weekly*, vol. XVII, no. 36, 4 September 1982.

Barret, M. & M. McIntosh. 'The "Family Wage": Some Problems for Socialists and Feminists', *Capital and Class*, no. 11, Summer 1980.

Bauer, M. *Deutscher Frauenspiegel* (München, Berlin, 1917).

Bazin, J. 'Guerre et Servitude à Ségou', in Meillassoux, C. (ed.) *L'esclavage dans l'Afrique pré-coloniale* (Maspéro, Paris, 1975).

Bebel, A. *Die Frau und der Sozialismus* (Dietz Verlag, (Ost)-Berlin, 1964).

Becker, B., Bovenschen, S., H. Brackert *et al. Aus der Zeit der Verzweiflung: Zur Genese und Aktualität des Hexenbildes* (Frankfurt, 1977).

Bennholdt-Thomsen, V. & A. Boekh. 'Zur Klassenanalyse des Agrarsektors', AG Bielefelder Entwicklungssoziologen Bd 5 (eds) (Breitenbach, Saarbrücken, 1979).

Bennholdt-Thomsen, V. 'Investment in the Poor: Analysis of World Bank Policy', *Social Scientist*, vol. 8, no. 7, February 1980 (part I); vol. 8, no. 8, March 1980 (part II).

————— 'Subsistence Production and Extended Reproduction', in: Young, K. *et al* (eds): *Of Marriage and the Market* (Routledge and Kegan Paul, London, 1981, pp. 16–29).

————— 'Auch in der Dritten Welt wird die Hausfrau geschaffen, warum?' (Also in the Third World the housewife is being created. Why?) Deutsche Gesellschaft für Hauswirtschaft e.V. DGH Bericht ü. d. 33. Jahrestagung am 22/23 9 1983 in Bonn.

————— 'Zivilisation, moderner Staat und Gewalt. Eine feministische Kritik an Norbert Elias' Zivilisationstheorie', (Civilization, modern state and violence: a critique of Norbert Elias) *Beiträge zur feministischen Theorie und Praxis*, Nr. 13, 1985, p. 23.

Bock, G. & B. Duden. 'Labor of Love – Love as Labor', *Development*, Special Issue: Women: Protagonists of Change, no. 4, 1984, pp. 6–14.

Bonté, P. 'Esclavage et relations de dépendance chez les Touareq de Kel Gress', in: Meillassoux, C. (ed.), *L'ésclavage dans l'Afrique pré-coloniale* (Maspéro, Paris, 1975).

Bornemann, E. *Das Patriarchat: Ursprung und Zukunft unseres Gesellschafts-systems* (S. Fischer, Frankfurt, 1975).

Boserup, E. *Woman's Role in Economic Development* (St. Martin's Press, New York, 1970).

Briffault, R. *The Mothers* (Atheneum, London, 1952).

Brooks, G.E. 'The Signares of Saint-Louis and Gorée: Women Entrepreneurs in Eighteenth Century Senegal' in: Hafkin, N.J. & E.B. Bay (eds) *Women in Africa* (Stanford University Press, Stanford, 1976).

Brown, J. 'Economic Organisation and the Position of Women among the Iroquois', *Ethnohistory*, no. 17 (1970), pp. 151–67.

Bunch, C. & S. Castley (eds). *Report of the Bangkok Workshop: Feminist Ideology and Structures in the First Half of the Decade for Women* (Bangkok, 23–30 June 1979).

————— *Developing Strategies for the Future: Feminist Perspectives*, Report of the International Workshop, Stony Point (New York, 20–25 April 1980).

Caldwell, M. *The Wealth of Some Nations* (Zed Books, London, 1977).

Capra, F. *The Turning Point* (1982).

Carr, M. *Technology and Rural Women in Africa*, ILO World Employment Programme, Research Working Paper (ILO, Geneva, 1980).

Centre of Education and Documentation (eds). *'Operation Flood: Development or Dependence?* (4 Battery Street, Bombay 400 039, India, 1982).

Chaki-Sircar, M. *Feminism in a Traditional Society* (Shakti Books, Vikas Publishing House, Delhi, 1984, 3rd ed.).

Chattopadhyaya, D. Lokayata: *A Study in Ancient Indian Materialism* (People's Publishing House, New Delhi, 1973, 3rd ed.).

Childe, G. *What Happened in History* (Penguin Books, London, 1976).

Cohn, N. *The Pursuit of the Millenium* (Paladin, London, 1970).

Collins, J. & F. Moore Lappé. *Food First – Beyond the Myth of Scarcity* (Institute for Food and Development Policy, San Francisco, 1977).

Corea, G. 'How the New Reproductive Technologies Could be used to Apply to Reproduction the Brothel Model of Social Control over Women', paper presented at 2nd International Interdisciplinary Congress on Women, Groningen, Holland, 17–21 April 1984.

Croll, E.J. 'Socialist Development Experience: Women in Rural Production and Reproduction in the Soviet Union, China, Cuba and Tanzania', discussion paper, Institute of Development Studies at the University of Sussex (IDS), September 1979.

————— *The Politics of Marriage in Contemporary China* (Cambridge University Press, London, 1981).

————— *Chinese Women after Mao* (Zed Books, London, 1983).

————— 'Chinese Women: Losing Ground', *Inside Asia*, February–March 1985, pp. 40–41.

Dalla Costa, M.R. *The Power of Women and the Subversion of the Community* (Bristol, 1972).

Daly, M. *Gyn-Ecology: The Metaethics of Radical Feminism* (Beacon Press, Boston, 1978).

Daswani, M. 'Women and Reproductive Technology in India', paper presented at the congress 'Frauen gegen Gentechnik und Reproducktionstechnik', Bonn, 19–22 April 1985.

Datar, C. 'The Anti-Rape Campaign in Bombay', paper submitted at the Anthropological Congress in Amsterdam, April 1981.

————— In Search of Feminist Theory: A Critique of Marx's Theory of Society with Particular Reference to the British Feminist Movement (Masters Thesis, Institute of Social Studies, The Hague, 1981).

————— 'The Left Parties and the Invisibility of Women: A Critique', *Teaching Politics*, vol. X, Annual No., 1984, Bombay 1984, pp. 71–82.

Davin, D. *Women-Work, Women and the Party in Revolutionary China* (Clarendon Press, Oxford, 1976).

Deere, C.D. 'Rural Women's Subsistence Production in the Capitalist Periphery', *The Review of Radical Political Economy* (URPE), vol. 8, no. 1, Spring 1976, pp. 9–17.

Diamond, N. 'Collectivization, Kinship and Status of Women in Rural China', *Bulletin of Concerned Asian Scholars*, vol. 7, no. 1, January–March 1975, pp. 25–32.

Diwan, R. 'Rape and Terror', *Economic and Political Weekly*, vol. XV, no. 28, 12 July 1980.

Dodge, N. *Women in the Soviet Economy: Their Role in Economic, Scientific and Technical Development* (John Hopkins Press, USA, 1966).

————— & M. Feshback. 'The Role of Women in Soviet Agriculture', in Korcz, J.F. (ed.) *Soviet and East European Agriculture* (University of California, USA, 1967).

————— 'Recruitment and the Quality of the Soviet Agricultural Labour Force', in: Millar, J.R. (ed.) *The Soviet Rural Community* (Illinois Press, USA, 1971).

Dross, A. *Die erste Walpurgisnacht: Hexenverfolgung in Deutschland* (Verlag Roter Stern, Frankfurt, 1978).

Dualeh Abdalla, R.H. *Sisters in Affliction: Circumcision and Infibulation of Women in Africa* (Zed Books, London, 1982).

Dube, L. 'The Seed and the Field: Symbolism of Human Reproduction in India', paper read at the Xth International Conference of Anthropological and Ethnological Sciences, New Delhi, 1978.

Dumont, L. *Homo Hierarchicus: Essai sur le système des castes* (Gallimard, Paris, 1966).

Dutt, P. *India Today* (Manisha, Calcutta, 1947, 2nd ed. 1970).

Ehrenfels, O.R. *Mother-Right in India* (Hyderabad, 1941).

Ehrenreich, B. & D. English. *Witches, Midwives and Nurses: A History of Women Healers* (Feminist Press, New York, 1973).

————— 'The Manufacture of Housework', *Socialist Revolution*, 26, 1975.

————— *For Her Own Good: 150 Years of the Experts' Advice to Women* (Pluto Press, London, 1979).

Eisen, A. *Women and Revolution in Vietnam* (Zed Books, London, 1984).

Eisenstein, Z. *Capitalist Patriarchy and the Case for Socialist Feminism* (Monthly Review Press, New York, 1979).

Elias, N. *Über den Prozeß der Zivilisation* Bd. I & II (Suhrkamp, Frankfurt, 1978).

Elson, D. & R. Pearson. 'The Latest Phase of the Internationalisation of Capital and its Implications for Women in the Third World', discussion paper 150, Institute of Development Studies, Sussex University, June 1980.

Engels, F. *Herr Eugen Dühring's Revolution in Science* (Anti-Dühring) (London, 1936).

————— 'Origin of the Family, Private Property and the State' (abridged) in: Marx/Engels *Selected Works*, vol. 3 (Progress Publishers, Moscow, 1976).

Epstein, S. *South India Yesterday, Today and Tomorrow* (Macmillan, London, 1973).

Evans, R.J. *Sozialdemokratie und Frauenemanzipation im deutschen Kaiserreich* (Dietz Verlag, Berlin, Bonn, 1978).

Farooqui, V. *Women: Special Victims of Police & Landlord Atrocities* (National Federation of Indian Women Publication, Delhi, 1980).

Fergusson, M. *The Aquarian Conspiracy* (Los Angeles, 1980).

First Congress of the Toilers of the Far East, Reports, Moscow, 1922.

Fisher, E. *Woman's Creation* (Anchor Press, Doubleday Garden City, New York, 1979).

Flandrin, J.L. *Families in Former Times: Kinship, Household and Sexuality* (Cambridge University Press, 1980).

Ford Smith, H. 'Women, the Arts and Jamaican Society', unpublished paper, Kingston, 1980.

————— 'From Downpression Get a Blow up to Now: Becoming Sistren', paper presented at the workshop, 'Women's Struggles and Research', Institute of Social Studies, The Hague, 1980.

Frank, A.G. *Capitalism and Underdevelopment in Latin America* (Monthly Review Press, New York, 1969).

————— *World Accumulation 1492–1789* (Macmillan, London, 1978).

Friedan, B. *The Feminine Mystique* (Penguin, London, 1968).

Fröbel, F., Kreye, J. & O. Heinrichs. *The New International Division of Labour* (Cambridge University Press, Cambridge, 1980).

Gandhi, N. 'Stree Shakti Sangahit Jhali Ho!' *Eve's Weekly*, 16–22 February 1985.

Gay, J. 'A Growing Movement: Latin American Feminism', *NACLA Report*, vol. XVII, no. 6, November–December 1983, p. 44.

Goodale, J. *Tiwi Wives* (University of Washington Press, Seattle and London, 1971).

Gorz, A. *Les chemins du paradis* (Editions Galilée, Paris, 1983).

Gough, K. 'The Origin of the Family', in Reiter, R. (ed.) *Toward an Anthropology of Women* (Monthly Review Press, New York and London, 1975).

Government of India, Ministry of Education and Social Welfare, 'Towards Equality', report on the Committee on the Status of Women in India, December 1974.

Griffin, S. *Woman and Nature: The Roaring Inside Her* (Harper Colophone Books, New York, 1980).

Grossman, R. 'Women's Place in the Integrated Circuit', *South East Asian Chronicle*, no. 66, 1979, and *Pacific Research*, vol. 9, nos. 5–6, 1978.

Guillaumin, C. 'Pratique du pouvoir et idée de nature. "L'appropriation des femmes" ', *Questions Feministes*, no. 2, Février 1978.

————— 'Le Discours de la Nature', *Questions Feministes*, no. 3, Mai 1978.

Hammes, M. *Hexenwahn und Hexenprozesse* (Fischer, Taschenbuch, 1977).

Handwerker, W.P. 'Changing Household Organisation in the Origins of Market Place in Liberia', *Economic Development and Cultural Change*, January 1974.

Hartmann, H. *et al. The Unhappy Marriage of Marxism and Feminism: A Debate on Class and Patriarchy* (Pluto Press, London, 1981).

Hawkins, E.K. Statement on Behalf of World Bank Group, International Bank for Reconstruction and Development (Washington, 1968).

Heinsohn, G. & R. Knieper. *Theorie des Familienrechts, Geschlechtsrollenaufhebung, Kindesvernachlässigung, Geburtenrückgang* (Suhrkamp, Frankfurt, 1976).

—————, Knieper, R. & O. Steiger. *Menschenproduktion: Allgemeine Bevölkerungslehre der Neuzeit* (Suhrkamp, Frankfurt, 1979).

————— & O. Steiger. 'Die Vernichtung der weisen Frauen Hexenverfolgung, Menschenkontrolle, Bevölkerungspolitik', in: Schröder, J. (ed.), *Mammut*, März Texte 1 & 2 (März Verlag, Herbstein, 1984).

Héritier, F. 'Des cauris et des hommes: production d'esclaves et accumulation de cauris chez les Samos (Haute Volta)' in: Meillassoux, C. (ed.): *L'ésclavage dans l'Afrique pré-coloniale* (Maspéro, Paris, 1975).

Honneger, C. (ed.). *Die Hexen der Neuzeit: Studien zur Sozialgeschichte eines kulturellen Deutungsmusters* (Suhrkamp, Frankfurt, 1978).

Hosken, F. 'Female Sexual Mutilations: The Facts and Proposals for Action', *Women's International Network News*, 1980.

————— 'The Hosken Report – Genital and Sexual Mutilation of Females' (2nd ed.) *Women's International Network News*, 1980.

Illich, I. *Gender* (Pantheon, New York, 1983).

Irrigaray, L. *Speculum, Spiegel des anderen Geschlechts* (Ed. Suhrkamp, Frankfurt, 1980).

Jain, D. *Women's Quest for Power* (Vikas Publishing House, New Delhi, 1980).

Janssen-Jurreit, M.L. *Sexismus* (Carl Hanser Verlag, München and Wien, 1976).

Jelpke, U. (ed.). *Das höchste Glück auf Erden: Frauen in linken Organisationen* (Buntbuch Verlag, Hamburg, 1981).

Kagal, A. 'A girl is born', *Times of India*, 3 February 1985.

Kapadia, K.M. *Marriage and Family in India* (Oxford University Press, London and Calcutta, 1968).

Karve, I. *Kinship Organisation in India* (Asia Publishing House, Bombay, 1965).

Khudokormov, G.N. (ed.). *Political Economy of Socialism* (Progress Publishers, Moscow, 1967).

Krishnakumari, N.S. & A.S. Geetha. 'Dowry – Spreading Among More Communities', *Manushi – A Journal about Women and Society*, vol. 3, no. 4, 1983.

Kumar, D. 'Male Utopias or Nightmares', *Economic and Political Weekly*, vol. XVIII, no. 3, 15 January 1983.

Lakey, B. 'Women help Women – Berit Lakey of the WOAR talks to Vibhuti Patel', *Manushi – A Journal about Women and Society*, March–April 1979.

Lalitha, K. 'Origin and Growth of POW, First ever Militant Women's Movement in Andhra Pradesh', *HOW*, vol. 2, no. 4, 1979, p. 5.

Land, H. 'The Family Wage', *Feminist Review*, no. 6, 1980, pp. 55–78.

Leacock, E. 'Women's Status in Egalitarian Society: Implications for Social Evolution', *Current Anthropology*, vol. 19, no. 2, June 1978.

Lee, R.B. *The Kung San: Men, Women and Work in a Foraging Society* (Cambridge University Press, London, New York, New Rochelle, Melbourne, Sydney, 1980).

Lenin, V.I. 'Imperialism, the Highest Stage of Capitalism', in Lenin, V.I., *Selected Works*, vol. I (Progress Publishers, Moscow, 1970, p. 666).

Leukert, R. 'Weibliche Sinnlichkeit', unpublished Diploma thesis, University of Frankfurt, 1976.

Lorenz, K. *On Aggression* (Methuen, London, 1966).

Luxemburg, R. *Die Akkumulation des Kapitals, Ein Beitrag zur ökonomischen Erklärung des Kapitalismus* (Berlin, 1923),
———— *Einführung in die Nationalökonomie*, Levi, P. (ed.) (Berlin, 1925).

Mamozai, M. *Herrenmenschen: Frauen im deutschen Kolonialismus* (rororo Frauen aktuell, Reinbeck, 1982).

Mandel, E. *Marxist Economic Theory* (Rupa & Co., Calcutta, Allahabad, Bombay, Delhi, 1971).

Mandelbaum, K. 'Sozialdemokratie und Imperialismus', in: Mandelbaum, K., *Sozialdemokratie und Leninismus*, Zwei Aufsätze (Wagenbach, Berlin, 1974).

Manushi, 'Delhi – "Women's Safety is Women's Right" Beldiha, Bihar – Mass Rape – Police, the Culprits', *Manushi – A Journal about Women and Society*, March–April 1979.

———— 'Such Lofty Sympathy For a Rapist!' *Manushi – A Journal about Women and Society*, no. 5, May–June 1980.

Marcuse, H. *Der eindimensionale Mensch* (Luchterhand, Neuwied-Berlin, 1970).

Martin, M.K. & B. Voorhies. *Female of the Species* (Columbia University Press, New York, London, 1975).

Marx, K. & F. Engels. 'The German Ideology', part one, with selections from parts two and three together with Marx's 'Introduction to a critique of political economy', Arthur, C.J. (ed.) (New York, 1970).

Marx, K. *Capital: A Critique of Political Economy*, Engels, F. (ed.), 3 vols (Lawrence & Wishart, London, 1974).

———— *Grundrisse* (Berlin, Dietz Verlag, 1974).

———— & F. Engels. *Collected Works*, vol. V (Progress Publishers, Moscow, 1976).

———— & F. Engels. 'Feuerbach. Opposition of the Materialistic and Idealistic Outlook', Chapter I of the German Ideology, in: Marx, K. & F. Engels, *Selected Works*, vol. 1 (Progress Publishers, Moscow, 1977).

Mass, B. *The Political Economy of Population Control in Latin America* (Women's Press, Montreal, 1975).

———— *Population Target: The Political Economy of Population Control in Latin America* (Women's Press, Ontario, 1976).

May, R.M. 'Human Reproduction reconsidered', *Nature*, vol. 272, 6 April 1978.

McKim, M. 'Little Communities in an Indigenous Civilisation', in: 'Village India, Studies in the Little Community', McKim, M. (ed.): *The American Anthropologist*, vol. 57(3), 1955, p. 181.

Metha, M. 'Urban Informal Sector Concepts, Indian Evidence and Policy Implications', *Economic and Political Weekly*, 23 February 1985, pp. 326–332.

Meijer, M.J. *Marriage Law and Policy in the Chinese People's Republic* (Hong

Kong University Press, Hong Kong, 1971).

Meillassoux, C. *Femmes, Greniers et Capitaux* (Maspéro, Paris, 1974).

————— (ed.). *L'esclavage dans l'Afrique pré-coloniale* (Maspéro, Paris, 1975).

————— 'The Progeny of the Male', paper read at Xth International Congress of Anthropological and Ethnological Sciences, December 1978, New Delhi.

Merchant, C. *The Death of Nature: Women, Ecology and the Scientific Revolution* (Harper & Row, San Francisco, 1983).

Mies, M. 'Towards a Methodology of Women's Studies' (Institute of Social Studies, The Hague), *Occasional Papers*, no. 77, November 1979.

————— *Indian Women and Patriarchy* (Concept Publishers, Delhi, 1980a).

————— 'Capitalist Development and Subsistence Reproduction: Rural Women in India', *Bulletin of Concerned Asian Scholars*, vol. 12, no. 1, 1980, pp. 2–14.

————— 'Social Origins of the Sexual Division of Labour', *ISS Occasional Papers*, no. 85, Institute of Social Studies, The Hague, January 1981.

————— 'Marxist Socialism and Women's Emancipation: The Proletarian Women's Movement in Germany', in: Mies, M. & K. Jayawardena, *Feminism in Europe: Liberal and Socialist Strategies 1789–1919* (Institute of Social Studies, The Hague, 1981).

————— & R. Reddock (eds). *National Liberation and Women's Liberation* (Institute of Social Studies, The Hague, 1982).

————— (ed.). *Fighting on Two Fronts: Women's Struggles and Research* (Institute of Social Studies, The Hague, 1982).

————— *The Lacemakers of Narsapur: Indian Housewives Produce for the Worldmarket* (Zed Books, London, 1982).

————— 'Landless Women Organize: Case Study of an Organization in Rural Andhra', *Manushi*, vol. 3, no. 3, 1983a.

————— 'Geschlechtliche und internationale Arbeitsteilung', in Heckmann, F. & P. Winter (eds): *21. Deutscher Soziologentag 1982 Beiträge der Sektions und ad hoc Gruppen* (Westdeutscher Verlag, 1983b, p. 34).

————— 'Wer das Land besitzt, besitzt die Frauen des Landes. Klassenkämpfe und Frauenkämpfe auf dem Land. Das Beispiel Indien' in: von Werlhof, C., Mies, M. & V. Bennholdt-Thomsen, *Frauen, die letzte Kolonie* (rororo, Reinbeck, 1983c, pp. 18–46).

————— (assisted by K. Lalita & K. Kumari). 'Indian Women in Subsistence and Agricultural Labour', World Employment Programme (WEP), Working Paper no. 34, International Labour Office, Geneva, 1984(2).

————— 'Frauenforschung oder feministische Forschung', *Beiträge zur Feministischen Theorie und Praxis*, no. 11, 1984b.

Militarism versus Feminism, an Enquiry and a Policy, demonstrating that Militarism involves the Subjection of Women (no author) (Allen & Unwin, London, 1915).

Miller, B.D. *The Endangered Sex: Neglect of Female Children in Rural North India* (Cornell University Press, Ithaka & London, 1981, p. 201).

Millett, K. *Sexual Revolution* (Doubleday & Company, New York, 1970).

Mingmonkol, S. 'Official Blessing for the Brothel of Asia', *Southeast Asia Chronicle*, no. 78, pp. 24–25.

Minkin, S. 'Bangladesh: The Bitter Pill', *Frontier*, Calcutta, 27 October 1979.

Mitchell, J. *Women's Estate* (Pelican, London, 1973).

————— *Psychoanalysis and Feminism: Freud, Reich, Laing and Women* (Vintage Books, New York, 1975).

Mitra, A. 'The Status of Women', *Frontier*, 18 June 1977.
————, L. Pathak & S. Mukherji. *The Status of Women: Shifts in Occupational Participation 1961 – 71* (New Delhi, 1980).
Mitra, M. 'Women in Dairying in Andhra Pradesh', term paper, Mimeo, Institute of Social Studies, The Hague, 1984.
Möller, C. 'Ungeschützte Beschäftigungsverhältnisse – verstärkte Spaltung der abhängig Arbeitenden', Beiträge zur Frauenforschung am 21. Deutschen Soziologentag, Bamberg, München, 1982.
Moraga, C. & G. Anzaldua. *This Bridge Called My Back: Writings by Radical Women of Color* (Persephone Press, Watertown, Mass., 1981).
Moselina, L.M. 'Olongapo's R&R Industry: A Sociological Analysis of Institutionalized Prostitution', *Ang Makatao*, January–June 1981.
Mukherjee, G. 'Laws discriminate against women', *Sunday*, 27 July 1980.
Muktadar, S. *Report of the Commission of Inquiry* (Hyderabad, 1978).
Niggemann, H. *Emanzipation zwischen Sozialismus und Feminismus Die Sozialdemokratische Frauenbewegung im Kaiserreich* (Peter Hammer Verlag, Wuppertal, 1981).
Oakley, A. *Sex, Gender and Society* (Harper Colophon Books, London, 1972).
Obbo, C. *African Women: Their Struggle for Economic Independence* (Zed Books, London, 1980).
O'Faolain, J. & L. Martines. *Not in God's Image: Women in History from the Greeks to the Victorians* (Harper Torchbooks, New York, 1973).
Ohse, U. 'Mädchenhandel und Zwangsprostitution asiatischer Frauen', *Evangelische Pressekorrespondenz*, no. 5, 1981.
Omvedt, G. *We will smash this Prison: Indian Women in Struggle* (Zed Books, London, 1980).
Ortner, B.S. 'Is Female to Male as Nature is to Culture?' in: Rosaldo, M.Z. & L. Lamphere (eds), *Women, Culture and Society* (Stanford University Press, Stanford, 1973, p. 67).
Pasquinelli, C. 'Feminism and Politics in Italy: Theoretical Aspects', paper presented at Women's Symposium of the International Union of Anthropological and Ethnological Sciences (IUAES), Intercongress, Amsterdam, 23–24 April 1981.
Patel, V. 'Amniocentesis and Female Foeticide – Misuse of Medical Technology', *Socialist Health Review*, vol. 1, no. 2, 2 September 1984.
Pearson, R. 'Women's Response to the Current Phase of Internationalisation of Capital', paper presented at Women's Symposium of the International Union of Anthropological and Ethnological Sciences (IUAES), Intercongress, Amsterdam, 23–24 April 1981.
Pestalozzi, H.A. 'Der neue Konsument – Fiktion oder Wirklichkeit', in: *Der neue Konsument* (Fischer Alternativ, Frankfurt, 1979).
Phongpaichit, P. *From Peasant Girls to Bangkok Masseuses* (International Labour Office, Geneva, 1982).
Radhakrishnan, P. 'Economics of Bride-Price and Dowry', *Economic and Political Weekly*, vol. XVIII, no. 23, 4 June 1983.
Rajaraman, I. 'Economics of Bride-Price and Dowry', *Economic and Political Weekly*, vol. XVIII, no. 8, 19 February 1983.
Rao, A., Vaid, S. & M. Juneja. 'Rape, Society and State', People's Union for Civil Liberties and Democratic Rights, Delhi, n.d.
Ravaioli, C. *Frauenbewegung und Arbeiterbewegung Feminismus und die KPI* (VSA, Hamburg, West Berlin, 1977).

Reddock, R. 'Women's Liberation and National Liberation: A Discussion Paper' in: Mies, M. & R. Reddock (eds): *National Liberation and Women's Liberation* (Institute of Social Studies, The Hague, 1982).
———— *Women, Labour and Struggle in 20th Century Trinidad and Tobago 1898–1960* (Institute of Social Studies, The Hague, 1984).
Reed, E. *Woman's Evolution from Matriarchal Clan to Patriarchal Family* (Pathfinder Press, New York, 1975).
———— *Sexism and Science* (Pathfinder Press, New York and Toronto, 1978).
Reiter, R.R. (ed.). *Toward an Anthropology of Women* (Monthly Review Press, New York and London, 1975).
———— 'The Search for Origins', *Critique of Anthropology, Women's Issue*, 9&10, vol. 3, 1977.
Richter, L. 'Tourism by Decree', *Southeast Asia Chronicle*, no. 78, 1981, pp. 27–32.
Risseeuw, C. *The Wrong End of the Rope: Women Coir Workers in Sri Lanka*, Research Project: Women and Development, University of Leiden, 1980.
———— 'Organization and Disorganization: A Case of Women Coir Workers in Sri Lanka', paper presented at Women's Symposium of the International Union of Anthropological and Ethnological Sciences (IUAES), Intercongress, Amsterdam, 23–24 April 1981.
Rowbotham, S. *Women, Resistance & Revolution: A History of Women and Revolution in the Modern World* (Vintage, New York, 1974).
————, L. Segal & H. Wainwright. *Beyond the Fragments: Feminism and the Making of Socialism* (Merlin Press Ltd, London, 1980).
Rushin, D.K. 'The Bridge', in Moraga, C. & G. Anzaldua (eds): *This Bridge Called My Back: Writings by Radical Women of Color* (Persephone Press, Watertown, Mass., 1981).
Safa, H.I. 'Export Processing and Female Employment: The Search for Cheap Labour', paper prepared for Wenner Gren Foundation Symposium on: The Sex Division of Labour, Development and Women's Status, Burg Wartenstein, 2–10 August 1980.
Sambrani, R.B. & S. Shreekant. 'Economics of Bride-Price and Dowry', *Economic and Political Weekly*, vol. XVIII, no. 15, 9 April 1983.
Schergel, H. 'Aus Fernost ein "Kätzchen fürs Leben" ', in *Tourismus, Prostitution, Entwicklung, Dokumente* (ed.: Zentrum für Entwicklungsbezogene Bildung, Stuttgart, 1983, pp. 89–92).
Schmidt, A. *The Concept of Nature in Marx* (New Left Books, London, 1973).
Schwarzer, A. *So fing es an* (Emma Buch, Köln, 1980).
Singh, N. *Economics and the Crisis of Ecology* (Oxford University Press, Delhi, 1976).
———— 'The Gaia Hypothesis: An Evaluation', discussion paper no. 9, Zakir Hussain Centre for Educational Studies, Jawaharlal Nehru University, New Delhi, 1980.
Sistren Theatre Collective. 'Women's Theatre in Jamaica', *Grassroots Development*, vol. 7, no. 2, 1983, p. 44.
Slocum, S. 'Woman the Gatherer', in Reiter, R.R. (ed.): *Toward an Anthropology of Women* (Monthly Review Press, New York, 1975).
Sohn-Rethel, A. *Geistige und körperliche Arbeit* (Suhrkamp, Frankfurt, 1972).
———— *Warenform und Denkform* (Suhrkamp, Frankfurt, 1978).
Sombart, W. *Liebe, Luxus und Kapitalismus: Über die Entstehung der modernen*

Welt aus dem Geist der Verschwendung (Wagenbachs Taschenbücherei 103, Berlin, reprint from 1922: Luxus and Kapitalismus).

Srinivas, M.N. 'A Note on Sanscritization and Westernization', *The Far Eastern Quarterly*, vol. XV, November 1955–August 1956, pp. 492–536.

—————— *Social Change in Modern India* (Berkeley and Los Angeles, 1966).

Srivastava, A. 'Police did it again', *Frontier*, 9 December 1978.

Stoler, A. 'Social History and Labour Control: A Feminist Perspective on Facts and Fiction', in Mies, M. (ed.): *Fighting on Two Fronts: Women's Struggles and Research* (Institute of Social Studies, The Hague, 1982).

Tanganqco, L. 'The Family in Western Science and Ideology: A Critique from the Periphery', Master's Thesis (Women and Development), Institute of Social Studies, The Hague, 1982.

Than-Dam, T. 'Social Consciousness and the Vietnamese Women's Movement in the 20th Century', unpublished paper, Institute of Social Studies, Women & Development, 1984.

Thomson, G. *Studies in Ancient Greek Society: The Prehistoric Aegean* (Citadel Press, New York, 1965).

Thompson, L. 'State, Collective and Household. The Process of Accumulation in China 1949–65', in: Smith, J., Wallerstein, I. & H. D. Evers (eds.): *Households and the World Economy* (Sage, London, 1984, pp. 180–198).

Thönnessen, W. *Frauenemanzipation, Politik und Literatur der deutschen Sozialdemokratie zur Frauenbewegung 1863–1933* (Europäische Verlagsanstalt, Frankfurt, 1969).

Tiger, L. *Men in Groups* (Random House, New York, 1969).

—————— & R. Fox. *The Imperial Animal* (Holt, Rinehart and Winston, New York, 1971).

Tourismus, Prostitution, Entwicklung, Dokumente. Ed.: Zentrum für Entwicklungsbezogene Bildung (ZEB), Stuttgart, 1983.

Turnbull, C.M. *The Forest People: A Study of the Pygmies of the Congo* (Simon and Schuster, New York, 1961).

Ullrich, W. *Weltniveau* (EVA, Frankfurt, 1979).

Unidad de Communicacion Alternativa de la Mujer – ILET, publicaciones alternativas de grupos de mujeres en america latina, Santiago, Chile, 1984.

Urdang, S. *Fighting Two Colonialisms: Women in Guinea-Bissau* (Monthly Review Press, New York, 1979).

Vargas-Valente, V. 'The Feminist Movement in Peru: Balance and Perspectives', paper presented at Women's Symposium of the International Union of Anthropological and Ethnological Sciences (IUAES), Intercongress, Amsterdam, 23–24 April, 1981.

de Vries, P. 'Feminism in the Netherlands', *International Women's Studies Quarterly*, London, 1981.

Wallerstein, I. *The Modern World-System: Capitalist Agriculture and the Origins of the European World Economy in the Sixteenth Century* (Academic Press, New York, San Francisco, and London, 1974).

Weinbaum, B. 'Women in Transition to Socialism: Perspectives on the Chinese Case', *Review of Radical Political Economics*, vol. 8, no. 1, 1976, pp. 34–58.

—————— & A. Bridges. 'Die andere Seite der Gehaltsliste: Das Monopolkapital und die Struktur der Konsumtion', *Monthly Review*, no. 3, September 1976, pp. 87–103.

von Werlhof, C. 'Frauenarbeit, der blinde Fleck in der Kritik der Politischen

Ökonomie', *Beiträge zur feministischen Theorie und Praxis*, no. 1, München, 1978.

———— 'Women's Work: The Blind Spot in the Critique of Political Economy', *Journades D'Estudi sobre el Patriarcat*, Universitat Autónomia de Barcelona, 1980.

————, M. Mies & V. Bennholdt-Thomsen. *Frauen, die letzte Kolonie* (rororo aktuell, Technik u. Politik, no. 20, Reinbeck, 1983).

———— 'New Agricultural Co-operatives on the Basis of Sexual Polarization Induced by the State: The Model Co-operative "Cumaripa", Venezuela', *Boletin de Estudios Latino-americanos y del Caribe*, no. 35, Amsterdam, December 1983, pp. 39–50.

———— 'The Proletarian is Dead. Long live the housewife?' in: Wallerstein *et al.*: *Households and the World Economy* (Sage, New York, 1984).

———— 'Der Weiße Mann versucht noch einmal durchzustarten. Zur Kritik dual-wirtschaftlicher Ansätze', *Kommune*, 2 Jhrg, no. 11, 2 November 1984, p. 61.

Werner, J. 'Socialist Development: The Political Economy of Agrarian Reform in Vietnam', *Bulletin of Concerned Asian Scholars*, vol. 16, no. 2, 1984, pp. 48–55.

White, C. 'Women and Socialist Development: Reflections on the Case of Vietnam', paper presented at PSA Conference, Exeter University, April 1980.

Wolf-Graaf, A. *Frauenarbeit im Abseits* (Frauenoffensive, München, 1981).

Women and Fascism Study Group. *Breeders for Race and Nation: Women and Fascism in Britain Today* (Bread and Roses, London, 1982).

Women in Russia. Almanac, Zamisdat, 1981.

Wood, R.E. 'The Economics of Tourism', *Southeast Asia Chronicle*, no. 78, 1979.

World Bank. *Integrating Women into Development* (Washington DC, 1975).

———— *Recognizing the 'Invisible' Woman in Development. The World Bank's Experience* (Washington DC, 1979).

Yamben, S. 'The Nupi Lan: Women's War of Manipur 1939', *Economic and Political Weekly*, 21 February 1976.

Youssef, N. & C.B. Hetler. 'Rural Households Headed by Women: A Priority Concern for Development', World Employment Programme Research, working paper, WEP, 10/WP.31, ILO, Geneva, 1984.

Zetkin, C. *Zur Geschichte der proletarischen Frauenbewegung Deutschlands* (Verlag Roter Stern, Frankfurt, 1971, reprint).

Newspapers, Magazines, Documentation

Der Spiegel, no. 43/1984.
Economic and Political Weekly, 26 July 1980.
Indian Express, 10 December 1980.
Maitrey, no. 1, April–May 1982.
Maitrey, no. 4, October–November 1982.
Sunday, 27 July 1980.
Sunday Mail, Harare, 27 November 1983.
Sunday Statesman, 10 August 1980.
The Times of India, 15 June 1980.

Index